RUSSIA'S
SHORTCUT TO FAME

Robert J. Morrison

ISBN 0-7090-3924-7

ROBERT HALE LIMITED
CLERKENWELL HOUSE
CLERKENWELL GREEN
LONDON EC1R 0HT

Mary Ellen Morrison Eterno, Editor/Advisor
Jean A. Morrison Kepenés, Editor/Advisor
Bud Morrison, Editor/Advisor

Designed by Susan Applegate of Publishers Book Works, Inc.,
Portland, Oregon

Cover art by Cao Uy, Vietnamese refugee, Portland, Oregon

Maps by John Tomlinson, Portland, Oregon

Printed by Artline Printing, Beaverton, Oregon

Morrison & Family Publishing House, Inc.
4701 Grant Street
Vancouver, Washington 98663

0-9618694-0-2

To Harry and Marie

PREFACE

The author hopes that readers will keep this book's purpose in proper perspective and within the context in which it was researched and written. *Russia's Shortcut to Fame* is simply a fascinating story describing how the Russian government fooled the world for more than 50 years. It is also the story of why Russia decided to stage several transpolar hoax flights to convince other nations, particularly its enemies, into believing that its aviation technology and daring pilots led the world in making the first transpolar flights from Russia to the United States (via the dangerous North Pole).

While not all the details of these 1937 hoax transpolar flights could be uncovered after so many years, an extensive investigation does prove beyond reasonable doubt that these previously accepted world aviation records by Russian aircraft were never achieved.

The research proved very interesting from different viewpoints, including the unique Soviet planning that was required to pull off the hoax flights and the central question of how the Russians managed to keep this major deception secret for 50 years. After all, these nonstop "transpolar flights" were acclaimed by the world as even more significant than Charles A. Lindbergh's Atlantic crossing in a single-engine airplane ten years earlier.

In retrospect, it seems almost unbelievable that governments, the news media, and aviation insiders worldwide never questioned the 1937 so-called polar flights, despite the many false statements, discrepancies, contradictions, and flaws in the official chronicles of these events. Furthermore, the record is full of impossible claims made by the Russian pilots and their superiors, led by Soviet dictator Joseph Stalin, other key Kremlin leaders, and the Northern Sea Route Administration, sponsors of the polar air explorations.

However, in all fairness to the news media (newspapers and radio), the Soviet government – with the generous assistance of the United States and Canada – kept the departure, destination, and other details of the flights under tight secrecy, giving out only after-the-fact scant information.

After receiving the initial information in 1983 that the first Soviet "transpolar flight" from Russia to Vancouver, Washington on June 18-20, 1937, a distance of some 5,300 miles, might have been a much shorter flight, the author did not expect to end up exposing these historic events. However, shortly after analyzing numerous newspaper clippings, photos, and United States government documents marked "Secret," it became increasingly apparent that major flaws had always existed in the Soviet polar claims, mainly because of the limited range of the aircraft used. Research into these Russian "polar flights" and the resulting book would have never been undertaken if it had not been for an offhand remark made by a young Indian to a neighbor nine years after the 1937 flight to Vancouver. The investigation was triggered upon learning that the Indian, Frank Eyle, once told his neighbor about how he helped the Russians carry crated airplane parts to a place south of Sitka, Alaska in 1937. Unfortunately Frank Eyle, apparently completely unaware of the claimed Soviet polar flights, and therefore not realizing the consequences of this remark, died long before any research began.

Another interesting aspect of the "polar flights" is the total lack of normal documentation for world records, such as eyewitnesses, the presence of the news media, independent observers, the sealing of gasoline tanks, proper installation and protection of barograph recordings, and other standard procedures required for official sanction. Whereas the English, through their magazine, *The Aeroplane*, immediately questioned the Russian flights, the rest of the world, particularly the United States, accepted and publicly praised the Soviets. Most of the free nations of the world were somewhat critical of the British aviation journal for calling the events "Flights of Fancy." Many viewed the few critics as just jealous or negative because the flights were accomplished by the only communist state in existence at this time.

The initial intent in researching the Russian flights was to alert our community leaders in Vancouver of possible future embarrassments that could result from basing a sister city relationship with a Russian city on the so-called Moscow to Vancouver transpolar flight in 1937.

I want to show my appreciation and acknowledge the numerous sources used in the research and writing of *Russia's Shortcut to Fame*, including the news media, public libraries, old-time and contemporary aviators, government agencies, aviation journals, books, and numerous other publications listed in the Reference Notes. I also want to personally thank my family, close friends, and others who rendered valuable assistance and support in completing this challenging research project.

CONTENTS

CHAPTER 1

Target Vancouver

Ordinarily the Columbia River Gorge, a picturesque river canyon dividing the states of Washington and Oregon, holds all who view it spellbound. The blue and indigo haze prevailing over the giant cliffs and timbered slopes cast a spell of primitive mysticism upon the ancient chasm. But on this late summer day in September, the attraction wasn't this showplace of nature. From the shores and small fishing boats, eyes had turned skyward as a small, silver-painted airplane caught the noon sunlight. Although those who watched had probably never seen this airship before, a few months earlier pictures of the plane were spread across every newspaper in the land. The year was 1927.

Now the celebrated ship was just above them. "Lindbergh," they called out, "that's Lindbergh's plane." And so it was: the *Spirit of St. Louis* conqueror of the Atlantic. There was magic to the sound of the young aviator's name and the ship he commanded. It seemed everyone realized the world had changed overnight when the two continents were bridged by the historic ocean crossing. As the *Spirit of St. Louis* passed over, following the Columbia River west, old men fishing for the bountiful salmon and estatic children waved in adulation.

After his famous flight Charles Lindbergh decided to tour various American airports to further promote aviation, a tour sponsored by the Guggenheim Foundation that included 75 U.S. cities. The young flier, now known as the "Lone Eagle," was scheduled to visit Seattle, Washington, before landing at Portland, Oregon's newly improved field at Swan Island. There was some concern the new turf would be severely damaged if thousands of people turned out to greet the famous aviator. Another airfield, a military installation just across the Columbia River

1

in Vancouver, Washington, was perhaps better suited for the historic welcome. This field, now called Pearson, had been a center of the area's early interest in aviation, and had even been involved in the delivery of the first airmail letter. Lindbergh originally got his flying experience with the airmail service. Also, Claude Ryan, the builder of Charles Lindbergh's plane, had been in Vancouver a year earlier to help set up a coastal mail service.

A friendly tug of war ensued between Swan Island and Pearson to host Lindbergh's visit. Vancouver could not hope to compete with the much larger and prestigious city of Portland but in this instance Vancouver's airfield might be the only answer since Portland's Swan Island field was under repair. Although Vancouver was the first port settlement in this area it did not grow nearly as fast as Portland. Other than the small business and residential districts, Vancouver remained basically a rural area. At this time Vancouver's population was about 15,000, spread over a relatively large area which included thousands of acres in prune orchards and outlying timber resources.

Vancouver's main distinction was its historical importance dating back to when Dr. John McLoughlin arrived in the Indian-dominated region in 1825 to lay the foundation for the Hudson Bay Company and eventually the city of Vancouver. In fact this highly educated pioneer was a giant in the social and economic development of the entire Northwest. In addition to the many noted industrial pioneers, statesmen and military leaders, Vancouver had also attracted other major leaders who contributed to the social development of the area, including "Mother Joseph." This action-oriented Catholic nun was a driving force in organizing and implementing a myriad of programs for Indians and disadvantaged settlers, raising the social conscience of the communities she served, long before such samaritan efforts were commonly accepted.

It was this pioneering spirit that may have inspired certain military and civilian aviation personnel from Pearson Field to optimistically believe there was a good chance Lindbergh might come their way. With expectations running high, the local citizenry rushed to Vancouver's riverside airdrome on this eventful September 14 afternoon. After a lengthy wait, it was evident Pearson had been passed by. *The Spirit of St. Louis* had already landed in Portland. There was great disappointment, but one man, Lt. Oakley Kelly, the commander at Pearson, would not give up. Kelly himself had a claim to fame since he was the first to fly nonstop from New York City to San Diego, California, May 2-3, 1923, a distance of more than 3,000 miles. Lt. Kelly completed this transcontinental journey in 26 hours and 50 minutes, flying a T-2 Fokker, now on display in the Smithsonian collection. With his undaunted spirit he went to see Lindbergh and implored him to visit Vancouver.

Over the years there had been great pride in Vancouver's progress in aviation, and Kelly was anxious to get some recognition for that city. Lindbergh was pressed for time but he did agree to one arrangement. In two days the young aviator was due to leave Portland; when that time came he would at least circle Pearson Field in a respectful salute to the local aviators and the people of Vancouver. Interestingly enough, by waiting two days, the Atlantic flier coincidentally chose to make his appearance on the very day of the second anniversary of Pearson's dedication.

So on the morning of September 16, a large crowd, including many school children, gathered at the military field. With great anticipation they looked toward the southern skies, searching for the first glimpse of the famous Ryan monoplane. Finally it roared into view, the drone of the motor gradually deepening. Soon it was over them, swooping down at the field. Thousands of admirers screamed their approval as the famous flier buzzed the ground so low it seemed he would surely land. Instead, Lindbergh dropped a message conveying his regrets for not being able to stop over. The message explained how he still had many cities on his itinerary, with limited time to complete his schedule. The famous flier thanked Vancouver citizens for their support of aviation. Although the event was over quickly, it left a wonderful feeling among the great throng. It would have been historically more significant for the city if Lindbergh had set down at Pearson, but such was not to be.

It was a credit for this small metropolis to have an airport; but of course this was primarily due to the fact that the U.S. Army financed the development and maintenance of the facility. The Army had been here since the late 1840s when Vancouver Barracks was built during the Indian conflicts before the Civil War. Some famous soldiers had passed through these portals, including Generals U.S. Grant, George McClellan, Philip Sheridan, George Pickett, and many other notable officers who were to take part in the Civil War.

As airplanes rapidly emerged as a military weapon, it was natural for Vancouver's Army encampment to become involved. So after the turn of the century, following the path set out by the Wright Brothers (Orville and Wilbur), the Army in Vancouver was determined to keep abreast in aviation. The land between the barracks and the Columbia River was an ideal site for a landing field. As early as 1918 the U.S. government authorized the development of a spruce production plant adjoining Vancouver Barracks. (Spruce was a popular airplane building material.) Believed to be an unprecedented encroachment into the normal private sector, the U.S. Army received appropriations to establish and maintain this large operation during the height of World War I. Operated by the Army's Air Division, the northwest plants' management and personnel grew rapidly, from 172 officers and 5,000 enlisted men in January of 1918 to 1,000 officers and 27,000 enlisted men by November of 1918 – in less than a year. Vancouver, headquarters for the Air Division, had the largest operations in terms of production and personnel. Evidently the Air Division of the U.S. Army desperately needed spruce for aviation and other military uses and couldn't wait for private industry to meet the immediate production demands. It was an expansive operation that included timber cutting, transportation, and refinishing in its cut-up plants for aircraft companies. Although this operation grew rapidly during the last year of the war, it was short-lived, closing November 11, 1918, the day Armistice was declared.

After World War I, government and military aviation interest in general subsided. Consequently, the bulk of the existing capital financing for aviation was withdrawn. Gradually a renewed interest began to return in the form of private financing. The development of the Pearson Field was helped along when the Army began maintaining a training facility and a squadron of airplanes there. Civil and military efforts combined to make Vancouver a principal aviation city. Because of this development, Vancouver was destined in 1937 to play an important part in one of the most celebrated feats in aviation history.

In the fall of 1929, it was noted in Vancouver-area newspapers that a Russian aircraft was headed for this country. It was to be the first time a Russian airplane visited the United States. According to reports, Semion Shestakov and three others had left Moscow in August and were scheduled to touch down soon in Alaska. The plane was coming by way of Siberia; its ultimate destination was New York City. It was learned this first-time visit by Russian fliers would be routed along the Pacific Coast, and San Francisco would be included as a main stopover. Cities such as Seattle, Vancouver, and Portland were situated along the route to the Bay Area, so there was much speculation that the large Soviet airship would be visible as it made its way south. There was also an outside chance the Russians would need to land somewhere before reaching San Francisco. If this did occur, where would it be? How large an airfield was needed for the Russian plane to land? What a magnificent occasion for some small city to host the aviators from the mysterious world of the Soviets!

According to Soviet news releases, the fall was not the best time of the year to fly the Siberian wastelands; therefore the progress of the plane was very slow, requiring many stops along the way. Early in September the big airship named *Land of the Soviets* reached Khabarovsk, a city situated on the Amur River near the northern border of Manchuria. At this point pontoons were substituted for wheels. The next landing had occurred at Petropavlovsk on the Kamchatka Peninsula. Petropavlovsk lies on the same latitude as the Aleutian Islands, the next scheduled landing area. After touchdowns at Attu, Unalaska, Seward, and Sitka, Alaska, it appeared the big Russian craft had a very limited range, probably not more than 950 miles, without refueling. After leaving Sitka on October 3, the plane incurred engine trouble and was forced down at Waterfall, a small port on Prince of Wales Island. Waterfall is only about 100 miles south of Sitka, indicating the plane wasn't in the air very long before problems developed.

Perhaps the Soviets felt at home visiting Sitka and this particular area as it once belonged to Russia. Many old Russian structures, including an historical museum and other reminders of the culture, are still in existence. These latitudes, which encompass the Alexander Archipelago, were rich in sea otter; and it was the pelts of these animals that attracted Baranof and Russian interest. Russian presence in Alaska and along the archipelago dates back about 35 years before American and British explorers arrived on the Pacific Coast. Actually, Russian ships controlled the waters from Kodiak, Alaska to a point north of San Francisco, California. The Russians were particularly interested in otter, whales, walruses, and certain types of fish. In the case of the otter, overzealous hunting led to an oversaturated market and a resulting decline in prices and profits. It was reported 10,000 walruses were slaughtered just to obtain the 20,000 ivory tusks. However, whaling remained a profitable enterprise.

As time passed, more and more American and British fishermen sailed northward into what had been considered Soviet waters, searching for the same quarry. The Russians realized it was only a matter of time before the Americans and British would dominate the Alaskan waters. Since the Czar was not on friendly terms with the English government at the time, he agreed to transfer ownership to the United States for the sum of $7,200,000. The sale was completed in 1867. After this, Russian exploration and territorial expansion pressed northward. In 1926 the Russians imposed the "sector theory of possession" by claiming everything between her northern boundaries and the North Pole.

And now after more than fifty years, four Soviet fliers had come to visit the old capital city and the famous Alexander Archipelago where Baranof once ruled. Alexander Baranof was the first governor of Russian-Alaska and eventually made Sitka its capital, and the island where Sitka is located is named Baranof in honor of this first ruler of Russian-Alaska. South of Baranof lies Prince of Wales, also in the archipelago, and it was here where the four fliers became stranded waiting for a new motor to be sent to Waterfall. It was nine days before it arrived, allowing the airmen a chance to get acquainted with the territory.

Finally a new BMW (Bavarian Motor Works) engine was installed and the big cumbersome *Land of the Soviets* headed south. On October 14, it was set down in Puget Sound waters just offshore of Seattle. From this point the plane would follow a land route while visiting cities in the United States, making it necessary for the Soviet aviators to convert back again to their original landing gear wheels. Upon hearing about the Seattle landing the city of Vancouver began to buzz with excitement as many people felt Pearson Field could be the next stopover. These hopes were dimmed when a Russian flight manager for the *Land of the Soviets* arrived in Portland to look over the Swan Island facility. He was only considering fields for emergencies, and said San Francisco was to be the next scheduled stop. The most local citizens could hope for now was to catch a glimpse of the celebrated Soviet plane in the event it should fly over Vancouver.

Radio broadcasts began to come into the Portland-Vancouver area; the *Land of the Soviets* had left Seattle and was soon due over the two cities. By automobile, by trolley, and on foot people hurried toward Vancouver's riverside airfield. Just as the noon hour struck, the huge monoplane was sighted off to the west. The craft had evidently followed the coastal route to the Columbia River and then headed inland following the river. It now appeared to be making its way toward Portland. There was a small American escort plane flying alongside. The occasion reminded many how two years before, Lindbergh had also passed them by. Part of the big crowd started homeward while others lingered a little longer as if hestitant to give up the vigil. After about ten minutes an airplane came into view, its silhouette growing larger and larger. Were the Russians coming back? Sure enough, for some unknown reason the huge craft was coming right at them. Murmurs from the crowd began and then open enthusiasm erupted as the plane's twin-motors roared over the field. Someone shouted, "It's going to land." It certainly was. Down it came, striking the sparsely grassed turf. The Russian aircraft was much bigger than what people in the Vancouver vicinity were used to seeing, and many spectators remarked about its size as they watched it taxi to a halt. On the ground the nose of the *Land of the Soviets* sat high in the air, angling distinctly upward. Scores of onlookers rushed forward to get a closer look at the mammoth craft.

In a few minutes the cabin door swung open. One by one, four very weary fliers worked their way to the ground. The chief pilot was Semion Shestakov. Several news reports had been written about him and his three companions as they threaded their way across the vast Soviet Union to America. And now they were here in Vancouver; indeed it was an eventful day! The more curious onlookers were told that a mechanical problem had forced the plane down at Vancouver. But why hadn't Shestakov landed at Swan Island since the aircraft was almost there? The navigator spoke a little English, and after a few minutes of difficulty in making himself understood, it was discovered the Soviets preferred a military field. The fliers had first been under the impression Swan Island was under Army control, but somehow learned otherwise. It was not clear just how they disovered the difference since the plane had not touched down in Portland. It should have seemed strange the Soviet flight manager had not learned Swan Island was a civilian field.

The general population, while caught up in the historic moment, assumed the *Land of the Soviets* was a Russian-built airplane. Art Whitaker, a young American pilot, knew this wasn't the case. Whitaker realized the plane he was looking at was a German Junkers model, or if not, an excellent copy of one. The Russian fliers had said the craft was – with the exception of the two German engines – all Russian-made and constructed in Soviet factories. The designer's name was given as A.N. Tupolev. A dead giveaway to the Russian claim of design and construction was revealed in the exterior covering of the fuselage. A special corrugated aluminum siding was a Junkers trademark. The same exterior materials were a part of the airplane now parked on Pearson Field. The Russian fliers also forgot to mention there was a Junkers factory in Filas, a city not far from Moscow. At this time the Filas plant was making the K-53, a fighter-reconnaissance craft being used by the

Soviet Air Force. The *Land of the Soviets* appeared to be a K-37 type, only a few of which were produced for the express purpose of carrying mail. The probability is the Russians purchased at least one of the K-37s and then converted it into the one now at Vancouver. Modifications and alterations were evidently made to disguise the German product. (Another airplane of this model was given to Japan as a gesture of friendship, and their engineers proceeded to develop a line called the Mitsubishi K-1/2.)

After the necessary repairs were made in Vancouver, the K-37, alias *Land of the Soviets*, was ready to depart for San Francisco. Many of the citizens who came down to bid farewell to Semion Shestakov and the other fliers watched as the big lumbering airship slowly gained speed for the takeoff. The onlookers wondered whether the plane would actually get off the ground. But it did and everyone breathed a little easier. Art Whitaker, who had been especially interested in the foreign plane, decided to lift off in his own small craft and follow the *Land of the Soviets*, hoping to take some in-flight pictures. To his great surprise, he was able to overtake the Russians before they had flown 30 miles. Whitaker later remarked, "My airplane would do only 85 miles an hour. It must have taken an awful long time to fly that airplane from Russia to Vancouver."

The Soviet fliers' welcome in San Francisco was somewhat marred by anti-communist demonstrations, but they were still royally honored by the city's officials. From San Francisco the plane made stops in Utah and Nebraska; after welcomes in Chicago, Illinois and Dearborn, Michigan, the celebrated airship headed east on the final leg of its intercontinental journey. On October 27 after flying 13,000 miles in two months, according to the airmen, the *Land of the Soviets* pulled into Curtiss Field on Long Island, New York. This was to be the end of the journey marking the first time Soviet fliers had brought an airplane into the United States. Thousands charged across the field to greet the foreign plane. Many waved flags in honor of the communist movement. So great was the enthusiasm that police had to regroup several times in an effort to control the huge crowd. Semion Shestakov, realizing the problem, wheeled the big ship around to blow up dust and give police a chance to restore some semblance of order. Then to everyone's surprise a familiar airplane swept down and hovered low over the airfield. It was an American Falcon, sporting blue and yellow colors, settling to the earth. In recent days Lindbergh had been flying this plane. "Lindbergh!" the crowd shouted in unison. This diversion allowed the

Russians to get their huge monoplane into a hangar. With the help of the police the American hero was able to join them, and in a few minutes they all appeared on the roof of the hangar. Choruses of cheers split the air as Shestakov made a gesture to Lindbergh in appreciation of his appearance. Eventually the noise subsided, as the huge crowd was eager to hear them speak. But unable to communicate well in the English language, the fliers were content to smile and wave their approval of this grand welcome. Although this first meeting between Lindbergh and the Soviets went well, less pleasant encounters were destined for the future.

The general public accepted the Russian visit at face value, but in reality it was much more than that. America was a land of opportunity for the Russian State, not in the usual sense but as an important resource for technology and manufactured goods. The Soviet Empire was the only communistic government in the world, and this isolation, along with the nation's relative industrial backwardness, made the ruling hierarchy reach out to America. Communist doctrine was being openly discussed in American society, especially among the intellectuals. There were also opposing factions at work in Russia. Joseph Stalin, the general secretary of the Communist Party, recognized these forces competing for support and sympathy from the United States. It was this situation that prompted the Shestakov visit. Specifically the trip was designed to secure a closer relationship with the American nation, but more in fact to initiate contact with aviation personnel in an effort to upgrade this industry in the Soviet Union. The Russians were probably not fooling themselves into thinking American experts were impressed with their altered Junkers on this 13,000-mile milk run that involved repeated repairs and fuel stops. The project was more of a social trip and would hopefully result in more friendly relations. In conjunction with the long air journey, General Secretary Stalin had arranged for the return of 86 American war dead. This was announced on the same day the *Land of the Soviets* arrived in New York. Although the soldiers had fought against the Bolshevists (the majority Communist Party), the bodies were apparently being returned as a gesture of goodwill.

Moscow heralded Shestakov's flight as a test of courage and industrial skill. (The Junkers' factory did not get a mention.) The Amtorg Russian-American Trading Company, headquartered in New York City, hosted the fliers and other American dignitaries, and told how the Soviet Union was making great progress in aviation. Not only did the

Soviets mislead the Americans into thinking they were flying one of their own planes, the vice-chairman of the Soviet Planning Commission declared, "Russia would soon surpass the United States in industrial production." Mr. E.J. Kviring was quoted as saying a total of $6.75 billion would be thrust into the First Five-Year Plan. The *New York Times'* reaction on October 27, 1929, was contained in the following quote:

> Scarcely had the Americans recovered from their astonishment at these enormous figures when Mr. Kviring revealed the government's Five-Year Plan was but a mere step in a general scheme for the entire reconstruction of Soviet Russia, along socialist lines, and the government was already considering the adoption of a much greater project which in fifteen or twenty years would completely transform the entire country and make it a dangerous rival of the United States.

Perhaps the speech would never have been made if it were not for the persistent economic troubles plaguing U.S. big business establishments and the stock markets during the month of October. Two days after the October 27 speech there was a major American stockmarket crash and subsequent massive bank failures. On this day (October 29) American confidence was shattered. Hindsight shows that the Soviet brags never materialized.

In Russia the Red newspaper, *The Worker's Gazette*, took advantage of America's general reception for the fliers by declaring it to be an important friendly gesture toward the Soviet Union. Walter Duranty, a *New York Times* correspondent in Moscow, relayed the Soviet government's reaction on October 30. *The Worker's Gazette* featured a four-column headline that read "America Honors the Land of the Soviets." A photograph showed the Red Russian flag flying side by side with the Stars and Stripes in the cockpit of the plane as it flew into Seattle. The article elaborated on the great welcome message included in the news item. It read:

> Twelve years ago, almost day for day, the American people learned that the workers had seized power in Russia, and immediatly it was deluged by a flood of calumny and hate. It became an article of faith with the average American that the Soviet State was a horror of mud and blood, hopeless and lifeless. Now, twelve years later, to this America which despised us, which refused to recognize our

"unaccredited ambassador," born on the wings of the wind, to show the American people what we have achieved unaided. [SIC]

Across unchartered Siberia they flew, and the savage North Pacific, whose conquest bore tribute to Soviet courage, skill and industrial development. This, at least, the American people must recognize, which is worth more than any newspaper recognition.

The *Worker's Gazette* article may have impressed millions of people in the USSR, but it would have had little effect on the American people. The American aviation community certainly was not impressed with this so-called act of courage on the part of the Russian fliers. The two-month sojourn in a made-over Junkers was hardly a tribute to aviation technology, and the fliers courage on the multi-stop flight could not in any way be compared with Lindbergh's feat or those of previous fliers.

Eight years later and three years after the completion of the First Five-Year Plan, Stalin was forced to acknowledge Soviet lags in industrial technology and agriculture and requested assistance. The discrepancies between Russian claims and performances would come to light during the second and third Russian air excursions to the United States. Meanwhile, the effects of the first visit were now wearing down as the Soviet fliers prepared to return home.

Publicly, Shestakov entertained the idea of flying the *Land of the Soviets* home by a northern Atlantic route and claimed the plane could fly 2,500 miles without stopping for fuel. The farthest the made-over Junkers flew at any one time was only 950 miles. Whether the many stops were for refueling or repairs, or both, is unknown; there were no indications the plane could fly very far on a single gas load. It was not surprising when the Russian government decided to ship the big plane by boat from a New York harbor back to the Soviet Union. Although the Americans were not impressed with the made-over Junkers, the Soviet fliers had used the occasion to make important contacts with aviation personnel. Lindbergh's appearance at the New York reception had been especially encouraging. Any association with his name would raise the level of respect for Soviet aviation, and the Russians desperately needed all the help they could get to offset their continued industrial backwardness.

Semion Shestakov and his crew had achieved a very humble beginning in Soviet-American relations. This was USSR's first move to contact American aircraft manufacturers in an attempt to upgrade the Soviet industry. The trip had not been easy; it was characterized by many stops that the Soviets claimed were for repairs. It had taken about two months for the plane to traverse the 13,000 miles between Moscow and New York, at an average of 150 miles per day. This fully illustrates the condition of Russian aviation at this time. The Junkers K-37 was a capable airplane before being renovated by the Russians to the *Land of the Soviets*. It appears Russian engineers and mechanics were not sufficiently advanced to convert and maintain the quality of the German product. Sponsorship of the *Land of the Soviets'* flight by a balloon-flying organization called the Osoaviakhim illustrates the novelty of Russia's entry into air travel between countries.

One of the factors leading to the shortage of technically skilled personnel was the Russian Revolution, during which thousands of skilled workers were killed or imprisoned because they had been identified with the czarist regime. Stalin's new government had been unable to initiate industrial development because many Russians were farmers. Despite this, the nation was still unable to produce sufficient foodstuffs to prevent widespread famine. Getting food to the marketplace was difficult because of poorly constructed railroads and unnavigable waterways.

The early 1930s were to mark the greatest advance in airplane technology since the Wright Brothers first achieved sustained motorized flight. Could Russia meet the challenge? Not without foreign help – as Stalin knew only too well. Since the political climate at this time was moderately friendly, America seemed to be the best answer. American aviation development was moving to Southern California because of its suitable climate for flying. This region would ultimately become the target of Soviet efforts to gather aeronautical knowledge. The Soviets would have excellent air access to the area from points in Eastern Siberia with refueling stops in Alaska and the Alexander Archipelago. Although Southern California was the general target for Soviet interests, Vancouver, Washington would remain in their plans for the next decade. Only time would reveal how this small unassuming community would play an important role in the exploitation of American technology by the Russians. Thanks to Semion Shestakov, Vancouver was to be a special target in the years to come.

During this period the Russians sought out American technology for mining gold in western Siberia. Stalin realized the need to increase the country's finances in order to purchase large amounts of American aviation technology and aircraft products, and gold was the logical means to expand its purchasing power. In 1928 Stalin sent a Russian industrialist to Juneau, Alaska, to make contact with John D. Littlepage, a highly respected American gold mining engineer. The industrialist, Alexander P. Serebrovsky, was introduced as a professor of mining at the University of Moscow. Actually, as the chief of all gold and oil mining, Serebrovsky was one of the most powerful industrial figures in the USSR.

At the same time Littlepage was being offered a lucrative position in Russia, hundreds of other American and German engineers and technologists were being recruited for special assignments in the gold fields. Serebrovsky informed Littlepage that Stalin's main interest was to trigger gold rushes to attract more Russians to the desolate and cold Siberian wastelands. The dictator was concerned about foreign intrusions into Siberia, particularly by the Japanese. With such small populations, it was almost impossible to protect this region from foreign squatters. Littlepage, in his book titled *In Search of Soviet Gold*, told how backward and inefficient the Russian gold mining efforts had been. He found their technology and methods deplorable, crude and dangerous to the miners, similar to the earliest gold mining operations in the United States. Eventually, Littlepage would spend almost a decade in trying to modernize the gold mining operations in Russia. He did not realize it, but his contributions would help Russia maintain a competitive image with the major foreign countries in aviation.

CHAPTER 2

Russia's Aerial Competition

There had been many famous airplane flights before Charles A. Lindbergh's dramatic crossing of the Atlantic in 1927; however, none so captured the imagination of people everywhere. His reception in Paris, although dominated by hero worship, fostered a new awareness of man's progress in mastering the skies. Traveling alone in a small single-engine airplane, the ex-mail carrier flew from New York's Roosevelt Field over the hazardous and expansive Atlantic Ocean to land at another major city in a different hemisphere. Through this act of courage the tall, boyish aviator brought the world almost to within a handshake. His feat in the *Spirit of St. Louis* covered 3,600 miles and took less than a day and a half. It was human nature for the public to view the epic flight as man against the elements; yet the aeronautical experts, including the pilot himself, were aware that this achievement was made possible by U.S. technology. Nevertheless, it took more than just technology to fly through rain, fog, sleet, thunderstorms, and the constant cold winds blowing against the small single-engine craft, with extra gasoline tanks jammed around him, even hampering navigation on this long and untried course. But the Ryan monoplane, with a 225 h.p. Wright J-5 Whirlwind radial engine, aircooled with nine cylinders, met the challenge. Its newly developed engine performed flawlessly, turning the propeller 1,700 to 1,800 revolutions per minute for 36 continuous hours. Lindbergh's achievement was not only sensational, but also marked a turning point in aviation through the public's acceptance of the reliability and safety of air flight.

The U.S. aviation industry also relied upon airplane development in Germany, England, France, and the work of such Russian notables as

Igor Sikorsky and Alexander Seversky, who emigrated to the United States after the first World War. These two were not alone in changing their citizenship because of an interest in aviation. Mikhail Gregor, Illya Islamov, Mikhail Waters, Alexander Pishvanov, Sepan Timoshenko, and several other talented engineers also came to America to become involved in airplane building. In time Sikorsky established an aviation firm in Connecticut and became famous in the development of helicopters. Seversky designed the first metal pursuit plane to exceed 300 miles an hour and invented an automatic bombsight that was purchased by the U.S. government. It appears these emigrating Russians saw no future for themselves in their home country. The main interest there was balloon flight. The absence of these men slowed Russian progress in aviation.

American and Russian aeronautical activity declined after World War I. The war had depleted treasuries and what monies remained were needed to rebuild the national economies. Once governments withdrew finances for aircraft construction, research and development suffered accordingly. In the United States small aeronautical companies began to emerge as they foresaw the enormous commercial possibilities of passenger and freight service by air. There was also a tremendous individual interest in flying retained by the young men who had been trained during the war. These and others struck by the "bug" to fly turned to barnstorming and circus flying in order to pay for their hobby. Daring young people, including Lindbergh, Wiley Post, and Amelia Earhart, sought sponsors so they could enter contests offering sizeable stakes. The sponsors gained the publicity needed to attract new investors and customers. This same pattern in aviation was also typical of other countries.

A different situation was transpiring in Russia, where the government was gradually becoming one big industry with the growth of communism. It would seem that having only one "corporation" to contend with, the Soviets should hold a distinct advantage in attaining national goals. In aviation this would depend upon how well industrialization caught on. Up to now the Soviet nation had not been able to mobilize its manufacturing potential; so airplane as well as automobile production still had a long ways to go.

Actually most of the airplanes used to set world records and make other spectacular flights were either German, British, French, or Italian. Lindbergh's Ryan with a Wright-Whirlwind motor was one of the first American-built planes to capture a world record. Although

Lindbergh's trip was the most publicized, perhaps because he did it alone, the Atlantic actually was crossed many times earlier. In 1919 John Alcock and Arthur Brown, two Britishers, went nonstop from Newfoundland to Ireland in a Vickers bomber. This same year, Albert Read and Walter Hinton, both Americans, flew from Newfoundland to London in a Curtiss seaplane. Shortly thereafter, French aviatrix Adrienne Boland attained an altitude of 12,700 feet in a dangerous leap over the high ridges of the Andes as she flew from Argentina to Chile. Then in a Dutch-made Fokker, Admiral Richard E. Byrd and Floyd Bennett claimed to have flown over the North Pole. One of the most grueling enterprises occurred in 1928 when James Fitzmaurice of the Irish Republic, along with two Germans, Herman Koehle and Gunther von Heunefeld, bucked strong headwinds while conquering the Atlantic from east to west in a German Junkers. It wouldn't be until 1936 when this dangerous crossing was flown solo. Beryl Markham, a remarkable woman, piloted a single-engine monoplane fighting terrible weather in a nonstop instrument flight from England to Nova Scotia.

The South Atlantic was spanned by the Italians Arturo Ferrarin and Carlos del Prete when they traveled from Rome to Brazil in an all-Italian craft. Every major country was getting into the act while Russia stood hopelessly by, occasionally making unverifiable claims. Soviet pilots were careful not to go outside the nation's borders because they had only foreign-made airplanes at their disposal. The few planes built by the Russians at this time were inferior. Stalin's regime, like V.I Lenin's before him, was continually beset by economic and political turmoil with the country still suffering from the loss of countless engineers and technical experts caught in the Russian Civil War. As the remnants of capitalism were systematically replaced by collectivism, many talented people in industrial technology were no longer available. It would take many years for the government to restaff these positions. Stalin was well aware how imperative it was to build a substantial airplane industry if his government were to survive.

Meanwhile American progress gained momentum as Wiley Post girded the earth over a northern hemispheric route and Amelia Earhart became famous as one of the country's bravest women pilots. Post's northern route must have been especially disconcerting to the Russians when he passed over their territory. The Russians have been historically bothered by infringements of their borders and Post's activities were a constant reminder they were far behind in aviation. America's James Mattern had crashed in Russia twice; it was apparent the world was knocking on her door by way of the skies. In 1933 two Frenchmen, Paul Codos and Maurice Rossi, reportedly flew farther nonstop than any other human. Beginning at Floyd Bennett Field in New York, they winged their way to Syria, 5,657 miles away. This is the record flight some thought motivated the Russians to attempt their own long-distance flight in 1937, a year that also marked the tenth anniversary of Lindbergh's flight. Realizing they were falling well behind the major powers, the Soviets had to find some way of getting into the international aviation picture, despite the fact their industry depended almost entirely on foreign imports, with the greatest percentage coming from the United States. The government was relying upon imported airplanes and parts and often purchased certain types of foreign planes to study and copy. Permits for the construction of foreign-designed craft were also secured.

CHAPTER 3

Enter Dr. Schmidt

The answer to Soviet prestige in aviation would not come about through the regular or usual channels. A strange situation was unfolding in the country's northern regions. Joseph Stalin, general secretary of the Communist Party, would be heavily involved; however, at the time he had no idea where his role would ultimately lead him. His government was experiencing serious difficulties in transportation, a vital component to the improvement of its industrial complex. Problems in transportation were compounded by the size of the country and the severe climatic conditions, since much of the USSR lies within the Arctic Circle. Because the nation's raw materials were largely located in Siberia the distance time factor in transportation was of major significance. Especially during the spring melting season, the terrain turned to mud in place of the typical hoarfrost and undermined efforts to build roads and railroads. The entire north coast of the Soviet Union was locked in by ice nine months of the year, resulting in limited access to the Atlantic Ocean in the west and restricting trade both at home and abroad. Frozen river waterways also restricted access to the north coast sea routes.

The transcontinental railroad system faced major difficulties, especially in the Siberian regions. The entire system was grossly underdeveloped, substandard, and inefficient. Stalin blamed the many interruptions in service on subversive elements, including the Trotskyites (followers of Leon Trotsky who was Stalin's most powerful political opponent) and other foreign agents. But the Soviet chief undoubtedly knew that natural factors and poor quality in construction were basically at fault. Whether Stalin realized it or not he had managed to

18

undermine both industrial development and collective farming programs by his lack of leadership and overzealousness in pursuit of political enemies. However, he took it upon himself to find new answers to the country's transportation problems. The attempt to push railroads into the eastern section of the country was severely handicapped because only eight percent of Russia's population was sparsely spread through 60 percent of the land known as Siberia. The purpose of developing railroads throughout this arctic country was to mine and transport the many minerals and other raw materials to western Russia for industrial purposes. It was difficult to draw sufficient workers to build railroad systems and obtain needed laborers for mining. Siberia later became known for its network of prisons and forced labor camps. Stalin recognized his country was 50 to 100 years behind the advanced nations, with limited time to catch up or be crushed in the process; therefore slave labor became part of the solution.

Due to the railroad transportation problems, the Soviets began taking renewed interest in channeling a shipping lane along the northern coast. Activity along this line dated back to the rule of the czars but for some reason ambitions for a new sea route waned. It was believed this was due to the lack of finances from the czarist government. When V.I. Lenin succeeded the imperialists as the first communist-socialist leader, he arranged for the purchase of several icebreakers from Britain. The main obstacle to passage were the great ice floes floating down from the north, jamming against the coast. Now Stalin was pouring considerably more money into the age-old project. If successful this would link the two great oceans, the Atlantic and the Pacific, and thereby increase Russia's trade potential. With the aid of new icebreakers Stalin set plans in motion to build many radio stations and encampments along much of the 8,000-mile coastline. But what did airplanes have to do with a sea route? There were two reasons why they were important: to service the radio station network entailing the delivery of supplies and equipment, and to forewarn ships about dangerous ice floes. It was important for the ships' commanders to know the speed, direction, and mass of the drifting ice-islands in order to better negotiate the channel.

There were many factors working against the idea of a continuous sea route along Russia's northern coast. Both Stalin and Lenin blamed the capitalists of the czarist regimes for not developing this mode of transportation, but there were other good reasons why shipping merchants had not exploited the idea any further. In earlier years when airplanes were in their embryonic stage, there was no efficient way to supply coastal stations. Since Russian progress in aviation was exceedingly slow, the use of airplanes in the development of the sea route lagged accordingly. But the major obstacle to the project was the weather. The entire coast lay within the Arctic Circle and was enveloped for most of the year in sub-zero temperatures. This extreme cold and frigid environment, besides keeping the coastal waters ice-ladened, also froze the rivers and their headwaters feeding the north seas. The rivers were especially vital to the overall water transportation system because they provided the link between the industrial cities along the rivers and the northern sea route. Another almost insurmountable problem was the manner in which the great ice floes continually crunched against the coast, ever deepening the layers of ice in the shipping lanes. Soon after the icebreakers broke through to provide passage for the freighters the floes would quickly close in and jam the channel again.

These were the age-old problems confronting efforts to open up the north sea channel since 1919. The new Communist government realized the importance of a modern transportation system if socialism were to prosper in the Soviet Union. Through the years, organizations by different names took on the difficult task of exploring the arctic seas and northlands, looking for the Northeast Passage. It was believed warm water currents flowed into the north seas of the Eastern Hemisphere, keeping open an ice-free sea lane. Various expeditions were directed toward finding this route by exploring the islands and the surrounding seas. One of the gifted minds tapped to organize these projects was Dr. Otto Y. Schmidt, a noted intellect from Moscow State University. Mathematician and geophysicist were titles often associated with his name. Dr. Schmidt had been a Communist Party member since 1918, and served on the board for Food, Finance and Education. He was one of the main organizers for higher education and science while at the same time helping to set up publishing houses. And since 1924 Professor Schmidt had been Editor-in-chief of the Great Soviet Encyclopedia. The educator-scientist also headed the All-Union Arctic Institute which essentially trained young men for duty in the arctic regions. One of his achievements was the establishment of a permanent camp on Hooker Island in the Franz Josef Land Archipelago. This large group of islands is situated only about 600 miles from the North Pole.

Dr. Schmidt then decided to get his feet wet by riding an icebreaker along the north coast from Archangel to Vladivostok by way of the Bering Strait so he could get a firsthand look at the problems presented by the massive ice floes. On July 28, 1932 an English-built icebreaker named the Sibiriakov headed east along the proposed northern sea route. An airplane was supposed to have been carried on the 23-year-old ship for the purpose of making reconnaissance flights, but the craft launched from the ship experienced innumerable problems and finally crashed into the sea. The aged Sibiriakov became a victim of the elements while sailing along the coast, coming up against frequent problems, including the loss of a propeller. Farther along, the remaining propellers broke, leaving the ship powerless and drifting at the mercy of wind and currents. In desperation, sails were rigged out of some old canvas, permitting the icebreaker to continue toward the Bering Strait. Finally Vladivostok was achieved in 61 days. The Soviet government hailed the feat as the beginning of the conquest of the northern route. It was the first time the channel had been negotiated in one season. In the company of Otto Schmidt two other Soviet explorers made the historic journey, both of whom were destined for important roles in polar explorations. They were Peter Shirshov, a hydrologist, and Ernest Krenkel, a radio operator.

On the basis of this recent expedition, Stalin became more serious as to the possibilities of fashioning a great shipping network, which would link and open up the industrial cities of Russia, many international trade opportunities, as well as providing a better system of defense for his country. In the process of gearing up for the northern waterway project Stalin formally established the "Northern Sea Route Directorate" in place of the former "All-Union Arctic Institute." It was not surprising Dr. Otto Schmidt was named as the new supervisor of its main staff. This full-bearded, stoop-shouldered walking encyclopedia hardly appeared to be Stalin's answer to the rugged north coast, but somehow he had weathered the long ice-breaking journey to Vladivostok.

After riding an icebreaker along most of the north coast it became apparent the massive ice floes were the primary problem facing the newly established Northern Sea Route (NSR) Administration. Dr. Schmidt realized icebreakers alone could not determine the patterns of movement characteristic of these gigantic islands of ice, making their way southward against the coast. Sightings from the air could be a possible answer but this would take a highly organized effort by the NSR. It was surmised that earlier efforts to free the channel had failed because these ice floe forecasts were not available. Seaplanes had been used for this purpose on occasion; however, a much more sophisticated aerial surveillance system was needed. There was a problem concerning the type of landing gear for these reconnaissance planes. It was dangerous for wheeled aircraft to venture too far over the seas but pontooned planes on the other hand couldn't put down on land and often were prevented from landing on water because of the ice. Skis might have been the answer for the immediate coastal areas; however, there was a more crucial need to monitor ice floe movements farther out over the water. An aircraft equipped with skis in the event of a forced landing at sea could mean death for all aboard. NSR needed a special type of aircraft to serve both purposes, one being to supply the stations and the other to scout the ice floes.

A.N. Tupolev, 41, a well-known Russian aircraft designer, had been working on a plane that would meet the requirements of the NSR project. Just as in the case of Shestakov's *Land of the Soviets*, he was not exactly working from scratch. Instead of starting with a German product he chose a French plane. The story of how this Russian designer got his hands on one of the latest French products was in itself an interesting revelation. It began in 1929, the year of the Shestakov flight to America. The French Air Ministry, a newly organized agency, was attempting to redirect the nation's aviation goals. One of the aims was to revise the Dewoitine type of aircraft. In previous years several of the Dewoitine models had been constructed but for some reason French officials decided to drop any further work with this line of airplane. Evidently the ministry saw some future in the plane, especially for long-distance flights. Because of the Lindbergh and other intercontinental air journeys, the French began thinking in terms of long-range flying. The Air Ministry wanted the Dewoitine Company to come up with a plane capable of breaking the world nonstop distance record, a feat which would undoubtedly gain international acclaim. In order to promote interest in long-distance flying, the ministry sponsored a contest to see which French entry could achieve a 10,000-kilometer (6,214 miles) nonstop flight in a straight line.

In 1930 Dewoitine announced the completion of a prototype of its entry and this plane was successfully flown in November. The new model was called the D 33 Trait d' Union and it was powered by a 12-cylinder, 650 Horse Power Hispano-Suiza engine. Sixteen fuel tanks had been installed in the wings, which spanned 92 feet. A wide-track landing gear and undercarriage helped support the large fuel load and wide span. Tokyo, Japan was selected as the in-a-line flight target for the Trait d' Union's try at the world record, but before this was attempted a long-distance flight confined to French air space was carried out in 1931, according to French aviation authorities. On the basis of this test, the D 33 was then scheduled for the Tokyo run on July 12, 1931. Marcel Doret, who had previously broken the world speed record in another model of the Dewoitine, was selected as the chief pilot. An aviator named LeBrix and a navigator named Mesmin would accompany him on this west to east transcontinental journey to Tokyo. The attempt got off on time from LeBourget Field in France (the same airport where Lindbergh's flight had ended five years earlier) and for 49 hours the Dewoitine, averaging about 90 miles an hour, continued trouble-free. Then it happened! The engine's cylinders froze up northwest of Irkutsk, a southeastern Siberian city across the border from Mongolia. Doret reacted quickly, jettisoning most of the fuel while searching the forested landscape below for a safe landing area. His two companions had other ideas and parachuted from the crippled plane. While descending, the chief pilot spotted a small clearing and headed into it; however, as the craft neared the ground the wide wings couldn't get through the opening unscathed. Both wings were ripped off, and as the ground was contacted the undercarriage collapsed. Miraculously, the skillful Doret was not injured, and LeBrix and Mesmin had fared just as well, and walked safely out of the woods after their hazardous jumps. They should have said goodbye to the damaged Dewoitine because this was to be the last time they would see it, at least in its original condition. The Soviets did not intend to return the ship to France.

Undaunted by their harrowing experience, the same trio of fliers, in less than two months, grabbed another D 33 and were again on the trail to Tokyo. But bad luck seemed to haunt the Dewoitine. After no more than 24 hours out of France the plane ran into violent turbulence causing severe vibrations and a loss of power. Doret chose on this occasion to parachute down while LeBrix and Mesmin stayed with the ship. The Ural Mountains loomed just ahead as LeBrix banked along the foothills, searching anxiously for a smooth section of land. This time LeBrix and Mesmin were not so fortunate; they perished in the wreckage while Doret floated down near the plane without a mark on him. How much of the second Dewoitine was salvageable was not learned, but in any event the Soviets also failed to return it to France. Both Dewoitines ended up at the Central Aero Hydrodynamics Institute in Moscow, and this is where Mr. Tupolev began his reconstruction of the damaged French planes. These acts of scavenging were certainly not the answer to Russia's deficiencies in aviation but they would play an interesting role in the next few years.

Stalin knew the chips were stacked against any major acquisition of American aviation technology, at least in the short term. But there was another facet to the problem of airplane building, namely, the need to establish workable transportation and communication systems. Mass production depended upon divisions of labor whereby each factory or industrial plant made certain items which would become a part of the total product, such as an airplane. This meant these parts must be machined accurately and delivered on a dependable schedule for the assembly line methods to be successful. However, assembly line or mass production systems depended on efficient transportation networks. Practically speaking, the Soviets were just as far behind in the development of transportation and communications as they were in producing large quantities of aircraft. One basic difference existed however, in that Russia felt she could do something about the domestic transportation problem by developing a northern sea route and by upgrading the country's railroad system. Stalin had given priority to the sea route project, which could be accomplished without appearing to depend heavily on foreign aid. Hopefully the Northern Sea Route project would be ready whenever Russian aviation technology was sufficiently advanced. Stalin and the Kremlin considered the Northern Sea Route project as the answer to the transportation problems. Such a channel would link some of the major rivers to the north seas and give an overall access to western Russia where most of the manufacturing was taking place. This is why the talented Schmidt had been summoned and also why some of Russia's top aviators had been hired by the Main Directorate of the NSR. It was a combination of these aviation personnel and other NSR staff which would ultimately bring about some dramatic events in the history of Russian aviation.

CHAPTER 4

The "Soviet Lindbergh"

Although Professor Schmidt was an important figure at NSR, another man, a pilot named Sigmund Levanevsky, was also to play a major role. He had been assigned to the Main Directorate staff to work with the airplane supply service. The 31-year-old flier had been an instructor in aviation, an experience preceded by Army training. Levanevsky, like most of the Revolutionists, joined the Red Guard in his early teens and later fought in the Russian Civil War. He then attended a naval flight school that provided the training for his position at NSR.

While on duty with NSR Levanevsky was called on to rescue an American pilot who had crash-landed in Siberia. The incident was to radically change his life and bring him close to the powerful Joseph Stalin. In the summer of 1933 James Mattern, a popular young American aviator, took off from Floyd Bennet Field in New York in a renewed attempt to break Wiley Post's record time for an around-the-world flight. This was Mattern's second try at circumventing the globe via a Russian route. Post, along with Harold Gatty, was also planning to better his previous record. So Mattern, all alone in a Lockheed Vega, lifted off from a Southern California airport and headed eastward to New York. The enterprising young Texan planned to reach Russia by crossing the Atlantic Ocean. A year earlier the young flier had tried the same route but the cover of the cockpit had ripped off, damaging the vertical stablizer and the uncontrolled plane crashed while traveling toward Minsk, Russia. Mattern's plane was just about a total loss.

But on this second attempt he reached Moscow via Norway, but not before being forced to make brief stops in the Russian interior. During one scheduled landing at Irkutsk, the tail of his new Vega was ripped off when the craft struck a tree stump on the airfield. Before reaching Khabarovsk, a port on the Amur River, Mattern ran into terrible weather conditions. And then after taking off from Khabarovsk the undaunted flier focused his sights on Kamchatka, a long peninsula extending down from the southeastern coast of Siberia. The flier had flown about 1,600 miles when he ran into the terrifying black storms often haunting these regions. As he climbed to clear the mountains ice began to form, and finally the discouraged American was forced to turn back to Khabarovsk, losing valuable time in his quest for a new solo world record for best time around the globe. After a good night's sleep Mattern returned to the skies, intent on reaching Alaska. Luckily a mountain pass opened up to him while clear skies showed the way through; the persistent flier thought the worst was now in his wake. He had survived a rocky landing on a Norwegian beach, raging storms, inaccurate Russian maps, and poor grades of Russian gasoline and oil. But though many hardships had been endured, still more serious problems lay ahead.

Just when Mattern could see promises of beating Wiley Post's around-the-world record, the oil pressure began to drop. The danger of this moment had no equal. The temperature began to plummet with the gauge creeping toward the red line. Heavy blue smoke invaded the cockpit and it was apparent the Russian oil was breaking down. Not sure whether he was over land or water Mattern speculated that he was at least near the coast. Should he chance a dash to Nome over the churning and cold Bering Sea or return inland and search for a level piece of land to bring the Vega down? Mattern sensed a try for Nome would be suicidal, especially since there was a loss of rpm's as well as of oil pressure. So down he plunged through the cloud mass hanging low along the coast. He then turned westward and inland, searching the rugged terrain for some clearing. There wasn't much time as the ground was rushing up fast to meet the plane. Unfortunately Mattern found himself right over a river and as the crippled ship glided downward he realized he must "ditch" quickly. A small island in the river loomed before him and with no time to hesitate the plucky pilot went right at it. The ground tore at the craft as it bumped along smashing wings and undercarriage. As it slid to a stop the American was thankful to be alive and able to walk away with minor injuries. But he was not out of trouble yet as he surveyed the stark isolation of his new island prison.

For weeks Mattern was confined to the island searching frantically for berries and small game to keep alive. In late July, having lost about

30 pounds of weight, he saw a band of Eskimos on the opposite river bank. The desperate flier set the tundra afire to attract their attention, but the flames swept over the entire island and consumed part of the downed Vega; luckily the ploy worked and Mattern was rescued. He quickly learned to his disappointment that he had come down in the Anadyr region several hundred miles from the east coast of the Soviet Union. The Eskimos guided him to the village of Anadyr where he was able to make contact with the outside world. When Moscow heard about the crash, aviation authorities were quickly summoned. What a great propaganda ploy it would be for one of Russia's ace fliers to go in after the American. Where is Levanevsky? At this time the Soviet pilot was down near the Black Sea. He must be called at once and sent to Anadyr, 5,000 miles away. It would take him two weeks to reach Mattern.

The Americans were already asking for permission to enter Siberia from Alaska. Somehow they must be stalled in order to give Levanevsky time to get there. An American Coast Guard cutter had been given permission to come alongside the Siberian coast but its crew was not allowed ashore. Meanwhile Mattern was several hundred miles inland waiting to be picked up and flown to Nome. While there was still a chance of bettering the world record, Mattern had radioed American stations requesting delivery of a substitute plane to Alaska. But now the Russian government had arranged it so he would have to wait two weeks for Levanevsky to traverse almost the breadth of the Soviet Union. This seemed senseless when Nome and American pilots were just a few hundred miles away.

Levanevsky, accompanied by his navigator, Alexander Beliakov, made his grand entrance into Anadyr two weeks later. He swept down in a large seaplane probably of foreign make. Mattern was more than ready to leave. The American aviator had supervised the crating of what was left of the Vega's instrument panel and motor for shipment back to the States. Then he and the Soviet pilot were on their way to Nome where Mattern would pick up the plane he ordered. Although the American flier had failed in his enterprise, he was surprised at the great welcome home he received. Mattern had not realized that most people had given him up for dead, so the tumultuous reception was actually in celebration of surviving this ordeal.

Levanevsky had fared even better, for now he was hailed for his dramatic – although unnecessary – rescue of Mattern from the wild and isolated Siberian regions. Furthermore, his government's efforts to enhance the reputation of Russian aviation had succeeded. The needed prestige not accomplished by airplane building was gained from this "rescue." Mattern's rescue had set the stage for Levanevsky to be drawn closer to Joseph Stalin. Presently he was serving on the Main Director- ate of NSR, an organization which would eventually fit into the govern- ment's plans to pump the United States for aviation technology. The Mattern rescue was invaluable in this sense because now Levanevsky might be much more welcome in America. His image also improved at home, with the Russian people now referring to him as the "Soviet Lindbergh." But for now the heralded Levanevsky must get back to the northern sea route project. There was much to be done to study the channel in order to learn the patterns of the ice floes. Professor Schmidt was planning another journey through the projected coastal route but this time, instead of an icebreaker, the professor would enlist a freighter to test how a regular ship would fare in the same route taken by the icebreaker last year.

As the Russians were busy trying to set up a new transportation route, the key for the development of mass production systems, other nations' fliers continued their conquest of the skies. But 1933 turned out to be a tragic year for oceanic flights, especially those challenging the turbulent Atlantic. Other than the Post-Gatty flight completed just after James Mattern's second crash in Siberia, there was not much else to cheer about. Many lives and planes were lost in the Atlantic by the end of summer. But early in August two Frenchmen, Paul Codos and Maurice Rossi, arrived in New York to start one of the longest nonstop air journeys ever attempted. Also in the Empire State at this time was General Italo Balbo who had just brought into the United States one of the largest airplane fleets ever assembled. Twenty-four huge seaplanes had crossed the Atlantic from Italy. The general hailed the undertaking as a tribute to Italian fascism. The event smacked somewhat of military posturing and would mark the beginning of a new wave of grabbing headlines for national prestige. Although most aviation industries throughout the world were under the auspices of civil control, there was still an awareness that aircraft had to be easily converted for military use whenever the need should arise.

International and intercontinental flights were also a way to moni- tor or spy on other nations. It was true a certain comradery existed among the world's fliers. However, there was also a higher order of things having to do with national security. No one was in a better position than aviators to know the great importance of the airplane in military strategy, and this was the underlying factor as each country strove to upgrade its own technology. It was to the advantage of each nation to negotiate the oceans in order to lay the groundwork for commercial airlines, especially routes including the United States, which looked to be the promising plum in aviation. Germany and Japan seemed reluctant to show off their wares and this is well understood in retrospect. Germany was secretly building up her military capabilities in defiance of the accords set down by the League of Nations. At the same time Japan was violating an agreement by militarizing and arming islands in the Pacific Theater. But the French weren't bashful about coming to America, a nation which had been a traditional ally. Codos and Rossi, with an excellent airplane in the Bleriot, were primed to reach India by way of New York and France. Although India was not attained due to a fuel leak, they eventually set a new nonstop world record for distance by getting as far as Syria.

As all of this was going on, Russia remained unusually quiet, not really content to sit on the sidelines but helpless to do anything about her lagging aviation industry. Government purchase of foreign planes allowed the Soviets to study some modern airplanes. But even though the Russians had established some schools and experimental institutions for design and development of aircraft they were not even close to setting up efficient assembly lines and production systems. Hopes of gaining this knowledge from the Americans required getting Soviet engineers into the U.S. However, aviation technology alone would not solve the dilemma. Transportation systems involving railroads and waterways needed improvement if mass airplane building was to become a reality. Stalin was depending upon Dr. Schmidt to pioneer an extensive waterway network which could serve all of the USSR. So indirectly Dr. Schmidt's work on the Northern Sea Route was the key to modernizing Russian industry and aviation.

CHAPTER 5

Fate of the *Cheliuskin*

Professor Schmidt and the NSR staff had been busy during the summer of 1933 preparing for another expedition over the northern sea route. The plan was to take a regular freighter from Murmansk and follow the north coast to the Bering Sea and beyond. A Danish ship with a reinforced hull was selected for the long journey through the dangerous ice fields. It was called the *Cheliuskin* in honor of one of Russia's former northern explorers. The primary objective of the expedition was to plot the most accessible route that could be used during the fall and winter seasons. They hoped to find the illusive warm-water channel which explorers referred to as the Northeast Passage. If successful this would increase the chances of establishing a year-round shipping season. Until this expedition was completed the Soviets would never know exactly what they were up against. Schmidt organized a party of 112 people, including the crew, scientists, and women. A young photographer went along to record the long sea excursion. His name was Mark Troyanovsky, son of the Russian ambassador to the United States.

On August 10, 1933 the *Cheliuskin* pulled away from the port of Murmansk on the Barents Sea and fittingly set out for Cape Cheliuskin. During the night of September 22, the ship was being tossed about in heavy ice-laden seas and became wedged between two gigantic bergs. It looked as if the expedition was going to spend the winter locked in ice. The *Krassin*, an icebreaker patrolling these waters, could not immediately reach the imprisoned *Cheliuskin* because of engine problems. There were no airplanes available in this part of the country so prospects of rescue would be slim if things were to become extremely serious. Meanwhile, the ice continued to batter the hapless freighter as it creaked and groaned under the tremendous pressure. Later seven men, including the ambassador's son, were evacuated from the endangered ship by dog sledge. After three weeks of this incessant pounding, in early October, there was a dramatic shift in the wind's direction. The ice floes were pitted against each other for a time resulting in new water leads or fissures through which the *Cheliuskin* could escape.

At last the freighter was free to continue its course toward the Bering Strait. But it wasn't long before more floating ice brought about a second major internment. Held viselike, the helpless ship was tossed unpredictably and aimlessly by wind and water. Three weeks later another wind change freed the *Cheliuskin* and miraculously blew it eastward toward its destination of Vladivostok, located on the underbelly of the continent. In order to reach this harbor just above North Korea, the Danish-made ship had to pass through the Bering Strait, a channel separating Siberia from Alaska. Just as Schmidt was in sight of the strait the ship became bogged down by crushing layers of ice piling up against its sides.

So for a second year the old professor knew what it was like to be at the mercy of the north seas. They must have realized it was sheer luck due to changes in the weather and not the ship's navigational abilities which had brought the *Cheliuskin* this far. Schmidt called out in desperation for help. The icebreaker *Litke* was nearby but like the *Krassin* the previous year it was partially crippled and could not come to the rescue. Its diminishing coal supply forced it to withdraw. The *Cheliuskin* was "sentenced to death" in the Chukchi Sea not far from the Bering Strait.

A dramatic and graphic account of the *Cheliuskin's* fate is told by George Simmons in his 1965 book entitled *Target Arctic*. One of the book's passages describes how Dr. Schmidt and the ship's Captain Vladimir Voronin, while on the bridge of the *Cheliuskin*:

> . . . anxiously listened to every sound coming from the shifting, grating ice as they stared silently into the blizzard. Behind a dense curtain of falling snow a thick ice sheet collapsed, as if crumpled by a gigantic invisible hand. Huge blocks of ice broke loose, and drifted menacingly toward the ship. Helpless, the fragile ship groaned. Glistening snowflakes on her tortured hull looked like tears as the moving ice-ridge crept on . . . the drum beat of pounding ice merged with the whine of tortured steel.

Other passages of *Target Arctic* narrated how Captain Voronin and Dr. Schmidt knew the ship was doomed:

The creaking grew into grinding and snapping as the ship's frame bent. Metal plates bulged, bursting along their seams, and heavy rivets started popping out like corks of champagne bottles. The *Chelyuskin* quivered, the port side of the ship split wide open. The ugly gaping hole, over 100 feet long, resembled a vast, thin-lipped mouth contorted in the agony of death....

The deck was teaming with bundled-up men and women. Their screams and curses were carried away by the wind as they jostled their way to predetermined stations and began lowering planks onto the ice.

Miraculously only one man died during the evacuation, and he was struck by a rolling barrel that broke loose from its moorings. At this time 104 people, including two children, scrambled to safety from the rapidly sinking freighter. On February 14 the first distress message was radioed by Ernest Krenkel to a Siberian wireless station. The message read: "Emergency-governmental.... Kuibyshev, Soviet People's Commissars, Moscow.... On Feb. 13th, at 3:30 p.m. the *Chelyuskin* was crushed by ice and sank.... Within two hours everything was over."

Confined to a cake of ice and with only the supplies they managed to haul from the sinking ship, the 104 survivors would remain stranded for two months. According to author Simmons, Schmidt realized there was no way to transport this large group safely over huge ice hummocks for long distances without more dog sledges. Dr. Schmidt also concluded the chances of an icebreaker reaching them in time were not good. He was resigned to one single rescue method – transporting everyone by aircraft – and he had to maintain discipline and morale in the camp. Would-be rescuers on the mainland had also reached the same conclusion of rescue by air. According to *Target Arctic*, "a primitive village arose; tents went up; scientific work was resumed, and community life continued." It was reported that Dr. Schmidt gave 33 lectures on a variety of subjects, including "Scandinavian mythology, history of South America, Freud's concept of psychoanalysis, socialism, fascism and the theory of evolution." The camp even issued a crude newsletter under the name "We Won't Give Up."

It is evident the Soviet government was ill-prepared to offer timely assistance to the expedition. Their old icebreakers were constantly in dry dock getting repairs and no airplanes had been made available in the eastern section of the country in the event something went wrong. No one knew better than the Russians the treachery of these waters but still no precautions or plans were devised beforehand to insure the safety of those people on board. Finally under the direction of V. M. Molotov, chairman of the People's Commissariat, several groups were organized to go to the aid of the Cheliuskin party. While two rescue groups were to make their way across Siberia to the stranded survivors, Sigmund Levanevsky and another pilot, Mikhail Slepnev, were ordered to Alaska by way of London and New York. From there American air-planes were to be purchased and made immediately available for search and rescue. It wasn't surprising to see the "savior" of Mattern being given this assignment. The objective was to promote Levanevsky as the "Soviet Lindbergh" and use him as an emissary to the United States in the interest of Russian aviation.

It appears the Americans were never asked to aid in saving the expeditionary party. It would have been a fairly easy matter for Alaskan airmen to land on the ice with skis and lift Schmidt's party onto the Siberian coast. But Stalin did not want to give the United States a chance to repay them for the rescue of James Mattern. Saving 104 Russians as compared with one American would place the Soviets in a position of gratitude, a situation the Kremlin hoped to avoid. The strategy was to groom Levanevsky with the idea he would be just the man to make important contacts in the United States. As it turned out, the government chose to make Schmidt wait until April before an air rescue was attempted. Mattern had survived his ordeal because he had found safety with a band of Eskimos; however, the *Cheliuskin* survivors were at the mercy of winter weather and dependent upon a limited supply of food and equipment to see them through. Schmidt must have been disgusted as he looked eastward toward Alaska, realizing how easy it would have been for the Americans to reach them. He must have been especially anxious since his own health was beginning to succumb to the extreme cold.

Luckily, sufficient food and other supplies had been salvaged from the crushed ship to sustain the survivors for a couple of months. Hopefully this would be enough time to allow for rescue. One search base was only 90 miles from the stranded party. Three separate search groups slowly closed in on the site where the ship had gone down and where they expected to find the survivors living on an icepack. There were constant stories of problems with the aircraft the Russians were using, and this coupled with poor visibility and subfreezing tem-peratures, made rescue progress move very slowly. Several aircraft were damaged in rescue attempts and some of these fliers themselves became stranded in isolated areas, touching off additional aerial searches and rescues by icebreakers.

Levanevsky and Slepnev passed through London and New York, reaching Alaska in good time, and leaving them in the best position to snatch the *Cheliuskin's* personnel from the ice. Two nine-passenger planes had been made ready by Joe Crosson, an Alaskan bush pilot, even to the extent of painting them bright orange. This was a tactic used to aid in spotting planes when they were down on the ice. Even this was not very effective because most arctic fliers attest to the difficulty of making visual sightings of ground objects from the air. A search plane has to fly very low to have a chance of seeing anything. Even so, Levanevsky and Slepnev's planes were well equipped in terms of radio and navigational devices.

On March 29, 1934, Levanevsky, along with an American mechanic, left Nome and began searching the north Bering Strait area for Schmidt and his expeditionary party. The weather was considerably stormy and Levanevsky overshot his intended target. The flier crashed on the shores of Siberia attempting to land and knocked himself unconscious. Levanevsky appeared to have sustained a fairly severe concussion, requiring rest and forcing him out of the rescue operations. Mikhail Slepnev was the next flier to embark from Nome in search of Dr. Schmidt's party.

Another rising star in Stalin's Northern Sea Route project was on hand. Mikhail Vodopyanov had volunteered his services to help his supervisor, Professor Schmidt. After much difficulty he had arrived in the general vicinity where the *Cheliuskin* had sunk. Vodopyanov was one of those key persons destined for a role in Stalin's questionable plans involving the North Pole. And now Vodopyanov and other members of NSR finally succeeded in reaching the 104 cold and neglected people who had made an ice floe their home for two months. The Schmidt party, braving subfreezing temperatures, blizzards, and other severe weather conditions, managed to smooth out and mark a landing strip on the ice floe; three additional landing sites had to be carved out of the ice to replace those damaged by shifting and melting ice floes. Before aerial rescuers could reach Schmidt's Camp, the ice floe continued to break apart, threatening its inhabitants and forcing them to move their tents and other facilities to more stable ice floes. Upon arriving the rescuers found Professor Schmidt needed medical attention at once; so arrangements were quickly made with the United States government to transport him to a hospital in Nome.

Slepnev was more successful than Levanevsky. He was one of the first fliers to reach the *Cheliuskin* survivors and airlifted some to safety. It took many aircraft and a number of trips to evacuate the 104 people, since some aircraft could only haul two or three passengers at a time. Often bad weather kept all the aircraft on the ground and the rescue efforts were stalled many times. Vassily Molokov, an old-time pilot, and reportedly a "man of few words" winged his way to Camp Schmidt three times in one day and rescued 14 people, even cramming two extra passengers in empty parachute containers strapped on his plane's wings. The last of the 104 survivors were airlifted to safety on April 13 after a two-month ordeal, according to *Target Arctic*. The book also quotes Radio Operator Krenkel as tapping out the last message from Camp Schmidt: "Nothing more to transmit; closing down station." Krenkel ended his communications by sending the call letters of the *Cheliuskin*, slowly repeating this two more times, in a deliberate and careful way to indicate he was part of history in the making. Krenkel made the last entry in the camp log: "transmitter disconnected at 2:08 a.m., Moscow time, April 13, 1934."

When Schmidt was examined in Nome he was found to be suffering from pneumonia. In honor of his efforts the New York Explorer's Club made him a lifetime honorary member, a distinction soon to follow for Sigmund Levanevsky. Such American contacts were important to the Soviets because they felt the United States was the best political ally they had.

During his long convalescence, Dr. Schmidt had time to evaluate the situation facing NSR. After riding the *Cheliuskin* down the coast he could personally attest to the problems posed by the great ice formations blocking passage through the north sea channel. This was particularly true during winter months. Even when an icebreaker escorted cargo ships through the ice blockades, the floes immediately closed in to seal off the channel once more. The presence and power of the arctic ice seemed insurmountable and the problem was not confined to the coastal route but extended up the rivers as the below-zero temperatures invaded the mainland for much of the year.

Perhaps if the expedition had known more about the patterns and movements of the ice through aerial surveillance, some of the bergs and floes could have been avoided. This might have resulted in the ships making better time. Practically speaking, seven months to travel from Murmansk to the Bering Strait was not an economical trip – a fact graphically underscored by the fate of the *Cheliuskin*. And even though the NSR organization claimed the exploration accumulated valuable information about the arctic waters, and even though the government planned to make heroes out of the rescued and the rescuers, the project was still a disaster.

Stalin and his government were not to be discouraged with the sinking of the *Cheliuskin*. The expedition was immediately hailed as a great success and propagandized throughout the nation. "Hail the Cheliuskinites," responded the people. Although the Russians claimed the expedition as successful, on the contrary it proved even a freighter especially built to withstand the ice-ladened arctic seas could not overcome these hazards. It had taken the *Cheliuskin* seven months to find its way to the Bering Strait; this was hardly a time-efficient passage on which to base a shipping route. However, in the face of failure the government declared the voyage an important breakthrough in the study of the arctic seas. Seven pilots in all received a newly created medal "Hero of the Soviet Union" for their part in the rescue. Although he was probably embarrassed to be so honored without being involved in the actual saving of lives, Sigmund Levanevsky received the commendation along with the other fliers.

The only unanswered question remaining was whether airplane assistance in spotting ice floes would have made a difference. Aircraft had occasionally been used to some benefit, but the winter season brought such great quantities of ice that early warnings of its movement might not help. However, it was worth a try to set up some kind of a coordinated network. This would require land-based radio stations communicating with aircraft and ships signaling information about the ice floes. Schmidt realized it would be an impossible task to fight the solid ice blanket with icebreakers and the only other alternative was to learn how to skirt them. Whether this was feasible remained to be seen, but it was certain some suitable planes were desperately needed. Hopefully, Tupolev would come through.

CHAPTER 6

Tupolev's ANT-25s

The Russian designer was working to restore one of the damaged Dewoitines but he was also engaged in another priority project being promoted by the Kremlin, one much more sensational. The plan was to build the largest airplane in the world to bring international recognition to Russia. Since the industry was lagging in production, why not make the biggest plane to attract attention and gain respectability? Government newspapers such as *Pravda* began a promotion to encourage financial contributions. In time enough rubles had been collected to start work on a giant airship to be called the *Maxim Gorky* in honor of the poor people's poet by that name. Gorky happened to be a good friend of Joseph Stalin and had supported the general secretary's plans to rebuild Russia. Stalin chose to honor his friend with the construction of this special airplane.

Tupolev's designs called for a wingspan of 210 feet, 65 feet longer than today's American 747. Eight motors would lift the mammoth craft, designed to accommodate a total of 70 persons, including a 20-member crew. The Communist Party wanted to use the plane to dispense propaganda leaflets and other materials to the populace. It was intended for the *Gorky* to tour the Soviet Union and bring party-line ideologies to more people. When finished the massive *Gorky* would have several printing presses and a small but complete cinema. It is apparent Tupolev got some ideas for styling from the Junkers planes being built by Germans near Moscow. The overall shape of the *Gorky* and the type of exterior siding would be similar to the German product. Tupolev was in the habit of copying from foreign models. Presently he was busy with salvaging the two damaged French Dewoitines, and now he also had to direct the *Maxim Gorky* project.

The world's largest plane was finished in the spring of 1934; however, the energetic designer did not complete work on one of the Dewoitines until late in that year. NSR had hoped to use the renovated Dewoitines to spot ice floes so that once and for all Schmidt would know whether the NSR was going to be able to open up the entire channel for shipping. The prospects didn't look good; however, they would give the spotter planes a chance to see what they could do. If Tupolev's new creations were effective this might help to increase the number of cargo ships using the channel and might in the long-run expand the shipping season to more months of the year.

As the end of 1934 approached, Tupolev showed off one of his finished products. His fascination for large wingspans was evident in the made-over Dewoitine. The wings of the first plane which crashed at Irkutsk had been severely damaged on impact, compelling Tupolev to add his trademark; the wingspan grew from the original 92 feet to 112 feet. A single spar running the length of the old span had evidently been damaged beyond repair because the new version was without this support. Only ribs of aluminum riveted together provided the wing strength and this assembly was covered with treated fabric, crudely and loosely applied. Evidently Tupolev did not want to take the time to replace the metal covering on the wings. Without the supporting spar it was impossible to retain the 16 fuel tanks; however, this didn't matter as the plane was only going to be used by NSR for relatively short runs. Tupolev decided on just six fuel tanks and these were placed well out inside the wings, leaving the wing stubs and fuselage without tanks for gas storage. Then the Russian designer came up with an innovative way to deal with the hazards of flying out over the water. The wing stubs and part of the fuselage were packed with inflatable rubber bags designed to keep the plane afloat longer in case it happened to be forced down in the north seas. This extra time would increase the chances for the occupants to be saved.

It is not really known whether a different engine was put into the new version of the Dewoitine or whether the original Hispano-Suiza was used. If the latter was true then some work to disguise it had taken place. In any event whatever power plant was installed, it thereafter became known as the M-34 and claimed as a Russian product. Like the Hispano-Suiza the M-34 had 12 cylinders; however, it differed in horse power if one can believe what was printed on the engine plates: 750

horse power vs. the 650 h.p. of the original motor. The so-called new Russian engine had a peculiarity that was difficult to explain since half of the parts were American-built.

Other parts of the Dewoitine which had been severely torn up were the landing gear and undercarriage. It was possible to use the damaged parts for patterns to construct a new assembly to support the much larger wings. It is also possible the original landing equipment was merely repaired, modified, and used again. Tupolev also retained the retractable mechanism controlling the wheel assembly. He added double wheels to enable the craft to land and take off in the snow. This was a compromise between pontoons and skis. After some exterior work involving paint and siding, the big monoplane was ready for duty with NSR. To the experienced eye the plane was still a French Dewoitine but Tupolev had managed to change enough features to fool the average person. With the restoration completed the great gliderlike bird was finally ready to be tested. Viewing the ship from the front and in silhouette, it appeared to have nice lines as it rested on the generous wide-tracked landing gear; however, in better light and up close the crudely painted gray fuselage and red wings were reminders of a patchwork job. Alongside any of the foreign-built aircraft Tupolev's newest creation would have stood out like a sore thumb, with the only distinguishing characteristic being the unusally large wingspan. A low bubble canopy covered the cockpit where the pilot and copilot sat. Another section toward the rear was reserved for the navigator. All quarters were somewhat confined. Tupolev was proud enough of his finished product to name it after the initials of his name, and thus was born the ANT-25, the numbers denoting the number of aircraft he supposedly designed.

Tupolev's ANT-6 was already being used by the Northern Sea Route Administration to transport large quantities of equipment and supplies to the north coast. And now one of the ANT-25s (renovated Dewoitines) would begin ferrying the cargo all the way to the coastal radio stations. If things went as planned the big gliderlike wings would slow the ANT's speed for landings in small areas near the radio stations. If the ANT-25 was ever to be used to distribute propaganda, its ability to land at small villages and townships was essential. Between the *Maxim Gorky* and the ANT-25 much of Russia could be traversed. Both planes would be touted as fine examples of Soviet ingenuity and thereby convince Russian people the USSR was making giant strides in aviation. However, such propaganda was not expected to last very long. The modernization of the industry was happening so fast that unless Russia got its act together quickly even some of the smaller nations stood a chance of passing her by. It was not likely the situation with airplanes was going to get better soon, and now with the Northern Sea Route project running at half speed, the picture was especially gloomy.

Professor Schmidt probably had no illusions that surveillance aircraft would make a major difference in opening up the north sea channel. However, the ANT-25s were given an opportunity to aid shipping by locating potentially dangerous ice floes. Despite this contribution there seemed to be no significant improvement in the amount of tonnage getting through. It began to appear only limited use of the shipping lanes would be possible. The most vital area where shipping service had to be maintained was the northwestern seas providing access to Europe and other parts of the world by way of the Baltic Sea. If worst came to worst the coastal route would have to be forgotten except during the summer months. A fortune in icebreakers could not keep the entire channel open throughout the year. This meant ships must negotiate the channel on their own both winter and summer. Icebreakers were barely able to break through the icy northern sea route in one season, so what chance did regular ships have? The Soviets could not afford to assign an icebreaker to every freighter seeking passage along the coast and up the rivers where the ice was almost as thick. One icebreaker leading several freighters through the channel at the same time had been tried but this required many of the ships to wait until others arrived. There was an explicit danger in waiting for icebreaker assistance, as illustrated by the *Cheliuskin*, because the pressure from the ice continues to mount, eventually sinking any imprisoned ship.

The professor could do no more now except to recommend a curtailment of further investments in the Northern Sea Route project. He probably did not relish the idea of making any more northern treks if only for the sake of his health. But maybe Stalin would consent to use him as an advisor instead of doing more field work. Both Schmidt and Stalin must have realized by this time that all the scientific expertise in the world was not going to move the massive ice floes out of the channel. Even the most powerful icebreakers became mired and needed to be pulled free on occasion. Gradually Stalin was learning why previous attempts to open the northern sea route had failed. He was the principal architect of this new thrust to join the two oceans and therefore there was no one else to blame for what was happening. Not even the Trotskyites were faulted, and apparently there was no sabotage connected to the *Cheliuskin* sinking. The Soviet chief had increased the number of icebreakers to eight, mostly through purchases from Britain; he had added a number of aircraft and ordered more radio stations to be established at the coast. Essentially there was not much more NSR could do; the tremendous ice formations proved to be the indomitable factor. One reason why Stalin might not have looked for a scapegoat for the failed project was the presence of the prestigious Dr. Schmidt. The professor had personally experienced the obstacles presented by the world of ice and snow and his integrity was not likely to be challenged around Moscow. The Main Directorate Administration offices were located in Moscow, where the professor was a highly visible and well-known person; any evaluation by him probably would be accepted without question. It is doubtful even the all-powerful Stalin would care to question the professor's judgment. In addition, Schmidt had plenty of impressive names behind him who could verify the problems encountered by NSR. These were the aviators who surveyed the northern ice fields; some like Levanevsky and Vodopyanov were celebrated heroes and it was surely not wise for the Communist dictator to question their efforts.

The project was not a total failure because some knowledge in shipping strategy was gained through Schmidt's explorations. However, for the most part the movement of cargo would be limited to the summer months. But of course this was not really an improvement over past years. Stalin's only alternative was to claim success instead of admitting failure – a common remedy to many deficiencies occurring in the Soviet Union. Under normal circumstances Stalin could have come down hard on the NSR staff, claiming their efforts weren't good enough and perhaps even casting some doubts about loyalty. But in this particular case the Soviet dictator could not readily admit his brainchild was in serious trouble. The strategy was to continue the impression that more and more shipping was being channeled through the Northern Sea Route. Stalin needed Schmidt and the NSR staff to carry on as if all were going well; moreover it was crucial for him to nurture the loyalty of the NSR aviators and pilots in general as the key to building an airway transportation system and a formidable air force.

CHAPTER 7

Wintering at Shelkova

During the winter of 1935 there was always much activity at the Main Directorate offices in Moscow. As things slowed at the coast many of the fliers and mechanics found themselves hanging around the administration building. Not far from Moscow, about 25 miles to the northeast, was the Shelkova military field. Shelkova was like a home away from home for NSR employees, as well as their families on special occasions. Even during better times, many fliers, engineers, and mechanics came here during the winter months. Bordering the airfield were two large barracks accommodating up to 500 people, and it was here relatives and friends could stay over for visits. All whose lives were touched by airplanes could exchange stories and experiences of the north coast.

Now as the cold winter days brought them closer together, the fliers and other employees of NSR discussed their futures, in view of the fact the channel project was not going to be running full steam. For pilots there was an opportunity to fly when the weather permitted. A new concrete runway was planned for this year. It would stretch more than a mile and make it much easier for the giant ANT-6s to land and take off. Two airplane hangars adjoined the field, now covered with snow; a two-story administration building and some store houses rounded out the complex. All of the buildings were constructed of either brick or stone and the entire facililty and grounds were surrounded by a low evergreen woods. Shelkova was conveniently close to Moscow; however, having Stalin and the Kremlin close by was not exactly inviting. The idled employees at Shelkova were a constant reminder that Stalin's NSR project was on the wane. They all knew the dilemma the Party and country faced in not being able to bring about a cohesive transportation system. Water routes were not the total answer, nor were railroads. A great airline network might be the answer since the country was so widespread. Perhaps large cargo planes along the lines of the *Maxim Gorky* could make up the difference. It appeared Stalin and the Kremlin were thinking in these terms. The government had hoped to solve the transportation problems first but this hadn't come about. The only alternative now was to go after American technology as quickly as possible.

Stalin began making arrangements to get A.N. Tupolev and some other engineers into the United States to study American production methods, and also some efforts were put forth to invite technical experts into the Soviet Union to help set up assembly line systems for airplane and automobile manufacturing. Although anxious to make some of their own products, the Russians would settle for foreign supervision and acquisition of foreign patent rights with the hope of producing large numbers of selected models. The American Douglas was of special interest to the Soviets but in order to mass produce the Douglas or any other type of airplane American technicians were needed. For that matter, any foreign experts were desirable. The Russians felt their chances of getting cooperation were better in the U.S. and Stalin wished to pursue this avenue whenever possible. The nation's aviators also were attracted to America, partly due to the fame of Lindbergh.

The greatest aerial activity was emanating from the U.S. and the competitive nature of the Soviets brought a focus on men such as Post, Mattern, and Lindbergh. But Stalin's reason to woo American help was more practical; he knew the U.S. had the best production systems in the world and the Soviet government desperately needed thousands of airplanes for domestic and military service. And last but not least, the political environment in America was more conducive to cooperation with Russia. There were signs this was changing, so the Kremlin must hurry if any advantages were to be gained. As things stood, A.N. Tupolev would be finished with the second Dewoitine-ANT-25 before embarking for America. The *Maxim Gorky* was also ready to roll out of the hangar and begin its great propaganda tour.

Many of the pilots felt compelled to help the aviation situation but wondered how they could contribute. If only one of their more popular fliers such as Levanevsky could make a world flight similar to Post's ventures. Despite two major rescues to his credit, the "Soviet Lindbergh" did not receive the international attention being accorded American aviators. There were no Soviet-built planes which could compete for speed and distance records, including around-the-world trips. Germany, England, and the United States had planes of this caliber but it would not serve any purpose to have Russian fliers use foreign aircraft to establish a world record. Doing so would just be an advertisement for some other nation's products and an admission of the Russian aviation industry's inferiority.

If the Soviets entertained ideas of making long-distance nonstop flights, the same quandary presented itself. There was no Soviet product capable of flights of exceptional duration, and again why use a foreign product? In the long run the most advanced countries in aviation were not spending much time and money developing planes capable of flying great distances without refueling. Other aspects of the industry held greater promise. Speed and maneuverability were the priorities in American factories so that passengers, cargo, and mail could get to destinations faster and more economically.

There was really no practical value in covering great distances without stopping to refuel. Sacrificing airplane speed to get the most mileage per gallon of gas was self-defeating when it came to delivering goods or people in less time. There was actually no demand for planes to fly farther than Lindbergh's trip across the Atlantic – a distance of 3,600 miles, enough to bridge the old and new worlds. In addition landing sites on islands were available. The Soviet Union almost touches Alaska in the North Pacific, so obviously there was no shortage of land for airfields in this part of the world. Essentially, flights such as Codos and Rossi's from New York to Syria were more for show than anything else. Nations falling behind in the aircraft field were prone to promoting publicity events designed to show that things were going well in their factories. From a governmental perspective long-range flights were a form of intimidation. They were a warning to unfriendly countries that their capitals and manufacturing sites were within bombing range. However, in Europe nations were so close to each other that excessive long-range capability was not necessary. Just as in commercial use, airplane speed was crucial to military strategy, since fast aircraft were more difficult to shoot down. During these years of peace, business promotions and contests inspired long-distance and around-the-world flights. Often, as in the case of Lindbergh, a financial incentive was involved in the decision to cross the Atlantic; aircraft companies could advertise particular airplanes and thus increase sales. But here again the long-distance flights were not the trend of the future; they were simply executed for show by either the government or private commercial enterprises.

Russia found herself in this very position. The only option open to the government was to do something for show. Recognizing this, the NSR avaitors wracked their brains to find ways of helping the aviation industry. There were many good pilots available, although only a few were known outside of Russia. But all of them were flying inferior planes and until this was changed there appeared to be no solution in sight. Even the "talented" Tupolev, who was both a designer and builder, had not been able to make a difference. This is why he had been scheduled to visit the United States. So now the boys of Shelkova would have something to think about. What could they do for show?

The Russian fliers didn't dare take any of the Russian-built planes out of the country and thus reveal their poor quality. Besides most everything the Soviets had was fashioned after German Junkers models. Tupolev's converted French products, the ANT-25s, were the best in the long-distance category with a range of 1,800 to 1,900 miles. But this distance did not begin to compare with foreign aircraft capabilities. It appeared the only alternative was an in-house or domestic attempt to establish a distance record. However, it was realized this enterprise would not generate any international interest. It might generate some international attention if foreign observers were allowed to witness the takeoff and terminus of such a flight. But the Russians could not permit any outsiders to be present no matter what plane was used, because of their limited ranges.

In order to qualify for a record, neutral observers had to witness the takeoff and landing; moreover the barographs on a plane were subject to examination at the conclusion of any try at a record. A barograph is an instrument attached to airplanes to plot the various altitudes of any particular trip. In this way officials would know whether a plane had landed secretly to refuel during a flight. Another way to insure against unauthorized refueling was the installation of gas seals. These seals are placed over the gas caps and must remain un-broken until they are inspected. Since the Russians had no long-distance aircraft it was impossible to comply with these regulations, and therefore was unrealistic to think any Soviet planes could qualify for world records.

The French had always been the keeper of airplane records, having set up the Federation Aeronautique Internationale early in the history of aviation. This was the organization to convince if the Soviets ever hoped to become known internationally. There was no way the Russians could meet the requirements of the Federation Aeronautique Internationale and if any record-setting flights were planned, some deception would be necessary.

It may never be discovered who was the first person to suggest using deception, but personnel from NSR and the Kremlin were heavily involved. The long winter days at Shelkova with Moscow next-door had brought together all of the elements it would take to devise a plan to fool the world. Many aviators and mechanics were present, as well as Mr. Tupolev, the designer. And not far away the offices of the NSR and the Kremlin were readily accessible. From this consortium was to develop one of the most bizarre stories in the history of aviation. Sigmund Levanevsky may have been the important link between the Kremlin and NSR, but he probably didn't realize where his cooperation would lead him, at least not initially. But now as rumors of deception surfaced, the celebrated flier began to grow anxious as to whether he was going to be asked to be a part of the skullduggery. If the NSR staff had any such plans, would the Soviet dictator approve of them? Levanevsky was quite aware his fame was directly attributable to Stalin since he had personally selected him for the Mattern and *Cheliuskin* rescues. Was Stalin now thinking about collecting on these favors? Levanevsky must have felt happy with the way his life was going at this point and leary of involvement in fraudulent enterprises. He was proud of his family which included his wife Natalie and two young children, a boy and a girl. It was not to his benefit to risk his good name and chance losing the respect of his family and friends. However, the "Soviet Lindbergh" must have known the difficulty he would face by refusing to cooperate with Stalin if the dictator were going to act in collusion with NSR. Levanevsky's fears would later be realized.

From the wintering camp at Shelkova, specific recommendations were being made to conduct a nonstop flight to America! How could this be when there was not a suitable world-class airplane available? But these were desperate times calling for desperate measures, and it was obvious the burden had been assumed by the idle employees of NSR. Whether this had come about voluntarily or as a result of pressure from the Kremlin is speculative. The NSR being the brainchild of Stalin put all of the employees in a subservient position. Stalin not only was the country's dictator, he was also their immediate boss. The NSR staff might have wanted to please him by conducting a major international event, or more in fact what might seem to be a legitimate flight.

Levanevsky's name was mentioned in connection to the plan. But the most amazing revelation was that the made-over Dewoitine was going to be used for the flight, a plane that couldn't fly more than 1,900 miles on a single gas load. A distance of 1,900 miles wouldn't even get the wide-winged monoplane to the North Pole, let alone to the United States. So what kind of flight was being considered? The news was enough to jolt even the wildest of minds. Yet there it was, a serious recommendation to sponsor a nonstop flight to America. In the ANT, this was ridiculous! Surely any flight plan involving the ANT would be a very short trip; perhaps NSR was thinking of jumping the ANT off from eastern Siberia if there were any hopes of reaching America without having to stop for fuel. But even then, everyone knew this particular airplane was still not going to make the American mainland and Canada – perhaps Alaska – but certainly not the United States.

There was talk California was to be the announced destination; this was of course ridiculous. What was happening at Shelkova? Were some of these people losing their minds? It appeared so when the final route to America was laid out. Levanevsky must have rocked back on his heels when he heard the words, "Over the North Pole." Was he expected to be part of this insanity? That was the actual recommendation offered by the NSR staff. They wanted to schedule a nonstop transpolar flight from the Moscow-Shelkova area to San Francisco, California. Naturally there was something wrong. The ANT couldn't make that trip, but that was exactly the point. NSR was not really going to go through with the flight. The plane was never going to be allowed out of Russia. The strategy was to advertise Tupolev's latest creation as being designed as a world flier. Who was going to know the difference? The ANT was a "new plane" and thus not familiar to airplane builders throughout the world.

Many world flights had been abandoned; one more shouldn't arouse suspicion. Even the original owners of the Dewoitine, alias the ANT, failed twice to get their plane to Tokyo, and the Americans also had their share of failures as illustrated by Mattern crashing twice on Soviet territory. All the NSR staff was trying to accomplish was to put the world on notice that the Russians had a plane capable of bridging the eastern and western hemispheres in a single hop. This idea was much more desirable than the dull in-house project contemplated earlier. Since there was no intention of completing the event, NSR could choose any route. Therefore why not take the most dangerous and dramatic path to America. A polar route would add to the affair's

prestige, suggesting to foreign governments and their airplane industries that the Soviets had the expertise and sophisticated navigational
equipment to negotiate the unknown sub-zero wastelands at the top of
the world. Although Richard Byrd was suppose to have surveyed these
regions, the excitement of the mysterious and relatively inaccesible
world of ice was still an intriguing subject. The other aspect of this
speculated venture was distance. Moscow to San Francisco was comparable to the Codos and Rossi flight. San Francisco was selected by
NSR because this destination would better the Codos and Rossi effort,
and would carry the message that the Soviets had an even better plane
than the French Bleriot.

The NSR employees wintering at Shelkova must have chuckled
heartily at the idea of taking one French plane and disguising it then
announcing plans to use it to better the record of Codos and Rossi's
Bleriot, another French product. The Bleriot, like the Dewoitine, also
used a 12-cylinder Hispano-Suiza engine. But it has not been determined whether Tupolev's M-34 was really a Hispano-Suiza in disguise.
If this was the case, the irony of pitting the French Dewoitine (presently
the ANT) against the world record-holder Bleriot was even more pro-
nounced. The practice of cribbing was not unfamiliar to the Russians;
their lot in life of being a struggling society had made it necessary to
pretend things were better than they seemed. In the area of aviation it
was extremely important to pretend they had quality airplanes because
this reflected on the technical ability of the Soviet engineers and designers. The number of Soviet planes could always be kept a secret, but the
quality was something that could not be faked – unless the Russians
were not going to venture outside of their own borders. In this particular case it was not a matter to worry about. Since the ANT would not
reach America, there was no reason to be concerned about the poor
quality of the plane being revealed.

No other nation was in the unique position or situation of being
the only bastion of communism on the face of the earth. Who could say
that the Russian people and their leaders were not genuinely afraid of
invasion, or for that matter of a collapse from within? In either case the
protection and control of the country depended upon the development
of aviation. Since no legitimate means were in sight, the government
and NSR were exercising their only alternative; in simple terms that
meant to cheat, or crib if you will. It is apparent these factions looked at
the matter as the end justifying the means. The seriousness of the
situation was probably at times tempered with the knee-slapping

humor of pulling one over on the capitalist nations, but in reality the times were so crucial no one could laugh for long.

Sigmund Levanevsky probably saw little humor to this outlandish try at world headlines. Even though he was not expected to leave Russia, the attempt to span the Pole would have to be announced beforehand, and for good reason this had to concern the "Soviet Lindbergh." Based on Levanevsky's reputation the Americans would think a genuine flight was going to be attempted. At least the Soviet flier was not scheduled to confront the citizens of the United States on the fake trip. Eventually Stalin had plans to send him to America in order to make contacts with some of the important figures in aviation. If this was to be, Levanevsky would sooner not have this fraudulent affair on his mind. He must have reasoned that this anticipated failure was not going to help improve his image; however, NSR was not so much interested in Levanevsky as it was in promoting the ANT as a capable world flyer. The "Soviet Lindbergh" already had enough prestige but Tupolev's renovation had none, and rightfully so. Therefore this was the focus of the Soviets; they wanted to plant the idea in foreign aviation circles that they had built a plane able to fly farther nonstop than any other aircraft in the world.

Understandably Levanevsky was concerned about trying to pass off the ANT as an example of modern technology, especially with himself at the helm. He must have wanted to delay his decision to cooperate as long as possible with the hope the NSR and the Kremlin would give up this folly.

Who were these men who had taken such an interest in staging a fake flight over the North Pole? Would Dr. Otto Schmidt stoop to taking part in these goings on? His expertise was along the lines of exploration and how to combat nature in the Northern Sea Route project. This unusually talented man was blessed with a wide range of abilities; he was not only effective as a man of learning in various fields but also had the practical mind to deal with the everyday problems that plagued the sea route. If the professor had not been of German extraction he might have attained greater heights in the Communist Party. But be that as it may, he still enjoyed a prominent position in Stalin's government and was highly respected in the Moscow area. In certain ways his situation compared with that of Sigmund Levanevsky. Both men had already garnered enough fame to last them a lifetime, so there was at least no personal need to become involved in this most illegitimate adventure.

But Professor Schmidt was still the chief of NSR and anything the staff and other employees were doing came under his responsibility. It was a ticklish situation for the plucky explorer. Was he going to tell Stalin he wanted out, or was he going to ride it out regardless of the outcome? From the Soviet perspective it is understandable why some individuals motivated by patriotism alone would agree to go along with what the government thought were necessary deceptions in the interest of promoting aviation. Schmidt was probably as patriotic as anyone and may have decided to cooperate. It is also possible the NSR employees were coerced to some degree by the feared dictator. Even if the professor did agree to mastermind the projected transpolar hoax flight, it was evident he would need help from other NSR staff. He would have to draw upon such veteran aviators as Mikhail Vodopyanov and Vassily Molokov. The latter was close to 40 years of age, experienced in arctic exploration, and had a strong background in naval flight training. Molokov joined the Party in 1925 which gave him a ten-year association with the Kremlin. He also was decorated for his part in the *Cheliuskin* rescue.

There were other aviators with the organization not so celebrated; they were younger and more ambitious, and therefore might have been looking for their place in the sun. Some of these men were certainly known around the Shelkova-Moscow sector as capable aviators who did not enjoy the fame of some of their fellow employees and therefore likely to be looking for opportunities to further their careers. One flier who fit this description was Valery Chkalov. He had no significant credentials but was known to be a good pilot. Chkalov had joined the Red Army at the youthful age of 15 and worked as an airplane assembler. Two years later he enrolled in flight school, specializing in aerobatics and bombing tactics. At 20, Chkalov was assigned to a fighter squadron in the peacetime army. Outside of a reputation for stunt flying and the testing of planes, Valery had not distinguished himself in any appreciable way. His aggressiveness and brazen nature were especially suited for the type of plan NSR was devising. Yet Chkalov lacked sufficient leadership qualities. He had a friend named George Baidukov who came up much the same way as he had; early service and flight training culminated in a job as a test pilot.

Baidukov had become somewhat incorrigible at the age of eight. He subsequently ran away from home and a few years later went to work as a laborer. Chkalov's background was more normal and he especially enjoyed the years accompanying his father who worked as a fireman on a boat which sailed the Volga River. Yet it is interesting that Chkalov rather than Baidukov was the rebel of the two. Baidukov was quite subdued in his behavior and probably more intelligent. He had some inclination to be a writer although not on the level of Vodopyanov. Baidukov was respected as a proficient pilot and had developed a particular skill in instrument or blind flying. Because of this talent he was in demand as a copilot while at NSR. Weather conditions in the arctic often required the ability to fly safely in low overcast skies. It was a good bet George Baidukov was mixed up in the NSR's proposal to fake a world flight.

No matter who or how many people from NSR were connected to the plan there had to be support and encouragement coming from the Kremlin. In the Soviet system there was no such thing as any civil group going out on its own concerning any project. Stalin had his thumb on every important element and in particular the NSR. Although he would never allow any direct connection to himself and a fake flight, there is no question the Soviet chief knew every move transpiring. The question then arises, who acted as the connection between NSR and the Kremlin? The person or persons must have held high office in order to promote this project and to influence Stalin. There were several who would benefit by such a promotion in Soviet aviation. They, like many other officials, were constantly under the gun to upgrade Russia's aerial defenses. And whether or not they wanted to be accomplices there was really no choice. Chief of the Air Force, General Iakov Alksnis, and Defense Minister Klementy Voroshilov were the two most probable figures involved as go-betweens. Mikhail Kaganovich, who was in charge of aircraft construction, and his brother Lazar, the Transportation Commission, were in a position to encourage the NSR plan. A major role was probably also played by Gregory Ordjonikidze, commissioner of Heavy Industry. Klementy Voroshilov, having been close to the dictator since the early days of the Russian Revolution, might have been the most trusted person to deal with this affair and would have been the logical link between Stalin and the NSR.

All these top officials knew the dangers if the plot to deceive the world were revealed. The repercussions would be enormous. If the Soviets had to resort to these kinds of tactics in order to convince the world of their prowess in aviation, wouldn't discovery signal just the opposite? If the Germans and the Japanese had any designs on invading Russia, this would be a great incentive. And there was Leon Trotsky waiting in the wings, in exile, for Stalin to make a serious mistake. If Stalin were caught in this fraudulent enterprise it might be enough to bring him down. What a blow this would be to the Communist movement. But in the face of almost insurmountable problems there appeared to be no legitimate way out of the aviation dilemma. The most frightening part was yet to come, namely, notifying the American government that a flight to the United States was being contemplated. A formal request to enter and land on American territory had to be submitted. Even though there was no intention of leaving Russia, this matter and other issues were necessary for appearances sake. And once it became known a world flight was in the offing, newspaper reporters from all over the globe would be descending upon Moscow. Their presence might increase the chances of discovery. The Americans and other correspondents could not be barred from Moscow because it would arouse suspicions. Of course there must be a takeoff from Shelkova if the flight was to have an authentic beginning. However, the greatest concern at this point was finding someone, preferably from the NSR staff, to take charge. Stalin did not want to give the impression that the government was the sponsor. Once it all got started a specific supervisor or spokesman must step forward and control the enterprise, otherwise the Soviets were asking for trouble. It wasn't likely any member of the Kremlin would volunteer because if the plan failed it meant almost sure death for this person. In the event of discovery, Stalin would be forced to move quickly to punish everyone before he was implicated. Many lives at NSR were at stake and probably a few from the Kremlin. If the green light was given, then it was obvious the government had to be involved as the approval could only come from the Soviet chief. Everyone who was a party to the fakery was placing life and career on the block; but since the flight was not going to reach America, they continued on with the plan.

All of the details had not been worked out during these winter months of 1935 but there was a positive feeling nevertheless that Levanevsky would take the ANT from Shelkova sometime during the year and then abort the flight shortly thereafter. The Americans would have to be notified soon of NSR's plans for the first transpolar attempt to span two continents in the history of aviation. It would be up to NSR and the Kremlin to convince the U.S. authorities that a legitimate flight was on the Russian agenda. This would mean going through all the protocol, diplomatic exchanges, and any other necessary formalities and the obtaining of permits.

CHAPTER 8

The *Gorky* Disaster

In the United States serious economic and unemployment problems were on the rise in the first month of 1935, so the situation in Russia was not unique when it came to the plight of the poor. The Roosevelt administration was again pressing for social change in the form of more money for public work projects. But even though some segments of society were suffering, technical advances in aviation and industry in general were without precedent. Wiley Post was conducting important experimental high-altitude flights. On one occasion he remained aloft in the stratosphere as high as 20,000 feet while dressed in a special pressurized suit. A leaking oil line interrupted the test. Following the flight an ominous prelude to his death developed when an analysis of the plane's engine revealed metal shavings and emery dust had been purposefully deposited in the manifold. Undaunted by this threat, the "gutsy" aviator began to plan still another air journey into the arctic wilds. This was to be the year of his last aerial adventure.

Wiley Post's experiments in high-altitude flying were an indication the U.S. had begun to think in terms of aerial superiority. Reconnaissance from high above the land was an important strategic advantage. Although war was not the aim, certain strategic precautions regarding aviation were quietly developing behind the scenes. For many years there had been an organized program to build airfields in the islands close to Japan. Starting in the Philippines, about 30 airports had already been constructed; the latest work was underway on Batan Island, only 130 miles from the Japanese island of Formosa. Although the airfields were claimed to be part of a general aviation development, it was noted the landing facilities were being constructed under United

States Air Force supervision. There is no question the Japanese government was concerned with this intrusion into its part of the world. Russia was probably glad to see the Americans put pressure on one of her arch enemies, but on the other side of the world the Germans were exerting some pressure of their own. Hitler was talking about moving against governments with significant German populations. And to back up the government's ability to accomplish these ends Hermann Goering, chief of the air force, declared Germany's air power second to none. A more comforting announcement in early spring of 1935 was that the Royal Air Force of Great Britain would be tripled in strength. Other European countries such as France and Italy were also gearing up their air defenses as the fear of war and invasion swept the globe. Stalin knew his country was not able to keep pace. It was a worrisome situation.

The position of the United States was to avoid entanglement with the military posturing in Europe. Economic woes had begun to loom again with 25 percent of the work force unemployed. Roosevelt had all he could handle without becoming enmeshed in foreign political problems. Something would have to be done for the growing lines of the poor and hungry, a situation which had worsened when some New Deal projects received less funding. Roosevelt made a dramatic move to turn things around and requested a tremendous increase in certain government-sponsored work projects. Among them was the Civilian Conservation Corps (CCC) which had been recruiting young men to work in the forests and state-federally owned lands in order to improve and preserve the country's natural resources. As a consequence of the new financing thousands of recruits were assigned throughout the nation, bringing the grand total to 600,000. Ironically it was this move by Roosevelt that was to have a bearing upon the Russian transpolar story. With the additional monies new ground was broken, taking the young CCC men northward to Alaska. Some recruits found themselves working in the Alexander Archipelago. It was this locale that would ultimately figure in transpolar events, and one young man from the Vancouver, Washington area – where Semion Shestakov had visited – was to play a very interesting part.

Six years after the arrival of Shestakov and his crew in the United States a new group was sent by Stalin to study American technology. Led by A.N. Tupolev, 15 aviation engineers and technicians began touring aircraft facilities. These were anxious moments for the Soviets because U.S. public opinion was turning against the Communist movement. Congress members were trying to bring legislation to thwart enlistment into the Communist Party. Stalin hurried to prepare a new trade agreement that would enrich Uncle Sam by $30 million. However, it appeared Russia was taking liberties with Soviet-American relations by encouraging American Communists to stir up striking dock workers at Pacific Coast ports. This meddling was beginning to enrage much of the American populace. If the trend kept up, Tupolev and his group of experts would never come away with any worthwhile information. Many of the industrial heads already resented their being allowed into the country.

In May of 1935 Tupolev and his entourage were busy studying production methods when a shocking announcement was issued from Moscow. The gigantic *Maxim Gorky* had crashed, killing all 48 of the crew and passengers. The designer's prize airship was completely destroyed, ranking it as the worst air disaster in the history of aviation. That spring the *Gorky* had been on a propaganda tour and as a special added attraction many Soviet citizens were given rides on the biggest airplane in the world. An important component of the Russian propaganda machinery was directed at building the "biggest of everything" in place of quality and realistic products, particularly aircraft. Tupolev had been immensely proud of his creation and now it was gone, and with it numerous close friends of the designer who were also noted aviation experts.

The circumstances surrounding the *Maxim Gorky's* demise were quite clouded. The government's account differed widely from witnesses'. Citizens who were waiting to take the next ride said the plane merely exploded in the air; but the official version said one of two small planes executing barrel rolls or loops had accidentally fallen into the great mother ship. The immediate reports reaching Europe seemed to agree with the civilian witnesses but the government quickly suppressed any further public statements. The pilot of the small escort plane was reportedly killed. He was posthumously condemned for "exhibitionism," lacking in social discipline, and for being an "air hoodlum." Regarding the *Gorky's* fatalities, all of the crew and passengers were listed as dead. No one survived according to official reports. However, in time there would be some evidence that chief pilot Nikoli Juroff had actually escaped death. Juroff was not the regular pilot of the *Gorky* but was sitting in for Mikhail Gromov, one of Russia's finest aviators. Gromov had not been able to assume his duties on this fatal day because of a stomach disorder.

The *Gorky* disaster was the third major one in the Soviet Union

within two years. In 1933 five important aviation executives and three
aviators died in a crash near Moscow. That same year 14 died at
Kharkov when the largest airship built prior to the *Gorky* crashed. The
possible cause of some of these accidents was described by William C.
Bullitt, American ambassador to Russia. In a confidential letter to
President Roosevelt, Ambassador Bullitt told of an incident reflecting
the primitive method of refueling planes in the Soviet Union (*For The
President Personal and Secret*, by Orville H. Bullitt, brother of William
C. Bullitt). Ambassador Bullitt was being transported by air when the
craft stalled as if out of gasoline. His American pilot struggled with the
airplane but it landed upside down in a marsh. There were no injuries.
Cause of the mishap appeared to be a clogged fuel line as the tanks still
contained gasoline. The ambassador explained that "there are no
pumps and cans of gasoline are simply poured in by hand which makes
it possible always that a certain amount of dirt will enter the tank."
(This might be contrasted with most U.S. airfields employing under-
ground fuel tanks outfitted with pumps and filtering systems since the
1920s.)

The fact that the Soviets were losing a few planes was not the main
impact of the disaster because almost every week other countries'
aircraft were falling from the skies. The only difference was the Russians could ill afford to lose their planes while the United States,
Germany, England, and France were producing more and more each
day. Stalin began making accusations of sabotage in Soviet airplane
factories illustrating how dear were each of these machines. One reported incident in particular might indicate the intensity of the times. A
young aviator was placed before a firing squad for what was described as
willfully smashing airplanes. The pilot, whose name was given simply
as Areflev, was accused of purposefully wrecking one plane while
engaging in stunt flying and damaging another by striking electrical
lines. Both times he was lucky to escape with his life, only to be
"executed."

The circuit court at the time of the trial warned the people to be on
the lookout for such wreckers of industry. Apparently this young man's
reported execution was to be a grim reminder of the consequences.
Whether Areflev was a real person or a government invention is a moot
question. It is possible the entire Areflev affair was fabricated in order
to bring those involved in aviation into line, but if the incident was
authentic this young man Areflev may have been allowed to join the
"walking dead." It was not uncommon under Stalin's rule to permit

certain people to go free if they changed their names and agreed to take up residence in some other part of the vast country.

Immediately after the crash of the *Maxim Gorky* the government moved quickly to instill confidence in the mammoth plane design. Sixteen more were ordered – but curiously enough the order was given to American manufacturers. Since Tupolev, the *Gorky's* designer, was in the United States at the time of the accident, newspaper reporters converged on him for a statement about the tragedy. He declined, explaining that he had been unable to get any information out of Moscow. The Russian government had immediately shut down all lines of communication in and out of Moscow – another reason to suspect something was wrong. For ten hours this silence continued, giving the appearance the Kremlin needed time to get its stories together.

At any rate the demise of the *Gorky* paved the way for a greater Soviet presence in America as U.S. companies began filling orders for 16 more of the monstrous planes. It appears contracts between Russia and the United States included the right of Soviet technical personnel to observe and even take part in the filling of Soviet orders. In order to do this the U.S. government had to bring pressure to bear upon private industry. Why was this done? The answer probably had much to do with the way Hitler was carrying on in Europe. If the Germans were going to run amuck in an attempt to build an empire, the allied nations led by England and France were going to need all of the help they could muster. Since Russia vehemently opposed fascism it was politically smart to woo them into the allied camp. Roosevelt and his administration decided to invite the Soviets into the country so they could upgrade their aviation industry. Stalin knew his nation held the balance of power in Europe; he would play this advantage of gaining American technology to the hilt. In spite of the encouragement offered by the United States there was a long road ahead before the Russians would be able to build large numbers of quality airplanes, a need vital to the modernization and perhaps the survival of Stalin's government. How to compete with the highly successful manufacturing techniques of the noncommunist world – that was the Russian dilemma.

In view of the situation Tupolev's effort seemed such a pittance but then again the Russians had to start some place. It was probably fortunate the stocky designer had been in the United States at the time of the *Gorky* crash. The Russian people had invested heavily in the construction of the plane and some very important people were supposed to have lost their lives. But now that the *Gorky* incident was behind him Tupolev could concentrate on the 16 additional *Maxim Gorkies* being built by U.S. manufacturers. Hopefully this would put him back in the good graces of Stalin and the Kremlin. At the same time the designer was busy doing his part, the NSR in Moscow was getting the ANT ready for the "transpolar flight."

Just who were going to make up the infamous crew was close to being decided. Levanevsky had held out about as long as he could but now it appeared he finally had given in to the Kremlin and Stalin. He was to bring with him navigator Victor Levchenko who had been one of his former students in flight school, and now Levchenko was going to follow his mentor in a pretended journey over the North Pole. It was probably not surprising to hear that George Baidukov had accepted the role of copilot in this misadventure. Baidukov's expertise at instrument flying was a perfect qualification to help convince the world the flight was really being made. The extreme overcast and cloud cover above the arctic and polar regions was well known and the choice of Baidukov addressed this problem well.

CHAPTER 9

Levanevsky's Dry Run

The signal that the "transpolar" aerial trip to America was definitely on became apparent when the Russian government applied for membership in the Federation Aeronautique Internationale (FAI). It was obvious the Soviets were now seeking world publicity. They had at last decided to give the impression their pilots were going to be flying into the territory of a foreign country. And since the flight was not going anywhere the barograph and gas seals wouldn't be examined by foreign aeronautical officials. There didn't seem to be any danger of the hoax-flight being exposed as the NSR would have complete control of it from the beginning to the end. From a political standpoint the gamble was evidently worthwhile. However, it would be wise to keep an eye on the foreign reporters. American newsmen were especially bothersome because they were more free from their government's control. Since San Francisco was to be named as the terminus for the "transpolar" air journey the American reporters could become a particular nuisance when trying to obtain information. The NSR directorate must be very careful in its management of the event.

In southern California Wiley Post was also planning a world flight but his intentions, unlike Levanesky's, were in earnest. It wasn't apparent at this time whether the partially blinded flier was going to go it alone or whether he would have a companion. There were rumors Will Rogers, well known humorist and western personality, might fly with Post for at least part of the trip. The proposed flight was to be routed over the northern latitudes and again was scheduled to fly over Russian territory. Naturally this required permission from the Soviet government, something the Kremlin soon must ask of the United States if the

NSR plan was to get underway this year. The most logical time for a transpolar flight was in July when the weather was most favorable. At the same time people were following Post's preparations another item of interest appeared in newspapers across the country. For the first time the American government and people became aware of the Soviet plans.

A brief article on July 13 told of a Soviet request for permission to fly over and land on American territory as part of a nonstop transpolar flight planned for that year. However, no specific date was given for the takeoff. Although the news was an eye opener, little interest was generated until a follow-up story hit the nation's front pages. It was learned that unfavorable weather reports were the only obstacle holding up the start of the North Pole aerial expedition to America. To make this flight believable the Kremlin had made arrangements to place one of their own radio agents in Seattle to translate and control all communications to and from the aircraft. Soviet sources declared that strict secrecy would be observed in relation to the flight in order to avoid any premature publicity and prevent the "possibility of an anti-climax." This secrecy also extended to Russia, where only a brief announcement was issued on July 17. It was apparent even local interest was being discouraged, probably to avoid a run on Shelkova by citizens living in the area. Meanwhile the Americans were being given more information. Sigmund Levanevsky, another of the Soviet Union's finest aviators, was to be the chief pilot. Internationally famous after rescuing James Mattern, he had become one of Stalin's favorite "falcons" of the airways. George Baidukov was named as the copilot and navigator Victor Levchenko had been selected to guide the plane over the "dangerous arctic and polar wastelands." A July 18 bulletin revealed the flight was being sponsored by the Northern Sea Route Administration but the article added, "all requests for information have been refused at the offices." Evidently American journalists had tried unsuccessfully to contact the NSR Administration. It was also noted the Central Aero-hydrodynamic Institute (TSAGI), where the plane was designed and built, was under heavy guard. Security was also tight at the Moscow airport "which because of its long runway is believed to be the field chosen for the takeoff." No details of the plane's construction were included other than to say it was "single-engined and entirely Soviet-built." Some accompanying material indicated American weather services would assist in the historic event.

On July 22, 1935 the Russians announced that an attempt to span the North Pole by air would begin that morning. The main objective of the flight was to "blaze the way for a regular aviation route between Russia and North America" while other benefits had to do with the groundwork to establish a permanent meteorological station at the North Pole. It was also reported a thorough exploration of the polar icecaps was scheduled. The Soviets focused hard on the commercial airline aspects of the project – not surprising in view of the political situation. The Soviets wanted to draw close to the Americans for obvious reasons and the airline was one way to do this. Of course this was only an excercise in blowing smoke screens because Levanevsky wasn't going to finish this trip. But the propaganda went on to predict that an air link with America was in the works. This was an effective tactic to give the impression the Soviets and Americans would soon enjoy a greater exchange. Shades of Shestakov! He too had dwelled on the prospects of an air link some six years earlier.

A July 22 news article told about the existence of 60 meteorological stations within the Russian Arctic Circle, most of which were equipped with radio apparatus; they would provide weather reports for Levanevsky's flight. The Moscow news releases gave a few facts about the plane scheduled to make the epic nonstop journey. It was an "ANT-25" adapted from a model used extensively in propaganda work. Americans became aware the plane was designed by A.N. Tupolev, who according to American news reports, was at this very time in the United States supervising the building of sixteen huge planes to succeed the *Maxim Gorky*. Tupolev's ANT was described as a long-distance model, low-wing monoplane with unusually long wings, short fuselage and landing wheels set wide apart. Other equipment included blind-flying instruments and other modern aides to navigation. The Soviets claimed to have a sun compass supposedly effective in the North Pole vicinity where magnetic compasses were not accurate. Two years later it was reported that the sun compass had been a gift from Richard Byrd.

According to Soviet documents, Professor Otto Schmidt, representing the Northern Sea Route Administration, was the man in charge of the Levanevsky flight. Schmidt's report declared, "the time is near when airplanes will carry research workers, equipment, food, tents, etc. to predetermined points on the eternal ice and leave them there for perhaps a year." It was speculated an observatory would be established to "broadcast weather reports, measure ocean depths, study ocean life, determine the laws of the ice movement and make magnetic studies." Levanevsky's flight apparently was to add to the Soviet knowledge of the arctic and polar regions which would make this so-called observatory possible in the future. The July 22 news article concluded with a claim that the ANT-25 could fly up to 8,000 miles without refueling. The Soviets had just added 2,000 miles to the already outrageous claim of a 6,000-mile range for the ANT-25. The Soviets also boasted this plane could carry 2,000 gallons of gasoline in six wing tanks.

It was getting late in July and in order to make the transpolar flight believable they would have to initiate a takeoff before adverse weather conditions would cast doubts on their story. Levanevsky and his two crewmen were ready. They had been staying at the airport awaiting the signal to begin the farce. Schmidt was being bombarded by foreign newsmen, particularly the Americans who wanted to interview Levanevsky. The NSR chief barred all but the Soviet writers from speaking personally with the flier. The Russian journalists were content to get whatever was given to them in contrast to the aggressive style of the Americans in their quest for information. They kept asking where the takeoff location was to be but Schmidt was careful not to reveal it. Harold Denny of the *New York Times* was very anxious to learn the location of the ANT and had for days shuttled back and forth from Moscow to Shelkova in an effort to spot the plane. He, like other American journalists, had come a long ways but was gradually finding out the Russians were leading them up and down blind alleys. When arriving at Shelkova the journalists were told the plane was back in Moscow, yet officials there would place the ANT back at Shelkova. This was repeated many times until Denny and his colleagues finally gave up. Denny said, "The most fantastic obstacles were being placed in their path to cover this great event." (*New York Times*, July 22, 1935.) Two of the reporters present had covered transatlantic takeoffs before, assignments considered difficult. According to the New York Times dispatches, the "evasiveness and secrecy employed by Russian officials seemed to be unmatched, . . . the incorrigible fondness for surrounding even the most innocent enterprises with dark secrecy. . . ." Even William Bullitt, the American ambassador to Russia, must have felt the restrictive policies of the Soviets as he learned he and no other outsiders would be allowed to attend the departure of Levanevsky.

Now that NSR had the blessing of Stalin and the Kremlin to move ahead, there was no turning back. The transportation and industrialization situation was not going to improve in the near future and there was growing internal unrest. Leon Trotsky, who was in exile, continued to criticize Stalin's leadership. Hitler was threatening aggression in Europe; Japan had already made a move on North China, an act that if successful would bring the Japanese very close to Soviet borders. These two arch enemies might soon threaten the security of Stalin's government. The more perceptive world political figures warned how things were getting worse each day. Especially terrifying was how any new war would be greatly magnified by the most deadly military weapon ever devised: the airplane!

Lindbergh recognized the peril in a notable speech in Berlin, an appeal to all nations to stem the tide toward another war. He warned of the great devastation befalling Europe as military fighters and bombers were unleashed. In many capitals the speech was hailed in the interest of peace. However, a curious reaction emerged from Moscow. On the same day of Lindbergh's presentation, July 24, an article was issued by the Soviet government and relayed to the international news services by *Pravda*, the Russian news agency. Although the text of the news item did not mention the Berlin speech, Lindbergh's name was the main focus (*New York Times*, July 25, 1935). The article contrasted Soviet aviators with Americans, "The former fly for their country," it said, "while pilots such as the Wright Brothers, Wiley Post, and Charles Lindbergh fly for individual glory and money." In a cruel remark referring to the infamous Lindbergh kidnapping, *Pravda* stated, "Charles Lindbergh bought personal independence with his feat and lost the stimulus to perform new feats. He sits in a far away place hiding his child and money from bandits. The brave Lindbergh is one of the most unfortunate persons in the world. He has lost both his son and his country."

Actually Lindbergh had been extremely active in aviation since his famous flight. Besides touring 75 American cities Lindbergh traveled 30,800 miles to 21 countries in 1933 and took a transpacific aerial journey to the Orient, all done in the interest of aviation development. He acted as a consultant to aircraft builders, served as an advisor to the government, charted various prospective commercial airline courses and had even invented an artificial heart during the mid-1930s, almost 50 years before American medical science made possible the development and implantation of the first artificial heart. It was apparent the Soviets were not closely following Lindbergh's career.

Moscow also described in the same news article a near world-record flight over dangerous arctic territory that had just been completed, but no specifics as to the names of the fliers and the type of plane were given. Apparently the claim was to bolster the credentials of the ANT-25 and the fliers who would soon "attempt the transpolar air trip."

What remains curious about the article is the slap at Lindbergh who had been held in great esteem in Russia. Levanevsky was still being referred to as the "Soviet Lindbergh." It is difficult to believe the comments would be issued on the same day as the Berlin speech but the Soviets may have been offended by the American aviator's visit to Germany, prompting them to draft a letter portraying the popular hero as egotistic and greedy. It is possible the Soviets spoke prematurely and may not have known the true contents of the speech. It was certainly in the interest of the USSR for Lindbergh to help slow down the trend toward war – for which the Russians simply were not ready. They needed more time to build up their country's aerial capabilities. Ambassador Bullitt phrased it in another way in secret letters to President Roosevelt. He informed Roosevelt there were reasons to believe the Soviets planned to wait out a European conflict; in fact Stalin was seriously thinking about signing a nonaggression pact with Hitler. Neutrality was in the interest of both leaders even though their reasons were different. Hitler dreamed of reuniting people of Aryan ancestry who made up major portions of other countries' populations. By keeping Russia temporarily out of the picture he could much more rapidly take over these countries and set up a German Empire. Russia simply wanted to keep the Germans out of her land until a capable defense system was built.

The Soviets had no need or intentions of invading any other country; however, by waiting out a European war they could more easily pick up the spoils. The spoils in this case were control of the states bordering western Russia, which could serve as a buffer zone. England and France feared the loss of Russia to the German side, knowing Hitler's dream of European conquest might become a reality. England and France and other sympathetic nations may not have known of the terrible weaknesses of Soviet ground and air forces, limiting the country's ability to carry on warfare outside of its borders. The Soviets lacked an efficient air force to protect their troops and tanks. This should have been apparent after the poor performance of Russian planes in the Spanish and Chinese theaters of war. But Stalin continued to speak boisterously about Russia's prowess and to some extent succeeded in intimidating her enemies. If the Germans had realized just how weak the Soviets were they would never have considered a neutrality pact. Yet it was this kind of agreement Stalin sought, and one that President Roosevelt wanted to avoid. This is why the American president applied pressure to the nation's airplane manufacturers to allow the Soviet engineers into their plants. Although Roosevelt advocated nonparticipation in the event of war, he felt compelled to help Russia in order to keep the allied cause strong and thus prevent Hitler from overrunning Europe. Stalin might have taken advantage of this situation when he gave his permission for the fake polar flight, knowing Roosevelt and the American government would discourage any serious probe into the affair if deception surfaced.

Levanevsky's hoax-flight was still waiting in the wings at Shelkova. If this "transpolar journey" was going to be believed NSR must get the plane off quickly. Weatherwise this was the best time to give the impression the Pole was going to be traversed; waiting longer would put the "flight" into a season of storms. It was also a labor to continue hiding the ANT and Levanevsky from the American news media.

As it turned out the ANT didn't take off on July 22, reportedly due to bad weather reports. Four days later *New York Times* correspondent Denny passed on to American readers the difference between the coming Soviet aerial attempt and the "individualistic exploits of Charles A. Lindbergh and Rear Admiral Richard E. Byrd" (*New York Times*, July 25, 1935). Although the Russians knew Lindbergh represented some aviation interests, and Byrd had the support of the U.S. Navy, they never missed an opportunity to blast away at what was perceived as individualism. This was a sudden departure from the previous accolades accorded Lindbergh. Just a year ago he had been welcomed in Moscow with open arms. The renowned aviator had gone out of his way to receive Pilot Shestakov in New York following his 1929 flight. It was baffling why the Russians would blast away at the American hero when they were making every effort to obtain U.S. expertise and technology in aviation, which in part had been furthered by Lindbergh.

The Soviet bulletins claimed the arctic and polar regions were being systematically tamed. Correspondent Denny wrote about the Soviet boasts, "there was not a point in the Arctic, including even the Pole, that Soviet planes cannot reach." Untold arctic riches in the form of natural resources were available for development. But the Russians had not begun to solve the transportation problems in these areas, let alone develop them.

What appeared to justify the intensive exploration of the Russian north was the notion of a natural ice-free channel that could link eastern and western Russia. The warm gulf stream rises to the surface somewhere in the arctic seas; however, in spite of all the expeditions by icebreaker between 1919 and 1935 this so-called warm water route had never been found. Even aerial reconnaissance had not discovered the mysterious passage. Correspondent Denny's July 26 article added, "Under the leadership of Otto Schmidt. . . seventy-three freight ships are now plying the Arctic Ocean between Soviet ports. Four ice-breakers, each assigned to its own section, keep the waters open." Considerable shipping activity is normal during the summer season but nothing was said about moving cargo along the entire north coast. The warm month of July would not require much icebreaker assistance to keep the western part of the channel free. It was in the political-military interest of the Soviets to exaggerate their accomplishments in the Northern Sea Route project. In this vein Schmidt continued to elaborate on the conquest of the northern regions, declaring "New plant strains capable of flourishing in the Far North are being tested in the hope that the Arctic can grow its own food. . . . New villages, towns and even cities are springing up on the Soviet Union's long northern coast. . . ." Schmidt was probably referring to the leftover radio station encampments serving the Northern Sea Route project. The news article concluded with claims of immense scientific benefits from the northern explorations and forecasts of a huge and advanced arctic population.

While Schmidt was expounding on the great strides being taken toward civilizing the arctic, Stalin and the Communist Party were busy attacking the Fascist cause throughout the world. The day before correspondent Denny's last story, Russia's Communist International, recognizing the great threat from Fascism, announced support for those nations opposing Hitler's expansionist plans. Stalin through necessity decided Hitler posed the greatest threat and therefore he placed a lesser priority on the international communist movement.

Although politically effective, this new policy was meaningless because the Soviets had all they could take care of at home. However, the Party line was softened in an effort to enlist international help against the Fascist menace. Two days later 2,000 American Communists attacked the crew of a German ship docked on the Hudson River. The riot lasted from midnight to dawn and resulted in many injuries to both sides. During the ensuing battle the Reds ripped the German flag from its mast and threw it into the river before hundreds of New York police could restore order. The policies of the Russian-based Communist International which encouraged such melees seemed to be working. Although the American government and public would not put up with Communist and Fascist sympathizers airing their differences on

American soil, the Soviet government felt it had the inside track because most Americans were vehemently opposed to the Hitler regime. The current plans for a "transpolar flight" were to cement Russian-American relations. So the grand hoax-flight of Levanevsky was to add the frosting to the cake. It was hoped the ANT and Levanevsky would come out of the affair with better credentials than before, even if the enterprise was doomed to failure.

While the Americans were waiting patiently during the last week of July for the big event, Schmidt was hurrying about Moscow and Shelkova trying to put the finishing touches on the takeoff ceremony. American Weather Bureau and Signal Corps stations had been asked to supply the three fliers with weather reports and information to help guide them once they reached the American side of the pole. The U.S. government had agreed to provide daily broadcasts to Levanevsky and his two associates who had been living at the Shelkova facility for days, reportedly waiting to get underway. Although numerous important government officials were to attend the ceremony it was not known beforehand if Stalin would show up. He had a habit of keeping the public off guard as far as his appearances were concerned. It was believed he feared assassination; therefore it was his practice to arrive unannounced and not spend much time before the public.

NSR offices, pressed by world interest in the flight, began releasing some personal information about the fliers as they prepared for the "historic" departure. Schmidt wrote, "For months the three aviators have been on special diets, designed to add weight in case the plane came down in an isolated area, and also rowing exercises were a daily routine in order to build up endurance." The plane was to carry "a small stove for heating food; ordinary rations of tea and various sandwiches; glazed fruits, concentrated lemon juice, chocolate, egg powder, canned meats, coffee, sugar, salt and numerous other items. The fliers, besides their normal clothing, were taking woolen underwear, fur-lined jackets, reindeer wraps, fur mittens and a medicine chest." These items were standard equipment for the ANT and other planes used in the north. No special adaptations were planned, although one which was certainly needed was de-icers for the wings. It was ludicrous for even a pretended trip north not to include de-icers; yet this was probably one more reason to keep the ANT well hidden until departure. Schmidt and Stalin's staff would have to carefully screen those attending the Shelkova ceremony. Since things were not quite ready at the airfield, Schmidt kept issuing news releases explaining weather problems.

The days of July 29, 30, and 31 ticked away with no signs the flight would begin. On August 1, it was reported Sigmund Levanevsky was confident the trip over the North Pole would succeed. According to the dispatch enough supplies were on board to sustain the fliers for three months in case the plane was forced down. A special wireless radio would be taken aboard in case the regular one was damaged. Schmidt had released an earlier report setting the tone for the expected failure: "Even if it [the flight] were not completed because of unpredictable circumstances, it would provide valuable scientific data regarding the polar regions and would blaze the way for regular freight or commercial routes...." Americans also were told that the fliers were only permitted to talk with selected Soviet journalists. Repeated requests from American correspondents for interviews with Levanevsky, Baidukov, and Levchenko continued to be turned down. This was puzzling since the flight was supposed to be a goodwill gesture between the two nations. It was imperative not to expose the fliers to the snoopy Americans; those experienced in aviation could easily spot something wrong, perhaps the absence of de-icers on the wings.

In the dead of night on August 2, activity around Shelkova began to pick up. Something was definitely in the air! Scores of NSR officials and personnel – many of whom were stationed in the field's barracks – began gathering at the airport. Throughout the night there was a bustling of flight personnel and Kremlin staff members whispering in small groups. The moment was almost at hand for Russia to enter the international aviation picture by sending her fliers on a pretended, nonstop transpolar flight to America.

While the NSR crowd was planning Levanevsky's dawn takeoff, Soviet officials went to the American embassy at midnight and spirited Ambassador Bullitt to Shelkova, along with Military Attaché Philip R. Faymonville. The attaché was given permission to attend the ceremony at the last minute after a previous announcement by the Kremlin that only Ambassador Bullitt would be allowed to witness the "historic" departure. As dawn broke several hundred Soviet officials arrived, among them Defense Minister Klementy Voroshilov and General Iakov Alksnis, from the Air Force. Adding a chill to the ceremony, Henry Yagoda of the secret police made his appearance. If anyone was thinking of making light of the flight or if questioning the capability of the ANT, Yagoda's presence would put a damper on that sort of thing.

By the morning of August 3, it was apparent that strict control of events at the airfield was the Soviet military's priority. A U.S. intelligence G-2 report described the strange scenario:

> Although several hundred Soviet officials were present, no other foreigners, except the press, were permitted on the field and no other foreigners are known to have visited Schcholkova (Shelkova). The greatest secrecy was maintained as to the location and even the name of the point of departure. Even after arrival at the airfield embassy chauffeurs who endeavored to ascertain general facts about the field were positively refused all information. Even the name of the field was refused them. The road, approaching the field, was lined for about two miles outside the field gate by a double cordon of soldiers at 10-yard intervals, and halts for identification purposes were frequent.

The G-2 papers concluded with a brief description of the airport, noting the "main runway across the front of the field is paved, 1,900 meters long and about 30 meters wide."

Professor Otto Schmidt was seen mingling with the crowd. The news media had often referred to him as the chief supervisor of Levanevsky's purported trip to America. Concern about security wasn't necessary; Schmidt's NSR men could be trusted to keep everything confidential. Foreign newsmen had no way of knowing a hoax was in progress because the soldiers kept them well back from the main gathering. Professor Schmidt made sure foreign reporters did not get close to Levanevsky. The "Soviet Lindbergh" might have been grateful to be spared interviews by the Americans.

Numerous relatives of the aviators, including Levanevsky's family, had stayed at Shelkova for several days awaiting the final countdown. The ANT was perched on a specially constructed elevated incline designed to give airplanes additional acceleration during lift-off. Levanevsky, George Baidukov, and Victor Levchenko appeared together amidst the applause of the carefully selected audience. After brief farewells with their families, the three shook hands with Ambassador Bullitt who gave them a letter to be delivered to President Roosevelt. The aviators turned to confer with Schmidt and the top Soviet dignitaries then quickly moved toward the wide-winged ANT. The fliers were dressed in their summer flying gear. According to Schmidt, because the cabin of the ANT would be well-heated by the large M-34 engine there was no need to dress in heavier clothing. In a few minutes the "polar trio" was inside the plane. All at once the roar of the motor was all one could hear above the din of the crowd. The pressurized oxygen tank used to start the plane's engine was quickly disconnected. Levanevsky continued to rev up the motor and then as the ANT lurched forward the fliers waved from the bubble canopy.

Levanevsky would have to hold the monoplane on the runway as long as possible. There was supposed to be 12,000 pounds of fuel on board (2,000 gallons), making the gross weight of the ANT about 25,000 pounds. If he were to take off too fast the foreign journalists might suspect there was much less gasoline on board. The ANT slowly moved along the 1,900-meter runway gradually gaining speed. Levanevsky would soon run out of concrete as the low woods began to loom closer and closer, but with 200 yards to spare the plane began lifting, finally clearing the trees as the chief pilot fought for altitude. Soon Shelkova was far behind as the ANT veered northward on course to the pole. Back at the airfield Schmidt was waiting for the appropriate time to tell the Americans and the rest of the world the "transpolar flight" was underway. NSR had decided to withhold the message as long as possible. Perhaps it would all be over before the bulletin was sent out.

At this very moment Levanevsky and his two flying companions were sailing along over the Russian countryside. The ANT was being kept at low altitudes as it skimmed the small villages and collective farms appearing on the landscape. Just how far would the big monoplane go on the limited supply of fuel? If there were no intentions of reaching America what did NSR have up its sleeve? What excuse would be used to abort the attempt? There was nothing to gain by flying too far north unless it was to convince the people watching from below that a bonafide North Pole flight was in progress. With only enough fuel to cover a distance of 1,800 or 1,900 miles, the fliers did not want to go too far. A point of no return must be calculated, otherwise the ANT would not be able to get back to Moscow.

During the next nine hours, according to Moscow radio, the fliers reported their northbound progress. Professor Schmidt reported that the fliers were 900 miles north of the Russian capital. If Levanevsky and the other two fliers were really where they said they were then a quick decision had to be made because they were fast approaching the point of no return. At 3 p.m. Schmidt received a distress call. There seemed to be a problem with the oil feed line; then Levanevsky signaled it was impossible to correct the defect and asked for permission to return. It was all over! The American government was immediately notified that it had been necessary to terminate the "polar" attempt. Signal Corps and weather stations were put at ease and the U.S. news media carried the disappointing bulletin. NSR had accomplished all it could hope for, which was to propagandize the idea that Soviet airplanes were capable of flying extremely long distances without refueling. Would this be believed after Levanevsky's short "polar trip?" Probably, since the Russian counterpart to Lindbergh was highly respected abroad. Unless someone "spilled the beans" the flight would be accepted as a legitimate effort to span the pole.

After receiving permission to discontinue the expedition Levanevsky turned the ANT around; but instead of aiming for the capital city he veered off to the right, a course on line with Leningrad. Leningrad, which is on the northwest coast of Russia, was the birthplace and hometown of Sigmund Levanevsky. If all went well the fliers would be arriving there sometime after dark. A total of 1,500 miles had been flown, according to Moscow dispatches, when the aircraft arrived over Leningrad. A flare was dropped from the plane to illuminate the landing field. But as the ANT neared the ground a dull explosion was heard and fire erupted from the left wing. Had the flare struck the wing, igniting the fabric? After a quick landing Levanevsky hurriedly shed his flying jacket and began smothering the flames. Soon two fire trucks arrived, and in a short time the situation was under control. News of this incident was not sent outside the Soviet Union for many years. Publicizing the fire would have reflected negatively on NSR's operation.

It wasn't long before government officials arrived from nearby Leningrad. A big black limousine pulled up close to the "fallen" ANT. The government men were there to remove $9,000, said to have been taken on board at Shelkova. Why was so much money being carried on a trip going nowhere? The Soviet consulate in San Francisco could have arranged finances for the fliers during a stay in America. Why carry such a large sum when it could be lost in the event of a crash? The three pilots were certainly not going to be able to spend any on a "nonstop" flight. Perhaps the money was intended to convince Leningrad officials that the flight was legitimate. The fact that both the fire and the money incidents were kept from the public only enhances the mystery. As the story goes, the mechanics at Leningrad easily repaired the oil feed problem and in a few days Levanevsky, along with Baidukov and Levchenko, flew the ANT back to Moscow. Experts there went over the oiling system and pronounced it sound. Thereafter the plane was supposed to have been flown on several successful missions and declared airworthy. Even though nothing was really accomplished by the Levanevsky flight it did serve to put the "Soviet Lindbergh" back into the international spotlight and to publicize the ANT as a long-distance flyer.

Four days after Levanevsky gave up on his "transpolar" adventure, Wiley Post, accompanied by Will Rogers, took off from Seattle for Alaska. His route included landings in Russia. It must have been disconcerting for the Soviets to see Post enjoy such access to their country when their own pilots lacked decent Russian-built planes for trips abroad. Post's incursions in northern Russia made his presence particularly undesirable. It was important to Stalin and the Kremlin not to let other countries see what they had failed to accomplish in the Northern Sea Route project. The number of arctic radio stations were probably exaggerated in Soviet news releases. There was no question Post would be in a position to get a good look at some of them. The irony of the situation was that the Russians needed the friendships and contacts with the American aviators but didn't want the Americans coming into their country and seeing the sad state of Soviet aircraft and general aviation technology.

By the middle of August, Post and Rogers arrived at Point Barrow, Alaska. Despite talk that Rogers would not continue, he apparently had decided to go to Russia. On August 15, the two close friends boarded the Lockheed aircraft; but something was wrong with the plane, prompting Post to get out. He was seen by U.S. Army Sgt. Stanley Morgan, radio station operator at Point Barrow, tinkering with the engine. Post then reboarded the craft and took off. Hours later a group of Eskimos rushed to the U.S. Signal Station at Point Barrow shouting and screaming, "A red plane, she blew up!" Sergeant Morgan hurried to an Eskimo sealing camp 15 miles away and spoke to the owner. The Eskimo identified Post and Rogers by describing them as "one wearing a rag on a sore eye, the other big man with boots." (Post had earlier lost the sight in one eye and wore a black patch.) On arrival at the crash scene Sergeant Morgan discovered both Post and Rogers entombed inside the partially submerged airplane. There was some mystery surrounding how the Army handled the affair. Sergeant Morgan was asked for details on the crash but declined, saying he was under strict orders not to give out any information. As fate dictated, this was Wiley Post's last trek to explore the northern territories.

CHAPTER 10

The Alaskan Plan

After Levanevsky's aborted flight, Stalin decided to send him to America to tour aviation factories. The Soviet leader also gave him permission to purchase a Douglas airplane. Both the Soviet Air Force and Civil Aeronautics Commission were interested in obtaining patent rights to produce this model. In keeping with past practices the Russian engineers would make slight modifications in the Douglas plane and eventually claim it as their own design. The Douglas craft was a good all-purpose transport plane. Stalin was probably also interested in a long-distance craft; one which Tupolev might copy to develop a Russian version that could later be used in a real transpolar flight. This was perhaps wishful thinking because the Americans were not interested in the production of long-range aircraft. The future of aviation was in speed and maneuverability. Actually the French Dewoitine would have been the answer for the Russians if Tupolev had not tried to alter it so much.

The NSR Directorate considered the "Levanevsky flight" as the first step in promoting Russian aviation. The only thing missing in the aborted affair was not getting the ANT into the United States. Of course this was easier said than done, judging by the ANT's limited range. However, until Russian aviators ventured outside their country no one was going to take them seriously in the field of aviation. There was no way the Soviet Union could compete with the faster planes of Europe and the United States; the only alternative was to continue trying to fashion some sort of long-distance feat. It was more likely an achievement in this aspect of aviation would be believed because of fewer demands on the planes' engines. Tupolev and other Russian designers had not yet mastered the technological skills required in

73

developing efficient airplane motors. The Soviets were thus forced to think in terms of cheating and hoaxes.

Because of its gliderlike appearance the ANT looked the part of a long-distance flyer; however, this is where the similarity ended. None the less, the NSR crowd decided to keep the renovated Dewoitine in their future plans. Certain factors were guiding their thinking. A long-range flight – or the appearance of one – seemed to be the only option open. It was a foregone conclusion that the destination had to be foreign soil, preferably the United States which was politically "the lesser of the evils." Although American Communists were losing influence, considerations involving technology and military alignments made the U.S. the most probable destination for a "world flight." Somehow a Soviet plane must end up in the United States while convincing the world an authentic achievement in aviation had taken place. And the only airplane that seemed to fit the bill for the proposed event was the ANT. Ideally a transpolar route would be the most exciting and spectacular.

In order for this or any other long-range route to be flown some cheating was inevitable. How were the NSR people going to get the ANT from Russia to America when the plane could only fly a maximum of 1,900 miles without refueling? The ANT would have to be started from a point relatively close to the American mainland. The only other option would be to plot a course where an airplane could land and refuel several times. The Soviets at one time must have considered making a multi-stop flight over the icecap and then trying to pass it off as an authentic nonstop achievement. This was really out of the question for one good reason. It would be difficult, if not impossible, to keep many refueling stops secret, particularly those on the American side of the pole. Therefore the NSR organization began looking for other solutions. If a route was directed westward over the Atlantic Ocean toward New York there would be too many miles of water to cross. Out of necessity the NSR staff began considering Siberia as a possible launch site. However, even this route was far from being problem-free. The eastern shores of Soviet Siberia are about 2,400 miles from the American Pacific Northwest, 500 miles farther than the plane's range.

Southern California, supposedly the destination of Levanevsky's flight, was an additional 1,000 miles. Semion Shestakov had flown the Siberian-Alaskan route in 1929 by stopping at the Aleutian Islands and the Alexander Archipelago before reaching Seattle. Even if the ANT were to carry some extra gas it would be extremely dangerous to attempt a North Pacific Ocean crossing given the possibility of navigational errors and adverse weather conditions such as headwinds. If only Tupolev's damnable contraption could fly a little farther on a single gas load the Siberian route might be an answer. But whatever plan was finally decided on, the intentions were to create the illusion a Soviet airplane was flying nonstop from Moscow to the United States. Yet as each route was closely examined it was determined excessive distance was the major obstacle. If the Soviets were going to succeed in this bizarre undertaking it would be necessary to get an aircraft much closer to the United States. The NSR staff must have felt the Siberian-Alaskan vicinity was the most promising.

Southeastern Alaska was both remote and close to the United States. An ideal sanctuary for refueling an aircraft was somewhere between the islands of Baranof and Wales in the Alexander Archipelago. Was it possible to set up a secret base in Alaska with the aid of some Russian sympathizers there? If they ever expected to get the ANT to California, one of the islands close to the North 55-degree latitude could serve their purposes. Baranof in particular was very familiar to the USSR. Rugged and mountainous terrain characterized the geography of Baranof. But perhaps in the southern regions around the Prince of Wales and smaller uninhabited islets were smoother and more suitable areas for landings and takeoffs.

People like George Baidukov and Valery Chkalov were apparently intrigued with the idea of refueling right on Alaskan territory and then reaching California from that point. The fliers had learned many things about the islands of Baranof and Prince of Wales from Semion Shestakov. There were many small islands and isolated areas all through the archipelago. A small landing party would have to precede a projected flight in order to set up a refueling base. It would not be difficult to sneak into Alaska at night as there were few American Coast Guard ships patrolling these waters. There was, however, considerable fishing and fur trapping. Fishermen and trappers would be the greatest threat to the secrecy needed for a refueling stop. If this strategy was successful they would be halfway to America. Everything depended on what could be arranged in Alaska. The details and other matters might be resolved once it was known for sure just how the ANT was to be refueled. But one difficulty remained relating to this speculated venture – the barographs. If the ANT were to land somewhere in Alaska the loss of altitude would show up on the barographic recordings, governed by changes in air pressure. It is possible to manipulate barographs to achieve desired results. This would have to be done. It is academic that new gas seals would have to be installed to disguise the refueling. The gas seals presented no problem but the barographs would have to be altered, at some risk of discovery. The barographs would most assuredly be inspected if and when an aircraft reached America.

The Federation Aeronautique Internationale (FAI) generally required a close examination of gas seals and barographic recordings to determine the authenticity of flights being considered for world records. The NSR planners somehow had to address this issue before making serious plans to visit America. The general plan was to announce a nonstop leap over the top of the world while the ANT was sneaking into Alaska to refuel. Misleading radio reports could be issued from Moscow and/or relay stations in Siberia to give the impression the ANT was en route over the North Pole. Radio operators could continue broadcasting a mythical flight over northern Canada and on to America. At some point from the archipelago the refueled aircraft would take over and the crew could begin radioing their geographic positions and receiving weather reports from U.S. stations.

Whether Stalin would approve this potential debacle was questionable. It differed from Levanevsky's flight route the previous summer since the new plan actually called for the ANT to make a landing in the United States. Not only would the hand-me-down ANT be exposed to the scrutiny of the Americans but the fliers as well. Too many things could happen to reveal the hoax and thereby embarrass the Soviet Union before the eyes of the world. Although NSR was to be the sponsor and planner for the fraudulent project there was no way for Stalin's government to extract itself from final responsibility. Every detail would have to be carefully worked out before the NSR could expect the Soviet chief's sanction. In any event it was too late in 1935 to pull off the scheme but the approaching winter months would give the boys at Shelkova a chance to rehash their wild plot.

How could a fake flight over the North Pole be made more believable? Radio broadcasts of plane positions alone offered no real evidence that the ANT was traversing the northern icecap. There had to be some way to dress up the affair, a way adding to its drama and believability. The northern radio stations used during the Northern Sea Route project would be helpful, in particular the Hooker Island camp. During any flight, weather reports are very important to fliers – especially over the arctic and polar regions. Even though only a mythical or phantom plane was to follow the polar route, receiving weather data from the northern stations was a vital part of the "master plan." Of course, the Soviets had no weather reporting stations north of Hooker Island. The NSR people had often talked about establishing a station right on the North Pole, an idea that surfaced during the study of ice floe movements in relation to the Northern Sea Route project. It had been theorized that the accurate prediction of ice floe movements increased when observations were made at the farthest northern points. As it turned out, however, the habits of the floes were less important than the unstoppable ice masses jamming the channel each season. There was no economical way to keep a shipping lane open. When the prospects of opening the channel looked hopeless, the northern radio and weather stations lost some of their importance; certainly no additional stations would be established in the polar region.

Supposedly there had been earlier Soviet efforts to reach the North Pole. A couple of icebreakers may have been lost during one expedition, discouraging further Russian polar overland explorations. These were the years when nations raced to get to the pole first. Such explorations commonly used dog sledges on the last leg of these journeys. Admiral Robert Peary and Dr. Frederick Cook attempted it 1907 and 1908. And now perhaps there was a Russian motive to conquer the top of the world and its hazardous and frigid environs. Reaching the pole and establishing a radio station would enhance and might help convince the world of their expertise to fly over the pole, at least under favorable weather conditions. Once it had been accepted the Russians were mastering the polar and arctic skies the only question remaining would be their ability to fly their aircraft long distances. Long-range and nonstop flights had already been demonstrated by Lindbergh, Codos and Rossi, and others many years earlier.

On paper the idea to refuel the ANT someplace in the more remote southern islands of Alaska looked simple enough, but in actual practice it might not be so easy. First a landing party would have to find a suitable clearing on south Baranof, Wales, or possibly some other smaller island. Sufficient fuel for the ANT would have to be transported. It would take some 250 gallons of fuel to reach Shestakov's old landing site at Vancouver, Washington, where the Soviets would get military protection from the U.S. Army. However, if the final destination was California, it would take 450 gallons for a trip of about 1,900 miles. The weight of the gas, estimated at 2,400 pounds, was more than a small aircraft could deliver to the archipelago, so other transportation – possibly a small boat – would have to be found. To set up a small camp they would need radios, tents, and aircraft tools, plus axes, saws, and other implements to clear trees and brush for a safe landing surface.

Furthermore, food would be needed to sustain a small work crew. Mechanics would have to be on hand in case of an accident, and because it was possible the wide-wing ANT would require attention after landing in the rugged Alaskan terrain. A daylight arrival from Siberia was required; the landing field was likely to be makeshift and possibly dangerous. Because of the many fishermen and hunters in the area, however, the large plane might be easily spotted and later identified as the one which had taken off from the archipelago. If it then could be proven that this same plane had landed in Vancouver, the "jig would be up." The risks were considerable.

It is difficult to say who finally came up with the answer to NSR's dilemma; probably Tupolev, the ANT's designer, had something to do with it. Since the risks of flying the huge monoplane into Alaska were evident, other ideas were analyzed. Could the plane be taken in by ship and then pulled to shore somehow? Tupolev might have reminded the NSR staff how the ANT could be easily disassembled, crated, and shipped to some selected island. The crated ANT could be transported at night to insure secrecy. While hidden from view amidst the island's trees the ANT could be reassembled by the camp crew. When the fliers arrived they would establish contact with Moscow by way of the Siberian radio relay stations. Close coordination and communication between the camp and NSR operatives were absolutely crucial if the master plan was to succeed. The pilots would have to be ready to take off on cue. The pieces of the puzzle had now begun to come together.

There were certain things working in their favor. Semion Shestakov had provided valuable information about the islands of Baranof and Prince of Wales and had identified islands in the region where an airplane could successfully take off. Although these areas were isolated and relatively uninhabited, some risks were inevitable. Only those few moments during lift-off posed a serious threat; but once the ANT was airborne and had attained sufficient altitude it didn't make any difference who saw the plane because it would simply appear to be en route to its destination. There were three major aspects to the plan: First, they would have to create the illusion the ANT was traversing the North Pole; second, a temporary radio station in the far north was needed for the sake of authenticity; and third, for the time being, the Northern Sea Route Administration would push the idea of disassembling the ANT for eventual shipment to Alaska. It seemed almost ludicrous to be thinking in these terms because of the extreme risks.

CHAPTER 11

Dream of an Aviator

A proposed permanent polar camp might be attractive to Stalin and the Kremlin because of its prestige. If things went wrong the Soviets could more easily control the situation and prevent adverse publicity. If Stalin was agreeable to the polar station enterprise it was not likely NSR would consider the use of icebreakers and dog sledges – which Admiral Peary and others had already used successfully. Besides, the Soviets had experienced difficulties in using icebreakers in the extreme north. If the icebreakers had been as successful as claimed, Russian explorers would have reached the North Pole long before. Now they wanted to do something spectacular. Perhaps they could fly to the North Pole.

The first explorer to suggest such an undertaking was Fridtjof Nansen, a famous Norwegian arctic scientist who held the Nobel Peace Prize for his supervision of the post-World War I famine relief program in the USSR. He was also a major influence in Soviet explorations. Nansen believed a radio station on the polar icecap would prove invaluable in weather forecasting. It was believed the polar basin was the "weather kitchen" for the Northern Hemisphere. Forewarning of storms and other climatic conditions would revolutionize weather science. A permanent village at this northernmost point would be an unprecedented achievement far outshining Peary's short visit to the pole. The flights of Admiral Byrd and Roald Amundsen may have started the Soviets thinking about the possibility of reaching the North Pole by air and somehow safely landing on the icefields, a unique and historically significant accomplishment. A landing at the Pole! It had never been tried; if successful the Soviets would gain world respect for great progress in aviation, navigation, and the ability to civilize the most

79

hostile of all environments. However, the Soviets did not have a plane with sufficient range to reach and return from the North Pole – with the exception of the two ANT-25s.

Why hadn't some country tried this before? Although it was commonly believed the northern icecap was a flat surface, Byrd had informed the Russians of certain pitfalls awaiting fliers attempting to land aircraft there. One hazard was the low fog cover and overcast obscuring the frozen surface. Another danger was the ice hummocks and ridges formed when different sections of the icecap jammed together. Planes attempting to penetrate the low-hanging fog would have little time to maneuver away from obstacles in the landing path. The Soviets also learned from the American admiral that the entire polar cap was constantly in motion; it was a gigantic ice floe continuously straying southward, away from Alaska and toward Greenland. Massive sections periodically break free and follow wide circuitous patterns southward, gradually melting while en route toward warmer latitudes. After an expedition calculated their position at 90 degrees north (North Pole), their readings would gradually change as the polar ice floe drifted.

Peculiar magnetic storms and disturbances interfered with compasses and complicated these readings. Aware of these problems, Byrd had conveyed his observations to his Russian counterparts and had offered them a special sun compass that negated the effects of magnetic deviations. But the NSR people were not listening carefully to Byrd on this matter of compass deviations. He had been speaking about Magnetic North and not Geographic North, which is 1,000 miles away. Magnetic North is where lines of force converge on the Earth and cause problems with navigational instruments. Eventually this misunderstanding would call into question certain Soviet polar claims. Admiral Byrd's special compass took bearings on the sun to determine direction and position.

Actually the Soviets had every advantage in establishing a base at the pole. The long fingerlike island of Novaya Zemlya and the Franz Josef Land group provided many stepping stones en route to the pole. The Franz Josef Islands are only about 600 miles from the Geographic North Pole. Hooker, the Soviet station, is situated in this group. Six hundred miles to the west lies Spitsbergen, from where Richard Byrd made his famous dash to the pole. On the Russian side of the world the closest land body to the top of the world is Rudolph Island, a part of the Franz Josef group. This would be the logical point to launch a polar aerial expedition. From here the pole was well within the range of

Tupolev's ANT-25. This plane's exceptionally long gliderlike wings enabled it to land at slow speeds, making it an ideal choice in combatting the unpredictability of fog and polar ice. At a gross weight of 12,500 pounds the ANT was not the lightest Soviet craft available, but it was the only type capable of flying to the North Pole and returning on a single gas load. The ANT-6s which had been used to ferry cargo to the north coast radio stations lacked the range to make a trip to the pole and back. This 72,000-pound monster, at one time the largest airplane in the world, had a relatively short range of 600 miles, less than half the distance required for a polar flight. The Russians actually were without any civil aircraft with long-range capabilities. Many aviation experts noted that the Soviets were obsessed with building the largest airplanes possible. These were characteristically cumbersome, with limited maneuverability, speed, fuel efficiency, and other restrictions. If NSR planned to use the ANT-6, the fuel capacity would have to be more than doubled and engine improvements made to give it sufficient range.

The Russians preferred to use a home-built aircraft to avoid publicizing foreign products, and thus suggesting a lag in Soviet aviation technology. Although the ANT-25 did not exactly fit the home-built category because of its French "beginnings," Tupolev's modifications gave it a Soviet appearance. The ANT-25 was the only type with a believable range for the task at hand; however, it was not capable of carrying all of the equipment and supplies needed to establish and sustain a so-called permanent polar village. Since there were only two ANT-25s in existence, a great many trips would be necessary to get all the cargo delivered to the pole – an impractical arrangement. Another consideration was the potential risk of damaging or even losing the two ANTs. If this were to occur the Alaskan "transpolar" project would end before it started. The only alternative was to use a bigger cargo plane like the ANT-6s but the range of these planes would have to be increased from 600 to 1,300 miles.

Before the NSR Directorate could proceed with these plans Stalin and the Kremlin would have to be approached. It was the intention of Professor Schmidt and other NSR staff members to make a presentation of the proposed venture to establish a camp at the North Pole. One NSR employee in particular was keenly interested in the North Pole; he was Mikhail Vodopyanov, author of *A Dream of an Aviator*, a three-act play and novel about a fictitious airplane journey to the North Pole and the establishment of a small village. Vodopyanov drew on his experiences with the *Cheliuskin* rescue squadron and his years working with

NSR. He had closely studied the accounts of Admiral Byrd, Roald Amundsen, and other explorers of the north. It is surmised the author-aviator capitalized on Fridtjof Nansen's plans for a polar radio-weather station. Nansen and Admiral Peary had been the first to suggest a transpolar airline between the eastern and western hemispheres. For Vodopyanov, an aerial expedition to the North Pole would mean the realization of a long-awaited dream dating from the early 1930s and his first writings on the arctic and polar worlds. In past years he had flown Tupolev's giant four-motored ANT-6s on freight runs to the north coast.

Most of the NSR employees were eager to participate in establishing a permanent station at the northernmost point of the world, an accomplishment certain to enter the history books and bring acclaim to the Soviet Union. Ernest Krenkel, a radio technician and *Cheliuskin* survivor, was a potentially significant contributor to the project. He had accompanied Amundsen in a dirigible flight over the North Pole in 1928 and was a member of Admiral Byrd's "Little America" expedition to the South Pole in 1934-35. It was possible Krenkel was purposely "planted" with this organization to gain first-hand information about polar regions. No other nation had succeeded in making a landing at the North Pole, let alone in setting up a permanent village. Such an operation would require strict attention to the smallest details. Every precaution would have to be taken to insure the safety and good health of the first polar pioneers. Food and supplies would have to be brought in regularly during favorable weather conditions. Since no one could be expected to remain for long periods in this desolate, ice-ridden, and eerie land, replacement personnel would have to be flown in on a regular basis. Any structures erected to defend against the elements would have to be portable and moved periodically back toward Alaska to maintain an exact 90-degree north latitude position.

Rescue arrangements, either by plane or dog sledge, were needed in case the expedition was unsuccessful and ended with planes damaged beyond repair or lost with men injured. The chances of a catastrophe were immense and the thought of wheeling those huge, lumbering ANT-6s through dense fog in an almost blind attempt to land was a chilling and sobering thought. The extreme dangers placed Professor Schmidt in a precarious position. All eyes of the world would focus on this historic undertaking. Heads would surely fall if lives were lost and the Russian efforts proved embarrassing before the international community. Was the gamble worth it or did the benefits outweigh the risks? The only way the NSR could carry out a legitimate aerial expedition to the North Pole was to somehow increase the fuel capacity of existing aircraft. Otherwise there was no hope of success.

In December of 1935 Professor Schmidt was scheduled to visit the Scott Polar Institute at the University of Cambridge in England. He planned to gather the latest information about the polar icecap. The greatest concern was whether a plane could be safely landed on the ice. The icecap was constantly in a state of change and no amount of preparation could guarantee a safe descent. It was hoped there were consistent patterns of ice formations in locations near the pole which would always have a smooth surface. Apparently the Soviets lacked firsthand knowledge of the icecap, at least there was no record of them ever scouting or conducting any aerial reconnaissance there. This seemed rather surprising when it was claimed the ANT-25 was capable of flying 6,000 miles nonstop. Why couldn't this plane be used to fully survey the North Pole. Perhaps this would eventually be done before the expedition got underway.

Finally, on February 13, 1936, Dr. Schmidt was asked to make a presentation to Stalin and the Kremlin staff. Schmidt laid out a plan to set up an airfield on Rudolph Island to be used to launch an aerial expedition to the North Pole. Dr. Schmidt was projecting the use of ANT-6s, despite knowing they were incapable of flying to the pole and back without more modern engine replacements to increase their ranges. It was claimed a supply depot on Rudolph Island would be established with the aid of icebreakers. Several ANT-6s were then supposed to make their way over Novaya Zemlya to Hooker Island, then jump northward 150 miles to Rudolph. From this northernmost land parcel Tupolev's big cargo planes were scheduled – at least on paper – to prepare for an air expedition to the North Pole. If the expedition was successful a permanent village could be established. Four men would be assigned to the camp for one year, then relieved by new personnel. Dr. Schmidt laid out the scientific benefits of the station, which included a study of the weather, water current patterns, and other scientific phenomena. Dr. Schmidt did not elaborate on the overall plan, this first meeting was designed to introduce general ideas, "test the waters," and try to extract a reaction from Stalin and the other government officials in attendance. It was already common knowledge among government insiders that Stalin was very interested in this polar camp plan. It was Stalin's nature when major projects were being considered to put people on record so there was no doubt who was responsible in case things went awry. The strategy of Stalin and his

Kremlin staff was obviously to play an active role in this northern project while maintaining a low profile until success was guaranteed.

This February meeting was a mere formality as it was a foregone conclusion the 57-year-old dictator would be agreeable to NSR's recommendations. Stalin would undoubtedly reap great political gains if Soviet scientists were able to erect and sustain a permanent polar base. The Russians would look down from the pole on the world's nations. The largest nation in the world would grow larger geographically. The average person might forget this added real estate was of no practical value; both the NSR organization and the government were aware of this fact. However, it was advantageous politically to declare a great conquest. If the polar landing could be accomplished the Russians would be respected as the hardiest of pioneers and gain much-needed respect, both at home and abroad. At the end of Professor Schmidt's presentation, as expected, Stalin gave tentative permission to begin preparations for the expedition. If carried out as Dr. Schmidt envisioned, it could prove to be the greatest death-defying act of the century. Even intercontinental flights like Lindbergh's or Codos and Rossi's could not match the uncertainty of a landing on one of the most mysterious and unexplored regions on earth.

It didn't take long to discover how impossible it was to find even foreign motors which could power the heavy ANT-6s to the pole and back. The idea of reaching the North Pole by air was now out of the question. Very large airships were mandatory if a year's supply of equipment and living needs were to be transferred; however, the range of the ANT-6s appeared to be limited to just over 600 miles, only half the distance required for a round trip to the pole. Although Schmidt and his NSR associates planned to give the impression new motors were going to be used, it is a matter of record in *Jane's Encyclopedia of Aviation* that the range of the ANT-6s was never appreciably increased. Even the bomber version of this aircraft (TB3), equipped with four BMW engines could stay in the air for only 620 miles. But somehow Schmidt must convince the world that the ANT-6 could make the trip if the Russians were going to pull off this great stunt.

The employees of NSR – including pilots, mechanics, radio-navigation technicians, and other personnel – were divided in two groups as far as the master plan was concerned. About 40-plus men were assigned or volunteered for the radio station project and possibly half that number were scheduled to take part in the Alaskan plan. This phase of the master plan called for numerous radio operators to command relay stations linking Moscow with Alaska and the Pacific Coast of North America. Other workers would be needed to supervise and assist in getting the ANT-25 to its ultimate destination in the Alexander Archipelago. Perhaps as many as three or four mechanics and aircraft assemblers would be sent into the secret camp at the appointed hour. The pilots themselves would round out this group. The northern radio station, wherever it ended up, was supposed to be in operation before NSR unleashed its mythical transpolar flight. It was a trade-off as to which project posed the greatest risk to life and limb.

Aviators like Mikhail Vodopyanov were vulnerable in arctic flying because none of the NSR planes was equipped with de-icers. The idea of personally engineering a hoax flight to the American mainland certainly was no cup of tea. Meeting face-to-face with high level American officialdom entailed terrifying possibilities if the hoax were exposed. Not only would the fliers be subject to world condemnation but the Stalin government might fall.

In view of these possible consequences one might wonder how any rational person would sanction these desperate schemes. This illustrates the dilemma which had befallen Russia, namely an inability to make the industrial progress necessary to secure the country, both from a domestic and international perspective. The most important aspect of industrialization was the development and mass production of civil and military aircraft. The Soviets had conceded the need to acquire American aviation technology. This was the motive for the "transpolar" scheme, a way to bring about direct contact between Soviet fliers and Americans in the field of aviation. The only way possible to carry out this mission was to attempt an outright hoax. Possibly the only ones who might stomach this kind of deception were the younger and more ambitious fliers. George Baidukov and Valery Chkalov fit this mold pretty well. They had few credits other than as capable test pilots. Maneuvering the gawky and inefficient ANT-25 to the U.S. from Alaska might take this particular kind of talent. It is not clear whether the "transpolar flight" idea had been mentioned during the February meeting; the official communiqués did not contain this information. It was logical for Stalin and the other associated Kremlin staff to keep the transpolar part of the master plan off the official records to avoid direct connection to this wild and wooly scheme. This part of the master plan was not fully under Soviet control, to say the least. Stalin and his crowd would avoid commitments until the danger of exposure had passed.

The NSR people undoubtedly were concerned about the fraudulent enterprise they were conceiving. It was one thing planning something while within the protection of one's own country but it was something else to take that damned old hand-me-down ANT and some unknown fliers on what was supposed to be the flight of the century. It might improve things if Sigmund Levanevsky warmed up to the Alaskan plan. He had recently returned from the United States after purchasing a new Douglas airplane. It is not known just how the American model was delivered to Russia; at least there was no record found indicating he flew the plane to his country. The Soviets planned to make a study of this particular Douglas model and then possibly ask for patent rights so the plane could be produced in quantity at some future date. In the meantime the Soviet flier was going to use the newly purchased craft to instruct the younger aviators. The "Soviet Lindbergh" could be the perfect person to take the ANT-25 to America. He was already known and respected in the States and his name would give automatic credibility to the NSR plan.

But it seems Levanevsky wanted no part of the second polar hoax. Besides, he had become interested in the American airplanes. There was some talk he was planning to ask Stalin's permission to fly the new Douglas over the North Pole to America at some time in the future. Since this new model was not a long-range plane, some stops would be required. Rumor had it the popular flier planned to make fuel stops during the trip. Perhaps a real flight over the North Pole would take away the bad taste in his mouth, after the August fiasco. He could perhaps face the Americans in a more candid and unabashed manner. Yet on the other hand, if he decided to take part in the hoax and was exposed, his ability to help his country's lagging industry would be nullified. It might be wiser to keep him free and clear of the Alaskan plan so he could continue to serve Soviet interests in the United States.

With Levanevsky out of the picture other fliers could be approached. It was a foregone conclusion that George Baidukov, left over from Levanevsky's aborted 1935 flight, would be one of three men selected to man the ANT, provided the project was approved. Another NSR employee, Valery Chkalov, was also an expected candidate. Chkalov had the intestinal fortitude to face the Americans on their own soil but he was far from being a good diplomat; his lack of discreetness and sometimes abrasive attitude would seem to eliminate him as a good choice. But it had to be remembered not everyone with NSR was going to volunteer to play a starring role in the scheme. The master planners might be grateful if Chkalov was willing. Bold and calculating people were needed to pull it off. The fliers selected would be exposed to some of the most astute and sophisticated officials in the U.S. military and industrial hierarchy, and to hundreds of journalists and large crowds. This experience would be exceptionally demanding and require a good measure of diplomacy, social graces, and self-control. Valery Chkalov came up a little short in these categories. George Baidukov, like Chkalov, lacked experience in socializing at this level but he did have a more even disposition. Whether this was enough to pull off the project was questionable considering the constant strain of living under the cloud of a faked flight. They would have to keep in mind at all times that the very salvation of Russia could depend on their conduct in America.

Because the main purpose for the "flight" to the United States was to bring in knowledgeable aviation people to study the latest American technology, Chkalov and Baidukov's experiences as test pilots were considered a plus. Both aviation and navigational instruments were priorities. The long Russian winters with months of overcast skies and poor visibility were good reasons why the Russians had a special interest in new navigational devices and weather forecasting technology and equipment.

The NSR realized there was much to be done before the Alaskan plan could be carried out. It was obvious every detail would have to be addressed. NSR was satisfied with the overall plan to get the ANT to America but one matter was unresolved: How to bring the plane back into the Soviet Union without divulging its limited fuel capacity. NSR could not permit the ANT to be flown anywhere once it reached the American mainland. The true fuel capacity – about 450 gallons – would be quickly discovered when the tanks were refilled. NSR hoped to convince the world that this particular airplane was capable of carrying 2,000 gallons of petrol in the six wing tanks. The only way to conceal the plane's limited gas capacity was by shipping it home. After his 1929 flight Semion Shestakov sent his *Land of the Soviets* back to Russia by boat in order to hide its true range and limited fuel capacity. At no time during his long trek across Siberia to New York had the renovated Junkers flown more than 950 miles, and yet in New York he claimed it could fly 2,500 miles on a single gas load.

Shipping the ANT-25 might be easier said than done. With a 112-foot wingspread that was supposed to impress the American public, the plane might become a nuisance upon arrival in the States. It could not be shipped intact to a port by truck or railroad due to the extreme length of its wings. The Soviets had to consider dismantling the ANT to facilitate shipping without revealing the gas storage limitation. There was a way to disengage the wings without overly exposing the fuel tanks; this separation would leave the fuselage with 10-foot wing stubs, only partially revealing the gas tanks. The ANT-25 did not have any fuel in these 10-foot stubs nor in the fuselage, with the exception of a 100-gallon reserve storage inside the cabin. The stubs contained only flotation equipment, oxygen tanks, and supplies. The dismantled wings could be shipped in crates measuring 43 feet in length and 14 feet in width. The fuselage-wing stub assembly was a greater problem because of its size – 26 feet wide and 45 feet in length. This might cause a problem in transferring it to a port.

Another crucial factor in the master plan was establishing a communication system. A three-way radio network was needed to coordinate the different areas involved. Besides their already established stations, including relay outposts, the Russians needed to "plant" one of their own radio agents somewhere on the Pacific Coast, preferably in the United States. It was important for Russian stations to have communication with the Americans for various reasons. NSR wanted to appear genuine in requesting weather information and sending out progress reports. The triangle could be completed by personnel assigned to the secret camp in Alaska. Besides the crew's regular plane radios, a special wireless and crystal set would enable them to signal Moscow whenever they were prepared to lift off and to maintain contact with NSR in order to receive the cue when the "transpolar flight" was underway. It was also important for the Alaskan camp to be able to listen in on the American-Alaskan stations for weather reports. The men in the archipelago would be able to converse in Russian with the special radio agent provided he could be placed at one of the American stations.

What NSR hoped to accomplish with the radio network was to mislead the world into thinking a real airplane would take off from Moscow, fly over the North Pole, and land at Vancouver without touching down during the entire flight. Through the use of phony radio broadcasts NSR planned to track a mythical airplane all the way from Moscow to some point over the southern part of the Alexander Archipelago. From here Soviet pilots in a real ANT-25 would take to the air and "intercept" the mythical plane and follow a predetermined route to the American mainland. The Soviet supervisors would draw the route in line with the secret camp in order to coordinate the timing of the "ph-ANT-om" ship with the planned departure of the genuine version.

The airmen of the real ANT-25 had the chore of getting airborne before the big craft was spotted; those few moments posed the biggest threat to the success of the hoax.

Once the phantom ANT was on the North American side of the world, U.S. officials would expect to be hearing directly from it. This, of course, would be impossible since no actual plane would be in the air to send messages. NSR was staging the entire affair right from its headquarters in Moscow. However, when the Alaskan fliers were getting ready to take over they would be able to send some plane position broadcasts while the ANT-25 was still on the ground. There was a hazard in doing this because it might appear unusual if strong radio signals were to be picked up in Juneau, Sitka, Wales, and other close stations when the ANT-25 was supposed to be hundreds of miles away. Several position reports would be necessary before it was time to depart from the secret camp. NSR planned to instruct the fliers to use a special radio frequency in making contact with the Soviet radio agent who would be on continuous duty during the "historic" event. Although this was an extremely serious undertaking from the official Russian perspective, the idea of a 52-hour mythical flight to Alaska without ever getting a plane off the ground must have provided some moments of levity for NSR fliers and other insiders.

CHAPTER 12

Making of Heroes

The NSR Directorate hoped to implement the "transpolar flight" and conduct the expedition north to establish a radio station and polar camp sometime during the summer of 1936. The permanent North Pole camp was not the main worry since it would be entirely under the control of Soviet personnel. Even if the project turned out badly the NSR and Stalin's group were in a position to hide any negative results. It was the Alaskan plan that apparently concerned the Soviet chief, because this venture was designed to end up in the lap of the Americans. Solid guarantees of its success were needed. It was risky business, to say the least, for any government to partake in such deception. What made the situation so politically volatile for Stalin was his close association with the Northern Sea Route organization; this might put the blame for any bad publicity at the door of the Kremlin. He probably had political escape routes lined up in case something went wrong; however, informed people would know of his part in the conspiracy. Although the dictator might fool the average person and survive exposure of the hoaxes, it was still in his interest to proceed with extreme caution.

The idea for a "transpolar flight" basically came from the NSR organization when the Northern Sea Route project disappointed expectations. In order to justify keeping the aviators with NSR after much of the work on the sea route had been curtailed, alternative types of programs were needed. Levanevsky's flight the previous year was an example of this and seems to have led into the fake transpolar plan. The NSR employees may have got in so deeply it was impossible to extricate themselves when some high government officials became interested. Certain expectations and pressures from high sources may have contributed in propelling the plan along. Now it had come down to the question of whether or not the government was going to chance entering the gates of America on the basis of a fraudulent transpolar flight. The American government was not expected to look very hard into the authenticity of such a flight, and there was no sense in offending or embarrassing the Soviet Union from a political or military perspective. The Soviet dictator knew the Roosevelt administration recognized that his country was holding the trump card in deciding the balance of power in Europe. Even though the United States was aware of Russia's industrial and military impotency, government leaders did not believe Hitler's first priority was to conquer European Russia, simply because of its distant geographical location. Stalin did not believe Hitler had any plans to attack Russia; history shows he made a terrible miscalculation. The Soviet dictator was considering signing a neutrality pact with Hitler as added insurance. Such an agreement was not in the interest of the Allied nations because it tended to give Hitler a freer hand in overrunning Europe. The United States, as a proponent of the Allied cause, did not want France, England, and many other European nations swallowed up by Hitler's juggernaut.

The Roosevelt administration was politically committed to neutrality and isolationism in the event of war. Somehow Roosevelt had to woo Stalin into the Allied camp; one way was to grant Soviet aviation engineers and technicians direct access to U.S. aircraft factories. The arrival of A.N. Tupolev and his entourage of "engineers" (actually mechanics) in the spring of 1935 was part of this controversial open factory-door policy. Many industrial leaders resented sharing years of secret technical developments without due compensation. Also, communist ideology was not compatible with most American business and government. Stalin recognized this problem and had sought ways to draw closer to the United States. Since aviation was the key to Russia's problems in transportation and defense, the Soviet dictator used the pretext of establishing a commercial airline link between his country and the United States in order to get direct U.S. technical assistance. Levanevsky's so-called 1935 transpolar flight was supposed to have broken ground for this projected enterprise. Six years earlier Semion Shestakov had also given the impression that his flight was dedicated toward a future airline link with the United States.

And now in 1936 the Soviet leadership was planning to resurrect the pretext of a commercial airline route over the North Pole. Neither the Americans nor the Soviet people had knowledge of plans concerning the North Pole expedition or of traversing the pole by airplane. This is understandable since hoaxes were involved. Every effort was being made to confine the affair to NSR staff and key members of the Kremlin. It was up to Professor Schmidt to maintain confidentiality among his trusted staff. The NSR chief also hoped to expand security for the project on the American mainland because of the many unforeseen events that could emerge once the fliers and the ANT-25 arrived there. The Soviets knew through the media how celebrating crowds in Paris had damaged Lindbergh's famous airplane. This could be disastrous in the case of the ANT. If fabric were torn from the wings and the true fuel capacity of the tanks was revealed, no one would believe a transpolar flight had been made unless the U.S. government was willing to cover up the truth. Otherwise, it would all be over. Everyone would have to run for cover. Keeping the ANT's actual fuel capacity and range secret was crucial. Civilian airports should also be avoided because of the difficulty in crowd control. Shestakov had convinced NSR that military airports were preferable, citing how he and his crew were well received and their plane properly secured at Vancouver's military airfield. Shestakov had also noted the friendliness of most Americans; this observation must have increased NSR confidence.

Many of the master plan's details were beginning to fall into place but there were underlying concerns needing more attention. Taking the crudely renovated ANT into the land of great airplane builders was bad enough; lack of access to fliers with sufficient credentials was worse. NSR was unable to enlist military aviators because Stalin did not want to have a governmental connection to the hoaxes, at least at this time. NSR had to concede that their fliers were the only ones available to carry out the master plan. It was formally agreed Valery Chkalov and George Baidukov would be the pilots. Alexander Beliakov, Levanevsky's navigator in the Mattern "rescue," was selected as the third member of the crew. However, something would have to be done to upgrade these men's flying credentials. Perhaps a highly publicized long-distance domestic or "in-house" flight with the ANT-25 would be an answer. Levanevsky's ANT-25 had been returned from the 1936 Paris air show, where the big gliderlike airship had attracted considerable attention.

It was imperative that Chkalov, Baidukov, and Beliakov become household names in Russia and respected throughout aviation circles if NSR ever expected to carry out the objectives of the master plan. Somehow a long-distance flight had to be arranged comparable in air miles to the 6,000-mile hoax flight to America. The Soviets needed to create the illusion of a nonstop air journey across the breadth of their country to promote the names of the fliers and to introduce the ANT-25 as a long-distance flyer. However, there were problems. The ANT-25 would need to make a number of fuel stops; witnesses might expose the fraud. It was paramount to keep these stops confidential. Russian loyalty to Stalin was not absolute, to say nothing of the many foreign agents the dictator claimed had infiltrated the country.

Because Chkalov and his crew were preparing for a so-called transpolar flight it would be appropriate to include at least some arctic landmarks on their mythical itinerary. NSR concluded that the mythical route should begin at Shelkova, proceed north to Queen Victoria Island in the Franz Josef group and from there continue eastward to the southern part of the Kamchatka Peninsula which juts down from the southeast coast of Siberia, much like Florida does in the United States. Chkalov, at least on paper, was supposed to aim the single-engine craft toward the Amur River bordering the Soviet Union and the northeast China frontier. NSR would announce to the Russian people that the flight ended on the Island of Udd, about 900 miles from Kamchatka. The journey would credit Chkalov and the ANT with a distance comparable to a transpolar trip from Moscow over the North Pole to San Francisco, about 5,800 miles.

Early in April word came down from NSR to start the in-house project immediately. Within a few days the necessary arrangements were made at Shelkova, where Chkalov, Baidukov, and Beliakov were ready on a moment's notice to make a quick takeoff because NSR did not want too much advance notice. Naturally NSR wanted some people present at the going-away ceremony but it was important to carefully screen and select the witnesses. The most logical groups to invite were the fliers' immediate relatives and close friends. At last, around noon on a sunny and cool, crisp day, the green light was given. The officials of the Northern Sea Route Administration appeared at Shelkova to conduct the takeoff show. A small crowd of about 25 assembled, and immediate family members said their goodbyes. The big ANT was parked nearby on the runway. In the background a black Packard sedan was winding its way toward the airplane and a small group of awaiting well-wishers. The automobile driven by ANT designer A.N. Tupolev rolled to a stop; Pilot Chkalov, Copilot Baidukov, and Navigator Beliakov exited the vehicle, carrying their arctic flight suits. They moved quickly toward the readied plane while the small group of people kept pace. Losing no time, Chkalov prepared to board the big monoplane; Tupolev stepped forward to embrace first him and then Baidukov and Beliakov.

After the farewells the wide-wing monoplane's single engine was started with a pressurized oxygen tank. The ANT began moving slowly along the concrete strip and after a short run lifted off in a northerly direction supposedly heading for the Franz Josef vicinity. Now one more step in the master plan was underway, a step it was hoped would add to the credibility of the ANT as a great long-distance flyer. Stalin and the NSR people planned to give great publicity to this so-called flight. It was ironic that this hoax flight was designed to better the credentials of the fliers in order to qualify them for an even bigger, international hoax. According to NSR's predictions and plans they would be able to get the ANT-25 into Alaska and have it ready to leave for the continental U.S. sometime in July. The strategy was to have Chkalov fly the ANT-25 to a remote island in the Amur River and be ready to take off for a refueling somewhere in Alaska. The exact refueling site was not yet selected, but hopefully that would be resolved soon.

At this time Stalin was ready to send Levanevsky and his navigator Victor Levchenko to the United States to make contacts with American aviation figures. NSR had a good reason for the visit. Realizing the "Soviet Lindbergh" would return with a new American airplane, they wanted him to fly over the Alexander Archipelago to survey possible sites for the secret refueling camp. The Soviet pilot arrived in the United States in late spring and proceeded to browse the various aircraft factories. He wasted little time in selecting a new Vultee model being produced by the Lockheed Aircraft Company. He had hopes of flying the Vultee back to Russia by way of southeast Alaska before arriving in Siberia, and intended to purchase cameras for photographing the Alexander Archipelago. When he arrived in Siberia on his return home he would deliver the aerial photos of the archipelago region to Valery Chkalov and George Baidukov, who would make the decision on where to land and refuel in Alaska.

Levanevsky had not foreseen any problem in getting U.S. government approval to carry cameras on his return trip home; as it turned out, there was a considerable delay in processing his formal application, jeopardizing his scheduled rendezvous with Chkalov and company. It was imperative for Levanevsky to deliver the archipelago photos in time for a "transpolar flight" in 1936. Levanevsky requested permission to take off from Los Angeles and fly over the Alexander Archipelago and the Alaskan mainland. His planned route included San Francisco, Seattle, Juneau, Fairbanks, and Nome. Apparently the United States government was not cooperating with Levanevsky's tight time schedule; the veteran pilot and his navigator had to wait through the remainder of July before receiving departure clearance for early August. Would it be too late to carry out this next stage of the master plan? Although the request to take cameras was initially refused the U.S. government rescinded the order with one restriction – the camera lenses must remain sealed until the aircraft reached Nome. This really put a damper on Levanevsky's plans unless he was willing to hide an unsealed camera somewhere in the new Vultee. It wasn't likely the Soviet aviator would chance violating a restriction that might lead to denial of his visa rights. Levanevsky realized that his value to Stalin centered on his ability to cultivate American cooperation and support in aviation. Although the veteran flier knew the NSR scheme had high priority, it was up to him to decide whether it was too risky to carry unsealed cameras.

Clearance for the return flight was not granted until the first week of August. It was getting late for NSR to try the transpolar scheme during 1936 but Levanevsky couldn't speed up American paperwork. After the Vultee airplane was fitted with pontoons at a Los Angeles port, Levanevsky and Levchenko finally departed on their long journey home, stopping over at San Francisco before flying northward above the coastal waters. Finally the two fliers were nearing the region of the archipelago where NSR wanted to locate a camp site. From these latitudes it was possible for the ANT-25 to reach Southern California. Levanevsky knew the American Signal Corps stations would be plotting his course and would expect his arrival in Ketchikan within a certain time frame. Despite U.S. expectations regarding his flight schedule, the Soviet pilot was determined to fly low, scouting for possible secret camp sites. The only way he could account for a delay was to claim that bad weather forced him to ditch the craft near some island. Eventually he identified this landing spot as near Goose Island, about 175 miles south of Prince Rupert, Canada.

He and Levchenko finally showed up at Ketchikan to take on fuel. The U.S. Signal Corps and Weather Bureau had no communications from Levanevsky after he claimed a forced sea landing at Goose Island because of poor visibility at 2:05 p.m. August 8. The Russian flier claimed he had received the hourly weather reports regularly and had acknowledged them. A U.S. Signal Corps report dated August 17 contradicts Levanevsky, noting there was no communication from the pilot for 46 hours and 45 minutes, until the Vultee landed at Ketchikan at 12:50 p.m., August 10. What did U.S. authorities think Levanevsky and Levchenko were doing in the archipelago for almost two full days? No one questioned them about their whereabouts or expressed concern for their safety during this long period of silence. Also, no one questioned them on why their new all-weather pursuit plane would be forced down by visibility problems. This ultramodern Vultee was capable of flying well above any adverse weather, particularly conditions involving visibility.

From Ketchikan, Levanevsky flew straight to Juneau and then Fairbanks for the scheduled first rest stop before continuing on to Nome, where the lense seals of the cameras were to be removed. It will probably never be known whether hidden, unsealed cameras were aboard. If not, then Levanevsky and his navigator were limited to making visual observations and sketches of areas suitable for NSR's future camp site. Four hours after leaving Fairbanks the pontoon-equipped Vultee landed in placid waters about 20 miles from Nome, where a U.S. Army Signal Corps technician of Russian lineage and fluent in that language removed the lense seals. After getting favorable weather clearance the fliers attempted a takeoff over the Bering Sea, but a low tide grounded the airplane on a sand bar, forcing a four-hour delay. When the aircraft managed to get airborne a heavy fog rolled in across the Bering Strait and forced Levanevsky to ditch the craft at nearby Tellar. When the dense fog cleared the next day the airmen winged their way westward toward Siberia, too late to rendezvous with Chkalov's group. So Levanevsky and Levchenko departed for Moscow. Ugelen was the first stop after Nome. Then came Ambarchik, Tiksi Bay, Shigansk, Yakutsk, Kirensk, Kransnoyarsk, Omsk, and Sverdlovsk. The two fliers arrived in Moscow on September 13, after covering 11,400 miles.

During the past several months the "Soviet Lindbergh" had inspected some of the best airplanes being made. He had been hindered by the policies of NSR and the Kremlin regarding utilization of foreign airplanes. But Stalin was not too proud to buy patents and actual models from the U.S. and other countries which could be altered and thus disguised as Soviet-built. Sigmund Levanevsky's ambitions at this point were being thwarted by Stalin's policies, probably causing him to rethink his role in NSR's master plan. Perhaps he would never join the ranks of such fliers as Lindbergh and Post, those who conquer the oceans in great leaps, bridging continents and welding one world from the great variety of nations. Nevertheless Levanevsky had hoped to become one of these selected few, and probably cared not what country's airplanes he used. After all, what part of the public remembered that Admiral Byrd had conquered the pole in a Dutch plane, or that Hubert Wilkins of Australia had gained his arctic flying fame in an American Lockheed? Age was also catching up with the veteran pilot as he neared his 38th birthday, then considered the twilight years for aviators. Levanevsky probably longed for one fling to make things right; then perhaps he could face the Americans with a clear conscience. He planned to ask Stalin for permission to fly one of the two American planes – either the Douglas or the Vultee – over the North Pole to some destination in Alaska. The NSR Directorate would oppose Levanevsky's request on the basis that it would lessen the "historical" significance of their so-called transpolar flight.

Levanevsky's medals in aviation did not buy any special favors from NSR. Offered a chance to cooperate in the Alaskan plan, he apparently declined. So NSR created new heroes out of Chkalov, Baidukov, and Beliakov. Each was to receive the "Hero of the Soviet Union" medal.

CHAPTER 13

Master Plan
Unleashed

A meeting of Soviet civil aviation officials and a host of fliers, most of them employees of NSR, was held October 9, in Moscow. According to an American intelligence report, the agenda for this conference was confined to discussing various commerical airline routes to the United States. This was a curious agenda since the past year the emphasis and publicity had revolved around a new transpolar route – as illustrated by Levanevsky's "flight." The American embassy in Moscow was encouraged to publish this information in U.S. State Department service journals. It was obvious the Soviets wanted to divert attention from the real designs of NSR and the Kremlin. The only routes discussed in the October meeting, according to the G-2 document, were those traversing Siberian regions and reaching the American mainland through Alaska and the north Pacific Coast. Each route evaluated included only basic information on distances and costs for airfields. The distance ranged from 6,960 miles at a cost of $16 million rubles to 7,920 miles at a cost of $54 million rubles. (The exchange rate was pegged at four rubles to one U.S. dollar.) There was no question this conference was orchestrated by NSR judging by attendance. The G-2 report listed the conferees as Chairman I.F. Tkachev, chief of the Soviet Civil Air Fleet; Pilots Levanevsky, Molokov, Chkalov, Baidukov, Beliakov, M.T. Slepnev, Levchenko, and other aviation personnel.

As things now stood, the earliest the master plan could be implemented was sometime in 1937. The coming winter months at Shelkova could always be used to refine the master plan. Perhaps the delay was an angel in disguise, in view of the many complications and the volatile nature of what they were trying to pull off. There really was no margin for error as far as timeliness was concerned, and this surfaced when the Americans did not immediately okay the use of cameras on Levanevsky's plane. In Russia, Stalin could simply call the shots, but the U.S. bureaucracy is much more complex, especially in national security matters. It would be a long winter for NSR to continue shouldering the apprehensions growing dramatically since the inception of these wild and politically dangerous aerial promotions. The ANT-25 was the only real concern as it remained parked and closely guarded at Udd Island.

The dictator's attention was focused on Russia's political relationships with the West. Communist ideology was steadily losing ground in the United States. Stalin was having difficulty arriving at agreements with France and England in relation to Germany's aggressive expansionist policies. Perhaps in part to counter Trotsky's personal attacks, the Communist chief agreed to make constitutional amendments. History shows that Stalin's change of heart was motivated by politics rather than by a desire to improve the lot of the Russian people. At least on paper, all citizens were given wide-sweeping rights – many of which rivaled the American Bill of Rights in terms of individual freedoms – including racial equality, women's rights, recognition of property ownership, and others. On the surface the new constitution seemed to suggest real change; however, the finer print stipulated that all of these human rights were secondary to the authority of a one-party political system protected by the secret police. This hollow constitutional manifesto was formalized by the All-Union Congress of Soviets on December 5, 1936. Russian citizens quickly learned that the new laws were of no benefit to them and that any complaints were negated in favor of the Soviet State and its only political party. The constitution was intended to impress foreign governments and to reduce the growing antagonism toward international communism.

In a surprising move at the end of 1936, Stalin authorized a westernlike New Year's celebration with traditional Christmas trees and holiday songs. "Grandfather Frost," Russia's equivalent to Santa Claus, made appearances at different gatherings. Hot dogs were served while people danced and children frolicked. The government's news organs described the events as the happiest ever seen in the Soviet Union. It was hoped the New Year would be more promising for Russian aviation as Dr. Schmidt prepared once again to implement the master plan. The time was not far off when Dr. Schmidt would be required to "go through the motions" of formally repeating the 1936 presentation designed to place Soviets at a "polar station" but more likely a post considerably farther south. The idea was to get some kind of expedition started by March. If Rudolph Island was the eventual location for a radio station, two months' preparation would still be needed to give the impression they were establishing a polar camp. Basically all NSR needed was an isolated, ice- and snow-covered area to resemble a polar terrain. The plan was to erect a radio station and encampment and include several ski-equipped airplanes parked nearby. The Soviet flag would be raised as evidence the group was actually at the North Pole. It must have been overwhelming for some of the NSR employees to see the small seed of the 1935 Levanevsky "flight" grow into this monstrous fraud.

Exactly one year to the day after the previous year's conference, Stalin summoned Professor Schmidt to the Kremlin. Since the 1936 "transpolar flight" plans had not materialized, NSR and the Kremlin would have to go through the motions again to implement the master plan. Apparently the dictator was interested in pursuing the hoax flight strategy and had given up on legitimate means of resolving the aviation dilemma. During this February 13, Wednesday meeting Professor Schmidt reiterated his 1936 presentation purportedly requesting permission to establish a polar camp. Schmidt traced on a globe the route he planned to use to place a small wintering party right at the North Pole. The plan called for a permanent camp and radio outpost to be established, serving a dual purpose of scientific research and as a possible refueling depot for a projected commercial airline route. For the record the professor outlined the flight plan to reach the pole. A temporary ice-landing strip was to be leveled off at a suitable site on Rudolph Island. This landing field would serve as a last refueling stop for planes to use before making the final jump to the top of the world, about 550 miles away. The dictator already had the NSR plans recorded from the prior year but apparently wanted to update the records to protect himself from any direct involvement.

As before, General Alksnis, Klementy Voroshilov, and Mikhail Kaganovich, commissar of Heavy Industry were in attendance, along with Henry Yagoda from the secret police. Ordinarily it would be strange for the chief of the secret police to be present for this type of an agenda but Stalin felt it necessary to have Yagoda there to apply sufficient intimidation to keep all of the conspirators in line, including both the NSR and Kremlin staff. For the first time in connection to the proposed hoaxes Valery Chkalov was allowed to appear and speak – a clear sign Stalin was committing himself to backing the Alaskan tactic of delivering an ANT-25 into the United States. Chkalov talked about the value of a polar station to advance a commercial airline route to America and informed the conference delegates that the Soviet Union now had planes capable of making the long flight to America without stopping to refuel. He spoke as if the officials present didn't know the capabilities of the nation's aircraft. After all, he was talking to the head of the Air Force, the Defense Minister and the Commissar of Heavy Industry, all of whom should know the exact range of all Soviet aircraft.

Stalin was obviously moving responsibility for the project away from the Kremlin and placing it on Chkalov and other members of the NSR. If the hoaxes were uncovered, he could refer to the official records to show how Chkalov had misrepresented the range of the plane. The shrewd dictator was an expert at trapping others and extricating himself from blame. Chkalov's presentation at the meeting was probably written by someone taking orders from Stalin, but the peasant flier might not have recognized the significance of the particular phrasing of his statements. If the Alaskan hoax flight was exposed, at this point Chkalov had just signed his own death warrant. And with the first serious sign of trouble Stalin would quickly backpedal away from the "sinking airship" by condemning the NSR organization for misrepresenting the ANT-25 as a long-range airplane. In this event the dictator would only have to admit gullibility. Those who were knowledgeable weren't to be fooled since it was obvious Stalin was the main conspirator; however, the general public couldn't be expected to know and understand these shenanigans. Chief Yagoda would make sure the dictator came out clean. Professor Schmidt's situation was equally perilous during this time but at least his role did not require him to leave the Russian side of the world.

Stalin made no commitment on record to Chkalov concerning a possible transpolar flight, but he did formally authorize Schmidt to proceed with the expedition to the North Pole. According to Soviet accounts of the February conference, Stalin asked Professor Schmidt why Sigmund Levanevsky's name was not mentioned in connection with the North Pole attempt. The professor reminded the Communist chief that Levanevsky had gone to America and was not expected back in time for the expedition. It is strange Stalin did not know the whereabouts of Levanevsky, but here again he wanted this information included in the official records. Levanevsky represented legitimacy in aviation affairs and would be a safer associate for Stalin than Chkalov. Therefore Stalin openly favored and officially selected Levanevsky to be the first to fly the polar route to America. Of course, the Soviet government had no intention of establishing a two-way commercial air link with America. The government simply could not risk exposure of the true backwardness of Russian industry and the country's economic plight. The whole idea of the hoaxes was to establish the belief the Soviet Union was on a par with the western nations, especially in aviation technology.

February, 1937 may have been the most crucial month in Stalin's reign. Although he had officially approved the polar station and unofficially okayed the Alaskan plan, it was always possible to stop these projects at a moment's notice. Was he to enter into the world of illusion by allowing NSR to proceed with its magic flying act or wait out the great aviation dilemma in the hope things somehow would change in time to prepare the nation against German and/or Japanese aggression? Unrest at home was unprecedented and the Soviet chief began worrying about political factions within the Communist Party. Communists in the United States continued to lose ground, and more and more public discontent was coming to the forefront, both from political sources and the leaders of aviation companies who did not want the Soviet engineers in their factories. Even more disturbing was the commotion being caused by Leon Trotsky, from asylum in Mexico. Trotsky had gained the attention of prominent figures in the United States and had requested an audience to hear his side of serious charges involving treason against the Soviet Union. A commission, headed by the American philosopher/educator John Dewey, had agreed to hear Trotsky's defense of himself. The former Soviet general secretary had been launching an incessant attack on Stalin and his direction of the Communist movement. Trotsky's exile began in 1929 on a small Turkish island where he remained until France allowed him entry. In 1935 Trotsky emigrated to Norway, where he remained until moving in 1937 to his last home, in Mexico. From here he continued to harass and irritate the stony-faced Stalin.

The Soviet leader was now up against the greatest threat to his rule; fearing different domestic factions and foreign elements would systematically whittle away his political powers and authority, he needed to draw the Russian people closer under his control. Stalin already faced a serious problem in not being able to defend the country in case of invasion, particularly due to its weak and ineffective air force. The seemingly calm, pipe-smoking Communist chief must have spent considerable time thinking about how to deal with the mounting pressures. Perhaps he even saw his political life flash before his eyes on occasion. Times had changed since Joseph V. Dzhugashvili dubbed himself Stalin, the "Man of Steel." Now he might have a chance to prove his new name.

He was born in Georgia Province about 1,000 miles south of Moscow, between the Caspian and Black seas, and spent his early years under the caring influence of his mother. She had become pregnant with Joseph by a Georgian political figure who did not wish to marry her. Dzhugashvili was the name of a shoemaker who was paid to become Joseph's legal father. The shoemaker turned out to be an incorrigible drunk who often beat the child unmercifully.

In later years, after discovering his bastard status, he began physically mistreating his mother. On one occasion, Stalin kicked his mother in the stomach during the final trimester of another pregnancy, also outside of marriage. At other times he openly and repeatedly referred to her as a whore in the presence of prominent people. Joseph Dzhugashvili showed no respect for either parent, nor for himself, as demonstrated by his stealing and petty larceny. During his tenure as a Communist Party official he was involved in expropriation of Party funds. He had spent some time in exile and concentration camps where it was noted he sought out the company of common criminals rather than his political compatriots. His first wife, Ekaterina Svanidze, died in 1907, presumably of pneumonia, after a three-year marriage. Stalin's second wife, Nadezhda Alliluyeva, many years his junior, died in 1932 under mysterious circumstances. Although some Soviet authorities reported the death as suicide, there is good reason to believe the dictator strangled his wife during a quarrel and then directed doctors to sign the death certificate as appendicitis. Another version recorded the sound of a gunshot coming from her bedroom just prior to Stalin's exit from the room. Never to marry again, Stalin took on mistresses, one of whom was Rosa Kaganovich, sister of Lazar Kaganovich, commissar of Transportation.

At the time of his mother's death in 1937, the "Man of Steel" had become remorseful and somewhat forgiving of her. At her funeral Stalin remarked to a friend, "She is dead and with her have died my last warm feelings for all human beings." This was a frightening eulogy from a man who had inherited all of Russia as his domain to lead. The five-foot, five-inch ruler had physical and psychological handicaps not matching his self-styled image of a "strongman" running the biggest nation in the world. As a child he fell beneath a horse-drawn wagon and suffered a permanently crippled arm, which became noticeably undersized. As if this handicap was not enough, the child also had congenital webbed toes. And since he often did not have shoes, although his father was a shoemaker, many of the children ridiculed him. There is no question that Stalin's stormy childhood resulted in the cruel treatment of others during his reign of terror. Stalin fit the model of childhood victims of abuse who become abusers of others, including children. He beat his own son and implemented a law making children 12 and older subject to adult punishment. By eliminating the offspring of his enemies he could prevent them from seeking future revenge. It is evident the Russian people in general substituted a dictator for the czar and viewed the "Man of Steel" as a strong father figure.

Stalin had broad features and strong hands, giving him an appearance of strength. He seldom smiled but instead wore a look of a chronic schemer and doubter. He could be described as a capable organizer of men but one who used arrogance and belligerence to humble and dominate. Professor Schmidt, Levanevsky, and the other NSR employees may have come under this spell of fear and intimidation, and then found themselves unable to back away from the runaway plan to deceive America and the world. The sober Stalin despised the truly intelligent and idealistic men of his time, probably because he related them to the past capitalist society, and because they made him conscious of his own inferiority. Stalin preferred the company of doers; those who were ready to accomplish something now, even if unethical or dubious in nature. In many ways this described the NSR employees, specifically those with ambitions in aviation. This fit in well with Stalin's conception of what was needed to build up the country's defenses and international image. It was fortunate that Stalin was a loner because his vain and jealous nature could destroy people (Maxim Gorky may have been one) close to him. Levanevsky, Dr. Schmidt, and a host of other people mixed up in the hoaxes were literally gambling with their lives. If the hoaxes were exposed the most they could expect was to join the "walking dead." With the help of Henry Yagoda of the secret police, Stalin could wipe out the entire NSR organization if he desired. But in this mad dash to secure the country from real or imagined invasion, the patriotic spirit of NSR employees was rushing to the fore. Would all caution be thrown to the wind and the final signal be given to launch the master plan?

After much deliberation Stalin made the decision to cooperate in the hoax – the go-ahead was finally given. Immediately Professor

Schmidt began organizing the expedition party for the northern air trek. Two pilots, Mikhail Vodopyanov and Vassily Molokov, and Ivan Papanin, who had questionable credentials as an arctic scientist, were the principal supervisors who would help Dr. Schmidt prepare four of the giant ANT-6s for the flight to Rudolph Island. Here were vintage ANT-6s with BMW diesel engines just barely able to reach the North Pole from Rudolph Island and no chance of returning. Despite this, the Soviets eventually claimed those four planes carried thousands of gallons of fuel to the pole in order to provide a depot where other planes could refuel in the future. In summary, the four ANT-6s were loaded to the hilt with far more weight than had they been carrying a full load of bombs. Also figuring in the gross weight were the 42 so-called explorers – as compared to the few crewmen normally assigned to the TB3, the bomber version of the ANT-6s.

Vodopyanov was in charge of all the equipment and supplies. In selecting these items he was allowed to draw on his experiences and the fictional version of a polar station he wrote about in *Dream of an Aviator*. Vodopyanov and Molokov were each scheduled to fly an ANT-6. Two other fliers to be named later would pilot two additional planes. Schmidt's chief navigator for the expedition was to be I.T. Spirin, also an NSR employee. Outside of NSR and key Kremlin officials, no one knew what was going on. It was important not to alert the public and news media prematurely since there was no real plan to reach the North Pole. NSR would settle for any remote location with sufficient ice and snow cover to set up a "polar" station. All that was needed was some film and perhaps some other documentation. Although an additional radio station in the northern regions was unnecessary since there was to be no flight, NSR intended to use this communication post to convince the public an authentic event was underway. Just like the plans of 1936, Schmidt's expedition was to follow the Kola Peninsula to the Franz Josef Archipelago and use the field at Rudolph, a landing site prepared the previous year.

In order to coordinate the existence of the northern camp with the Alaskan plan, the aerial expedition would have to get underway sometime in March. It would take about three weeks to reach Rudolph Island due to the limited range of the ANT-6. These craft would have to be refueled several times between Shelkova and the northern tip of the Kola Peninsula. This would enable the four-engine ANTs to reach Hooker, about 400 miles away, and from there it was only a short hop to Rudolph in the same island group. NSR planned to claim a polar conquest in the month of May. They must arrive on Rudolph in April to guarantee a snow cover, not only for landing their ski-equipped aircraft but also for making the film documentation. Ordinarily Rudolph had an abundance of ice and snow well into the month of May; however, NSR was not about to risk an unusual warming trend that might leave them without a substitute polar camp environment. It wasn't critical to establish this northern camp as far as the Alaskan plan was concerned. Other advantages could be derived from its existence if the world actually believed a permanent village had been founded in this most foresaken of territories. If the Alaskan hoax were uncovered the Russian government could still salvage considerable fame from an unprecedented permanent camp at the "pole." However, since both northern projects were being sponsored by the same NSR organization discovery of a transpolar flight hoax might mean discovery of the North Pole station hoax.

NSR was satisfied with their overall strategy. At the start it was concluded the film of the 1936 staged Arctic-Siberian takeoff ceremony could be used to authenticate the forthcoming "transpolar flight." Another avenue was always open to NSR and that was to take advantage of having twin ANT-25s at their disposal. One ANT-25 could be used in an actual takeoff from Shelkova while another ANT-25 waited for a signal to fly from the archipelago to the United States. Apparently Levanevsky could not locate a safe landing site in Alaska so NSR decided to dismantle the ANT-25 and ship the parts to an isolated island in the archipelago. The plane would be reassembled and made ready to fly to America on cue.

It must have occurred to the master planners that everything hinged on whether the ANT was going to be airworthy at the prescribed hour to embark from Alaska. What if Chkalov failed to lift off and reach America? All of the plans and work would be for naught. The major thrust had always been to improve Soviet aviation. Failure of the "transpolar flight" might make the program unsalvageable. The so-called North Pole achievement with the 1925 ANT-6 models would add nothing revolutionary to the field of aviation. The overriding objective was the success of a "transpolar flight." Everything must be done to insure a successful takeoff in Alaska without being discovered. One way to do this was to forego a 1937 takeoff ceremony at Shelkova and ship a second ANT to the archipelago. This would double Chkalov's chances of getting one ANT off the ground and on its way to America. There was another advantage in having a backup airplane. If one ANT had mechanical or weather problems and crashed, another standby crew could make a second try at any time. Considering the ANT's crude workmanship and the M-34's poor engine performance, a second plane could prove a blessing. Besides, Berdnik and his crew of mechanics would have to reassemble the ANT in the wilderness without the benefit of shop facilities. Something could go wrong. NSR at this time began to lean toward sending the twin ANT to Alaska and using the staged 1936 takeoff ceremony for its documentation of the "transpolar flight."

If this eventually were the final decision, NSR had to face the reality of no actual takeoff ceremony from Shelkova in the summer. They were planning to execute an historic and unprecedented aerial bridge between hemispheres, with no takeoff being contemplated: It seemed ludicrous to say the least. This conjecture was further complicated by not being able to invite the American ambassador, Joseph Davies, who had been officially assigned to Moscow in January. Like William Bullitt before him, Ambassador Davies probably would expect to attend this once-in-a-lifetime happening. If NSR pursued its present plans, some way would have to be found to distract the new ambassador away from the takeoff point at Shelkova. Another consideration related to the Federation Aeronautique Internationale's (FAI) expectations for neutral witnesses to be present at attempted world records. Both the takeoff and landing had to be authenticated and the gas seals must arrive intact at the destination point. The proper barographic evidence showing an uninterrupted flight must also be demonstrated. It is apparent NSR and the Kremlin were not worried about complying with FAI regulations. The important objective of insuring American aviation contacts had the greatest priority.

Only in Russia could such a stunt be pulled off. The Russian people were rarely told much anyway, and apparently accepted what was provided without question. It would still take some doing to stage a fake takeoff, but the element of surprise might help. The American government would have to be informed of Russia's impending "transpolar flight" plans in order for them to obtain landing permission, exit visas for the fliers, and weather and communication assistance. But the Soviets planned to withhold any requests for U.S. permits until the last few weeks prior to Moscow's official announcements of the "flight." It was hoped the U.S. government would agree to keep these communications secret as long as possible. The Russian populace need not be told anything until the affair was almost completed. No one, including the

American government and foreign press, was to be informed as to the takeoff time and location. *Pravda* and *Tass,* the official Soviet news agencies, could be given detailed accounts of a near-dark takeoff ceremony after it was over. Those government-controlled publications would never question whether there was an actual takeoff. As an added precaution the secret police could make Shelkova off-limits to those not involved.

Dr. Schmidt had been busy throughout March organizing for the trek northward. Four big ANT-6s had been made ready to transport 42 NSR employees and many tons of equipment to Rudolph Island. Finally, on March 20, the expedition got underway.

The benefits would be immeasurable if the Russian people could be convinced that the North Pole had been conquered by air and that a transpolar flight had set the stage for an air link with the United States. It would substantially raise Stalin's political image and make it possible for him to survive the ill effects of his purges and inhumane policies. It could add years to his political life and keep his regime intact. Stalin wanted to let Germany know the Soviets were developing closer ties with the United States; the "transpolar flight," if successful, was designed to demonstrate to Hitler an airline route had been established, free from Nazi interference. The Soviets had to convince the world they possessed long-range aircraft. They also had to show that their fliers could negotiate the arctic and polar regions by using advanced navigational aids, which actually they didn't have.

In order to heighten the mystery of how the Russian fliers were able to operate in the arctic wildernesses, NSR did not intend to install any de-icing equipment on the wings of their airplanes. This was partly because the Soviets did not produce them; it would be rather embarrassing to use foreign types that could be easily spotted when the ANT-25 arrived in the United States. After all, the Soviets were trying to prove that their aviation industrial progress was right on target. The Soviet pilots would surely be credited with extraordinary abilities if people believed they could survive the polar atmospheres without de-icers. Even with special equipment there was no guarantee against severe icing problems, but it did give the pilot a fighting chance in most circumstances. To fly to Rudolph in the spring would require short hops for periodic removal of ice, or coating the wings with oil or some other anti-freeze solution. Naturally Chkalov could get by without these devices on a hop from Alaska to America; however, one would have thought precautions against icing would have helped project the illusion of a polar flight. The surface temperatures at the pole in June hover around freezing, and atmospheric temperatures where planes fly sometimes drop to 30 degrees and more below freezing.

Whether Stalin was going to allow NSR to carry out the Alaskan plan or bail out at the last minute hinged on the conditions in the coming months. If the outlook of holding his government together was bleak or threatened by Trotskyism and foreign agents, the Soviet dictator might have no choice but to proceed with the hoaxes. The problems in aviation, and especially the lack of good air defenses, placed the Soviets in great jeopardy. For these reasons and the incessant verbal bombardment by the exiled Trotsky, the aerial hoaxes appeared to be the government's only salvation. Trotsky continued his relentless attack on Stalin's leadership. Mexico had given the ex-Soviet political asylum and a base for launching attacks on the direction of the communist movement under Stalin. Trotsky offered to bare his complete archives to answer the treason charges leveled against him and – what was worse – certain important Americans were listening. Stalin shot back at the exiled Russian, accusing him of ordering the overthrow of the government. It was reported several high-ranking Soviet officials admitted complicity with Trotsky involving sabotage, treason, assassination threats, and advocating the return to capitalism. Trotsky quickly replied through the world's newspapers how Stalin's rule had always been based on lies, calumny, and falsification. He said, "They are afraid in Moscow of the fact that with American public opinion, I have a certain sympathy. They want to make it impossible for me to go for one day to the United States, or even to remain in Mexico" (*New York Times*, February 19, 1937).

Alexander Troyanovsky, the Russian ambassador to the United States, took up the battle in support of Stalin at a meeting of the American-Russian Institute in Washington D.C. Besides attacking Trotsky, the ambassador said the world misunderstood Russia under the New Constitution. The Soviet Union's true intentions were "friendly cooperation with all democracies" and his country was following a direction of socialism and not communism, declared the ambassador. His softened approach was no doubt designed to offset growing support for the exiled Trotsky. The Stalinist government proceeded to execute 13 people charged with being in league with Trotsky. But this was only the beginning. It appeared the Kremlin was intent on unleashing a major purge, coincidentally coinciding with the tenth anniversary of Trotsky's expulsion from the Communist Party. Hundreds of former

Communist leaders were seized and charged with sabotaging railroads, grain production, coal mines, etc.

In Trotsky's next major news release he offered evidence disproving collaboration with a prominent Russian journalist assigned to *Izvestia*. The documents suggested the exiled dissident was in a different region of France and therefore could not have met with the journalist, who had decided to testify for the Stalin government. It seemed Stalin was caught in a deliberate lie. If things continued like this the Russian government's inroads into the U.S. industrial empire of aviation and navigation might come to a halt.

Perhaps the serious domestic situation in Russia is what spurred Stalin's approval of the next and most crucial step in the Alaskan plan. This objective was to get the two ANTs into the Alexander Archipelago along with the men who were going to put the planes back together. Recently the names of several NSR aviation mechanics had been confirmed who would make the trip; they included Vassily Berdnik, Eugene Karlovich, and two men not fully identified. By this time their trip was well in progress. Eventually, Berdnik and his working party arrived in the southern waters of the archipelago, which is composed of literally hundreds of small islands. It is surmised that the work party made contact with a small group of Indians in the area. It may have been a chance meeting or it could have been planned. They knew the task of reassembling the two planes was going to be time-consuming and worried about meeting a deadline. NSR did not want to attract too much attention by sending in a large party, knowing native Alaskans (Indians) would be available to assist them. Somewhere along the coast of Baranof or near northern Prince of Wales the Russian party encountered these Indians who may have been fishing the waters. It appears the natives were wooed by offers of generous salaries and a bonus of all the vodka they could consume. They had to know everything was not on the up and up when it was revealed the crates contained airplane parts. Shouldn't it have appeared unusual for Russians to be unloading airplane parts in Alaska? There were plausible explanations that may have crossed the Alaskans' minds. It was not unusual to meet Russians in Alaska; they had been present in great numbers for years. And it was not uncommon to use airplanes to spot game and schools of fish.

Apparently the arrangement between Berdnik's group and the Indians was workable. The airplane parts were unloaded and packed inland where a clearing had been previously reconnoitered.

The American public was also thinking about airplanes at this time; Amelia Earhart was preparing to take her $80,000 Lockheed "flying laboratory" around the world. The brave and celebrated aviatrix planned to follow the equator in one of the longest air journeys ever undertaken, a distance of 27,000 miles. On March 17, a few friends and relatives bid her and navigator Fred Noonan goodbye at Oakland, California. After reaching Honolulu, Earhart attempted to take off again when an accident occurred and forced her to temporarily give up the around-the-world trip. The route was thereafter changed to an easterly direction and scheduled a couple of months later. Miss Earhart's aerial activities had drawn great interest in the United States and she was considered to be one of the greatest women pilots in the world. Miss Earhart used a Lockheed product; her model was an Electra and not the smaller Vultee purchased by Levanevsky. The Soviets wanted the best and were willing to pay for it. Anticipating large purchases from American companies, the Russian government transferred huge amounts of gold to the United States. Some of the products acquired were already being used by Russian pilots in the Spanish Civil War. In April of 1937 Soviet fighter planes were performing extremely well against the fascists, but as it turned out the planes were all equipped with American Wright-Cyclone engines.

During April, Leon Trotsky was granted an appearance before an impartial commission. John Dewey acted as chairman while Trotsky presented evidence of being unjustly accused of advocating the overthrow of the Soviet government. Trotsky admitted opposing Stalin's ruling party while still favoring a communistic-socialistic nation. Evidently Trotsky's ability to attract an American audience was creating a problem for Stalin and the Kremlin because Ambassador Troyanovsky went after the dissident again, labeling the "trial" as a flop – a premature judgment since the commission had not yet released its findings. Stalin as usual announced the liquidation of more spies; this time the Japanese were found to be in league with the Trotskyites. Before April had passed there was a national campaign against graft. Henry Yagoda of the secret police was arrested as an example of high officials enriching themselves at the expense of the people. Many other important officials and supervisors in industry were caught in this latest dragnet to "purify" the economic system.

In the same breath the Soviet government, represented by Lazar Kaganovich (the brother of Mikhail Kaganovich) announced a gigantic modernization program using American methods in mass production in their factories. He talked about Sigmund Levanevsky's work in familiarizing Russia with American products. Already, contracts had been signed with the Douglas company, Glenn Martin, Bendix and others. The Kremlin looked forward to the day when the skies would be full of Soviet-built aircraft that could be paraded before thousands of Muscovites. But until this time arrived they would have to be content with disguising foreign products. When May Day came Red Square was brimming with the customary military parades and overhead, according to Soviet news reports, 800 airplanes of all types blackened the skies over Moscow. There was no doubt many foreign-built planes participated in this special occasion, but the average Russian citizen was none the wiser. An effigy of Trotsky was carried along dressed in a yellow shirt with hands bloodied. It was obvious Stalin and the Kremlin were becoming more preoccupied with this exiled political figure and needed to generate public antagonism against him.

The purges didn't seem to quell the anti-Stalinist movement; however, the dictator continued his wholesale arrests. Numerous Trade Union officials were seized as the government began to cut into its own personnel. Sanctions were placed on Red Army generals in a desperate move by Stalin to lessen the power of any individual official. In the exercise of his rule the dictator had always guarded against bestowing too much power on any one person because he feared they might successfully challenge his leadership. People who did gain prominence were in mortal danger. More and more Sigmund Levanevsky fit this description. The key to Russian progress in aviation was America, and fortunately Levanevsky had the most access to U.S. factories. The "Soviet Lindbergh" was not the only Russian touring the American factories. A fairly large number of "engineers" and mechanics had been diligently studying the production and assembly line techniques ever since Tupolev first opened the door for other Russians.

CHAPTER 14

"On Top of the World"

It had been ten years since Lindbergh's historic Atlantic crossing; but this anniversary, like his Berlin speech, was about to be upstaged by the Russians. This time the Soviet claims were more spectacular. Towards the last part of May front pages of newspapers throughout America carried the banner headline, "RUSSIANS LAND AT THE NORTH POLE." There had been no prior hint of the endeavor. Some talk about a polar station was mentioned in 1935 during Levanevsky's "attempt," but nothing since then.

Most Americans were startled on May 22 when newspapers across the country carried the story of Soviet fliers safely landing at the North Pole. This announcement was a complete surprise to the Russian people as well. No one outside of the Kremlin and NSR knew this so-called polar landing was a part of a gigantic master plan to deceive the world. This purported feat was unprecedented, and therefore historic. More than just the landing claim caught the public eye; the Russians also said they intended to set up a permanent scientific station at the top of the world. This wasn't the extent of the "revolutionary news." The Soviets reportedly were planning to build an airfield that would link their country with America.

To the unsuspecting Americans it almost seemed as if the Russians were about to conquer the world from the most advantageous position on Earth. The Americans learned from recent Russian propaganda how this new socialistic empire had been systematically civilizing the arctic regions for years with many camps and small villages. There were claims of untold riches in the form of minerals and oil resources there for the taking. Bountiful fish harvests were projected in what heretofore was thought to be a lifeless environment. Earlier explorers, probably including some Russians, reported schools of fish, 300 to 500 miles from the pole, but far from bountiful. The Soviets continued to magnify their expected scientific achievements. People wondered if this new ideology of communism held the key to successful government. Was Russia moving as one great cooperative to dominate the world? Here was the largest nation in the world seemingly expanding its territories. The fact that much of the Soviet Union was already a part of the arctic didn't seem to matter as people visualized almost unlimited new territories under her rule.

The average person didn't know that outside of a few islands in the north seas and Arctic Ocean there was nothing but floating ice; in fact the polar icecap itself was nothing but a gigantic ice floe. There were certainly no accessible minerals – such as gold – under this ice, but only plenty of frigid water. When the Soviets spoke of the arctic they were really speaking of the northern regions of their own country. Very few of these areas had been developed simply because the Russians lacked an efficient transportation system. All they could handle was keeping the trans-Siberian railroad free of serious problems that would completely break the line down. During the last few days NSR had issued statements extolling Soviet explorations in the northern regions, including the success of the northern shipping channel. The world in general did not realize the Northern Sea Route project was a failure. Professor Schmidt alluded to the 50 or 60 camps and radio stations established in the arctic as if they were examples of Russia's ability to populate and civilize the most inaccessible lands. Schmidt was actually referring to the leftover radio stations placed strategically along the coastal channel. Not even the nearby island of Novaya Zemlya had been developed or settled to any extent. In truth there was little going on to "civilize" the northern regions; however, the average foreigner imagined the Soviets making great strides in conquering the "richly endowed" arctic and polar wildernesses.

With the claimed landing of Vodopyanov's ANT-6 at the pole for the purpose of establishing a permanent village, the Soviets declared the territory for their own. The Stalinist government cited traditional international laws governing acquisition of new territories as proof of their ownership of the pole, from the time their flag was driven into the icy surface. It was furthermore argued that Peary had missed the pole by 100 miles, but even if others had successfully preceded the Soviets no country had ever tried to set up a permanent residency. Most major

U.S. newspapers carried Russian stories and pictures of "polar camp" activities. One photo showed three raised Soviet flags symbolizing the conquest of the North Pole. One flag displayed the NSR insignia, a second bore the portrait of Joseph Stalin and a third carried the Russian "hammer and sickle." Stories included biographical sketches of Professor Schmidt's life in connection with previous explorations and his work as supervisor of the Northern Sea Route project. The pictures and stories certainly looked impressive.

The world completely bought the enterprise as one of the great achievements of the times. According to news articles, the Soviet scientists were busy setting up a temporary tent city to carry out their work of erecting a prefabricated building to become a part of the permanent settlement. A radio station and a smoothed-out ice field airplanes could use for a proposed commercial airline route between Russia and America were scheduled to be built. Moscow radio reported the polar pioneers were busy unpacking and storing tons of scientific equipment needed for future investigations of the pole's climate and underlying waters.

According to stories emanating from the Russian capital, Vodopyanov's plane was only heard from once after he left the depot on Rudolph Island. Reports indicated his plane was carrying 13 passengers, including Dr. Schmidt and the four men to be left at the camp for one year. Absolute silence followed until finally Russian sources relayed word the polar party had successfully landed near the 90-degree North Geographical Point. According to the reports received by the American news media from Moscow, Professor Schmidt radioed personally to Joseph Stalin and V.M. Molotov, the Soviet premier, informing them the expeditionary party had made it to the North Pole. Supposedly Schmidt told Stalin the plane's radio had ceased functioning, causing delays in transmission. A quote attributed to Professor Schmidt read as follows, "We feel that by the interruption of communications we have inadvertently caused you alarm. We are very sorry. Hearty greetings. Please report to the party and the government the fulfillment of the first part of our task."

The communiqué stated that the exact number of men transported to Rudolph Island was 42, and that 13 of them were now at the pole setting up a "tent city." The tents would be used for the storage of an 18-month supply of food, equipment, etc. Three more huge ANT-6s were expected in the next few days, with enough cargo to supposedly sustain four scientists for a year. (The chances of all three airplanes safely landing on the pole defy the odds considering the hazardous conditions such as ridges and hummocks rising as much as 18 feet, unpredictable snow storms, numerous meltwater ponds, and low and foggy overcast.) An 80-pound prefabricated hut measuring 7 by 10 feet was to serve as the men's permanent dwelling. A radio station weighing half a ton and powered by a windmill would be installed. A gasoline motor was brought along to insure a power source. The news item explained how the camp was designed for scientific study and the comfort of the four men. Vodopyanov's fictional research was beginning to show through as the Soviets described in considerable detail what was involved in the establishment of a permanent polar camp.

On the following day, May 23, the Soviet government formally claimed the North Pole as its own to "have and to hold forever on the grounds that it was the first to establish a permanent settlement in the vicinity." However, the American government was quick to note why this region could not be annexed because there was no land, only ice floating on international waters. This same day, according to Professor Schmidt, the radio station was completed and ready to send weather reports back to Moscow. Heavy fog over the pole now limited visibility to about a mile. These conditions reportedly would forestall any attempt by the three ANTs on Rudolph to join Vodopyanov. Professor Schmidt said scientific work had already begun but its nature wasn't mentioned.

The chief Soviet newspaper, *Izvestia*, explained why conquest of the pole was important to the country. One benefit was in learning the weather pattern in the polar basin, referred to as the weather kitchen; the second related to airline links with the rest of the world; and the third was a political benefit because "our plan of conquest of the Arctic Pole and the polar spaces was so enormous and majestic that its fulfillment became possible only by means of the perfect, powerful technique of socialism...." The newspaper *Pravda* joined in proclaiming that "Soviet polar workers will conquer the North Pole as they have already conquered and inhabited many points of the distant Arctic. What was too much for decrepit capitalism will be successfully done by the country of the Soviets."

To the Russian citizens at home *Izvestia*'s headlines screamed out, "The North Pole had been taken...by the power of Socialistic technique, the courage of our people, the quality of our machines, the valor and will of our nation which has given such brave sons to the country, and the clear wisdom of the leaders of our country, who suggested and inspired the plan of conquering the Arctic." Indeed it must have been a wonderful and proud day in the Soviet Union to hear of these great accomplishments the people thought were happening. The Russian people were "on top of the world" in their rejoicing, and had no inkling their explorers were not actually at the top of the world. Instead they were sitting on Rudolph with a make-believe polar camp.

Dr. Frederick Cook must have believed the Russians. Cook had been carrying on a running battle with Robert Peary over which one reached the North Pole first. Dr. Cook had received the worst of the scuffle as the major governments sided with Peary, claiming his evidence was more credible. Cook's life appeared to be shattered when witnesses from his own expeditionary party denied the explorer had even come close to the pole. Now at 72 years of age he hoped the Russians would verify his claim and end 30 years of frustration. He said, "the most important information about the North Pole since I was there on April 21, 1908, will come from the Russian scientists.... Their description of the land they flew over before reaching the Pole will prove I actually was the first." Apparently the Soviets weren't going to let Cook die happy because they proceeded to throw aside all previous claims to the North Pole.

Byrd and Amundsen's accomplishments apparently didn't count, and how they came to the conclusion Robert Peary missed the pole by 100 land miles is beyond comprehension. Since the North Pole ice formations undergo perpetual change due to their constant southern movement, how was it possible to know who had been there and who had not? Cook's reference to the Russians passing over land before reaching the pole is interesting because there isn't any to pass over. After Rudolph there is nothing but water and ice. At any rate, Cook's last hope for verification seemed gone as the Soviets were not willing to share all their newly conquered ice. Actually there was evidence showing why Dr. Cook missed the pole by several hundred miles. Even Admiral Peary was criticized for his neglect to document his journey and for his admitted failure to take instrument sightings to prove his location. It would be interesting to see whether the international scientific community would demand equal proof from the Russian explorers.

Admiral Byrd took it all in stride as he enthusiastically congratulated the expedition, and revealed how he had been consulted concerning Soviet plans to take an air expedition to the pole. It was Byrd's assessment that the Soviets had been very thorough in their preparations. Americans learned how Byrd had reminded the Russians why the polar camp would have to be moved back in the direction of Alaska every so often in order to maintain a precise position at 90 degrees North. Although Byrd did not know for sure which direction the polar ice floe would follow, he thought Spitsbergen or Greenland could be the terminus. Vilhjamur Stefansson, president of the New York Explorer's Club and a friend of Professor Schmidt, echoed Byrd's feelings. Stefansson said he wasn't surprised at the announced Soviet accomplishments because of his familiarity with their general exploratory and aviation programs. Here were two noted experts who believed the Russians had indeed conquered the North Pole by air. It was curious that the international scientific communities with all their knowledge and skills, and their governments with even more financial and other resources, never made the expected follow-ups to determine whether the Russians really reached the North Pole. All other explorers – including Admiral Peary, Dr. Cook, and others – had been put through grueling inquiries to determine the legitimacy of their polar claims. This wouldn't be the last time Soviet claims were blindly accepted by the world.

But for now the drama continued as the Russians released biographical sketches of some of the major figures in the expedition, including Dr. Otto J. Schmidt, Mikhail Vodopyanov, Ivan Papanin, Ernest Krenkel, Peter Shirshov, and Eugene Federov. Schmidt, NSR supervisor, named Krenkel, Shirshov, and Federov as the crew to remain at the "polar station" under the supervision of Papanin. At age 43, Papanin, the senior member of the group, had been a principal organizer of the Soviet secret police and later served as a military commissar before becoming a radio operator for NSR. Other biographical data described Krenkel as a 32-year-old radio operator; Shirshov, at 27, the youngest, a hydro-biologist; and Federov, 32, a magnetologist. A dog named Jolly, said to have been brought along to warn the camp of polar bears, rounded out the team. The American public was informed for the first time about Vodopyanov's *Dream of an Aviator* story and how it had inspired this "historic achievement." Russian news articles credited Vodopyanov for the idea of using airplanes to establish a permanent polar village. Vodopyanov revealed how he had been influenced by Admiral Byrd's aerial efforts at both poles. Moscow honored the author-flier by staging his three-act play *Dream of an Aviator* at this time.

Shirshov, according to Professor Schmidt, was to act as the permanent camp physician. The Soviets had apparently been surprised by questions concerning the lack of medical precautions being taken. No doctors had been mentioned among the 42 persons making up the expeditionary party, and this may have prompted some reporter to inquire why there was no medical physician assigned. It was explained how Shirshov had taken a crash medical course and "performed several operations, including amputations of arms and legs," before leaving Moscow. This explanation seemed weak. The Soviet government revealed in various news bulletins during the month how NSR had been preparing for the past two years. In view of this much advance planning it would seem the Soviets could have found a certified medical doctor for this physically dangerous "mission." Admiral Peary had enlisted Dr. Frederick Cook as his physican to go along on one of his tries at the pole, even though his crew would only be there a short time.

The Soviets said Schmidt and his party of 13 were still awaiting the three supply planes on May 24. If weather prevented a landing, there was a possibility men and supplies could be dropped by parachute. In a news release Professor Schmidt recounted how he had made a presentation, based on Mikhail Vodopyanov's theories, to Stalin and eight high government officials. During Schmidt's presentation a new aviation personality was introduced to the American media. According to Schmidt's story, a flier named Valery Chkalov rose to his feet in the presence of the Soviet dictator and declared, "The shortest road to America lies across the North Pole. Study of the central polar basin will make realization of the Moscow-North Pole-San Francisco flight possible. . . . At the same time we have airplanes in which it is possible to make nonstop flights from Moscow to San Francisco via the North Pole. . . ." Chkalov was referring to the same plane Levanevsky had used in his "failed" attempt in 1935. The news story went on to announce how Sigmund Levanevsky was expected to use the polar station first on a projected trip to America. The choice of Levanevsky was supposedly made by Stalin himself. No date for the renewed effort by the "Soviet Lindbergh" was given.

The following day, May 25, a curious bulletin was issued from Moscow stating how unusually warm weather at the pole had resulted in the melting of some ice-blockhouse structures and that the floe on which the 13 men were camped had begun breaking up, causing alarm. It was therefore decided the permanent camp might be given up any day. Shortly thereafter, another statement was issued from Russia denying there was any truth to the first message. Why this was done is not clear but speculation might offer an interesting answer. The Soviets feared American pilots might come looking for the polar airfield and not

CHAPTER 15

In the Archipelago

At this very time Joseph Stalin had summoned Valery Chkalov, George Baidukov, Alexander Beliakov, and Sigmund Levanevsky to the Kremlin to make their case for a "transpolar flight." The May 25, 1937 meeting included several important Soviet leaders. Baidukov previously had been required to write a letter asking for permission to make the flight, and before meeting with Stalin and his advisors the fliers had been instructed to go to the office of Klementy Voroshilov, apparently for a briefing. It appears that Defense Minister Voroshilov was acting as a go-between. Several hours later as the fliers entered the conference room, Stalin rose behind a long table where Molotov, Nikolai Yezhov, and Voroshilov were seated. Yezhov had recently been appointed to replace Henry Yagoda as chief of police, and he came forward to greet the NSR fliers. A model of the ANT-25 was on a nearby desk.

"So the Earth is not good enough for you?" Stalin joked in a questioning manner. "You want to fly again? And where do you intend to go?" Stalin continued. Then he paused for a moment, looking inquisitively at each aviator, before asking, "Which of you will make the report of your plans?" Although Stalin knew the answer to each inquiry, the questions were carefully framed for the official record and to prove that NSR people were the driving force behind the "transpolar" plan and that he was merely listening to the presentation before deciding whether to grant approval.

Klementy Voroshilov spoke next, informing the dictator that there were actually two factions being represented: "Levanevsky and Chkalov have different plans about this flight, but both want Baidukov as copilot." Stalin motioned for Chkalov to speak first. Chkalov spelled out his intentions to fly nonstop from Moscow to America, adding how the ANT-25 had been tuned up, and "our crew. . . our troika (trio) of last year. . . is ready to fly." Then Levanevsky was permitted to tell of his plan to use a four-motored plane in a one-stop flight to America. Previous to the meeting a rumor had circulated that Levanevsky planned to use his two-motored American Douglas for a transpolar journey. For some reason George Baidukov was asked to speak and indicated a preference of making the "journey" with Chkalov in the ANT-25. Stalin turned to Molotov, Voroshilov, and Yezhov and asked them if they approved of the plan detailed by Chkalov. The dictator was wrapping them up neatly into a "package" of instigators. But there were some staff members missing who also had a part in this affair, namely, General Alksnis and Mikhail Kaganovich. Since the Soviet chieftain was not about to let them off the hook, he asked they be summoned.

George Baidukov later talked about this conversation, noting how Stalin and Voroshilov showed an extraordinary comprehension of technical aeronautic details. He related, "The questions they asked were acute and precise, showing both a broad perspective on the general progress of aviation in our country and concern for impregnable air defenses in case of war." As they continued to wait the arrival of Alksnis and Kaganovich, the subject turned to American planes. As the conversation wound down Stalin introduced the topic of the North Pole landing reported just three days ago. The Communist chief said the new polar station would make a transpolar flight easier. At this point Mikhail Kaganovich entered and Stalin asked point blank for his opinion on the flight. Kaganovich looked at the fliers first and then gave his okay. General Alksnis stepped in to meet the same question. "How about it? Is it possible to fly across the pole to America?" The Air Force chief had to say, "yes." It was reported Stalin then addressed V.M. Molotov and asked him to record the decision.

After the meeting concluded, Baidukov wrote, "we went directly to the airport to have a look at our great red-winged bird ANT-25 as she stood in her hangar." This was his way of placing the plane in the Moscow area when in fact it was being assembled in a remote region in Alaska. The next tactic was to transfer Chkalov, Baidukov, and Beliakov across Siberia to Alaska as fast as possible. There was no specific time limit involved but NSR wanted to begin implementing this phase of the master plan in June. The fliers should be there early enough to make sure everything was in readiness. It was clear there was to be no going-away party because there was no plane to use for the occasion.

The only people who presented a problem were the relatives and friends of the fliers who naturally expected to be there. The family situation was abruptly and decisively handled by the government; officials simply told them they could not attend! In any other country this ruling would have been viewed as outrageous, but in Russia it was "par for the course," the rule rather than the exception. In order to account for the disappearance of the fliers, now on their way to Siberia, the families were told go home because the three would be confined at Shelkova airfield until the "takeoff."

Now that the fliers were on their way, the Russian government must move quickly to contact the U.S. authorities. The Americans must be given at least a few weeks advance notice in order for everything to look proper. This early departure of the fliers for Alaska via Siberia posed a particular problem in securing passports and exit visas. The Kremlin did not want the passport applications made too early for fear of tipping off the American embassy in Moscow before NSR was ready. The Soviets admitted they wanted to limit the number of people who knew about the proposed flight, including the Russian employees working in the embassy. The Soviet government directed its embassy in Washington, D.C. to prepare and send a document to the U.S. State Department giving notification of two planned transpolar flights from Moscow to the United States scheduled for the summer. The Russian embassy complied and issued a message to the U.S. Secretary of State on May 29. The contents of this communication said the first nonstop flight would take place "June 10 or later depending on favorable weather conditions." The plane was to be piloted by "Valeri" Chkalov; copilot George Baidukov, and navigator Alexander Beliakov. The single-engine monoplane would bear the markings of URSS 025. Also contained in this message was the announcement of a second flight over the same route to take place July 15 or later, depending on favorable weather conditions, but this aircraft would make a landing in Fairbanks, Alaska.

The second flight, according to the message, would be made with an aircraft powered by "four AM 34R engines and marked URSS HGI 09." This plane would be piloted by "Sigismund" Levanevsky and would carry five additional crewmen to be named later. Both flights were to be conducted under the sponsorship of the Central Administration of the Northern Sea Route. The Soviet government at this time was appealing to the United States for strict confidentiality concerning these announced flights. The Russians said the secrecy requests resulted from the embarrassment incurred when premature news releases announced the Levanevsky flight of 1935 that ended in total failure. The American governmental officials involved in this request for confidentiality must have thought it strange why a planned aviation venture of this magnitude would go unannounced until the plane supposedly crossed the North Pole into the Western Hemisphere.

There was nothing secret about Amelia Earhart's plans to make a world flight. She had been trying for months to get her Lockheed Electra into the air. The day did arrive though, and early in the morning of June 1, she and Fred Noonan, her navigator, took off from Miami and pointed her specially equipped airship eastward into a hazy sky. The United States government and its people were to follow her progress closely. A Coast Guard cutter was ordered from San Diego to Howland Island to help guide Miss Earhart on the last leg of her flight. Newspapers and radio stations throughout the land featured the historic attempt to set a world record by following the equator around the world. Because of the equatorial bulge this was the longest possible route to take. Now, if only the Soviets could get their hoax flight successfully underway; they could steal the headlines away from Miss Earhart's great attempt.

Despite the intentions of the Soviets to ask for permission to land in California, NSR and the Kremlin staff's real plan did not involve sending the unpolished Chkalov and the relic ANT into this sophisticated hub of aviation. The actual destination for the "transpolar flight" was to remain a top secret with only a few people knowing the exact location of the projected landing. The little, unsuspecting city of Vancouver, Washington had been the secret choice ever since the "transpolar flight" plans had been on the drawing board. When the time came it would be up to Chkalov and his companions to find believable excuses why they brought the plane down at Pearson Field instead of going on to California.

By June 2, the Russian embassy in Washington, D.C. had passed another message to the United States Department of State requesting permission to land on American territory and seeking assistance as far as weather reports and directional signals were concerned. For several days there was an exchange of documents between the two countries covering a variety of subjects, including restrictions on photography and regulations on flying over restricted military facilities. An interesting document was received by the State Department on June 5, involving a change in the markings of the Russian planes scheduled to make the polar run. The first bulletins had shown the ANT-25's markings to be URSS 025, but later N was added to make the wing markings read URSS N 025. The change might have had something to do with not knowing for sure which ANT Chkalov would use when he departed from Alaska. Correspondence continued to be exchanged confidentially between the two governments until June 10.

Finally the curtain of secrecy was lifted on the proposed flights. It came about, according to U.S. news sources, through private talks involving American and Russian diplomats in Moscow. As a result the U.S. State Department released a very brief bulletin describing Soviet intentions to span the North Pole by air and reach the pacific coast of the United States. There was no information concerning the time of takeoff from Russia and the terminus of the event. It was crucial for the Soviets to keep everyone guessing as to when it would all happen. The Russian and American governments cooperated in withholding the names of the fliers. Rumors were floating around that Sigmund Levanevsky was going to try again after his 1935 failure. Any attempts by reporters to obtain more information from the State Department were referred to the Soviet embassy in Washington D.C. But this source became a dead end as Russian officials there professed ignorance of the project.

The breakthough had come on June 10 when the American government acknowledged that the Soviet Union had asked permission to fly over and land on U.S. territory. In the meantime the Soviets were reminded not to violate an "Executive Order" of August 12, 1935 restricting flights over "air space reservations and other important military and naval establishments." This presidential order also prohibited taking photographs over any United States territories. The U.S. War Department said it had no objections to the flights as long as the restrictions were honored and told the U.S. State Department it would cooperate and facilitate in a necessary communication system to give the fliers periodic weather reports. An advisory segment of the G-2 (military intelligence) message listed several emergency Alaskan landing fields for the fliers.

The Weather Bureau began setting up a system June 12 to assist the Soviets in the flight "across the Pole." Besides a regular 24-hour service, the Russian embassy asked for weather reports at three-hour intervals. On June 15, an arrangement was made to obtain weather reports from ships at sea which would give a larger overall picture of climatic conditions over the Pacific Ocean. The Soviets reasoned how this request might enhance the impression that a long and time-consuming flight was being proposed. A Russian radio agent, A.A. Vartanian, had already been assigned to a U.S. Signal Corps station at Seattle to handle the incoming reports. Vartanian would also translate the Russian fliers' messages and relay them to U.S. agents. As it turned out, Vartanian was the same radio agent assigned to the Seattle station in 1935 to conduct operations for the Levanevsky "transpolar flight." Mr. Vartanian was no stranger to the American scene, having been employed for many years by the Amtorg Trading Company, an import-export house in New York. He had arranged for the purchase of millions of dollars worth of airplane parts and other technical equipment for the Soviet government. In earlier years when the United States and Russia did not have a formal relationship, Vartanian had been the unofficial Russian representative in the United States. The radio agent had arrived in Seattle a number of days earlier and was setting up a communication system connecting American stations with those in Vladivostok and Khabarovsk, the latter serving as relay outposts to Moscow. Vartanian was going to be working under the U.S. Weather Bureau, a branch of the Department of Agriculture, and the U.S. Army Air Force's Signal Corps.

When the time came, Moscow radio would pretend to track the progress of the mythical flight and send coded information in Russian to radio agent Vartanian, who would then translate for the Americans. The main U.S. stations offering assistance ranged from Nome to San Francisco, with Seattle, Juneau, Fairbanks, and Anchorage rounding out the main communication network. By the middle of June, weather reports were being issued in compliance with Russian requests. On June 15, a document was sent from the Soviet embassy to the State Department requesting permission to bring a third airplane into the country. This new announcement made it apparent the Russian ground crew in the archipelago had both ANTs assembled and ready to make the dash to the American mainland.

At this time the Russian airmen in Alaska were waiting for the weather reports to come in from Vartanian and the other coastal stations. They were not at all interested in fair weather reports but rather were looking for low clouds and overcast to better hide the ANT on takeoff at the appointed hour. During the last few days a low overcast had been blowing in from the Pacific Ocean, extending from Juneau to Seattle. On June 16, the overcast continued, except more of the Pacific Coast was clouded over, driven by strong southwest winds aloft. The southern regions of the archipelago in the vicinity of the Russian camp was included in the overcast, and with the exception of some minor breaks the cloud cover blanketed the entire Pacific Coast, from Ketchikan to San Francisco. These were precisely the conditions needed to hide the big ANT-25. The Russians repeatedly requested an inordinate amount of weather and radio communication assistance from U.S. agencies, including minute details on receiving and transmitting radio frequencies. However, they appeared evasive in providing the U.S. with the most basic information on their own receiving and transmitting ranges and frequencies.

Previously, on June 2, the Soviets had listed one aircraft as being equipped with a 20-watt transmitter, operating on "frequencies ranging from 20 to 40, and from 50 to 80 meter bands. The receiver works on frequencies of from 25 to 1,800 meters," the Russian memo said. A second airplane with a 150-watt transmitter operates on frequencies ranging "from 25 to 80 and from 600 to 900 meters. The receiver works on frequencies of from 15 to 1,800 meters." One communication specialist said that all this information is "totally meaningless and would not be of any value to the pilots or the stations." It is obvious these vague responses to U.S. inquiries were deliberate; the Soviets wanted to listen in on American broadcasts but did not want their whereabouts known.

The United States warned the Russians that their signal stations could not proceed in establishing a communication link with the planes without reasonable information. The Russians knew that. But that is precisely why they withheld the communication information – because there would be no plane coming over the pole. And at all costs they certainly couldn't allow the real plane to be monitored from Alaska to America. It was critical not to permit foreign stations to track the real ANT from point-to-point, and thus expose the low speed of the plane, particularly if those low speeds were matched against the much more rapid speed of the mythical plane. NSR could not schedule the plane on the phony route at speeds less than 80 mph because in reality such low speeds would cause a plane of this type to stall out, especially with the heavy load of gas it would have to carry for such a long trip. Gradually the Soviets would be forced to increase the speed of the plane on paper to make it appear the decreased load of fuel was having an effect upon how fast the plane could then travel.

Although no one in the United States knew what kind of Russian plane was to be flown over the North Pole, some important information was being gathered by the Federal Bureau of Investigation. The FBI, operating out of a Portland office, had previously planted an informant in one of the Communist Party cells in this area. In the middle of June the spy made contact with two government agents and divulged a secret about the Russian flight to America. The agents were surprised to learn that the Soviet aircraft in question was scheduled to land at Pearson Field in Vancouver. Up until this time the U.S. government had been led to believe that San Francisco was the projected destination, although the Soviet government had not actually stated this. The assumption that San Francisco was to be the terminus for the so-called polar venture was based upon Levanevsky's plans in 1935.

It appears the Russians decided to enlist some of their American comrades to help out when the ANT-25 landed in Vancouver. This is why the Communist cell in Portland learned that Vancouver was to be the flight terminus. NSR and Stalin's staff were worried that an over-enthusiastic reception might result in damage to the plane and thus reveal the true fuel capacity. It is highly possible that Portland Communists were recruited to meet the incoming flight to protect both the aircraft and the fliers, without giving away their communist affiliations.

After learning that Vancouver was the selected landing site, the FBI moved quickly to alert Army officials at Pearson Field. The exact time and date of the meeting is not known at this writing; however, according to an unimpeachable witness, it was in the early morning sometime in the middle of June. This witness said two FBI agents met with the commander of the airfield and a Lt. Carlton Bond. (Lt. Bond had the distinction of being present when Shestakov arrived in 1929.) The commander at this time was Maj. Paul Burrows but there is some question whether he was on duty that day, or whether Lt. H.A. (Hap) Reynolds was in charge. In any event, the officer in charge heard the FBI story about Vancouver's eventual role in the "transpolar flight."

On June 16, the United States government notified news services of permission granted three Soviet aviators to fly over and land on American territory. This was supposedly the first transpolar trip in the history of aviation where two continents were bridged by air. The Soviets had not waited for U.S. permission, because on June 14, two days earlier, visa applications to the American embassy in Moscow had been filed. The visas were granted June 16, but, of course, the fliers had long since departed Moscow for their Alaskan camp. Soviet couriers would just have to deliver the visas secretly to the United States. Again the time of the "transpolar flight" departure and the destination were not given but the U.S. was led to believe that the plane would land in

San Francisco, the same destination reported by those in charge of the 1935 Levanevsky project.

On June 17, the Weather Bureau privately acknowledged to the Soviets that it would furnish reports every three hours, including specific times for the broadcasts. By knowing the precise time of the broadcasts Chkalov and his crew could conveniently tune in without having to man the radio all the time. The Alaskan crew had wireless and small crystal sets at their disposal besides the regular radio equipment in the planes. There were additional replacement parts in the wing stubs of the ANTs. It is not clear exactly which units were to be used; however, the Alaskan crew was well equipped to meet all circumstances.

The fliers had to be able to listen in on Moscow's phony plane position reports via the Siberian relay stations and follow the phantom ANT over the North Pole to the vicinity of their secret camp. In this way the pilots could make a timely ascent from the camp and be en route to the United States before anyone knew a real plane had taken over for a mythical one. The fliers needed to keep in touch with Moscow to alert NSR when and if the ANTs were airworthy. With the cooperation of the United States the Russians had established a three-way communication system under their complete control.

Either the Soviets came on so fast that the U.S. did not have sufficient time to study and evaluate the situation, or else the Americans thought it was in their interest to support the Soviets' plans. This was going to work to the advantage of the NSR organization as it prepared to sneak the phantom ANT over the pole and down into the archipelago where Chkalov and Baidukov were waiting to fly the real one out. While the Soviets were trying to decide when to unleash the first hoax flight to the United States, the U.S. State Department was receiving the names of the fliers who were expected to make another "transpolar" attempt in a single-engine plane. The chief pilot was identified as Mikhail Gromov, the copilot as Andrew Yumashev, and the navigator as Sergei Danilin. A low-winged monoplane with the markings URSS 025-1 was to be used. Other than this description there was no way to know what type of aircraft was coming to the United States.

On the evening of June 18, it was obvious "something was in the air." A little after 8 p.m. eastern standard time, the Soviet embassy contacted American officials in Washington, D.C. The news media were alerted and received statements from Russian embassy officials

Gregory Gokhman, acting consul, and Constantine Oumansky, counselor. One statement read: "Three Soviet fliers had passed over the
North Pole and were now 500 miles on the American side en route to
San Francisco." The report came 24 hours after the Soviet plane had
supposedly taken off from a military airfield outside Moscow. The
Russians had stayed with their plan not to release any information until
after the mythical ship was on its way to America, and the U.S.
government had kept its confidence by not issuing any information
about the enterprise. Although no one noticed, the report put the
plane's speed at 120 miles an hour. Even Gokhman was rather puzzled
by the message. He told reporters he had received an earlier bulletin
placing the Russian airship 250 miles short of the pole after 18 hours of
flight, which figured out to be 120 mph, in the face of headwinds, a
cyclone, and a plane that under the best circumstances had trouble
attaining 100 mph. A scant 90 minutes later the Russian embassy
official notified American correspondents that the plane was now at the
North Pole. The Russian monoplane, still handicapped by more than
7,000 pounds of fuel, supposedly covered the 250 miles to the pole at a
speed of almost 170 mph, but no one noticed this discrepancy. Adding
to the confusion, Gokhman received another announcement from
Moscow placing the airship at the North Pole after 27 hours of flight
time. It appeared NSR had the wayward plane back on a more believable schedule. Its time of 27 hours and 10 minutes to the pole from
Moscow, a distance of 2,352 miles, meant an average speed of 90 mph, a
much more believable pace for the ANT-25.

Why these contradictory time frames were being transmitted is a
mystery; the discrepancies probably deeply embarrassed the Russian
officials. Even the Russian embassy officials seemed honestly puzzled
by the various contradictory reports. Possibly communications got out
of hand and no one could immediately regain control of these plane
position mix-ups, causing Gokhman to throw up his hands in frustration. First the Russian emissary was told by Moscow the plane was 250
miles short of the pole, after 18 hours of flight. Then 90 minutes later
the ANT was reported at the pole; followed by another report the plane
was 500 miles past the top of the world, after 24 hours. After giving
these plane positions to the press, another Moscow bulletin came in
putting the Russian plane "back to the Pole where it belonged," judging
by its normal cruising speed. Apparently the radio operator in Moscow
was learning by trial and error.

It seems as though the problems didn't end with the "polar" mix-ups. Just after midnight Vartanian received another report reading, "Everything all right. I am trying...establish communication with America. Cruising speed 200 – Patrick Island – Beliakov." The navigator didn't say whether the speed was in miles or kilometers. If he meant kilometers this translated to approximately 120 mph. What should have been shocking about the report was how the plane got to Prince Patrick so fast from the North Pole. According to Moscow, the ANT had averaged 85 mph on the Russian side, then this was eventually to be increased to 125 mph after a good share of the fuel had been spent. The navigator had reported the expedition over Prince Patrick Island just three hours after it passed over the pole, an astounding time since Prince Patrick is at least 800 miles from the top of the icecap, requiring an average speed of 252 mph.

If Vartanian had a map in front of him showing latitudes he would have instantly discovered that the navigator's report did not make sense. Beliakov, who wasn't at Patrick anyway, would be hard pressed to explain this sighting since Prince Patrick was the first land mass the fliers would have encountered on the 120-degree meridian, on the American side. Prince Patrick is an island jutting 1,000 feet above sea level at its highest point, and measures 20 by 150 miles. This should make the island distinguishable from any waters, even if frozen. At least part of Prince Patrick lying in the Parry Group should have shed some of its snow and ice by June, and the contrast between sea level and land and/or terrain and water would be evident. There are large islands of ice between Prince Patrick and the pole called paleocrystic (ancient ice) islands. Beliakov could not have mistaken these islands for Prince Patrick because they only measure two to three miles in diameter as compared to the 150-mile-long Prince Patrick. Vartanian was specially placed in the role of coordinating all communications between Soviet and American radio stations concerning the "transpolar flight." Apparently the Russians thought he could handle this job; however, the mistake in the Prince Patrick report was so flagrant there wasn't much he could do. This gross misrepresentation of the plane's position was immediately detected by U.S. station operators who were only able to read the latitude and longitude portion of the broadcast due to the language barrier. The information ended up in a secret U.S. government file and was never divulged to the press. Vartanian understandably was not about to give out this information. He hoped the U.S. authorities would overlook one more unexplainable report coming from Moscow. At this stage it was very difficult, if not impossible, to determine who knew what, and when. Is it possible Stalin did not take his own embassy officials into his confidence, or was it wiser and safer for them not to know what was going on? Would they seem more natural in their roles if they were ignorant of what was transpiring?

It is hard to believe any well-orchestrated plan would be so riddled with errors. The Moscow operator should have simply reported the phantom plane at Franz Josef after 20 hours and at the pole after 27 hours. This was the schedule NSR had set for the flight, time frames based on an average speed of 90 mph. What had caused the mix up? There is possibly one good explanation, related to the different time zones involved. Officially, Greenwich time was being used in logging the illusionary air expedition. According to the Soviet sources the plane had taken off from Shelkova, a military airfield outside Moscow, at 1:05 a.m. Greenwich time. This was 4:05 a.m. in Moscow, a three-hour difference. Since the Soviet embassy in the U.S. was involved, the radio operator might have been thinking in terms of eastern standard time, all of which became confusing and led to the mistakes in plotting the progress of the phantom airship. Luckily, as newsmen hurried to prepare their stories for the morning editions, no one questioned or challenged Gokhman's statements.

The *New York Times* headline read, "THREE RUSSIANS OVER ARCTIC ON MOSCOW-OAKLAND FLIGHT." In smaller print the article described the fliers as battling bad weather 350 miles short of the pole after 18 hours, contrary to the 250 miles reported by Gokhman. From either point, the fliers said they made it to the pole in 90 minutes. If one accepts Gokhman's plane position report, then the average speed was 180 mph, and this would increase to 220 mph if the *Times* article were to be believed. Fortunately for the Russians the media did not dwell on these contradictions and discrepancies. It seems everyone was on a "different wave length."

People on the Pacific Coast were most excited about the "transpolar" flight. If all went well a Russian plane would be passing over their respective cities. One small metropolis especially interested was Vancouver, host of Semion Shestakov's *Land of the Soviets* in 1929. The destination of the "transpolar flight" was the San Francisco-Oakland area; Vancouver citizens could only hope for and dream of a Russian repeat performance.

In an official statement, Alexander Troyanovsky, Soviet ambassador to the United States, who had just arrived in San Francisco by air, said he had received information from Moscow via Washington, D.C.

that three Soviet fliers were en route from Moscow to San Francisco on a nonstop flight over the North Pole. The ambassador described the plane as a single-engine, low-wing monoplane, and identified the fliers as Pilot Valery Chkalov, Copilot George Baidukov and Navigator Alexander Beliakov. He said they were attempting the longest nonstop flight in the history of aviation. On this same day, June 18, the Canadian Signal Corps station at Edmonton, Alberta heard the same message supposedly from a Siberian station, but curiously the takeoff time was given as 2:05 a.m. instead of 1:05 a.m. Greenwich time. This same discrepancy also appeared in newspapers. According to the reports coming from Moscow the fliers were running into bad weather. What had happened to their elaborate weather reporting stations throughout the arctic? To make matters worse the American stations had issued bulletins warning Moscow that the entire Pacific Coast was enveloped in cloud cover with low overcast.

Chkalov and the others in the archipelago needed cloudy skies to hide their eventual takeoff. Everything seemed to be falling into place. It is interesting, but not coincidental, that the date selected for the "Shelkova takeoff" was an overcast day.

And now, Chkalov waited on a lonely island in southeast Alaska ready to make his great debut in America. The pressure of being chief pilot and spokesman for the crew must have weighed heavily on his short but sturdy frame. According to the schedule laid out for the mythical plane, 50 hours would have to elapse before the real plane could take off from its Alaskan base, calculated on the distance from Moscow to the archipelago. This would place the mythical ANT-25 at a latitude where Chkalov must become airborne for a timely start of the real and last leg to the United States. This "rendezvous" was to occur at about 9 p.m. pacific standard time Saturday, June 19 as dusk approached.

When Americans awoke on Saturday they were greeted with new stories about the "transpolar flight." There was a picture of the three Russian fliers in many of the major newspapers, along with a drawing of a globe marking the route of the "transpolar flight" to America. One news article declared: "PEOPLE IN RUSSIA IGNORANT OF FLIGHT," and went on to tell how the takeoff from Shelkova was kept secret, long after the aviators were well on their way toward California. Included in the report was a review of the general precautions taken in the name of secrecy. The Soviet embassy admitted bringing vigorous diplomatic pressure on the United States government to suppress all news about the start of the three Russian aviators on a nonstop flight from Moscow to San Francisco. "The embassy sought to have each government department whose cooperation it had requested refrain from making any announcement," one news story related. These departments included State, War, Commerce, Agriculture and others. As a result of this censorship all inquiries to these bureaus were referred to the Russian embassy in Washington, D.C. But Constantine Oumansky, upon being approached, emphatically denied any knowledge of the flight, leaving the reporters at a dead end. The imposed secrecy affected the Russian people as well, and had to be more strict around Shelkova airport to hide the fact that there was no takeoff. The Soviet government did not want a horde of Moscow citizens making a run on the Shelkova airfield only to find it vacant. By waiting 24 hours before issuing any announcement, who would really know whether a plane had left for America? NSR figured the people could read about it in the government-controlled newspapers the next day.

In the United States a navigational expert commented on the problems the Russian fliers were due to face in the polar region. Clarence Williams, a U.S. Navy lieutenant, elevated a few pulses when he cautioned, "the navigator will have to work like a fiend, figuring his directional problems," adding that the arctic played tricks with the instruments. Another American official, Allan Bonnalie of the National Aeronautical Association, was asked to be ready Sunday morning to check the plane's instruments, including the barograph and gas seals. Mr. Bonnalie described it as a Russian-built craft, type ANT-25, powered by a single twelve-cylinder water-cooled motor. It carried 2,000 gallons of fuel, a capacity equal to the largest four-motored Clipper planes then being used in the United States. This fuel supply, according to Bonnalie's report, was enough to sustain the ANT in the air for 100 hours.

The June 19 radio communications between Nome and Anadyr estimated that the red and blue monoplane should complete its journey to San Francisco the next day (Sunday). Ambassador Troyanovsky was now in the Bay City awaiting the arrival of the ANT and the three aviators. The Soviets distributed sketchy biographies of the fliers to the international news services, providing Americans with some background on their lives and careers. Both Chkalov and Baidukov had been awarded the Order of Lenin for "quick thinking" and "heroism" as test pilots, and all three of the airmen held the "Hero of the Soviet Union" medal in recognition of their 1936 nonstop flight across Siberia, the news report said. The Russian event completely dominated the news throughout the country. Otherwise, more people would have noticed that Amelia Earhart had just left Burma to continue her dramatic around-the-world attempt.

(Only NSR personnel, Stalin, the Kremlin, and the Indian helpers knew the exact location of the secret camp. Circumstantial evidence eventually placed the camp somewhere on an island south of Sitka. Sigmund Levanevsky's spy mission in 1936 suggests the site was north of Prince of Wales and south of Baranof Island. The range of the Dewoitine after Tupolev removed most of the fuel tanks was reduced to 1,900 miles or 20 hours aloft. If the destination of the Russian plane was San Francisco or southern California, then this would correspond with the vicinity between Prince of Wales and Baranof as the starting point. One only had to look at the crude workmanship applied as the two ANTs were reassembled in the wilderness to realize the Russians did not have access to a regular aviation workshop. If the starting point had been some city in Siberia, the Soviets would have done a much more polished job on the ANTs; so this seems to suggest someplace outside of the USSR was used for the secret camp. An isolated southern island in the Alexander Archipelago would have been the logical alternative. Perhaps someday the site of the secret camp will be discovererd. Surely some materials such as rivets, small tools, or discarded camp items would be left behind after the Russian fliers and mechanics left the scene. Later the Soviets would supply a map showing how the route to America passed directly over the area scouted by Levanevsky.)

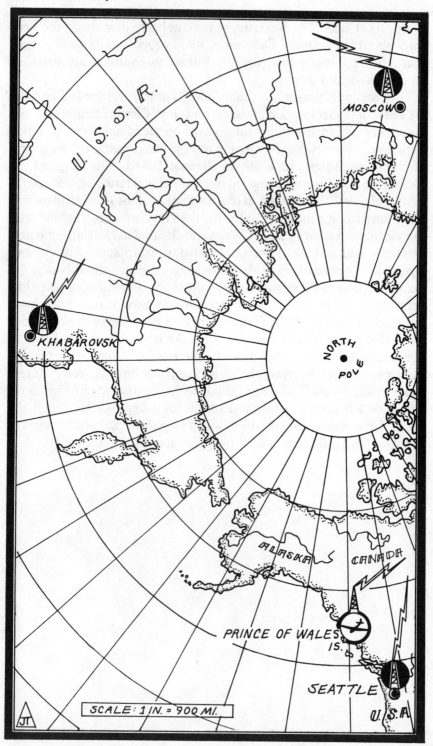

The communication network between Moscow, Khabarovsk, Seattle, and the
ANT-25s.

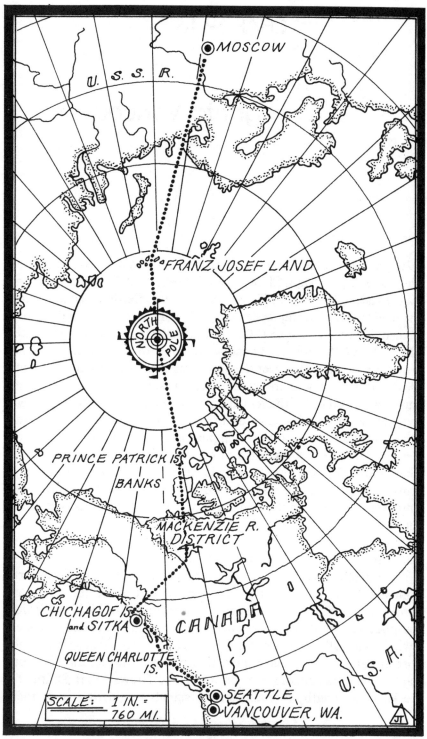

The route the Russian fliers supposedly followed to reach the United States.

CHAPTER 16

Flight to Vancouver

On this particular Saturday afternoon on a remote island in the Alexander Archipelago, Chkalov, Baidukov, and Beliakov were getting ready to take off on a "world" flight of their own. Berdnik had long since dismissed his Indian employees and with Karlovich, Korf, and Stoman readied the ANT-25 URSS N 025 for the final lap to America. The other ANT URSS 025-1 was ready and waiting for Mikhail Gromov and his two crew members whenever the signal was given for them to proceed to Alaska. But for now there were not too many hours until dusk; they must make good use of the remaining precious time. All the equipment and gear had already been loaded on the two ANTs; both must be ready in case one failed to lift off. The important part was finished; they had met the deadline, taking much of the pressure "off their shoulders." Their Indian helpers had been paid generously in both money and drink and apparently departed with good feelings for their Russian employers. The Russians could only hope the Indians would not speak out of turn and spoil their big secret. But now the airmen must make their final broadcasts as they tracked the illusionary ANT down the 120-degree meridian toward the United States.

Strangely enough, the only station receiving radio position reports from the "plane" was Fort Smith, located just above the northeast border of Alberta Province, Canada. The grounded ANT-25s were well equipped with radios whose frequency and transmission bands spanned a wide range, allowing any station to pick up their signals. Why only Fort Smith? A reasonable explanation was that the Russian aviators wanted their transmissions to be limited to faraway Fort Smith, by special wave length, to avoid strong signals originating from their hidden location. To guard against this a special secret frequency was set up through Vartanian in Seattle and Fort Smith, blocking all other stations from listening in and possibly tracing the strong signals to the secret camp. All radio reports were relayed to Vartanian by the Canadian Signal Corps station at Edmonton, about 700 miles south of Fort Smith, in central Alberta. Fort Smith, said its radio operators received four reports they thought came from the "transpolar plane." The first one came at 4 a.m. PST Saturday, June 19, 35 hours from the time Moscow said the aircraft left. This message said, "Everything okay, traveling 200 kilometers (120 mph), location Patrick Island, 800 miles south of the pole on the American side and about 1,100 north of Fort Smith. Included in the message were Beliakov's words, "I am trying. . . establish communication with America." About eight hours later at 12:25 p.m. (PST) the station received a second message: "Latitude 64, Longitude 124 (degrees). Everything okay, plane 100 miles south of Fort Norman," (Northwest Territories) and 38 minutes later at 1:03 p.m. (PST) a message said, "plane over Mackenzie River." And the last broadcast – supposedly heard only by the Canadians – placed the ANT slightly south of Fort Simpson at 2:24 p.m. (PST).

The first radio report apparently received by the U.S. Signal Corps stations came at 3:40 p.m. (PST) and said the "Russian plane had passed into Alberta." The flight logs published by wire services and a number of major newspapers said the "plane" passed over Great Slave Lake before entering Alberta air space. These logs gave the time as 8:40 p.m. (PST), a five-hour discrepancy between the U.S. Signal Corps report at 3:40 p.m. This position at Great Slave Lake would have taken the "plane" in an easterly direction, some 250 miles off of their 120-degree meridian course. It wasn't determined whether the grounded fliers or some other Soviet station made these errors in the position but what was to follow is more interesting. After making the mysterious 250-mile dog-leg to the east, a subsequent message supposedly from the "plane's" crew radioed they were turning westward toward the Pacific Ocean ostensibly to "avoid the Canadian Rockies" (mountains). Other newspaper "flight logs" did not include the Great Slave Lake-Alberta run and instead had the "plane" turning westward at 3 p.m. (PST) from the Mackenzie district, about 350 miles northwest of the Alberta position. Since radio agent Vartanian in Seattle was translating all messages for the U.S personnel and news media, it is evident he tried to smooth out this mess by arbitrarily dropping the Great Slave and Alberta position reports. There was a constant and wide disparity among the

American press reports on just about every detail, including locations of the "plane," times, directions, and the actual contents of the messages themselves; but the media did not publicly raise any questions, despite all of them getting their information from the same source. Vartanian was probably getting "flack" from the U.S. Weather Service because none of their weather data was being recognized. Of course, it was impossible to answer those weather reports because there was no plane out there yet and the crew in Alaska couldn't respond for fear of disclosing their hideout.

Without realizing it the Russian party in the archipelago had already made a terrible mistake; the mythical ANT had been placed too far south, threatening a timely "rendezvous" over the archipelago. How could such a thing happen? Was it the long ordeal catching up with them? The pressure of pulling off a great hoax on the world? Too many time zones to accurately compute? Excessive refreshments in the form of vodka and cognac clouding their minds?

Chkalov and his two flying associates had to review their situation. The plan was to take off at dusk and hope no one was around to witness the ascent. Vancouver with its small military airfield offered plenty of security without excessive exposure to the public. Chkalov and Baidukov intended to follow the coast south to the mouth of the Columbia River, using the waterway as a guide to Vancouver. Information already acquired from Shestakov alerted the fliers about this small southwest Washington city located about 80 miles inland from the ocean, and its east-west airport runway was not far from the Columbia River's banks. According to Shestakov there were two bridges across the Columbia, providing excellent landmarks when and if they got that close.

Even Vancouver was somewhat frightening, considering that an international hoax might be terminated there. Could they look their American hosts in the eye without giving away their Alaskan secret? One thing for sure, it was too late to back out now as the phantom ANT was closing in on them. The Americans were expecting the "plane" to follow the 120th meridian through Edmonton, Alberta and Spokane, Washington and were unaware NSR had abrubtly changed the mythical course in conformance to the master plan, designed to hide the air speed of the real ANT-25 when it departed for America. The new route would pretend to take them from the Northwest Territories in Canada down through the Alexander Archipelago and then to the United States. Tupolev's craft was not capable of matching the speed of the mythical plane reportedly flying now at 120 mph. The one thing NSR didn't have to worry about was crashing the plane as it "traversed the northern worlds," but the real test was ahead. Would the crudely converted Dewoitine in the Alaskan camp hold up long enough to reach the American mainland? There had been no way to make a test run after the two planes had been reassembled, other than to taxi them about. It was going to be a little scary during those few moments when the pilots tried to get one of the ANTs into the air. One thing remaining in their favor was the cloud cover still blanketing the Alaskan skies. They had received weather information every three hours and the extended outlook was for the overcast to persist all the way to San Francisco. The low ceiling was ideal for hiding an airplane; this, along with the dim light of dusk, would add to their chances of escaping the island undetected. Berdnik and his two helpers would be glad to leave the camp and get back to Russia, but until Gromov showed up to fly the second ANT out they must remain to assist him. They still had to get this inferior airplane to America and convince experts in aviation it had really made the trip, supposedly to be authenticated by the barographs. Crew members had installed three of these devices on the N 025, the ANT finally selected to make the trip. The barographs were placed underneath the wings.

NSR and the Kremlin were counting on not receiving negative feedback from the U.S. government in view of the political and warlike situation in Europe, knowing it was in American interests for the "flight" to succeed. This is why the fliers would seek out a military airfield when it came time to bring the ANT down on American soil. The tension and apprehension brought about by the many unknown factors ahead may have prompted a few extra drinks of cognac in order to bolster sagging spirits. However, the fliers must be very careful regarding alcohol consumption. Life and limb were dependent upon maintaining a sober condition, to say nothing about the great expectations of the dictator himself. The airmen had to remember their families back in Russia who might suffer if the Alaskan plan went wrong. If something did happen to expose the hoaxes, the crew of the ANT could always ask the U.S. for political asylum. But, of course, this would not help their families.

They must proceed with the utmost care and guard against every possibility of failure. The main problem was not to overindulge before or during the flight. There were ways to control this: taking castor oil before drinking, and lemon and tea afterwards. Russians commonly used lemon for this purpose. But the best prevention of side effects and disorientation came from breathing in oxygen, plenty of which was on board. Actually, the Soviet fliers carried oxygen for two reasons – to start the motor and to inflate the airbags in the wing stubs and fuselage in case of an emergency landing at sea. The regular purpose of oxygen, of course, is to sustain breathing at high altitudes, but it wouldn't be needed on this flight from Alaska to America.

There was a definite danger of pushing the American government too far with outlandish claims, particularly concerning the fuel capacity of the ANT-25s. Even Chkalov and Baidukov must have wondered how they could get away with saying each wing section contained 1,000 gallons of fuel with a total weight of 12,000 pounds aboard. In addition, there was also the weight of the six "huge" gas tanks to be considered. The designer had claimed the tanks reinforced the wings but with no reinforcing spars there was no way to keep the wings from breaking off. The lightweight soft aluminum ribs could never hold up under such tonnage. This would be the same volumewise as placing 20 fifty-gallon barrels of gas out on each wing section and expecting them to hold up without proper supports. It must have seemed like it was going to be a great chore selling the American aviation people on the merits of the ANT in light of these various problems. Of course, NSR and the Kremlin should have thought of them long ago. And now the burden fell on these three country fliers to hold up under the scrutiny they feared from the Americans. No one could blame them if they reinforced themselves with a few extra drinks for the road. As long as the oxygen held up everything would be okay.

The grounded fliers knew full well they had placed the mythical ANT too far south, resulting in the loss of five to six hours of time. Now there was no way to get this mythical plane to the archipelago on time for Chkalov's dusk takeoff in the real ANT.

There is one probable explanation why the wilderness trio let the mythical ANT get too far south. They could have mistaken Great Slave Lake for Great Bear Lake, the latter being 300 miles to the north in the Mackenzie district. Instead of altering the route just past Great Bear Lake, it appears Beliakov had implemented the change of direction south of Great Slave Lake. Regardless of what or who caused this colossal mistake, Vartanian and the Russian fliers had no intention of telling U.S. radio operators they had decided to turn the plane toward the coast from the Mackenzie district. The Americans would not learn of this sudden route change for seven more hours.

Regardless of the errors and previous problems the trio must now rise to the occasion if there was going to be a chance of pulling off this bizarre magic act. The ANT was posed among the trees as the three plucky fliers made their way to the "gawky bird." In this wilderness setting it looked like a giant pterodactyl about ready to take to the air. In aviation terms the ANT-25 was somewhat prehistoric. Now the question was, would Tupolev's "masterpiece of aviation" be able to make it to America? After the wide-wing airplane had been reassembled the only thing they could test was the engine. It had been started many times to keep the batteries charged in order to operate the radio transmitter. Other than testing the engine the aviators did not know for sure how the ANT-25s would fly after being boxed in those crates for almost one year. It was now 8:40 p.m. PST, Saturday, June 19. They were about to leave their home away from home.

Realizing there were only a few minutes before takeoff time and no turning back, the excitement bordered on panic. Carrying their personal effects and several maps Chkalov, Baidukov, and Beliakov moved to the left side of URSS N 025 and entered the cockpit from the port wing. The pilot and copilot occupied the cabin situated beneath a shallow bubble canopy and the navigator was positioned to the rear; his seat was an oxygen tank. There was not much room in the cabin and the fliers had to stoop or crawl whenever they moved about. The supplies, equipment, and food had long since been packed. Some bottles of cognac and possibly vodka were among the items brought on board. A breath freshener in the form of eau de Cologne was a necessary item to pack and would come in handy in disguising their drinking en route. Berdnik and a mechanic identified as "Stoman" had moved to the front of the ANT. One of the oxygen tanks had been attached to the engine.

After a year of waiting; this was it. The moment of truth was here! The skies were heavily clouded over and darkness was rapidly approaching. It was up to George Baidukov to begin the flight. He was the expert on "flying blind." He often remarked, "that's my speciality." Baidukov motioned to Berdnik to "crank it over," the signal was acknowledged and the motor roared! Its noise drowned out the sounds of the ocean. At last there was a "takeoff ceremony." The fliers waved goodbye to the mechanics. All of them must have wondered whether they would ever see each other again. It all depended on how the ANT URSS N 025 held together. The copilot pushed the throttle forward and the huge plane lurched ahead, steadily picking up more speed. Leaving the grassy turf behind, there was not much beach property in front of them as they aimed the craft directly at the water; hopefully the big double wheels would not sink too far into the sand. Moving faster and faster, the wide-wing monoplane managed a slow liftoff; it did not need a great deal of room to take off, but any miscalculation would quickly end the project, at least with one of the ANTs. There would be some nervous moments until the ANT gained a respectable altitude. Once this was accomplished who was to know the plane had not traversed the top of the world? The seconds rushed by as Baidukov pulled hard on the controls lifting the huge ship steadily higher above the sandy beach. The motor coughed grudgingly as more altitude was attained. The fliers could only hope no outsiders had seen the takeoff.

The hour was about 9 p.m. and Beliakov was scheduled to radio the first plane position from the air. In order to hide their location the fliers agreed to falsify their plane's position to about 200 miles south of their actual location to reduce the risk of being spotted by the Americans. As Chkalov was falling asleep navigator Beliakov sent a message in code to Vartanian in Seattle. The radio agent translated the message for the U.S. Signal Corps Seattle station, "Everything going well over Queen Charlotte Island, 500 miles north of Seattle," adding they would follow the "inside shipping lane to Seattle." Baidukov finally leveled off above the ocean and in actuality set a course due south toward Queen Charlotte Island and then on to Vancouver! But there was something terribly wrong with this last position report, and the problem was so great there was nothing Vartanian could do to correct it. Only 28 minutes ago, stations had received word the ANT had turned west from Alberta. A staggering distance of 700 miles was just covered in only 28 minutes, requiring the ANT to travel the astounding speed of 1,500 mph. The age of rockets had just been ushered in prematurely; it seemed even a phantom ship could not stand much more of this incredible reporting. At this time none of the American stations knew the mythical ANT had been "backed up" to the Mackenzie district for "another run at the archipelago." The Great Slave Lake error had played havoc with the illusionary flight schedule. But there it was in the lap of Vartanian, a most capable radio agent, but not a magician. He probably sent out the message before taking a good look at the time factor. All of the newspapers were preparing to print the flight log in their following morning editions and Vartanian could only hope the Great Slave Lake-Alberta position report went unnoticed.

Meanwhile George Baidukov, Valery Chkalov, and Alex Beliakov were sailing along over the Pacific Ocean. They planned to skirt Queen

Charlotte Island and stay a good distance from the coastline on their trek toward the United States. But somewhere in the vicinity of Charlotte it appears the plane began to experience problems. The Canadian National Railway Telegraph wired the U.S. Signal Corps stations, indicating the Russian plane was "down" near the north tip of Queen Charlotte. The usual procedure was to send everything to Vartanian in code; he would translate for the U.S. officials and they would give it to the news media. Vartanian may have been the one who denied the plane was down, claiming an error in the interpretation of the word "down" had occurred. No one will probably ever know what actually happened, but there could have been some engine malfunction. Sometimes the atmosphere over bodies of water is saturated with moisture, causing motors to miss. Perhaps the ANT's engine faltered, prompting the fliers to send out a distress call, and after the message was sent the motor might have smoothed out when an adjustment was made to enrich the gas mixture.

At this point the aviators needed to get word to Vartanian or the Russian consulate in San Francisco, and at 12:02 a.m. Sunday Beliakov prepared the following message: "Your radio without number received, the height is 4,000 meters (about 13,000 feet). Will make landing in the morning. If will [SIC] not have enough fuel to reach San Francisco will land at one of the airdromes between Seattle and San Francisco." This radio message bypassed the normal channels in Seattle and went directly to the U.S. Signal Corps Station in San Francisco. Apparently the fliers found it urgent to contact their consulate to have their visas delivered to them in Vancouver. No location of the plane was included in the report but an hour earlier they reported themselves 50 miles west of the north tip of Vancouver Island, about 350 miles from Seattle. It was imperative for Ambassador Troyanovsky to be ready to travel quickly to whatever airfield was finally chosen to deliver the fliers' visas. They needed to have their travel documents as soon as possible to guard against any embarrassment that might arise.

In San Francisco another embarrassing situation was developing. Ambassador Troyanovsky had just received the plane's latest broadcast from Vartanian in Seattle. The message from Navigator Beliakov reported, "I am receiving you well San Francisco and Anchorage. How are weather conditions? My position is Queen Charlotte Island. We already have expended 10,463 liters of gas." The navigator might have been under the influence when he gave this figure. A San Francisco reporter converted the amount from liters to gallons and found the

ANT had used 600 more gallons than the amount "loaded at Shelkova." The plane appeared to be manufacturing fuel while in flight. Supposedly 2,000 gallons were loaded at takeoff. But Beliakov claimed 2,619 gallons had already been consumed and the plane was still about 1,200 miles from San Francisco. Vartanian probably let this report out before he had made the conversion to gallons. Not only were the fliers testing the juggling ability of Vartanian but his patience too.

Although the fuel was in very short supply, it is apparent the ANT was performing satisfactorily as it plugged on southward through the overcast night. With the exception of those moments when moonlight filtered through the clouds Baidukov was essentially flying blind. They had been in the air about four hours with midnight well behind them and sunrise less than five hours away. Sunday, June 20, is here; the day this strange expedition was to arrive in the United States. Most Americans were no doubt sleeping as the ANT flew along at 80 per. None of the fliers was in any hurry to meet the American reception. Considering what they were trying to pull off, it is natural they would have deep anxieties as they came closer to their destination and no doubt hoped the couriers, Evsei Charapov and Fedor Ivanov, would deliver their visas on time to the consulate in San Francisco. Visas for the couriers were issued June 15, while visas for the three fliers were not ready until the following day. However, this should allow sufficient time for the couriers to get to San Francisco before the fliers arrived. It might be hard to explain why the airmen weren't carrying their travel documents when these normally would have been issued at the American embassy in Moscow before departure. At any rate, someone would have to quickly get the documents to Vancouver.

It was now 4 a.m. (PST), and the airmen were well out to sea. After a quick conference through the talking tube between Baidukov and Beliakov it was decided a message must go to Vartanian telling him of their plans to land in Vancouver and having him relay this change of destination to Troyanovsky in San Francisco. Protocol demanded the presence of Russian representatives and U.S. officials to carry out a reception and witness the end of this "historic flight." And there was still the little matter of the missing passports to resolve. Visas and protocol weren't priority items right now because somehow the airmen had drifted off course. Visibility and the desire to stay away from the North American coastline probably were contributing factors. Baidukov, with the "help" of Navigator Beliakov, may have steered the ANT too far out to sea and had problems getting back to the coastline in the darkness.

As Chkalov slept, Baidukov worked steadily to locate the Pacific coast at the expense of valuable time and fuel. They were already well behind schedule because of the Alberta mix-up and wanted to make up some of the missing hours. But now they were losing time in the real flight. The ANT had been in the air seven hours since flying over Charlotte, and Baidukov was eager to get his bearings on the American mainland. He directed Beliakov to radio Bellingham, Washington for a beacon, and the copilot turned the big craft east following the signal. At last they spotted Seattle's lights well ahead. All they had wanted was a bearing so they could return to the coastline route before sunrise, now less than one hour away. Yet all possible precautions had to be taken to avoid being seen; there would be no way to pad their mileage if someone spotted the ANT. At this point the airmen knew the Columbia River mouth was about 150 miles south. Two hours passed as the Russian plane droned on toward the big river.

The overcast and dense fog were making it difficult to define the coastline. Copilot Baidukov was beginning to worry about the amount of fuel left and realized they must find the Columbia River fast. He awakened the "chief pilot" for assistance. There was no way to see the river from this altitude; they must descend and take a chance on being spotted. Down came the ANT into a thinner layer of clouds. The three fliers scanned the landscape in search of the waterway. Finally, the clouds and fog opened and they saw the Columbia's mouth appear below. A great sigh of relief came over them; now it was just a matter of following the river to Vancouver, 80 miles to the east. Baidukov guided the big birdlike craft straight into the gaping mouth of the mighty Columbia. He must be able to see the river and still hide the Russian plane as much as possible. Unbeknown to the crew the ANT was spotted for the first time in flight by sailors on a U.S. Coast Guard cutter. Although this information appeared in the newspapers, no one bothered to calculate the time and distance, typical of the lackadaisical coverage of the many discrepancies and strange happenings throughout this so-called transpolar flight. The sighting of the plane near Astoria, a port city located on the northwestern tip of Oregon, would reveal its speed to be less than 60 mph since leaving Charlotte. To compensate, the fliers might eventually have to admit they had become lost. This was not desirable because it cast doubts on the navigational ability of the fliers and on the modern equipment supposedly directing the ANT on this "most historic occasion."

As Baidukov wound his way along the river, he knew they were not far from Vancouver. Chkalov had slept during most of the flight and Beliakov, with the exception of a few broadcasts and navigational duties, was able to nod off frequently. It had been a lonely flight for Baidukov. Though the two were connected by a makeshift speaking device, the heavy drone of the M-34 engine made talking with the navigator very difficult. Chkalov decided to take the controls for a few minutes to give Baidukov a chance to don his arctic gear. Perhaps there was time for one more little bracer before facing the Americans. This, of course, must be chased with eau de Cologne to disguise the cognac. Despite flying the entire distance from the archipelago, Baidukov was still in the best shape of the three. The copilot had been careful not to drink to any serious degree because it had fallen on his shoulders to get the ANT through the overcast and darkness with his "instrument flying capability." Baidukov broke out some apples and oranges. There were several months supply of food on board; but they never had any need for nourishment on this short trip, packing it merely to convince Americans a "transpolar" flight had taken place. No one had much of an appetite after drinking during the previous hours. Chkalov refused any of the fruit but Baidukov and Beliakov helped themselves.

The chief pilot must now gather his wits for the greatest challenge of the entire master plan. It appears he asked Baidukov to take over the controls again to give him time to better prepare his composure for the dreaded meeting with the Americans. He must have asked himself hundreds of times how he ever let himself get into this mess, and the same question probably occurred to the others. However, most of the pressure was on Chkalov as he was the appointed spokesman for the expedition. It was up to him to convince the Americans that the flight was authentic. Apprehensions and fears were surely crossing their minds as they flew closer to the landing site at Vancouver, a city with a population of about 15,000. If this great shortcut were discovered the fury of Stalin and the world would come tumbling down upon them.

Vancouver was only 25 minutes away: a good thing since the gas supply was down next to nothing. They would be fortunate to make it to the landing field; but they knew they could find it quickly because it runs along the river's edge. Chkalov wanted Beliakov to tell the listening stations that they were bringing the plane down at Swan Island, Portland's main airline terminal. The Americans and the entire world had been told the ANT-25 could fly 100 hours or 8,000 miles without refueling. Now what would they tell the Americans, even if they could convince them that a transpolar flight had been made, after only a "63-hour" trip? They would have to make up a reason for landing at Vancouver, 700 miles short of their announced destination in San Francisco. Baidukov and Beliakov were in favor of admitting that the ANT was out of gas, but Chkalov advised his navigator to report that a fuel pump problem was forcing them to make a premature landing. By giving the false radio report of a Portland landing, Chkalov hoped to divert the Americans away from the Vancouver airfield and give the military a chance to secure the plane before people had an opportunity to gather in great numbers.

After deciding on this diversionary strategy all three airmen focused their attention on the river below in search of the first signs of the city. They had learned from Semion Shestakov that there were two bridges spanning the Columbia. The second bridge was not far from Pearson Field; once the steel structure was spotted it should only be a lapse of a few minutes until the airport was in view. They must get down quickly because of the gas situation. It wasn't long before the first bridge was spotted through the overcast, and seconds later the second bridge caught their eyes. The tension was growing with the awareness of the magnitude of their deception dominating each passing second. Apparently Chkalov wanted Baidukov to take the plane down because he made no move to take the controls. They spotted Pearson Field off to the left. The closely cropped grassy landing strip was fairly short but there was no concern as the slow-flying ANT could land at 30 mph. As a result, ANT designer Tupolev had never felt the need to install brakes on either of the two planes.

From across the airfield several human figures could be seen pointing upward at the plane. It appeared Chkalov's ruse had worked and this gave them a feeling of excitement. Everyone must have gone to Swan Island. This was perfect; they had arrived at the military field, literally vacant. (Baidukov, a year later, described how he had made the landing. "I fly low and take a good look at the landing field...I dip toward the earth, and the red wings skip close to the fields. We clear the treetops by a few feet. A swamp flashes by. I cut off the motor and the plane, lighter by several tons of fuel, hovers a long time over the ground, then starts its glide. I can see that I'll have to pull the nose up a trifle or we'll land in some sort of plowed field. The engine idles down again and the plane drops gently to the earth. I pull back on the controls and our wheels touch the ground...I switch off the ignition and the plane bounces once more.") It was evident now the four figures running onto the field were soldiers. Baidukov wheeled the ANT around and taxied slowly northward toward the airfield offices. Chkalov and Beliakov watched the soldiers with curiosity as they approached closer and closer to their aircraft. The copilot finally cut the engine and "unbeknownst" to him had stopped the Russian plane on almost the same spot where Semion Shestakov had parked his aircraft some eight years earlier. He had also come to rest on the old famous Hudson Bay territory, where Dr. John McLoughlin had supervised the building of the Hudson Bay Company. The three anxious fliers were not aware of or concerned with history, but rather with what lay ahead.

It was comforting to know that Shestakov and his crew were treated royally at this very place; but the circumstances were quite different, since Shestakov had not misrepresented his flight. Now Chkalov and his two flying companions must be careful not to make a slip of the tongue that would disclose the hoaxes and in turn throw the Russian-American political relationships into a turmoil. The "journey" was over; in the next few minutes they must climb down from the ANT and face the unknown consequences. But this was not a moment of triumph; more in fact, the fliers felt reluctant to deal with the many unknown factors which the American reception might present. None of the Soviet fliers had any idea if the hoax was already publicly exposed. Would the crowd tar and feather them or welcome them as heroes? What had the press said about their flight? Did the various western signal stations report all the mix-ups and unexplained happenings? Did the government and the military know, and if so, would they tell? All these questions and more were running through the fliers' worried minds. Surely Vartanian would have informed them if serious problems had developed.

CHAPTER 17

American Reception

The American public and Vancouver, Washington were caught completely by surprise when the wide-wing monoplane, bearing Russian markings, URSS N 025, settled down on this small airfield rather than at the larger and more important airdrome in Portland. The latter, generally referred to as Swan Island, had hosted the famous Charles Lindbergh arrival just ten years earlier.

From the American perspective there was the anticipation and excitement of a once-in-a-lifetime experience. This was especially true for people living along the coast in cities with airports. All indications had San Francisco as the chosen terminus for the historic flight. It wasn't until 8 a.m. Sunday morning when anyone had an inkling where the celebrated Russian airship was really going to land. Local radio stations in the Vancouver-Portland area received the electrifying word the plane was going to set down at Swan Island very soon. Thousands of early risers rushed to the island airport north of Portland's city center. Many people, including newsmen and photographers, had kept an all-night vigil in the hopes of seeing the Soviet "transpolar" plane fly over en route to San Francisco.

The scene was later described by a local newspaper: "Hundreds were gathered at Swan Island expecting to cheer them on their way, but never even saw them through a thick haze that arched the field.... Conflicting rumors and scanty reports from the craft caused diminishing interest as the hours dragged by, and many spectators left disappointedly for home." One news blip said, "...only occasionally did a credible shred of a message from the plane to the U.S. Signal Corps pierce the murk in which the plane was flying blindly." Another press report said, "with accurate information unavailable from the fliers as to the speed they were making and their location, it was impossible last night to estimate the time and their position over Portland." The press had to be suspicious at this time but failed to inquire properly. The Russian plane was the "star" of this magnificent show but no one witnessed the takeoff, no one saw it in route, no one heard accurate position reports and yet no one's curiosity was aroused.

If the American people and radio station operators were confused about the Russian flight they certainly could have found sympathy among the Canadian operators. The Canadian government statement summed it all up: "as far as we know the Russian aircraft did not hear any of our stations"–these included Ft. Resolution, Aklavik, Ft. Norman, Cameron Bay, Ft. Smith, and Edmonton. Ironically, Vartanian had made a special plea for all information gathered by Canadian stations to be sent to Ft. Norman and then passed on to him in Seattle. Canada broadcast extensive weather reports and alerted her operators to be prepared to transmit radio beacons to help guide the plane along the 120th meridian. However, there were no indications from the Soviets or the aircraft that any of the transmissions were received or acted upon. The Soviets bombarded the Canadians and the Americans for more and more detailed weather reports, keeping the fatigued station operators on duty around the clock. From his station in Seattle, Vartanian was able to control all American and Canadian broadcasts, and therefore be in a position to make any corrections or other adjustments necessary to avoid detection. He also gained permission from the Canadian government to place one of his radio agents at one of their stations; however, apparently there was no need to implement this part of the plan. One Canadian document attempts to explain away the lack of communication with the Russian aircraft, noting the possibility of static interference with radio signals. But the Canadians were aware the "static" disappeared on June 19 when the real airplane was nearing the U.S. border. It is fair to say the Canadians were as much in the dark as the Americans who were gathering at various Pacific Coast airports to catch a glimpse of the elusive "polar fliers."

But now at last everyone at Swan Island was bubbling with enthusiasm as they waited for the grand entrance of the pilots and for what they innocently thought was the greatest flight in the history of aviation. People patiently watched the skies for the first sign of the now famous Russian plane. But it was all for naught. In a few minutes word began to fly through the crowd that the Russians had just landed at

Aviator Charles A. Lindbergh (with his famous *Spirit of St. Louis* in the background) is greeted by Portland's Mayor George L. Baker at Swan Island Airport, Portland, Oregon, September 14, 1927. Lindbergh was on tour following his New York to Paris flight. (Clark County Historical Museum)

Throngs of people inspect Semion Shestakov's *Land of the Soviets* after the aircraft landed at Vancouver's Pearson Field, following a multi-stop flight from Moscow to New York in the fall of 1929. The huge plane is believed to have been converted from a German Junkers K37. (Clark County Historical Museum)

Dr. Otto Schmidt, director of Russia's Northern Sea Route Administration, gathers information about the arctic region, ostensibly to establish a permanent camp at the North Pole in 1937. The author believes there never was a sincere effort by the Soviets to accomplish this project. (AP/Wide World)

Arctic expert George Ushatov (center), flanked by Soviet pilots Sigmund Levanevsky (left) and Mikhail Slepnev, study maps prior to leaving Nome, Alaska to participate in an aerial rescue of 104 passengers aboard the *Cheliuskin*, a Russian freighter that was crushed by ice and sank in the frigid Chukchi Sea. All but one passenger escaped from the foundering ship and remained on an ice floe for more than a month. (AP/Wide World)

This photograph was used by the *New York Times* to identify Russian pilot Nicolai Juroff, a picture that later raises questions since it was used again by the same newspaper to identify Sergei Danilin, navigator on an alleged trans-polar flight from Russia to San Jacinto, California in July of 1937. (AP/Wide World)

Dr. Otto Schmidt, center, director of the Northern Sea Route Administration, is flanked by Ivan Papanin (left) and Mikhail Vodopyanov, prior to an alleged trip to the North Pole. This photo was probably taken in Moscow in 1936. (AP/Wide World)

The Soviets distributed this photograph to depict Dr. Otto Schmidt at the North Pole with an ANT-6 aircraft. The scene is probably Rudolph Island, 550 miles from the North Pole, where the Russians did have an arctic camp. (AP/Wide World)

The Soviets claim this scene shows the main tent of their drifting polar expedition to the North Pole in 1937. The scene is more likely a base camp at Rudolph Island. (AP/Wide World)

Ivan Papanin (left), receives a traditional Russian embrace from A. Ostaltsev, skipper of a ship that rescued Papanin and three others from a polar ice floe that the Soviets claimed drifted from the North Pole to near the Greenland coast in 1938. Another ship crewman in the background is not identified. (AP/Wide World)

One of the original French Dewoitine Trait d'Union D33s, before Russian aircraft designer A.N. Tupolev converted them to the ANT-25s. (Smithsonian Institution)

From left to right, A.N. Tupolev, who renovated the French Dewoitine aircraft to Russian ANT-25s; Alexander Beliakov, navigator; Valery Chkalov, pilot; and George Baidukov, copilot, the crew of an ANT-25 that the Russians claim flew over the North Pole from Moscow to Vancouver, Washington, June 18-20, 1937.

Meeting at a military airport near Moscow are (left to right) Soviet Dictator Joseph Stalin; Sergei Ordjonikidze, head of Heavy Industry; Alexander Beliakov, navigator; an unidentified airman; and Valery Chkalov, pilot. This Russian photograph was used to give the impression that it was taken just prior to Pilot Chkalov's departure on a nonstop "transpolar flight" to the United States June 18-20, 1937. Actually Ordjonikidze died under mysterious circumstances on February 18, 1937, four months before the "transpolar flight."

Army General George C. Marshall, commander of Vancouver Barracks, Vancouver, Washington, quickly orders soldiers at Pearson Field to throw a tarpaulin over the cabin of a Russian ANT-25 and places guards around the aircraft after it landed June 20, 1937, following an alleged nonstop flight from Moscow, via the North Pole. (Oregon Historical Society 42122)

Attired in arctic flight gear, three Russian fliers (left to right), Alexander Beliakov, navigator; Valery Chkalov, pilot; and George Baidukov, copilot, pose at Pearson Field in Vancouver, Washington shortly after their arrival on June 20, 1937. (Oregon Historical Society 26115)

Army General George C. Marshall, along with his wife Katherine (in background) and stepdaughter Molly Brown, host the Russian fliers. Standing next to General Marshall's stepdaughter is Soviet Ambassador Alexander Troyanovsky. (Marshall Historical Museum)

Crews load the ANT-25, an aircraft the Soviets claimed flew nonstop from near Moscow to Vancouver, Washington, at Vancouver's Terminal No. 2 for shipment back to Russia. None of the alleged 2,000 gallons of fuel were in this section of the plane. The wing tips were removed for easier shipment. (*Oregonian*)

Colonel Carleton Bond of the U.S. Army Air Corps reportedly received an FBI tip from a communist cell in Portland that a Russian aircraft destined for San Francisco, California would actually land at Vancouver's Pearson Field, where Bond, then a lieutenant, served.

Crowds gather around a Soviet ANT-25 aircraft that landed at a ranch near San Jacinto, California, July 14, 1937, allegedly after a nonstop flight from Russia, via the North Pole. Numerous discrepancies have been uncovered by the author concerning the "transpolar flights." (AP/Wide World)

The tail section of the Soviet ANT-25 aircraft parked at San Jacinto illustrates the poor workmanship of the big craft, a fact quickly discovered by U.S. Army Air Corps technicians and personnel from the War Department's Intelligence Division, assigned from nearby March Field. (National Archives)

Consul General Grigori Gokhman, assigned to the Soviet embassy in Washington, D.C. (in a suit) poses with (from left) Pilot Mikhail Gromov, Copilot Andrei Yumashev, and Navigator Sergei Danilin after the crew landed an ANT-25 near San Jacinto, California. (AP/Wide World)

A six-member crew poses near their Soviet ANT-4 airplane that the Russians claim disappeared August 14, 1937, over the North Pole while attempting a nonstop flight from Moscow to Fairbanks, Alaska. The Soviets identified the crew (left to right) as Radioman N.J. Galkovsky, Second Pilot N.G. Kastanaov, Flight Commander Sigmund Levanevsky, mechanics G. Povezhimov and N.N. Godovikov, and Navigator V.I. Levchenko. The author believes these men never left Russia and that Levanevsky and possibly others were executed shortly after this picture was taken. (AP/Wide World)

This photo from a 1977 book titled *Chkalov* shows Chief Pilot Valery Chkalov, his wife Ina and son Igor, at a Moscow parade honoring the Soviet flier for an undocumented long-distance aircraft flight across Russia in 1936. The same photo was used in Russian newspapers and a motion picture to depict a parade ceremony honoring Chkalov and other flight crewmen for a "transpolar flight" one year later.

This photo, taken after the "transpolar flight" to Vancouver, is of Copilot George Baidukov, who in 1938 published a book about the episode titled *Over the North Pole*. (AP/Wide World)

This photo from *Over the North Pole* shows Chief Pilot Valery Chkalov supposedly smoking his last cigarette just prior to departing on the "transpolar flight" from Russia to Vancouver, Washington on June 18, 1937. The same photo was published in Soviet newspapers in 1936, a year before the alleged flight. (Harcourt Brace Jovanovich, Inc.)

Another photo from *Over the North Pole* supposedly shows the historic takeoff of an ANT-25 aircraft (with no markings on the right side of the fuselage) on a nonstop flight from Russia to the United States on June 18, 1937. When the aircraft landed in Vancouver, Washington two days later it had lettering on both sides of the fuselage. (Harcourt Brace Jovanovich, Inc.)

This photo, taken shortly after the ANT-25 landed at Vancouver's Pearson Field in Vancouver, Washington, clearly shows lettering on the right side of the fuselage, which translates to "Route of Stalin." (Oregon Historical Society)

This photo was reproduced from one frame of a video tape of a film produced by the Soviets to show the takeoff of an ANT-25 aircraft from Shelkova airport, near Moscow, to the United States June 18, 1937. No markings are detectable on the aircraft. (Dick Powers of Photo Art Studio)

A Vancouver committee sponsored the erection of this Chkalov Monument at Pearson Air Park in 1975, in honor of the Soviet's "transpolar flight" to Vancouver.

Arriving in Vancouver, Washington for the dedication of the Chkalov Monument in June of 1975 are (left to right) Alexander Beliakov and George Baidukov, the then only surviving crew members of the "transpolar flight," and Igor Chkalov, son of Valery Chkalov who the Russians said died one year after the "transpolar flight" in a plane crash caused by sabotage. (Vancouver Historical Museum)

Placing flowers on the Chkalov Monument June 20, 1984 in a symbolic peace offering is Irina Beliakov, widow of the late Alexander Beliakov who was navigator on the so-called nonstop Moscow to Vancouver flight in 1937. Standing (from left) are Igor Chkalov, son of the pilot Valery Chkalov, Colonel General George Baidukov, copilot, and Vladimir Kirilov, a Russian delegate participating in the forty-seventh anniversary of the flight. (*Oregonian*)

Frank Eyle (center), now deceased, with two other unidentified Native Americans, at about the time Eyle, from Charter Oaks near Vancouver, reportedly helped the Russians in the Sitka, Alaska area unload aircraft parts in 1937, information that triggered the author's investigation that convinced him the Soviet nonstop transpolar flights were actually faked. The author is attempting to locate the two unidentified friends of Eyle who may have accompanied him to Alaska. (Rosemary Kalama)

Vancouver. Heads dropped as the news was made official by airport personnel. Now Portland knew how Vancouver felt when Lindbergh passed their city by. But many rallied from their disappointment, realizing Pearson Field was not far away. It was only a 15-minute drive to Vancouver. Undauntedly, they began rushing for their cars, with the newsmen leading the way. Once across the Interstate Bridge linking Oregon and Washington, Pearson was just a few blocks away.

The sighting of the Soviet airship over the mouth of the Columbia River by the American Coast Guard is the only report of official record. However, several people spotted the big foreign craft when it reached the skies over Vancouver on this misty morning which just happened to be Father's Day. One witness to the plane in flight was a 14-year-old paperboy named David King. Young David had risen early to deliver the Sunday edition of the *Oregonian,* a Portland newspaper. He had permission to sell his papers to the parishioners of St. James Catholic Church, so he was hurrying along to catch the churchgoers between masses. As he waited on 12th Street in front of the gothic cathedral the heavy roar of an airplane caught his attention. He had often watched the regular biplanes flying in and out of Pearson Field, but never had he seen such a huge monoplane as this one. He stood fascinated as the strange low-flying aircraft veered east about a half mile from his vantage point, so he assumed the big plane was going to make a landing at the local airfield. David, at this time, didn't know he was watching the "famous transpolar" airship, but he was aware there was something different about this particular plane. Little did the young paperboy realize that some day he would learn a very important fact about this Russian exploit, and that his story would become a principle piece of evidence in this bizarre adventure.

Before the thousands of people on hand at Swan Island heard the message the Russians had landed, the American reception in Vancouver had already started, although only a handful of people were there to greet the fliers. It is difficult to say who were the first persons to reach the Russian plane, but among the first eight were four or five soldiers and three photographers. Charles Alexander, corporal of the guard, was on duty at the gate this Sunday morning. He recognized the plane as the "polar flyer" and immediately ran over, with rifle in hand. A few other soldiers began converging on the plane. Chkalov knew it was now or never as he swung open the modified bubble canopy. He crawled slowly out and made his way down the wing, at first ignoring the soldiers and several photographers who had gathered. Realizing there was going to be a problem with translation, Corporal Alexander returned quickly to his guard post and telephoned his commander, Brig. General George C. Marshall, reporting that the Russians had landed at Pearson Field. As Chkalov's feet struck the ground the curious Americans noticed a slight buckling as the aviator struggled to regain his balance. Another strangely dressed aviator supposedly from "arctic worlds" descended from the foreign ship and began eyeing the Americans.

The two fliers were surprised when one of the American soldiers stepped up and greeted them in their own language. "Xallo" cried out the soldier! A broad grin spread over Chkalov's face as he recognized the word "hello" in Russian. The pilot immediately grabbed the soldier's hand and shook it vigorously. Baidukov also stepped forward and shook the young soldier's hand. Beliakov had remained inside the plane up to this point, appearing reluctant to leave. Every few minutes he would glance out to see what was happening. Finally, he rallied enough courage to join Chkalov and Baidukov. Just as the navigator touched the earth, an attractive dark-haired woman approached with hand outstretched. She also gave a greeting in Russian and then proceeded to carry on a conversation with the navigator. "I am very happy, but disappointed, and very tired," Beliakov was quoted as saying. The navigator asked the Russian-speaking lady to join the fliers; but she declined, later explaining to the press that they looked very tired.

A photographer from the *Oregon Journal* finally succeeded in lining up the arctic-dressed aviators alongside their plane for pictures. The photographer, Ralph Vincent of Portland, captured the only still photos of the airmen attired in their arctic flying gear. Photographer Vincent was to receive $5,000 from a major news organization for his efforts, and his pictures became famous the world over. Another cameraman and his wife saw the Russian plane prepare for a landing. They rushed through the gate and arrived in time to take motion pictures of the "historic event." Jesse Sill worked as an independent motion picture photographer. On this occasion he happened to be under contract with Pathe News. His wife assisted him as he recorded the only motion pictures taken at the terminus of the "great transpolar crossing." The Sills wasted no time in sending the film off to New York where it would undergo sound synchronization. Universal News would then send it back for its first showing at the Mayfair Theater in Portland as a special feature of the Oregonian-Universal newsreel.

Eugene Spencer, a civilian mechanic, was among the first to spot the big, lumbering Russian plane as it approached Pearson Field from the northeast. Verl Buroker, 17, was at the east end of the airfield where his father's flying service and shop were located. As the wide-wing craft swung westward roaring low over the hangars, young Buroker and other civil aviation personnel took off on a dead run, knowing the plane was about to land. Other people had also witnessed the event. A maid employed at the Vancouver Barracks looked up just in time to see the big ship coming in. Although the Soviets knew from the beginning that they were going to end this adventure in Vancouver, everyone else had to guess where the aircraft was going to land. Young Buroker later reported that word was "flying around" the airport that the fliers had been looking for an airfield by the river. The information had been translated either by the mysterious lady from Portland or by the young student/ soldier who happened to be at the field. This shows that the fliers knew where Pearson was located. After mechanic Spencer was absolutely sure the foreign plane was going to land, he hurried to alert the local newspaper office. On his return he talked with the aviators through the young soldier who was fluent in Russian. One question Spencer asked was, "How much horsepower does the engine have?" Chkalov answered, "750." This was 200 horsepower less than the amount Moscow was telling the American public. Perhaps the pilot was afraid Spencer was going to look at the inscription on the engine plate and thought he had better tell the truth. The mechanic then informed the Soviet flier that by American standards it would take 1,500 horses to turn the three-bladed propeller. Chkalov did not comment further.

But there they were, standing on this strange soil, nervously waiting for whatever was in store for them. The few moments which had passed must have seemed an eternity; but at least they had each other for moral support. They did look like triplets in their dress. Each one had on a brown turtleneck sweater, leather trousers, spotted seal-skin boots, (mukluks), grayish-brown caps, and light-leather jackets. A strong odor seemed to come from their many layers of clothing. Most people probably did not notice it because the fliers were standing downwind. However, the young soldier-interpreter must have caught the smell when he shook their hands. It is unlikely the soldier thought too much about the unusual odor considering these men had supposedly been in the air for almost three days, confined to the cramped quarters of the ANT.

As the reporters perceived them, Chkalov was the most reserved, "He seldom smiles and seems to see nothing but his ship and his mission. He suffers the attention of the press and photographers, and the adulation of the crowd. . . ." The chief pilot was short of stature, but had a stocky and muscular frame. In this situation he looked the part of a prize fighter who was defensively awaiting his adversary. George Baidukov was more boyish-looking which was understandable since he was the junior partner in this "historic" episode. Though the copilot showed a wide-eyed interest in the reception, he "seldom smiles and says nothing except to answer questions," one press report said. Alexander Beliakov "was all business when he returned to his familiar cockpit to unload equipment." Asked to pose for pictures he caustically replied, "I'm busy." A reporter thought he added something else the interpreter didn't see fit to translate. In Washington, D.C. reporters were busy interviewing Mikhail Beliakov, the older brother of the plane's navigator. The elder Beliakov had been working alongside U.S. Weather Bureau personnel but firmly denied his presence in America had anything to do with the flight – it was simply coincidence.

By this time other reporters and photographers had arrived at the field. One of the newsmen described them as ". . . peering at the rain-soaked country through eyes reddened by lack of sleep." (The buckling of legs and reddened eyes could surely be caused by lack of sleep, but drinking alcoholic beverages can bring on the same symptoms.) The reporters pressed closer, eager for some personal comments from the fliers, bombarding spokesman Chkalov with questions. The services of their newly found interpreter were invaluable. Who was this young man who had been one of the first to greet the Russian fliers as they disembarked from the now famous airship? His name was George Kozmetsky, an ROTC student from the University of Washington. Was his presence merely coincidental or had he been assigned by the United States government at the request of the Soviets? Was this same procedure used at other airports along the route of the flight in case the fliers dropped in? Kozmetsky was an assistant to a language professor at the university and was adept at speaking and understanding Russian.

It was equally strange that a Russian-speaking woman was one of the first to greet the aviators. A Portland resident and fluent in Russian, her presence should have seemed unusual when everyone else had gone to Swan Island. Was she asked by the Soviet embassy in San Francisco to go directly to Vancouver in order to translate and to make the foreign visitors more comfortable? No one inquired. As the reporters pressed the fliers with many questions, Chkalov shouted, "No! No! No!" and then bolted from the group. Kozmetsky followed him as he went toward the field offices.

Brigadier General George C. Marshall, commander of the Vancouver Barracks, was just arriving at the airfield to take charge. His breakfast had been abruptly interrupted when word came that the Russians had just landed. The news media reported that General Marshall was wearing pajamas under his overcoat when he reached the field, only several blocks away from his residence. Corporal Alexander, who let General Marshall through the gate, said many years later the pajama story was incorrect because he remembered the general arriving fully dressed. General Marshall was never in the habit of being improperly dressed, but the unexpected arrival of the Russians may have forced him to hurry that morning.

There is no evidence that Marshall was informed by the FBI about a Vancouver landing. One would think the general would have been contacted immediately as the overall commander of the military complex in Vancouver. At this time the Air Force was under the auspices of the U.S. Army so it is curious why the FBI approached Air Force officers at Pearson. It is possible Major Burrows passed the FBI story on to Marshall; however, there is another argument that this didn't happen. Marshall's integrity may have been a bothersome factor in this situation and the FBI could have been reluctant to involve him in any "game playing." The FBI had encouraged Lieutenant Carlton Bond and whoever was in command of Pearson on this day to show surprise whenever the Soviet fliers arrived, otherwise their informant's life could be placed in jeopardy. If the Communist cell in Portland really did not want any information leaked to the FBI, someone might be at risk. On the other hand, it is possible the Communist cell was instructed to provide this information to the FBI to improve military security at the field. Marshall, as well as other commanders of military airfields along the proposed route of the Russian flight, were probably advised of the possibility that any one of several landing sites could be the eventual destination of the Russians.* When the "transpolar" journey had begun there was no evidence the U.S. government knew a hoax was in progress; however, when reports started to come in indicating excessive plane speeds in the polar vicinity and Prince Patrick Island, station

---

*Around 1954, Lt. Bond, who had later been promoted to the rank of colonel, was having dinner with David King, his neighbor. [David King was the young paperboy who had first spotted the Soviet plane over Vancouver in 1937.] Col. Bond told King about the FBI visit to Pearson Field. King told this story to a few close friends but nothing was ever made public concerning the information provided by the Communist cell in Portland.

operators and supervisors must have become a little suspicious. When the Alberta-Great Slave Lake run to Queen Charlotte was reported to have been negotiated in 28 minutes it is inconceivable high American officials were not notified. Because of these unbelievable discrepancies people like Marshall were no doubt alerted of a problem with the "transpolar" flight. This would present a grave situation. Any disclosure that a hoax was being perpetrated on the American people could have far-reaching ramifications. It was imperative for General Marshall to proceed with the utmost caution and to guard against any possibility of some incident or slip of the tongue occurring. The officers and men under his command wouldn't be sleeping in on this Sunday morning. Out of their beds they tumbled to help control the crowds and guard the Soviet airship.

And now the general stood face to face with the Russian chief pilot. George Kozmetsky, the soldier-interpreter, had joined them in the field office. Marshall made use of his services in posing a few questions to Chkalov in behalf of the news media. The Russian flier quickly and decisively denied any mechanical failure had brought them down. (This was in reference to the fuel pump problem radioed by Beliakov at 8 a.m.) It is amazing Chkalov could make this statement after many stations had picked up the message. But this wasn't the extent of his brazenness. Knowing full well the ANT was almost out of gas he went on to tell the general there was still enough left to travel another 750 miles. (This meant they could have reached their San Francisco destination.)

In the close quarters of the small field office, the smelly "arctic" clothing probably became overwhelming to the general and other officers present. Marshall should have known something was radically wrong with the flight claims. Anyone would naturally presume the fliers had started out with clean clothing, just 63 hours ago from Moscow. After supposedly traveling most of the way in chilling temperatures it was not possible to get so dirty and smelly in 63 hours. Either the airmen had started out with filthy clothes or else there was some other explanation for their appearance. Perhaps the general considered the possibility they had been on the road much longer than the 63 hours claimed. In any event, Marshall must deal with the affair as it now stood. It was apparent the chief pilot was uncomfortable. A news reporter described his demeanor in this way, "His eyes darting nervously about the small office room and never resting on any one object for more than a second's glance, the sturdy aviator licked his lips repeatedly and then apologetically requested a glass of water. When it was brought by one of the officers, he gulped the contents down hurriedly and then returned to the ship and his two companions. Strangers in a strange country, the trio seemed uncertain of what to do...." After eyeing the propeller, someone in the crowd suggested that one of the three blades was "out of line." This statement drew a curt admonishment from Chkalov who blurted out, "you're cross-eyed," Kozmetsky translated. The three foreign visitors were obviously beginning to feel like they were in a fishbowl. But the American audience was elated with the great flight they thought had been accomplished, one that seemed to surpass Lindbergh's in distance, duration, and – according to some – danger. It appears Chkalov, Baidukov, and Beliakov were having trouble recognizing the Americans' genuine appreciation of the "transpolar flight," and that this, coupled with their guilt for the sham being perpetrated, made them all extremely uncomfortable. These feelings were compounded as more and more people flooded onto the field.

At this point the Army took over, halting the oncoming hordes behind a rope barrier about 100 feet from the Russian ship. Soldiers with rifles sobered the frenzied crowd. A local lawyer tried to get through the ropes to get a closer look at the plane but was ordered back by a young soldier named Felix Cruz. But this lawyer insisted on getting to the plane, prompting Private First Class Cruz to fix bayonet. When the intruder continued, the soldier pushed him down with the rifle, according to Corporal George Gollehon who presently resides in Vancouver. General Marshall became exasperated when reporters and others continued prowling around the Russian plane. He hadn't realized it but one over-exuberant individual had already climbed into the cockpit and secured a souvenir, a bottle containing liquid. But now Marshall ordered a tarpaulin thrown over the cabin canopy and threatened to impose strict Army control. The general had already invited the Soviet fliers to his Army post home.

By this time Chkalov and his two companions were ready to bolt the gathering. They pushed their way quickly through the enthusiastic crowd and headed back toward the field offices. As they fled, cheers and applause rang out and many elated onlookers slapped them vigorously on the back. A newspaper reporter recorded their reactions, "They paid little heed to the adulations, walking rapidly toward the Army vehicles." General Marshall had ordered the cars to transport the fliers to his home. They quickly climbed into one of the vehicles, accompanied by the general and one of his military drivers. Kozmetsky was the sixth passenger. During the ride the driver, a sergeant, in an effort to make "small talk," commented on the knives the fliers were carrying, saying he admired their fine quality. Baidukov bragged how Chkalov was an expert at throwing them. Kozmetsky translated the chief pilot's reply, "How would you like me to demonstrate this on you?" The crude remark must have rung empty on this historic occasion. Chkalov was certainly demonstrating his lack of social graces.

By the time the party got to General Marshall's house, his wife Katherine and his stepdaughter Molly Brown had already started preparing for the three unexpected guests. Katherine had been cooking bacon and eggs for the family when word came the Russians had landed in Vancouver. Their breakfast would now go to the three hungry fliers. But first the trio asked for water, and then made a request for some cognac. A search was made through the battalion but this item was not among the regular supplies. An extended search took the orderlies into the city's nearby business district and two bottles of cognac were delivered to Mrs. Marshall. She was somewhat surprised when the three men set upon the two bottles and "drank the works."

In the course of the conversation the fliers were interrupted by repeated calls from all over the world and the United States. However, only three calls were recognized by these new "heroes." One was from Moscow, apparently from a high dignitary; the second was from the Soviet Consulate in New York; and a third was from San Francisco, presumably from Ambassador Troyanovsky. Marshall's personal papers show at least 14 long-distance telephone calls were received that first day. Thinking the fliers must be very tired, General Marshall offered them baths. But it appears something was either gained or lost in the translation because Chkalov replied, "We do not go into the river in winter in Russia." It was then explained there were facilities upstairs in the building, specifically three bathrooms with tubs. Baidukov and Beliakov decided to retire upstairs to bathe but Chkalov seemed eager to remain behind to socialize with the general. Marshall was also anxious to ask the chief pilot some questions in the interest of the reporters who were waiting patiently for interviews.

Through the young interpreter, Chkalov said they had not eaten since leaving Moscow, but had drunk tea, lemonade, and a little brandy while in flight. He continued telling his small audience the plane they flew to Vancouver was the same one used in a long-distance flight of 4,700 miles, undertaken in July the previous year. (Other reports emanating from Moscow had set the distance at about 5,700 miles.) But on this 1937 air expedition just completed the course as traced by Chkalov on the general's atlas, claimed the route had taken them over the Kola Peninsula to Franz Josef Land and on to the North Pole. From the "roof" of the world the ANT was steered southward to Prince Patrick Island. Kozmetsky translated additional accounts of the "transpolar flight" from information provided by Chkalov, noting the most trying portion of the flight had been from the Barents Sea to Patrick when they were confronted by the danger of ice forming on the wings and cyclonic storms blocking their path. After passing Great Bear Lake and the Mackenzie district the plane was veered west past Ft. Simpson and on to the Pacific Ocean, the Russian pilot told General Marshall. (Chkalov wisely omitted the Great Slave Lake run. Vartanian apparently alerted the fliers to this gross exaggeration of having the ANT flying 1,500 miles an hour.)

Once the fliers had reached the ocean, according to the Russian spokesman, they proceeded over Chichagof to Sitka, Alaska. This, of course, was an entirely different route than was sent by radio to the various American stations listening for the plane's position. The official flight log already had been printed in papers throughout the United States. Even the San Francisco station from where Ambassador Troyanovsky was monitoring the flight acknowledged the "transpolar" airship had passed into Alberta from Great Slave Lake and then turned to the coast to a point over the Queen Charlotte Islands. Only the latest reports told about the last-minute route change. General Marshall and the public had been under the belief the airplane followed a course through the Canadian interior and knew nothing about the coastal route until newspapers had reported it. It would be difficult to fault the American news services because everything they were printing was coming from Russian radio agent Vartanian, who supposedly based his reports on direct information from the plane.

It appears the pilot was on a storytelling "roll," probably stimulated by the substantial amount of cognac consumed a few minutes earlier. He went on to explain how magnetic disturbances at the North Pole caused some concern, but they were ready with a sun compass to find their direction. Admiral Byrd had given the Soviets this sun compass several years ago. It was an invention of a cartographer from the National Geographic Society. The chief pilot said the extreme cold in the northernmost regions had caused ice to form on the wings, and even their drinking water had frozen. Chkalov "surprised" General

Marshall with his detailed knowledge of the North American coastline, surprising since this was reported as a last-minute route change. With the exception of the last leg, the fliers had enjoyed "daylight from the time of takeoff," said the Soviet pilot, adding the engine had performed perfectly, not missing a beat the entire journey. First, he said, they passed over Vancouver and Portland and ventured as far south as Eugene before the three airmen agreed it was too dangerous to go on with poor visibility. This contradicted the American weather reports indicating there was clear weather to the south; this forecast was radioed to the plane.

Chkalov had no idea their plane had been spotted at 7:15 a.m. over the mouth of the Columbia by the Coast Guard, and felt safe in adding the extra miles to Eugene and back, a distance of 200 miles. Since the plane landed in Vancouver at 8:16 a.m., this meant Chkalov was claiming to have flown a distance of 280 miles in one hour and one minute, an outrageous speed for this aircraft, even giving him the benefit of the doubt on the obvious time consumed circling Swan Island several times and the time spent in the flight landing pattern at Pearson Field. He felt it was imperative to "pad" the flight mileage because it had taken, according to their own reports, 11 hours to fly from Charlotte Island to Vancouver, a distance of 700 miles at a speed of 65 mph. The time taken on this leg of the trip would cast doubts on their navigational ability and would not conform with their announced speed of more than 100 miles an hour. It is speculated three of these missing hours resulted from placing their plane ahead of their actual position just after leaving the archipelago. Apparently the fliers did not want to radio their actual positions for fear of being spotted. To compensate for lost time the Eugene trip was fabricated. There was a bigger hole in their story. Since they earlier expressed serious concerns over the dwindling fuel supply, why would they venture to the Eugene area and back, a distance of 200 miles?

There is another unexplained factor concerning Swan Island. According to the fliers they saw thousands of people swarming over the airdrome below, and fearing their airplane might be damaged by the crowd, decided to seek out the military field in Vancouver as their final destination. What is particularly unreal about this explanation is that not one of those thousands of people saw the plane as it supposedly circled low over the field a number of times. Later Baidukov (who claimed he and not Chkalov was flying the plane) said he brought the ANT down within 150 feet of the ground before deciding to fly to

Vancouver. Here was an airplane with a wingspan of 112 feet, hovering above the Portland airport at 150 feet, and no one in a crowd of thousands got a glimpse of it despite a weather ceiling of 600 feet visibility at the time. The fliers said they could see people waving their arms and yet the people could not see this huge aircraft. These time-consuming maneuvers were just another way to pad the distance of the flight and make up for discrepancies in time.

As it turned out, the Soviets emerged "smelling like red roses" because someone apparently asked the Coast Guard to reconsider its sighting of the ANT, and subsequently this report was changed to state that only the sound of a motor was heard. If the report had been allowed to stand, newsmen would have easily noticed the 280 mph speed claimed by Chkalov. Considering all of the unbelievable plane speeds from point-to-point on the way down to Vancouver, anyone would be hard-pressed to think the situation went unnoticed. But with Vartanian ironing out the difficulties in Seattle and the Americans looking the other way, the hoax was still intact. However, the Soviets had a long ways to go if they were really going to spend a month in the United States, answering questions. Allowing Chkalov to get away with so many untruths seemed to encourage more carelessness.

Only one of the airmen got any sleep, related Chkalov. Baidukov had sprawled out in the cabin and took a little nap. Then the chief pilot made the preposterous claim of never leaving the controls for the entire 63 hours and 17 minutes; he alone flew the plane. His version had Beliakov also remaining awake to guide the ship to America. It's a good thing Baidukov had left the room before Chkalov started to rant and rave; otherwise he may have shown visible signs of displeasure at his diminishing role. Baidukov was dealt another severe blow when Chkalov claimed credit in landing the big ANT at the Vancouver field, describing in detail how he brought the big plane down. As Kozmetsky translated Chkalov's version of the landing, he did not "drag" the field but merely settled the ship down, took a good look at the turf field in front, and landed with part "throttle." He gave himself plenty of leeway to get off again if the field proved rougher than it looked. When he felt the big wheels on the smooth ground he reduced the throttle, taxied to the edge and with a flick of the wrist, cut the engine.

Perhaps, in order to emphasize the ordeal the chief pilot informed Kozmetsky they had smoked hundreds of cigarettes in the course of the flight. This was probably true because it had been noted Chkalov "smoked like a chimney." (As harmless as the statement appeared it was bound to have repercussions later when people began contemplating the dangers of smoking while sitting atop a "large fuel load.") It all appeared to be a grab for glory knowing his copilot would not ruin things by calling him a liar. Satisfied he had made a good impression with Marshall, Chkalov left the room to join his comrades upstairs. But General Marshall was not likely taken in by what the Soviet spokesman said. He may not have known how this "transpolar flight" had been pulled off but one thing must have caught his attention: These men, looking as they did, with filthy clothing and oilstreaked faces, had not gotten this way by coming over the North Pole from Moscow 63 hours ago. But the general's main duty was to avoid anything that might cause a politically explosive incident. He had kept the reporters and writers at bay by asking their questions for them. Now that it was done, Kozmetsky could relay the stories to the news people while he checked on his orderlies who were attending the fliers upstairs. In the course of meeting with reporters the youthful interpreter offered a comment of his own, "They did not appear exhausted or all in." His remark demonstrates his innocence in the affair.

Meanwhile, the orderlies were having quite a time with the fliers who seemed reluctant to leave the confines of their bathrooms and tubs. Unable to operate the water faucets, an orderly helped them draw the water. Mrs. Marshall had been waiting a couple of hours to feed them; still they were not in a hurry to eat, despite their previous claims of not eating during the "63-hour flight." Finally, the general's wife directed the maids to take food up to the bedrooms. There was still no response from the bathroom occupants; in desperation the orderlies passed the bacon, eggs, orange juice, toast, and coffee through the bathroom doors to the Russian guests. Orderlies opined the fliers ate their breakfast while in the tub. There is such a thing in American culture of "breakfast in bed," but eating in the tub was altogether new. Perhaps it was some sort of custom in Russia. Possibly the fliers were not hungry and/or did not want to interrupt the effects of the alcohol they had consumed. They had cognac and brandy during the trip down, and now finished off the two bottles provided by Mrs. Marshall. This, coupled with the hot baths and lack of food might make them a little tipsy. Was it possible to get the warmed-over and greasy breakfast down without getting sick? The fate of the food was not disclosed. However, in their position three good flushes would have solved the problem and at the same time convinced the world the three "heroic" aviators had just eaten a well deserved, hearty breakfast.

At last, the three well-washed fliers emerged from the bathrooms attired in pajamas provided by the Army. Three maids had just finished "fluffing up" their beds and were on their way out of the room. General Marshall had scaled the stairway to wish them pleasant dreams. It appears the fliers had the wrong idea at this point, perhaps because there were three of them and three maids, suggesting the royal treatment being enjoyed might get even better. In any event, the tireless Chkalov had his eye on one of the girls who was especially endowed. Feeling his great "transpolar" feat had earned him this favor, he approached the frightened young lady, intent on pulling her into the bedroom. Despite the language barrier the general, using demonstrative sign language, was finally successful in convincing the flier that girls did not come with the service. General Marshall now fully realized that his difficult job of controlling the Russian situation was going to be made even more difficult if he had to protect all the women in the camp. He quickly assigned a soldier with a rifle to guard the three maids. On one later occasion a soldier followed one of the maids into the bedroom occupied by Chkalov, who again reached out for her before he noticed the soldier staring him down with rifle in hand. The flier pulled back at once. Forgetting he was a married man apparently wasn't too difficult for Chkalov who received "red roses" from his fiancee in Moscow, delivered by a Vancouver florist, according to Mrs. Marshall. Were these the "arctic scientists" who methodically were conquering the most inaccessible parts of the world; who knew at all times where they were and what they were doing? This image was further tarnished when an orderly came running to General Marshall with a fistful of one-hundred dollar bills, apparently blown or thrown out of an upstairs window. Were the Russians, made happy with cognac, throwing away their money, or could it be blamed on some gentle June breeze and an open window? The general had done all he could; he posted guards at their bedroom doors to prevent newsmen from getting to them. By this time Mrs. Marshall graciously had invited some 60 members of the press inside for sandwiches and coffee.

General Marshall's behavior began changing dramatically after the Russian fliers arrived. The general was known for a healthy "Irish temper" but kept it well under control. However, the Russian visit seemed to have irritated him to no end, a fact which begs for some speculation. Did he realize a hoax was taking place? Had the Army ordered him to cover up any discrepancies concerning the flight? Marshall was not the kind of person who would quietly sit still for such phoniness. Yet he was also a loyal soldier obligated to take orders from his superiors. Had all of this brought the general to a point of desperation and frustration?

An observer close to the Marshall household described the general as grim and disturbed – on the verge of "blowing up." He appeared as if his mind was "racing 60 miles an hour." This otherwise well-controlled and efficient soldier was now giving the impression he was having a difficult time coping with the Russian situation. Ordinarily General Marshall was up to any challenge but this event was definitely gnawing on his nerves. Had the FBI failed to notify him of the Vancouver landing and not given him time to prepare for this highly publicized international event? And it wasn't just the first day of the ordeal that bothered the general. He remained irritated and uneasy on the following day as well.

General Marshall probably breathed a little easier when the three Russians were finally bedded down. Marshall's role in this kind of diplomacy was new to him. His primary duty was supervising Civilian Conservation Corps (CCC) camps and many public works projects in the Northwest, in addition to his regular command of the barracks. His next step on this eventful day was to name a committee to check the plane's instruments in order to prepare an official report to the National Aeronautical Association. Any barographs or gas seals were destined to go to Washington, D.C. for evaluation. There also was a matter of finding suitable clothing for the Soviet aviators. They had not brought anything but their flying gear, which was a bit unusual since they intended to stay in the United States for a while. Now it was necessary on Sunday, Father's Day, of all days, to contact some clothing store and ask for special service. The general set in motion arrangements to buy clothing. Meier & Frank, a large department store in Portland, agreed to supply a full wardrobe to the men without charge. They wouldn't be the easiest to outfit because Chkalov and Baidukov had short legs and might not fit into regular sizes; however, this was overcome by sending a tailor or two along with the clothes. A small room was converted to accommodate the tailors, translators, and other storekeepers. A large Army truck delivered an assortment of suits, vests, shirts, ties, underclothing, and shoes of all types and sizes to the barrack's temporary fitting room.

General Marshall finished selecting his committee of five to oversee the removal of barographs. Among them were Major Paul Burrows, field commander at Pearson, and a man by the name of Harry Coffey, who represented the National Aeronautical Association. Coffey also acted as the official who was to report his findings to the Federation Aeronautique Internationale (FAI).

The day continued to be a busy one with Vartanian dropping in from Seattle at the Marshall residence to meet Ambassador Troyanovsky who was arriving from San Francisco that afternoon. While General Marshall entertained Vartanian, Mrs. Marshall directed the table setting in the dining room for the expected guests. A chartered plane was flying the ambassador and his party into Swan Island Airport about 3 p.m. and special automobiles had been dispatched to transport them to Vancouver. Accompanying the ambassador were Vladimir Begunov, military attaché; Stanislav Shumovsky, aeronautical engineer, and several others. When the entourage arrived at Portland the dignitaries were quickly hustled into the waiting cars, and police, with sirens screaming, escorted the delegation to the now famous city, marking the end of what was envisioned as the greatest air flight of the decade, if not the century. Aside from all the hoopla, Troyanovsky's main concern was getting the fliers' visas to them as quickly as possible.

When the ambassador and his group arrived at the barrack's home of the general many journalists and reporters had already gathered. They were still waiting for personal interviews with the "heroes" of the day. But the Russian emissary shot right by them as they crowded around the front porch. Once inside Troyanovsky inquired about the aviators. "Yes they were asleep," was the reply. His response was "let the fliers sleep," but he did want to take a look at the sleeping "heroes." With that said, the short, round-faced ambassador with a button nose quickly climbed the stairs and disappeared. (The visas were delivered at last.) He returned shortly and joined the main body of people on the front porch. "My country has become air-minded," he said to his eager audience. The ambassador went on to applaud the many fine airmen and planes in Russia. Between telephone calls from New York and San Francisco, the diminutive Russian talked about trade relations with America. He was asked about the airfields in the United States and was complimentary in his response. "They [the fliers] told me they wished you had a larger one here in Vancouver." How the ambassador learned this is not clear since the fliers were supposedly sleeping.

Troyanovsky told his audience that the plane would likely be reassembled in Moscow and flown again. Apparently this cleared up the problem of how the ANT was going to be returned to the mother county. There had been some speculation by Russian officials that the

ANT might be taken on an air tour but Troyanovsky erased this speculation. He said, "One reason why the plane will not be flown further here is that a thorough inspection of its equipment will be made to determine what must be overcome in the Arctic. The information is important for scientific purposes." Of course, it was out of the question to let this aircraft go on tour, thus divulging its limited fuel capacity when the tanks were refilled at American facilities. It had also been reported the fliers were going to donate their arctic flying clothes to the Smithsonian Institution. (It was later learned the Smithsonian did not receive the apparel.)

It was time for the ambassador to awaken the fliers and give the tailors an opportunity to take measurements for their new attire. They would have a choice of suits, vests, and other matching items, including socks and shoes. Downstairs on the porch the newsmen were clamoring to interview the now "famous" Russians but the ambassador held out, telling them they would soon be presentable. But despite all the new things at their disposal none of the three would give up their much-worn silk underwear. The fliers appeared smartly dressed in dark double-breasted suits, white shirts, and conservative ties. Finally the patient newsmen and radio reporters got their pictures and interviews, but the information was essentially the same material Chkalov and Troyanovsky already presented. But newsreel cameras ground away as the story of the "transpolar" adventure was being readied to send all over the world.

Then it was time for the "polar birdmen" to go to the airfield to help in the removal of the barographs. Major Burrows asked Chkalov where they were located but the pilot appeared "dazed" and was not able to find them. This was especially strange since he reportedly had been flying the same plane on a "record flight in 1936." It is possible Chkalov did not want to admit knowing the location of the barographs to take away any supposition that he had tampered with them. Or was he suffering from a hangover, leaving him disoriented? He climbed into the cockpit and busied himself by throwing out some knapsacks. Major Burrows and Coffey and the other members of General Marshall's committee scoured the bottom of the big ship and subsequently found the barographs; two were together under one wing and the third was attached in another area. Chkalov rejoined the committee members and offered his assistance in removing the barographs. Using the knife previously admired by Marshall's driver, he began prying one of the instruments loose. Blood spurted out when the aviator accidentally cut his finger, and handing the instrument to Major Burrows he said, "Please do everything possible to make our record complete and official."

That evening a worldwide radio broadcast had been scheduled directly from Marshall's residence. At 6 p.m. the National Broadcasting Company (NBC) began beaming the latest news of the "great event." The Russian ambassador was the first to speak and proceeded to tell the people of the world that the fliers were scheduled to visit many of the American aircraft factories. Was this a message to the Germans that Russia had the inside track with the United States in terms of political and military opportunities by having direct access to U.S. companies? Troyanovsky was speaking from the game room, set aside for the broadcast. The three now "celebrated airmen" approached the microphone to take their turn in addressing a world audience.

The neatly dressed Alexander Beliakov spoke first. His message concerned the great possibilities of building a transpolar airline between the two nations. Chkalov was then asked if he could have flown farther. He answered, "Yes, Los Angeles." The name of the city was clearly audible, but the ambassador's translation of the answer was only, "They could have gone farther." It appeared Chkalov never gave up as he kept insisting on taking the ANT on many more miles without any gas. He proceeded to tell his world audience that the first time they experienced any serious difficulty with the plane's radio was when the trio flew over "Baffin Land." As he spoke Baidukov and Beliakov nodded in agreement with this statement. Baffin Island, not Baffin Land, was 700 miles east of the 120-degree meridian, their "polar route." There must have been thousands of geographers listening to the broadcast throughout the world, but apparently no one thought to challenge Chkalov's ridiculous mislocation of Baffin Island. As things went on a correction was quietly made before the papers went to press, so again the hoax was saved from exposure.

The ambassador rescued the microphone from the chief pilot and turned the attention to the congratulatory messages coming in from around the world. Joseph Stalin had sent his high praise of the "feat" earning them the love and admiration of the Soviet people. President Franklin D. Roosevelt also recognized the "skill and daring" of the Soviet fliers. Vilhjalmur Stefansson, noted arctic explorer and president of the New York Explorer's Club, issued a statement saying he was not surprised by the latest polar achievements. He based his evaluation on his own studies concerning Russian efforts to conquer the northern

regions, a project going on for many years. And then this particular
ordeal was finally over; however, Troyanovsky knew full well the days
ahead were marked with unknown dangers and pitfalls. He must keep a
tight reign on these three peasant fliers, especially Chkalov, the
spokesman for the crew. The main problem was keeping the airmen
away from the booze. Having just lived through the fright of an international radio broadcast, perhaps everyone would sleep very well on this
first night in America. Troyanovsky and his party had also been invited
to stay at General Marshall's military domicile.

The Russian guests arose at 8:15 a.m. the following day and were
served breakfast. General Marshall then took them for a stroll through
the barrack's compound. He had planned a small parade in honor of the
fliers and Ambassador Troyanovsky. This got underway shortly. The
usual protocol and dialogue was carried out, and then the ambassador
was honored with a 19-gun salute. When the ceremonies were completed the fliers, while shopping for raincoats, ducked into the nearest
Vancouver liquor store and bought several bottles of vodka and cognac,
undoubtedly without Troyanovsky's knowledge.

The Portland Chamber of Commerce had invited the Soviet party
to a luncheon at noon. This seemed fitting as the city felt somewhat
cheated out of hosting the "great event." As the Russians arrived on
Fifth Avenue in motor cars, thousands of enthusiastic Portlanders
waved and shouted their approval. Inside, the podium was bedecked
with the flags of the two countries. As the food was being served the
ambassador was recognized and rose to give appreciation for the great
hospitality provided by General Marshall. He went on to recap the
Russian interest in forging a commercial airline route over the pole
linking these two great nations. Portland Rose Queen Dorothy Hardin
approached Chkalov and placed a wreath of flowers about his neck and
gave him a royal kiss. The flier's face turned a "beet red" during this
gesture; he quickly rallied himself and began discussing the merits of
the airline concept. (Did the aviator blush because of feeling shame for
his part in the hoaxes?) He was a married man with two children; it
seems he should have been the master of this attention. When the short
celebration was over the Russians were scheduled to appear at one of
Portland's largest hotels for additional personal get-togethers with the
American hosts. As the party reached the Chamber of Commerce door,
they found many more thousands gathered to welcome them. The three
blushing airmen hurried to the waiting automobiles in order to escape
the crowd's wild appreciation.

At last they were safe from the hordes in the sanctuary of the Multnomah Hotel. This gathering proved to be much more intimate and casual. The fliers said they hoped to make another "transpolar flight," but this time to New York. They added a hope that some American aviators would return the visit. Chkalov then described the "polar" achievement, commenting, "They said it couldn't be done. So we started to gather the data about the impossible area, the bald spot on top of the world. It took long scientific study. It took much hard work to gather the data we needed." It seemed as though he was once again about to say too much or trying to be overly technical. Cognac was offered to him and the others, but they quietly declined and accepted weak tea. Had Troyanovsky put a damper on their drinking? Nothing but tea and ice water was touched during this session. So another milestone had passed by with the great deception still under wraps.

The plan now was to take the show to San Francisco. The ambassador could better monitor events with a little more control from his consulate headquarters. The three heralded "polar" birdmen and Troyanovsky's entourage were transported to Swan Island International Airport just before 3 p.m. to board the same chartered airliner that had brought the Russian welcoming committee to Portland the day before. It was to be about a three-hour flight to the Oakland Airport in California. The fliers passed some of the time speaking with United Air Lines pilot Joe Smith and his copilot. All three of the Soviet pilots were allowed to take the controls for a brief time. Chkalov displayed his knowledge of Pacific Coast cities by naming each one correctly as they passed over them. He knew all the cities from Portland to San Francisco. Pilot Smith was able to carry on his own interview with the Soviet aviators.

It appeared he was the only one who thought to ask them if they had seen the "Russian polar camp" when passing over the North Pole. They didn't see anything but a lot of ice, was their answer. The fliers said they wore dark glasses to counter the sun's glare and sometimes it had been necessary to skirt high above the clouds to avoid too much ice forming on the wings. They told the American pilot that contrary to popular opinion storm clouds in the polar vicinity rise to more than 19,000 feet, requiring them to scale the clouds at this height to avoid icing. In the course of the conversation, distance claims for the ANT increased more and more. The pilots affirmed they had actually flown 7,000 miles, 400 miles more than Chkalov's account to General Marshall. And in the same breath it was stated the plane could have flown twice as far as it did. This meant the ANT could travel 14,000 miles nonstop. The next remark might have indicated the Russians did not understand that America had a national news network, because upon their arrival in the United States the fliers first told of smoking "hundreds of cigarettes on the 'trip,'" and now they changed the story to pipes. Someone must have said something to caution them about the use of cigarettes while supposedly carrying 2,000 gallons of gasoline. It is unbelievable the story would be changed in midstream but this had become the practice more than the exception.

Two thousand people were anxiously waiting at the Oakland Airport for the popular "Heroes of the Soviet Union" to arrive. A strong delegation of Communist Party members led by Anita Whitney were ready to greet the airmen when they stepped off the chartered airliner. At exactly 6:40 p.m., the plane arrived and again the "heroes" of the day stepped into a "sea" of people. Oakland's mayor was there to direct the festivities in their honor but the Communists pushed forward to shove huge bunches of red roses into the fliers' arms. The French song "Internationale" rang out, "Arise ye prisoners of starvation," the song continued, as Communist clinched fists were raised. Police moved in to break a pathway for the three fliers.

Chkalov, Baidukov, and Beliakov moved quickly to a small raised platform where they began breaking off the red blossoms and throwing them into the crowd. There was "wild pandemonium" as applause thundered beneath the low overcast. It would have been impossible to quiet the throngs for the purpose of speech-making. Even Mayor James de Paoli was virtually swept aside by the onrush of still and motion picture cameramen. The aviators and the ambassadorial party were hustled into yellow limousines to take them to San Francisco. A police escort accompanied the parade part of the way, but finally the Oakland police escort left and the special automobiles continued across the Bay Bridge to downtown San Francisco. Through the murk and moisture of the early evening the motorcade pressed on to the Russian Consulate. A crowd was beginning to gather here, too.

Ambassador Troyanovsky and Gregory Gokhman, acting consul from the Russian embassy in Washington, D.C., wasted no time in ushering the unpredictable Chkalov and his flying associates through the massive doors, and away from the exuberant masses pressing toward them. Gokhman must have been aware of the inconsistent reports which had the Russian plane "dancing about the Pole," and Troyanovsky's experiences the last two days were enough to warn officials these men needed to be watched much more closely. The consulate was alive with local Russians of all classes shouting to their heroes. Once Troyanovsky had the three fliers inside the walls, he was more able to plan the next move. A representative of San Francisco Mayor Eneas Kane arrived to apologize for not meeting the fliers at the Oakland Airport and said, "this was perhaps an oversight of San Francisco's head but not of her heart; we expected word and did not receive it." Apparently the Soviet strategy was to keep the San Francisco people off guard in order to minimize the number of people greeting them, a consistent pattern since the fliers' arrival in Vancouver.

That evening Ambassador Troyanovsky hosted an invitational affair to introduce the fliers to the Bay area. Certain American military personnel were invited and the ambassador took on the role of interpreter to answer a "volley" of questions fired at the aviators. There wasn't anything really new in the exchanges but rather a rehash of the interviews held in Vancouver and Portland. At least there was not any glaring contradictions this time around.

James Mattern, the American pilot who had twice crashed in Siberia, was invited to the festivities. This was an opportunity to revisit Alexander Beliakov. The Russian navigator had accompanied Levanevsky when the latter had come to the "rescue" of Mattern. Mattern told the gathering he intended to fly to Moscow via the North Pole in the near future. His announcement posed a big problem for the Russians. They could not afford to have this experienced aviator mixing with Russian pilots around Moscow and Shelkova Airport, where some aviation personnel might know about the hoax. Although the American flier didn't understand or speak Russian, he might be told things by bilingual Russians. Such a flight would require the Soviets to reciprocate the hospitality accorded their pilots. Mattern might expect to visit Russian aviation facilities. The Soviets wouldn't want this professional aviator seeing their backward systems of production. They didn't have to worry long because American officials turned down Mattern's request to travel to the Soviet Union.

Meanwhile the gala celebration at the Russian consulate was coming to a halt and the "exhausted" airmen were allowed to go to bed. San Francisco newspapers generously lauded the Soviet achievement. One newspaper said, "no migrating swan or goose had ever done what this man-made bird had done. It sailed across the top of the world . . . linked Moscow-Portland-Vancouver . . . joined the United States and Russia in the first feat of its kind in world history . . . ushered in a new transpolar era of air flight." An editorial page typified the appreciation of the reported feat:

> Chkalov, Baidukov and Beliakov knew when they took off from Moscow that over the Arctic part of their route nothing must happen or they would most likely never be heard of again. Only intrepid men can embark on such an adventure. These Russians show us they share to the full the intrepidity exhibited by flying men of other nations. . . . We have been hearing a good deal about Russian flying feats. This one was performed under the eyes of the entire world and all saw that it was first class.

These observations were seconded by Russian Attaché Stanislav Shumovsky when he was quoted from Vancouver as saying, "The USSR has made much more progress in aviation than is generally believed," adding "they [the pilots] are not glory seekers, but scientists doing a matter-of-fact job in the world's greatest attempt to build planes for long-range flying." Perhaps Shumovsky did not know Chkalov belonged to a Soviet sport flying club in Moscow. His next remark should have been left unsaid because it cast suspicion on the 1936 flight across Russia. The attaché said this flight had occurred in January when Chkalov, the *Great Soviet Encylopedia*, and other sources said it took place July 20-22. At least the attaché had the claimed distance of some 5,800 miles right—more than could be said for Chkalov who shortchanged the distance by 1,000 miles. It would seem the chief pilot would know the length of a "nonstop journey" for which he, Baidukov, and Beliakov received the "Hero of the Soviet Union" medal. In summary Chkalov had the date correct but the distance wrong while Shumovsky had the distance correct and the date wrong.

In spite of the many unexplained inconsistencies, the Soviet strategy was on course, thanks to generous U.S. government assistance and an apparent attitude of "turning their heads the other way." There was still a strong possibility something unforeseen and devastating could happen, but so far the flight had not been challenged.

The Soviets took advantage of their newly recognized long-distance flying by going on the offensive. Strongly worded bulletins were issued from the Kremlin warning the enemies of the Soviet Union to be aware of Russia's ability in aerial warfare. Articles threatened that Russian bombers could now reach the capitals and industrial centers of nations potentially hostile to the Communist State. The general public did not know this was one of the major reasons why Russia had launched all of its polar and aerial hoaxes in the first place, namely to scare her adversaries. No one questioned any phase of the "flight" nor thought to ask the fliers if they had taken photographs of the Pole and their trip. Privately it appears someone asked about the absence of cameras because the Soviet embassy was requesting permission for Gromov to carry cameras on his "flight."

Another prime objective for the hoax flights would get underway in a few days; the fliers were to take a closer look at U.S. airplane factories. Numerous Soviet engineers and technicians had already entered the country to accompany the three airmen to major aviation facilities throughout the U.S. In a lighter vein Chkalov, Baidukov, and Beliakov toured a Hollywood movie studio and met "America's little darling," Shirley Temple, who gave them a few bars of "Good Ship Lollipop." If the Russian airmen had been able to understand the words of her song they might have joined in because they too had a "Good Ship Lollipop." Other hours were spent visiting some of the agencies and departments which had assisted the "transpolar flight."

In Vancouver, General Marshall prepared the sealed barographs for shipment to Washington, D.C. While the ANT remained at Pearson Field under guard, a Russian engineer was said to be en route from Russia to disassemble the craft. As the Army waited for his arrival some of the local mechanics gave the plane the "once over." Apparently Major Burrows, the field commander, gave them permission. Eugene Spencer, the mechanic who first spotted the plane as it approached Pearson, simply stated that the Russian aircraft contained, "no apparent revolutionary features... either navigationally or aerodynamically." Art Whitaker, who had been present when the *Land of the Soviets* had arrived in 1929, gave his general impression of the Russian monoplane. He said the ANT-25 was put together with bolts more typically used on farm machinery; it was crudely built and the wings were poorly wrapped with fabric. He also noticed that one half of the engine parts were U.S. products. This contradicted the Soviet claim the plane was entirely Russian-built. Perhaps if Whitaker had known the plane had been reassembled in the wilderness, he would not have been so critical of its workmanship. Corporal Gollehon, who was in charge of the guard detail for the airplane, agreed with Whitaker on the poor workmanship of the Russian plane.

It appears Chkalov didn't realize the ANT's gas tanks were going to be emptied before the plane could be transported on U.S. roads because he was still bragging there was sufficient fuel to fly to San Francisco, and farther. Fortunately he was out of Vancouver during the draining of the tanks and was spared answering any questions. On June 23, Major Burrows stepped on the field to inspect the gas seals, his final official check of the flight. After the gas seals were removed, he opened the petcocks of the wing tanks and drained the gas. To everyone's surprise only 10.75 gallons dropped in the bucket.

Mr. Stanislav Shumovsky, a Russian aeronautical engineer who arrived in Vancouver with the ambassador's party, witnessed the operation. He declined comment on the "dribble of gas" drained from the tanks, denying any knowledge about the makeup of the airship. Burrows was pressed for an explanation as why there was only a small amount of fuel in the plane. The commander "pointed out emphatically that this does not necessarily mean the amount removed was all the gas in the ship. What was done was simply to drain all the gas that would come out of all the outlets that could be found." This answer indicated the possibility there were other tanks somewhere in the wings or body, and maybe the drains were so situated they would not completely drain the tanks without siphoning or pumping. "We know nothing about the construction of this ship and do not know where to look for what may be in it... so none of us can do more than guess. I am not willing to even do that because it is unwarranted." Burrows went on to say he did not know when a further check of the fuel situation might take place, explaining that a Russian engineer was en route to Vancouver and would arrive some time in the next 15 or 20 days. Perhaps this person could shed some light on the subject. Major Burrows had to be concerned about the small amount of gas found and knew the Russian craft had to be completely purged of gasoline before shipment.

The Soviets had stated on record that the plane carried enough fuel for 100 hours in the air, with 63 hours supposedly used up; what had happened to the remaining 37 hours of gas? There is no explanation for this discrepancy. No matter how much mileage was tacked on to the flight, the only factor relevant is the air hours. There is an exception and this has to do with greater air speeds requiring more fuel. But this wasn't the case with the slow-flying ANT. The Russians claimed they averaged 100 mph, a slow plane speed relatively speaking. It is apparent the American public and newspaper people got so caught up in the "transpolar" flight they failed to put two-and-two together. On one hand, American officials were told the ANT had six "huge" fuel tanks in the wings, totaling 2,000 gallons; and now Major Burrows was saying "hidden" tanks somewhere in the fuselage could account for the missing gas, about 740 gallons, equivalent to some 37 hours of flight time. This gas would require a very large storage space. Although the wings on the ANT were exceptionally long, the fuselage measured only 45 feet. Was it possible to store the equivalent of 15, 50-gallon barrels of airplane fuel in a very narrow fuselage, cramping the fliers in the widest section? Assuming such a fuel load could have been carried in the fuselage, is it reasonable to believe the pilots smoked hundreds of cigarettes in the presence of all that gas?

The real plan called for carrying only enough fuel to reach Vancouver with 100 gallons in reserve. Difficulties in finding the mouth of the Columbia River required burning the reserve fuel. This is why Baidukov and crew limped in on "fumes." This left open the possibility there was still fuel on board but it could not be pumped. Chkalov had another excuse ready for the shortened flight, citing visibility problems over the "Eugene area." All of this was done without the realization the Americans were going to demand complete removal of all gas before the ANT could be transported by truck to a port in Vancouver.

Outwardly it appears Mr. Vartanian and the fliers were the only ones who knew the ANT was going to be brought down in Vancouver. Radio agent Vartanian said he had received word from the fliers that they would land in Vancouver but he did not acknowledge this until about ten hours after the Russian plane landed. In retrospect Mr. Vartanian spoke out of turn in divulging he knew of the plane's destination four hours prior to the landing. His admission undermined Chkalov's excuse that the Vancouver selection was a last-minute decision, throwing suspicion on the pilot's story about flying to Eugene and back, and made it obvious Chkalov purposely diverted the public away from the Vancouver airfield.

CHAPTER 18

Crippling of Russia

In Moscow, Joseph Stalin must have been tremendously encouraged by the public's acceptance of the "transpolar flight." This is what he had hoped for, a major distraction from the political turmoil now beginning to envelop his country. Was there an organized campaign against Stalin or did he manufacture the degree of dissent in order to pull the Russian people in tighter under his control? Stalin must have recognized that in the event of any serious trouble it would be a monumental task to control such a large country with a highly dispersed and diversified population. Considering the very poor transportation system, it was next to impossible to politically secure the remote areas of Siberia, in close proximity to Japan, a traditional enemy that the dictator had previously warned when Japanese forces moved into north China, threatening Russian borders. And then there was Leon Trotsky who was receiving international attention with his attacks on the Soviet chief. Now when Soviet aviation was getting new respect from America and the rest of the world, Stalin was more confident in moving against his so-called political enemies. Even before June 20, the date marking the end of the "transpolar flight" and landing at Vancouver, Stalin had begun to purge various factions within his own party.

On June 12, the Kremlin chief announced the executions of eight Red Army generals. They had been accused of collaborating with the Nazis, allegedly in a plan to turn over the western states of the Ukraine and White Russia to Germany, in the event of a European war. Earlier, the regime had informed the world it had been necessary to execute 44 persons from Svobodny in the Far East for conspiring with the Japanese secret police.

Twenty-eight more were shot in that general area for sabotaging the new Amur railway system. Seventy others were reported liquidated as spies for the Estonian intelligence service. Even southern Russia did not escape the criticism of the Red Party. The heads of the Uzbekistan Republic and numerous other officials were ousted. This particular group was responsible for the training and education of millions of reserves for the Red Army. It seemed as though the country was coming apart at the seams.

The dictator was not only confronting certain elements outside of the Party, such as the Trotskyites, but striking deeply into the Communist Party itself, arresting and executing people who had been with the Revolution from the beginning. As early as 1933, 800,000 members were purged; the following year an additional 340,000 got the axe. Stalin blamed many of those purged for the sad state of agriculture and other economic deficiencies. The military took the brunt of the most ghastly punishment. For example, 75 out of 80 members of the Supreme Military Council were executed; three out of five Field Marshals, 14 out of 16 Army commanders, eight out of eight Naval admirals, 60 out of 67 Corps commanders, 136 of of 199 Division commanders and 221 out of 397 Brigade commanders paid the supreme penalty after being found guilty of what later turned out to be unfounded charges, according to Martin McCauley's 1964 book, *The Soviet Union Since 1917.*

Labeled as the "Great Show Trial" it began March 2, 1938, and when the court cases ended more than 35,000 officers, half of the officer corps, were either executed by firing squad or imprisoned, reported McCauley. Was paranoia now taking over? Was madness showing through in the face of what seemed to be insurmountable problems in industry and collectivism? If he were not truly desperate, then why else would Stalin have risked his nation's prestige by approving the hoax transpolar flight and misrepresenting the North Pole expedition. Stalin didn't have to be reminded that a second ANT-25 was about to be delivered into the United States. But this time three military fliers were going to make the trip. Hopefully this arrangement would result in fewer questionable practices.

American journalists assigned to Moscow were beginning to report major upheavals taking place. One *New York Times* correspondent wrote on June 24 that "The continued denunciation of thousands of men, including many who had stood near the very top of the state and party organization, gave the Soviet Union the appearance of being engaged in a gigantic Salem witch hunt." The Red chief of White Russia was reported to have killed himself after being accused of conspiring with foreign agents.

The purge continued with the chief of the Georgian state (Stalin's birthplace), being expelled. Joseph Umschlicht fell from one of the highest positions in the powerful Central Committee of the Communist Party. The industrial complex and agriculture's collective farm system were becoming disorganized; a severe crisis loomed over the nation. *New York Times* writer Harold Denny had covered the 1935 Levanevsky flight and was in Moscow again reporting on the alarming events taking place. His forthright and perspective articles seemed to capture the basic causes and effects of Stalin's move toward greater consolidation and centralization of power.

Denny said the execution of the eight Red Army generals, whom many believed to be innocent, caused considerable disenchantment among the older generation. A curtain of fear permeated every level of life. Many people feared involving themselves in political discussions, particularly with strangers and foreigners. University professors reverted solely to the books of Karl Marx for their teachings. They even worried about making casual statements to students and faculty that might be used as evidence against them. Under ordinary circumstances the situation might have led to open revolt against the ongoing cruelty from the Stalinist regime. However, the news of the flights was sweeping the country, a convenient diversion from all of the arrests and executions. Had their leaders miraculously brought the Soviet Union to the forefront in aviation? Was this all a sign the socialistic system was now beginning to produce? Even after Stalin learned in January that the country's population, according to the national census, was short about 25 million people, he persisted in eliminating many more. The death penalty was often evoked for simply attempting to flee the country.

On June 25, "smack" in the middle of what was now a major purge, Stalin and the Kremlin took time off to honor the returning members of Dr. Schmidt's "North Pole Expedition." Moscow announced 38 arctic explorers were due at the airport the following day, but Papanin, Krenkel, Shirshov, and Federov remained at the "pole." A temporary grandstand had been erected at the airfield to conduct the June 26 ceremony and about 1,000 people gathered to watch some of Russia's top officials greet the "Polar party." Premier Molotov and Klementy Voroshilov were on hand for the occasion. Another man who eventually would walk in the "boots" of Stalin stood nearby. He was

Nikita Khrushchev, who eventually would become first secretary of the Communist Party. Did Khrushchev know what was really going on with the polar hoaxes? Stalin himself made a sudden and surprise appearance.

All at once over the horizon came the four giant ANT-6s, carrying some of the "angels" who were supposed to save the dictator from falling from power. In a few moments the planes were on the ground and flower-bedecked limousines transported the "heroes" to the grandstand. Pilots, mechanics, and other expeditionary workers rushed from the automobiles to their waiting families. It was described as one of the most demonstrative meetings ever seen in Russia as family members embraced the gallant "heroes" of the north.

The group led by Dr. Schmidt approached Stalin and the Kremlin officials to exchange greetings. It was said the Soviet chief impulsively embraced the bearded Schmidt and "kissed him full on the lips." I.T. Spirin, chief navigator for the expedition, and others also received a royal weclome from Stalin, Molotov, and Voroshilov. Apparently the dictator was extremely grateful for the accomplishments of the "North Pole Expedition" and he demonstrated his approval by whisking up some of the flier's children and hugging them in an open display of affection. The small children represented Stalin's political salvation. His recent efforts at reorganizing the Communist Party were addressed to the young, with many more opportunities destined for the youth. The dictator had become suspicious of the older generation and the Old Guard, a group more difficult to manipulate.

But where was Stalin's favorite aviator, Sigmund Levanevsky? If anyone should be at the ceremony it would be this national hero of the skies. His absence was indeed mysterious! Levanevsky's close friend, General Iakov (Jacob) Alksnis, chief of the Air Force, was also unaccounted for. Rumors were circulating that both men had been arrested. Surely this could not be true in the case of Levanevsky. He was due to make a historic flight to America in July. Supposedly his flight, carrying a crew of five, was to be the forerunner for a commercial airline Russia was proposing to develop in the near future. Rumors were always part of the Moscow scene, especially since the purges. But now there were unofficial reports saying the "Soviet Lindbergh" was accused of trying to leave the country without authorization. It is surmised Levanevsky and his friend General Alksnis actually were in deep trouble. It was known the Air Force chief had been linked with one of the eight Red Army generals who had just been executed for treason. The rumors of

Alksnis' arrest died down when he was drafted to sit on the court trying the generals. If he wasn't in trouble why hadn't he appeared at this great historic occasion honoring the polar party? And in the case of Levanevsky, is it possible he had become disenchanted over the hoaxes and decided to flee to America? Had Stalin become suspicious of his favorite flier and placed him in confinement?

Vice Premier Vias Chubar had been selected as the spokesman for the day's events and he rose to give the official welcoming speech. The tone of his address was strictly political, noting the "difficulties of the polar adventure not only were due to the backwardness of technique at the time of the Revolution, but also to German and Japanese Fascists, who together with their Trotskyist agents and traitors tried to hinder our progress.... But we have crushed them mercilessly. We know that the enemy is preparing to attack us but after the destruction of... [refers to the execution of eight army generals], we know our people, who have created heroes such as we are welcoming, will more than ever be devoted to the cause." Chubar's charges were, of course, preposterous; the Northern Sea Route Administration, sponsors of the North Pole Expedition, had been under the tight and watchful control of Stalin himself. There had been no previous complaints of any element or group interfering with the progress of this project.

What was especially interesting about today's affair was that Russia's "historic polar crossing" to America was not mentioned. It would have been a perfect opportunity to publicize and propagandize this so-called world achievement in aviation. Those attending the ceremony and the general public must have thought it strange no mention was given to a once-in-a-lifetime event they had just heard about a few days earlier. However, here again, Stalin was reluctant at this early date to embrace the "flight" as authentic. Any premature recognition of the event would make him look the fool if something were to occur in America discrediting the Russian polar claims. The Kremlin boss surely had to be aware, five days after the landing in Vancouver, that serious discrepancies were now known to U.S. officials. It was prudent to wait longer for American reactions before using the "transpolar flight" to further his popularity. If he extended too much credence to this event and it fell through, then his association with the hoax flight was sure to be revealed. However, as the head of state, he did have to send his congratulations to the fliers at Vancouver.

On the other hand, Schmidt's Polar Expedition did not pose any serious credibility problems because it was always under local control and did not involve foreign governments. Even though the expedition had never reached the North Pole, it was unlikely it would get challenged because visibility on top of the northern icecap was hampered by fog during the summer months. It is reasonable to believe the camp at Rudolph Island was legitimate because this site was only a hundred miles from Hooker, a well-established camp. It appears the Soviet plan called for placing four men and equipment onto an ice floe in the Rudolph Island vicinity. The four explorers would then attempt to ride the floe to Greenland in a circular route of about 1,300 miles. Once Papanin, Krenkel, Shirshov, and Federov were safely aboard the floe no one would ever know they had not been at the North Pole. Stalin was now free to exploit the conquest of the "North Pole" for all it was worth without fear that the hoax would be exposed. The Soviet dictator had already directed his ambassador in America to downplay the government's part in the "transpolar affair" as much as possible and stress NSR's role. The day was one of celebration for the Communist Party as it hailed one of the greatest feats in aviation. This was the first landing at the North Pole and the first time a permanent camp had been erected, or so the people were told. This was an opportunity to rejoice over the only significant aviation achievement up to this time.

Professor Schmidt, the pilots, and the rest of the northern explorers were attempting through any means, even if only symbolic, to portray a new Russia, an air-minded generation that ultimately would solve the crucial transportation and communication problems of the nation. This was at least the Russian government's dream, but it was only a dream. Stalin was now ready to capitalize on the "conquest" of the North Pole by parading the illustrious Dr. Schmidt and his aviation "heroes" through the central streets of Moscow. Ironically, these Russian "heroes of the sky" were riding in American Packard and Buick limousines. The Russians had not yet built a decent automobile or airplane, suggesting how far behind they were in transportation technology. Only the flowers decorating the cars in the parade were homegrown. The dictator perceived the purges as a step in the direction of providing a more efficient and productive nation, once the country's enemies were removed. Though a major share of the populace didn't believe his premise, their fears and apprehensions made them too reluctant to complain; they really began ignoring the political process. While Schmidt and his expeditionary party were being honored in Moscow the three "transpolar fliers" were en route to Washington D.C. for an appearance at the White House.

In America in the latter part of June, Ambassador Troyanovsky and his "polar heroes," Chkalov, Baidukov, and Beliakov, arrived in Washington, to meet with President Franklin D. Roosevelt. After an informal welcome by several Air Force officials, the group rested in preparation for a White House reception the next day, at which they were to visit briefly with President Roosevelt and Secretary of State Cordell Hull. Hull's department had handled most of the Russian requests for assistance during the "flight." After the White House reception, which had been merely a formality, the Russian entourage attended a luncheon sponsored by the Overseas Writer's Club and the National Press Club. The ambassador took this opportunity to minimize the significance of the upheaval and the economic woes now being experienced in the Soviet Union. He hurriedly tried explaining how many people were confused about what was taking place in his country, "The purge... is due to the government's will to protect the liberties of the people and to foster their creative spirit." It is apparent Troyanovsky used this emphasis on creativity as a lead-in to the "transpolar flight."

It was essential to avoid giving an impression that Stalin's office was the driving force behind "the flight." He said this achievement was "due in large part to the initiative of the airmen themselves." Troyanovsky noted how the flight was an example of the programs in the Soviet Union and the encouragement of individual achievements. "I want to say that we have not only made it possible for the creative impulse to function freely but also to defend the rights of our people for freedom against any internal or external enemies." In a few lofty and high-sounding statements Troyanovsky gave the illusion his countrymen were unshackled. The speech was broadcast by NBC's worldwide radio network.

At a later ceremony honoring the fliers, Ambassador Troyanovsky was somewhat jolted by the behavior of Chkalov. The pilot had misinterpreted a question by a young American, and curtly shot back an answer not appropriate for the inquiry. "How far do your American planes fly?" was his haughty reply. The ambassador wisely said that the fliers would not be answering any more questions during the reception. These must have been anxious moments for the emissary and he had a month to go before the unpredictable and ill-mannered Chkalov would be on his way home with the other two fliers. Furthermore, there were still two more flights supposedly on the agenda. What did the ambassador really know about the flight at this time? Was he aware of NSR's polar hoaxes? He should have known quite a bit if he was closely following the flight and all of its contradictions and strange happenings. He could have received an alert when the couriers brought the fliers' passports to the Russian consulate in San Francisco. Hopefully, the next set of fliers would not present the problems caused by the first trio. It is doubtful even Troyanovsky knew the precise time when the next "transpolar flight" was due to start. It seems the Soviet government and the NSR organization did not trust anyone with advance notices.

The next thing on the agenda for Chkalov, Baidukov, and Beliakov was to tour the many American aircraft and navigational factories. Troyanovsky's task was to nurture them through the following 30 days and hope no serious incidents occurred, particularly any adversity reflecting negatively on him and his government. Currently the USSR was facing all the problems it could stand.

In the Soviet Union, "rampant distrust and the venting of personal grudges were taking place within the Party itself," Denny of the *Times* wrote June 25, "...but for a decade now the revolution has been devouring its own. The men whom the regime has been destroying in the past year or two, who are now imprisoned or under a cloud, included the best brains and the loftiest characters of the Bolshevist Revolution." Denny went on to record that, "Apart from the younger, more thoughtless element, the prevalent reaction to these executions (eight generals) was not callous indifference but stunned incredulity. If these were guilty, then who could be trusted? For nearly every mind that might have disputed with Stalin for leadership has been destroyed by execution, exile or imprisonment. If Lenin was to return to life in this Red State that he founded, he would see few familiar faces."

Denny questioned, "whether this purge is directed at a counter-revolutionary movement on a large scale or is a frame-up to enable a little ruling clique to rid the country of outstanding personalities who might threaten it." He observed that "...this system as now administered has destroyed the last vestiges of personal initiative." Thousands of workers were leaving their jobs because of low wages and difficult working conditions. A general lack of interest and cooperation was complicated by fear of making mistakes that might then be attributed to a lack of loyalty. In one city alone 5,362 members of the Communist Party were removed; thousands more were ousted in the Ukraine and the eastern section of the country. It was estimated the Party's Central Committee membership had been reduced by 70 percent as the majority of high-ranking officers were being purged.

What kind of a man would it take to carry out such vengeance against his own people? In retrospect the dictator has been analyzed and studied by all kinds of psychologists and other students of the Stalin personality cult. He was basically described as a man with ingrained distrust for just about everyone and as having a great inferiority complex regarding the more educated and intellectual members of society. When dealing with the "intelligentsia" Stalin remained silent and reserved, and often stood back from the group, observing from a distance. He was not diplomatic, not subtle, not eloquent, nor charming, and had no ability as a writer or deep thinker. What did show through to those close to him was his arrogance, harshness, boundless vanity, jealousy, intolerance, belligerence, and cold, calculating manner. By the time the Communist Party discovered Stalin's true nature, he had become so powerful no one could bring him down. Fear and repression would rule Russia until he either died or was removed from office.

To make matters worse for Stalin at the time of these ongoing purges, Japan pressured his government into evacuating some islands in the Amur River, causing more domestic turmoil. Evidently Japan was not impressed with previous Russian threats of being able to bomb Tokyo and other industrial cities.

The American industrialists were also compounding the Russian dilemma. U.S. aircraft companies were going public in denouncing U.S. government pressure to allow the Soviet engineers and technicians into their factories. The situation had been bad enough before the Chkalov flight, but as the number of visiting Russians grew, the presidents of some large corporations lost patience with the Russians. "Get them out of here," they cried, "They're taking for nothing what it has cost us to acquire over the last 20 years." The American government quickly noted the Soviets were buying aircraft materials in such large quantities they should be permitted to oversee the making of these products. The Soviets, in their own defense, claimed their purchases from the U.S. were four times their total worldwide imports of all materials and foodstuffs. Still, according to the large U.S. companies, Soviet import business wasn't worth giving away such hard-earned technology. In some cases the Russians were willing to pay ten times the normal cost of the product just to be able to observe it being produced. It was no wonder such offers were being made. The Soviets had dramatically increased their gold production in the past few years to upgrade their own aviation industry as quickly as possible. American mining expert John D. Littlepage was instrumental in increasing Russia's gold output by almost 600 per cent by 1937. During this year of the terrible Stalin purges, Littlepage noted how engineers and other professional people were particularly subjected to extreme dangers. After about 10 years in Russia he quickly left and returned to America. Without the help of people such as Littlepage it is doubtful that the Soviets would ever have been able to make any significant improvements in aviation.

The secrets of technology in mass production systems were worth more in terms of military defense than the gold itself. Of course, Russia's stability in these tense times was in the interest of America and its allies. Russia without advanced technology was still considered a deterrent to Hitler's expansionist policies in Europe. It was better to supply the Soviets in a war against the Germans than to become militarily involved – assuming Russia was going to align with England and France if war did break out. There was no guarantee of that because a neutrality pact with the Nazis was still a viable option for the Russians. There was some risk in turning too much information over to the Soviets because it might end up being used against the allies. The neutrality pact under consideration called for a greater trade between Russia and Nazi Germany. It was up to American experts to monitor the situation and decide just how far to go in modernizing the Soviet Air Force. There is no question the U.S. government was aware of the very poor quality of airplanes being produced in the Soviet Union. The ANT-25 still parked on the airfield at Vancouver illustrated this point very well. The Russians had called this a "masterpiece of their aviation technique." If this was an example of their latest aviation capability, Roosevelt and the American government must realistically weigh what Russia could contribute as an ally and what harm she might pose by signing a neutrality pact with Germany.

The "polar flights" were one way to determine what the Russians had in aircraft engines and navigational devices. Major Burrows at Vancouver had already been ordered to go over the ANT with a fine-toothed comb, giving special attention to any navigational equipment on the plane. The U.S. Army Air Corps was especially interested in knowing if the Soviets had developed revolutionary guidance systems superior to those being produced in America. The investigation by the Air Corps, under the command of Brigadier General Henry H. "Hap" Arnold, was top secret. Major Burrows was cautioned not to divulge any of his findings to anyone except Air Corps executives. While the Russian engineer was en route to Vancouver, Major Burrows had plenty of time to make a complete report on the ANT. One observation he made was that all gyro instruments appeared to be copies of instruments manufactured by Sperry and Pioneer, an American company.

On July 6, the Russian engineer showed up at Pearson Field and began making arrangements to dismantle the Soviet plane. Vassily Berdnik, who claimed to have assembled the ANT in Moscow, said through an interpreter that he had checked all six tanks and found them dry. He was under the impression a Russian engineer had already drained them, not realizing Major Burrows had been in charge. Berdnik would not comment or express any opinion on how much or how little gas might have been in the craft. It must have appeared strange that he did not know the capacity of the fuel tanks of a plane he claimed to have assembled in Moscow prior to the flight. It was fairly certain "Engineer" Berdnik knew the Americans were puzzled about the fuel situation. He must now be careful not to let anyone see inside the wings where the gas tanks were located. It was Berdnik's desire to ship the aircraft intact and so the Great Northern Railroad Company was offered $1,500 cash to transport the ANT-25 to an eastern port for delivery to Russia via France. Railroad shipment of the ANT, with its wingspan of 112 feet, was rejected as physically impossible. Transporting it a short distance by truck to a Vancouver dock was also out of the question due to its size.

Berdnik was forced to remove two, 43-foot wing sections from the plane. This left a fuselage with 10-foot wing stubs. Each of the 43-foot wing sections housed three fuel tanks; the tanks were visible from an end view only and left to speculation the length and total volume. For some unexplained reason a Russian representative requested permission to bring in some California people to help with the aircraft dismantling. Because the Soviets had not gone through proper channels the request was turned down. The Air Corps notified Major Burrows there were plenty of qualified personnel in the Vancouver area who could help with this work. Berdnik decided to recruit a few civilian mechanics at Pearson to help him crate the gigantic wings for shipment. Loads of lumber were brought to construct shipping crates for the wings, tail, rudder, and other fragile equipment. Berdnik and his crew began packing these aircraft parts.

Some of the local mechanics watching the dismantling became quite amused at the antics of "Engineer" Berdnik. The men noticed he only had three crude tools in his tool box: a hammer, a wrench, and a screwdriver. The engineer kept calling for his *molot* (hammer), which hardly seemed to be the proper instrument to dismantle an airplane.

While Berdnik was going about his business in Vancouver, his comrades, Chkalov, Baidukov, and Beliakov were touring Wright Field in Dayton, Ohio. After being taken on the regular tour for foreign visitors, the fliers complained they had not seen anything of interest to them. To the surprise of the American Air Corps executive, Chkalov made a special request to see a particular gearbox used to calculate latitude and longitude. This device was still in an experimental stage, yet the Russians knew it was being developed. The fliers also asked to see the Norden bombsight and a side type engine super-charger, both on secret status. Naturally they were not allowed to see these projects. As a consequence, the three fliers and a few other aviation experts visiting from Russia showed visible discontent and left the airfield in a huff.

The officer in charge at Wright Field immediately contacted his superiors to explain the situation, noting they could expect a complaint from the Russian attaché who accompanied the touring airmen. Brigadier General A.W. Robbins, a division chief at Wright Field, had been alerted to the possibility the ANT-25 was equipped with a "gyro magnetic compass" which may be of special interest to the Air Corps, General Robbins indicated this in a letter, July 7, to Air Corps Chief "Hap" Arnold. During the Russian fliers visit to Wright, General Robbins tried to "draw out" information on the compass from the Russians but they informed him it was of "no interest whatsoever and they could not explain it." In this case, the Russian airmen were actually telling the truth. The "gyro magnetic compass" turned out to be a nonfunctional device with unconnected wires. Drawings of the compass had been prepared by Major Burrows and forwarded to General Arnold. Apparently American experts thought the Russians had invented a miraculous type of compass and they wanted to know more about it. General Robbins told General Arnold he was trying to "do a little horse trading" on this mystery compass in an apparent exchange of information the Russians were seeking. The U.S. report on the visit stated, "The whole time they were here they were very intense in asking many questions and trying to get information. . ." The trip to Wright Field was only one of the many facilities Soviet aviation personnel were going to tour during July. Only time would tell how the impatience of Chkalov would fare in these next visits.

CHAPTER 19

Gromov's Phantom Number Two

If the plans for the next "transpolar flight" were on schedule Chkalov, Baidukov, and Beliakov would soon be joined by a second trio of fliers – Mikhail Gromov, Andrew Yumashev, and Sergei Danilin, who were on their way to the secret archipelago camp. Unlike the first trio they had applied for visas on an earlier date and probably would be bringing them along.

Again there was to be no takeoff ceremony. American Ambassador Joseph Davies in Moscow must be distracted once more while NSR faked the start of the flight from Shelkova. Before Gromov and his companions departed for Alaska, they reportedly met with Ambassador Davies in order for him to say his goodbyes early. This arrangement was apparently made to discourage Davies' expectations of attending any takeoff ceremony at Shelkova Airport. Basically the same plan was to be followed for the second "transpolar flight" as was followed in the first one. According to Moscow dispatches, the formalities at Shelkova for the second "transpolar" takeoff were minimal. None of the Kremlin staff, including Stalin, was reported present. In fact Professor Schmidt and a "few others" were reportedly the only witnesses at the airport for the alleged July 12 takeoff at 12:22 a.m. Greenwich time (3:22 a.m. Moscow time). This was an hour earlier than the June event; although press reports didn't agree on the precise "takeoff" time.

Again there were no neutral observers, no foreign news media identified, no American embassy officials named, and obviously no filming at this conveniently arranged takeoff, in almost total darkness. And like the first "flight" the Americans would not be told of the "takeoff" until a full day had passed. The destination of this flight was rumored to be Chicago, Illinois. The Soviets had no intentions of telling the American government of their destination and confused the situation by requesting weather reports ranging from the Eastern Seaboard to weather ships in the Pacific Ocean and hundreds of cities in between. The Russians had never planned to fly to Chicago or any eastern location; this was another diversionary tactic to get the slow-flying ANT-25 into the United States without being seen.

Because of the many errors, omissions, miscalculations, and other problems encountered during the Chkalov event it was decided a minimal amount of information would be released on the second hoax flight. Dr. Schmidt would personally supervise the radio reports on the mythical plane's position. The Americans had been told of two more "transpolar flights" being planned for the month of July. Since U.S. newspapers had carried stories of Levanevsky's rumored arrest on June 26, the American public did not know whether this famous flier would be attempting a "polar crossing." However, according to the government's secret files, there was no change in the status of the proposed third flight. As far as the U.S. State Department was concerned, Levanevsky was still going to pilot the second flight while Stalin was preparing to substitute other fliers in this second hoax. In selecting the aviators for the second flight the Kremlin reached into its list of Air Force pilots. Stalin apparently felt secure enough with the progress and acceptance of the first hoax flight to approve a plan to send the second ANT-25 into the United States from Alaska. Stalin was undoubtedly encouraged by the gracious cooperation of the American government and its people.

Also, because of the acceptance of the first "transpolar flight," the dictator could risk using some of his Air Force fliers on the second hoax attempt. One of the new pilots being considered had a familiar name, Colonel Mikhail Gromov, the regular pilot of the ill-fated *Maxim Gorky* which crashed in May of 1935. Gromov was scheduled to fly the huge *Gorky* on this fateful day but reportedly suffered from a stomach ailment and missed the flight. The selection of Colonel Gromov as chief pilot of the second polar hoax possibly was connected to his arctic flying in the early 1930s. Presently he held the rank of colonel in the Red Air Force. Major Andrew Yumashev and Captain Sergei Danilin were lower grade officers in the Air Force. There is no question these fliers would make a better impression than Chkalov and his crew. Besides being of military rank, they were all much more socially polished and able to confer with aviation experts on a more professional basis.

Gromov, the 38-year-old son of a doctor, was a professor of aviation and an accomplished pilot. He, like the members of the first crew, had been decorated for a reported long-distance "closed-circuit" (domestic) 7,500-mile nonstop air journey, supposedly completed in 75 hours.

The type of aircraft was never identified by the Russians but they said the flight occurred in 1934. It is doubtful Gromov flew an ANT-25 because Tupolev did not renovate this craft until late 1934. If he claimed this record in an ANT-3 or ANT-9, the airplanes he had been flying on his previous so-called record flights, this 7,500-mile journey would have been impossible to complete in 75 hours. The maximum speed of the vintage ANT-3, according to *Jane's Encyclopedia of Aviation*, was only 106 mph with a range limited to about 450 miles. The ANT-9 was a pre-1930 model with no appreciable increase in speed and range, casting serious doubts on all Gromov's record flight claims. His previous alleged flight records occurred in 1926, in an ANT-3, 4,300 miles, 34 hours; and 1929, ANT-9, 5,400 miles, no time listed. The 1934 "flight" won Gromov the "Hero of the Soviet Union" medal. The Soviet propaganda machine manufactured the 1934 7,500-mile nonstop flight to build up Gromov's credentials to be used later in the transpolar hoaxes.

The Soviets referred to Gromov's plane as an RD-25-1, commonly known as ANT-25, and claimed it could carry about 2,500 gallons of fuel, giving it a range of 4,350 miles. Russian records show they installed a "geared" engine that increased the range to 6,200 miles. Somehow they said a "smoother exterior surface was added, upping its nonstop capability to 7,500 miles. After polishing the wing surface, the range was increased to 8,000 miles, they claimed.

Andrew Yumashev, Gromov's copilot in the 1934 "flight," and serving in a similar capacity for this "transpolar excursion," had one credential making his selection believable. He was a high-altitude test pilot, a talent needed according to Chkalov, to escape "arctic and polar storms" occurring upwards of 19,000 feet. (Weather scientists and commercial airlines dispute these high arctic and polar storms.) Yumashev's selection, like Gromov's, was based on his social adaptability, his general technical knowledge of aviation, and his military background. His social refinement was augmented by a flair for painting and ballroom dancing. Yumashev, now a major in the Red Air Force, was sure to be an asset during the projected reception in America. He also had a sister living in the San Francisco area.

The navigator was a questionable choice for this extremely sensitive project. His name was given as Sergei Danilin but a 1935 photograph in the *New York Times* identified this flier as none other than Nikolai Juroff, who supposedly died in the *Maxim Gorky* crash in 1935. Did Juroff actually live through this aerial catastrophe and assume the name of Danilin? Had Stalin allowed Juroff to join the "walking dead?" If so he had to change his flying credentials too, from pilot to navigator. Did Gromov and Danilin (Juroff) owe something to the dictator? Some bizarre story was hidden behind the crash of the *Gorky*. What really happened? "Danilin" also served with Gromov on his 1934 "flight." This is interesting because if he was Danilin he didn't become Juroff until May of 1935.

On July 12 the suspense of the second "transpolar flight" ended. Front page headlines in bold type told the story: "THREE RUSSIANS CROSS THE NORTH POLE IN STORM." As in the first "transpolar flight" the announcement was delayed for more than one day. Although the flight wasn't for real, Russia's northern weather stations were again doing a poor job of advising the invisible fliers as to when it was safe to fly. For the first time the photographs of the three fliers appeared in American newspapers. Sure enough there was Danilin, alias Juroff, in an identical photograph of the one printed in 1935. Would anyone recognize the ex-*Gorky* pilot?

It was reported that Mikhail Gromov and his two-man crew crossed the pole after 24 hours in the air, besting the other flight by three hours. This first report was said to have been intercepted by the U.S. Signal Corps Station at Seattle on a relay from Anadyr, Siberia. Coincidentally, Seattle is where Russian radio agent Vartanian was headquartered. It is not surprising Vartanian was the first to get this message, considering he had orchestrated most of the guarded communications in the first hoax flight.

It is clear, judging by these initial bulletins, that there were not the mistakes in the plane position reports which had plagued the first "attempt." Who, of all people, was said to be at the helm in Moscow? None other than Professor Otto Schmidt. According to the official news releases, Schmidt was now supervising the Gromov "transpolar" attempt to reach America. In describing the scene at Shelkova airfield, if the Moscow information is to be believed, Dr. Schmidt was the ranking official present at the airfield to bid the fliers goodbye. There was no mention of crowds, nor any indication government officials were present. Typically, the Russians wanted to "keep everything quiet on the Eastern Front until the hoax was well underway on the Western Front." The main strategy was aimed at keeping everyone off guard while the

ANT-25 crew was preparing to "rendezvous" with the second phantom ANT, the same act followed in the first hoax flight. News releases from Moscow said Gromov had been summoned to the Kremlin June 10 and was "shown into a room where sat Joseph Stalin, Vyachesiaff M. Molotoff (Molotov), chairman of the Council of People's Commissars; Defense Commissar Klementy E. Voroshiloff and other party and government leaders."

Premier Molotov asked with a smile, "Well, what is it you want? Gromov answered, "We have only one request. . . . Permit us to fly from Moscow to America over the North Pole." The *New York Times* (July 13, 1937) article goes on to say how Stalin asked "detailed questions," such as "how far did he intend to fly?" and whether "his plane was ready for it." After hearing Gromov's explanation, the news article said Stalin granted permission after discussing the subject with others present. Always cautious, the dictator again put the fliers on record as being responsible for the hoax flight. By getting official recommendations from his top staff, Stalin also made them a part of another hoax.

It apparently did not seem odd to launch a second hazardous leap over the pole without reviewing in depth the problems encountered by the first crew. This recklessness is difficult to fathom when Chkalov and his crew had told the world of the dangers they faced in the first "polar crossing," including icing of wings, cyclonic storms, radio transmission and receiving difficulties, excessive oxygen demands, frozen radiator, fuel pump problems, visibility limitations, and other factors and information valuable to protect the fliers. There was a simple reason why the Soviets threw caution to the wind; they weren't worried about a mythical plane and three invisible aviators. Though there was no "takeoff ceremony," news articles continued to publish some information describing the final moments of the "takeoff." According to these bulletins, the ANT crew took off knowing the weather near the pole was bad. Other messages emanating from the Russian capital said atmospheric conditions being reported by their "northern stations" were favorable. Professor Schmidt said precautionary measures had been taken to deal with icing. It is apparent, judging from his answer, that questions had been asked as to why the flight began in the face of polar storms.

Perhaps Schmidt did not realize this second ANT was also without wing de-icing equipment when he claimed precautions had been taken to deal with icing problems. The NSR chief went on to tell about the "takeoff" from Shelkova. He related how the ANT had become airborne with about 200 yards to spare, a statement later contradicted by Gromov. That was about all the information the world's press corps would get, with one additional "disclosure" of the "takeoff" being witnessed by "foreign correspondents watching." Those correspondents were never identified. Another "historic flight" had just been launched without the presence of American Ambassador Davies.

However, in the course of the illusionary journey from Moscow to the north of Banks Land, a distance of some 3,300 miles and about 27 hours into the mythical flight, it appeared ANT Number 2 was manufacturing more gas in flight than ANT Number 1. This latest report originated from NSR in Moscow where all plane positions and other messages were supposedly received from the plane. There was no evidence that any Canadian or American station had communicated directly with the plane. Beliakov on the first "flight" had reported the fuel consumption near Queen Charlotte was 10,463 liters (2,700 gallons), 700 more gallons than they said was taken aboard at takeoff. According to Beliakov's figures the plane had already consumed about 2,700 gallons of fuel with 500 miles more to travel to Vancouver, Washington.

It is evident this serious contradiction on the part of the navigator was relayed by Vartanian from his Seattle office, warning Professor Schmidt about the first flight crew claiming excessive fuel consumption. Vartanian's warning was apparently not fully understood by the NSR chief or his radio operators. This apparent misconception resulted in an even sillier predicament. Moscow, pretending to relay a message from the plane north of Banks Land, said the fliers still had 10,589 liters (2,750 gallons) of fuel left. Besides manufacturing extra fuel while in flight, this ANT was not burning any fuel. The Russians said Gromov's ANT took off with 2,500 gallons of fuel, and after 3,300 miles an extra 250 gallons somehow got on board. If this rate should continue, ANT No. 2 should show a "profit" of 500 gallons by the time it reached its U.S. destination. Unfortunately for the Russians, this preposterous fuel data reached the newspapers and was now being viewed by millions of people. But as luck would have it, no one, including the news media, bothered to analyze the fuel situation and thus the second Soviet hoax was preserved. The Russians could only hope the discrepancy went undetected while phantom ANT No. 2 plied its mythical route over the wilds of British Columbia, with Mr. Vartanian relaying the details of the epic journey to the anxious American audience.

Vartanian's messages contained episodes of difficulties supposedly encountered by the fliers of ANT No. 2, fighting their way through two cyclones and avoiding icing conditions by high-altitude flying. During these first reports, the second phantom was recorded traveling at believable speeds of 100 mph, increasing to 120 mph on the American side. One incident probably caused Vartanian some concern. The plane supposedly radioed from northern British Columbia (via Moscow) giving a latitude of 55 degrees north and a longitude of 120 degrees west. "I don't receive you, everything all right," Moscow quoted the fliers as reporting. American weather stations were aware of showers blanketing these regions which, of course, the fliers failed to mention. This is understandable considering the "fliers" were 500 miles away in the southeast Alaskan camp, awaiting their turn at the helm of a real plane. But in the meantime the "invisible aviators" were reporting trouble with their radio, the same ploy used by Chkalov to explain why they had not communicated for much of their "flight."

Those who were orchestrating this part of the master plan had apparently simplified Gromov's itinerary. The mythical route was not going to pass over Sitka this time around. Instead Gromov, Yumashev, and Danilin (Juroff) would depart at the appointed hour from their Alaskan camp, staying far offshore and high above the Pacific Ocean on a southern course for California. In following this course the fliers would be gambling against being seen while Moscow continued to plot the make-believe airplane on a route following the 120-degree meridian, about 450 miles inland of western Canada. From the eastern British Columbia border the 120th meridian runs directly toward San Francisco. Chief pilot Gromov was planning to hide his ANT in the prevailing cloud cover until taking advantage of darkness to fly inland to intercept the mythical path of the phantom ANT. Again, it was very important to create this diversion to hide the true speed of the ANT-25, lest someone were to make a quick calculation and uncover the hoax.

Following the report from Banks Land at 12:37 a.m. PST, concerning the fuel situation, five additional messages from the plane were also reportedly relayed by Moscow. These alleged radio messages were punctuated with unbelievable plane position reports, including excessive speeds and unusual hours of complete silence. In fact, other than one disputed direct radio message the Canadians said they intercepted, all reports were received by radio agent Vartanian in Seattle, on a Moscow relay system. Another glaring "speeding infraction" had the mythical ANT traveling at a preposterous 225 mph between the northern border of British Columbia and a point 100 miles south of Fort St.

John, a distance of 300 miles covered in one hour and twenty minutes. An earlier position report was also interesting because it indicated the ANT was then traveling at a near crawling speed of 70 mph (close to the aircraft's stalling speed), between Novaya Zemlya and 600 miles from the Russian side of the North Pole. The 70 mph average speed had to be explained somehow. The loss of time could be accounted for by a roundabout course but not by any serious weather problems faced during this part of the "flight."

This "transpolar flight" was characterized by the lack of information supplied to American and Canadian signal stations. In addition to a radio blackout the first 24 hours of the "flight," there were several long intervals later when nothing was heard. Far off in the nation's Capitol the lights were burning overtime and top officials of the U.S. Weather Bureau were awakened in their homes by Russian embassy officials.

Shortly after midnight Tuesday an "urgent" telephone call was received by Willis R. Gregg, chief of the United States Weather Bureau, from Constantine Oumansky, a Russian embassy official. Mr. Oumansky made the following appeal: "Please wire urgently survey synoptical processes of regions of Mexico and California, as well as forecast of weather on the line San Francisco, Mesatlan, Mexico City."

This sudden request may have appeared strange to the sleepy-eyed officials but yet it was another piece of the continuing master plan saga. This information would be needed later by Gromov in order to pad extra miles onto the "transpolar flight." By familiarizing himself with climatic conditions in lower California and Mexico, Gromov and crew could use this current information to convince the public they had flown over those territories. Despite all the advanced communication planning for the first and second "transpolar flights," the Russian embassy apparently felt it necessary to contact Chief Gregg personally. There was already an elaborate and intricate ongoing communication network supplying weather and other data to Moscow, and presumably to the fliers. Again, the Russians had their reasons to bypass the lower echelon and go directly to the "top" for this weather information.

The Russians did not want to reveal the purpose for weather information or who was requesting it. A memo dated July 13, apparently prepared for Chief Gregg, quoted Mr. Oumansky as appealing for confidentiality on the previous request. When told by Chief Gregg the U.S. Weather Bureau had no means of getting these reports unless the Mexican Meteorological Service was asked for them, "he (Oumansky) quickly informed me and requested if we asked the Mexican government for these reports that we should not mention to what use they would be put to. . ." Chief Gregg immediately directed his officials to try and obtain the San Diego and Mexican weather data and contact Mr. Oumansky at the embassy. When contacted by telephone at 12:50 a.m., Mr. Oumansky also requested the "latest reports and forecasts from San Diego to El Paso to San Antonio" (Texas), a 1,500-mile swath. The weather data was assembled and given directly to Mr. Oumansky before 1:35 a.m. and he said it was ready for "immediate transmission to Moscow," where it would be relayed to the fliers. Why Moscow? All weather data and communications for the "transpolar flight" were being handled by the U.S. Signal Corps and Weather Bureau at Seattle, where the Russian radio agent Vartanian was on around-the-clock duty with American technicians and supervisors.

Meanwhile the real ANT-25 in Alaska had taken off about one hour before the mythical plane reportedly reached Fort St. John on the 120th meridian; approximately 10:30 a.m. pilot Gromov took a southwest heading over the sea and circumvented the west coast of Queen Charlotte Island, following the same route Chkalov flew. Gromov did not plan to make any radio contacts with Alaskan or American mainland stations, a lesson he learned from the Chkalov "flight." While the radio remained mysteriously silent from the mythical and real ANT, people became increasingly concerned for the safety of the fliers. During this silent interlude and generally throughout the first 50 hours of the "transpolar flight," American weather bureaus and signal stations were "breaking" the radio silence by constantly transmitting climatic conditions in the "path" of the Russian plane, all at the request of the Soviet government. This assistance was never recognized or even used, merely serving their diversionary tactics. Despite lack of communication from the plane, the Russian Consulate in San Francisco appeared unperturbed and handled inquiries in a routine and unemotional manner. Did they know something not being shared with the anxious populace?

As the hours dragged by there was one person especially worried about the continuous silence from the Russian ship. Andrew Yumashev's sister Tamara Yumashev Mamay lived in the Bay Area. She had waited anxiously and under great stress throughout the night at the Oakland Airport yet all during this time there were no reports from the fliers. Tamara, in the company of her aunt and uncle, was beside herself waiting for the brother she had not seen in 20 years. Searching the skies for a glimpse of the plane she reminisced about the days when she last saw her fair-haired, blue-eyed sibling in Russia during the devastating days of World War I. The low ceiling over the airport would dim any view of the airplane but she reacted wishfully at every sound of a motor overhead. Each motor sound proved not to be the right one and a hopeless feeling swept over her. Sobbing aloud, the young woman turned often to her aunt for some comfort. From reports received previously, she had worried her brother and the other two airmen through storms and cyclones, having no idea the plane's silence was all part of the plan.

Tamara had treasured every message from the "plane" reporting the fliers were safe. The cruel hoax was temporarily lifted for Tamara when Moscow radio said the plane had weathered nature's worst conditions and finally reached British Columbia. This information gave her a chance to breathe a great sigh of relief. Then the dreaded silence fell again. Thoughts of airplane crashes and death refused to be brushed away. Hours passed as the distraught young woman paced the airfield, often stopping people to ask if they had heard any news. The thousands of excited welcomers were unaware of Tamara's personal stake in the flight. The lights of the field had been turned on for hours. Earlier, 10,000 people had gathered for the historic landing scheduled at the Oakland airdrome, but these numbers were gradually diminishing.

Andrew Yumashev also must have been thinking of his sister, but it was not possible for him to let her know he was all right. The success of the entire master plan depended on the airmen's silence and on hiding the real ANT in the overcast while flying south over the ocean. It wouldn't be long before darkness fell, affording them an opportunity to sneak inland, intercept the mythical ANT on the 120th meridian and continue to California. There was a slight gamble in taking this aerial path because commercial airlines and general aviation frequented this airway and might spot the Russian plane. Decision time was coming up within a half hour; the sun had dropped below the ocean horizon and dusk was upon them. They would wait a short time until nightfall covered their entrance over the populated beaches and inland towns. Hoping ships at sea had not been able to identify the "transpolar plane," Gromov, Yumashev, and Danilin bid farewell to their ocean "sanctuary" and banked southeast toward the darkened Oregon shoreline at about 9:35 p.m. PST, maintaining tight radio silence.

Eventually the fliers would reach the 120th meridian and then go due south to some destination in California. When the ANT was over Roseburg, 400 miles north of San Francisco and 200 miles south of Portland, luck ran out. By chance a commercial airliner crew on a flight from San Francisco to Portland spotted the wide-wing monoplane at 10:25 p.m. PST Tuesday and reported this sighting. The United Air Line fliers said they recognized the plane from previous news photos. The Associated Press issued a bulletin on this sighting that failed to spark any curiosity or trigger a line of questioning by the news media, even though the "transpolar flight" was being covered closely by every major and minor newspaper and radio station, including the prestigious *New York Times*. Either the Russians didn't see the airliner or thought it was now too dark for the ANT to be properly identified. Being spotted in this location could prove disastrous to the credibility of the Russian claims, because now someone could compute the speed of the plane by comparing the last latitude report with the Roseburg sighting. The Americans had been told the Russian plane had arrived at latitude 55 degrees north at 11:20 a.m. PST, Tuesday. Roseburg is situated near latitude 43 degrees north, which is about 800 miles from latitude 55 degrees, just south of Fort St. John in Alberta, Canada. According to these figures the ANT-25, enjoying tailwinds, had only averaged 88 mph between Fort St. John and Roseburg, contrary to the fliers claim of 120 mph. The fliers had no intention of acknowledging the Roseburg location at 10:25 p.m. because of the radical difference in average speed.

The Russians had recently upped the ANT-25s range to 8,000 miles, forcing the Soviet aviators to convince the world of this claim, one way or the other. Approaching midnight, the fliers had actually been in the air a total 13.5 hours since their takeoff in the archipelago. Using the moonlit Coast Range as their guide they continued their odyssey. It had been many hours since they began receiving the additional weather synoptics (temperatures, barometer readings, humidity, wind readings at various altitudes, visibility, and the ongoing forecasts from locations in San Diego, Mexico, and Texas). There was no way the Soviets could fly this plane to Mexico, much less Texas and dozens of midwestern and eastern cities, even though they had requested weather information from those areas; they didn't have sufficient fuel. When the ANT crossed into California at about 11:40 p.m. it only had about 220 gallons of gasoline or about nine hours of flying time left.

Gromov was attemping to demonstrate the long range of the aircraft in order to help Stalin send a message warning their country's adversaries of the plane's range and its high altitude capabilities to bomb distant enemies of Russia. The only way to carry out this threat was to stage an exceptionally long, nonstop aerial journey over the pole and hope to win U.S. support by linking Moscow with America. If they had flown the entire transpolar route the total distance into Southern California would have been about 6,000 miles. The Soviet pilot hoped to increase this figure to 7,000 miles claiming a side trip into Mexico. Chkalov had done a little "padding" in the first "transpolar flight" by claiming their ANT-25 had reached Eugene, Oregon before circling and returning to Vancouver, Washington. Adding extra miles to the already flawed air journey was probably on the fliers' minds while they winged their way deeper into California, passing well to the east of the San Francisco-Oakland area where Tamara maintained her long vigil.

While Americans slept the ANT plugged along with the lights of Fresno to their right and off to the left the silhouetted melting snowcap of the 14,495-foot Mt. Whitney, the highest peak in mainland United States. It was now about 2:30 a.m. Wednesday, July 14. They would land somewhere within the next four to six hours, based on a fuel supply that should carry them through the dark hours and into the early dawn. This would give the fliers an adequate opportunity to seek out a suitable place to bring the big gliderlike monoplane to earth. The ANT droned on steadily, turning southeast along the winding Coastal Range.

These must have been anxious moments for Gromov, Yumashev, and Danilin. There were three more hours of gas at this point when the first light of dawn began lifting the shadows of night from this beautiful world of valleys. There had been no opportunity to see much of the American countryside up until this time. Only water was traversed during the jaunt down from the archipelago; then at dusk they had ducked into the American mainland en route to Roseburg. This was the first time the green earth had come into their view. It provided a quiet time for the fliers to gather themselves together emotionally.

Soon it would all be over. How would they be received? As well as Chkalov, Baidukov, and Beliakov, they must have hoped. The sun was now above the horizon basking the entire countryside. March Field at Riverside was not far away; this was the landmark they had been waiting to see. It was a military airfield, one of several situated along the route. All of the Soviet fliers who had come into the United States were well versed on the major Pacific Coast cities and airfields, especially the military facilities. Gromov, as Chkalov before him, knew the dangers of landing at civilian airports. If each souvenir hunter tore off just a small piece of the wing fabric, it would be enough to disclose the actual size of the gas tanks. March Field was much larger and busier than Pearson at Vancouver, and in addition there was considerably more brass and sophistication at this California facility. This could work for or against them. More brass or authority might give the fliers and the ANT more protection; but more sophistication or experience among the American aviation personnel could prompt suspicion and subsequent detection of the Russian hoax. There was some consolation in knowing the American government had not raised any issues over the first flight, in spite of the many contradictory and outlandish claims made. Based on the first "transpolar flight" and the cooperation afforded by the military and other agencies, there was no reason to think the American government was going to discredit this flight. It might all depend on how well the fliers conduct themselves while in the country.

The time was now about 6 a.m. PST, Wednesday. March Field was very close, probably to the left of the airship. Gromov and his crew soon spotted the airfield, located about 70 miles east of Los Angeles; after viewing its large complex of buildings they decided to pass it by and look for a suitable landing site in the rural sector. Soviet broadcasts had succeeded in convincing West Coast signal stations the Russian plane would land in Oakland; the diversion worked again. The strategy was to ditch the plane quickly at an unpopulated location. The chief pilot probably wished for a small military field more on the order of the Vancouver facility, something a little less intimidating. The fliers conferred on the landing field choice while entering the San Jacinto Valley, marked by the 10,000-foot San Jacinto Peak.

Circling an area about 25 miles southeast of March Field, Colonel Gromov began a slow glide toward a large field near the tiny farming community of San Jacinto while Major Yumashev hand-cranked the wide landing gear into position. Captain Danilin aided the two pilots in selecting the safest field to set the big ANT down. Easing back on the throttle Colonel Gromov reached over and switched on the carburetion heat, lowering the flaps when the plane was in its final approach, slowing to about 30 mph. The long flaps on the wide-wing aircraft allowed Gromov to glide slowly to a landing without stalling the heavy ship. The pastoral field was coming up fast now and Colonel Gromov pulled back on the controls and let the ship settle down on terra firma, bouncing along the rough cow pasture. The big ship rolled across the field slowing with each turn of its big double wheels. The flight was finished! There the fliers sat, alone in a beautiful but strange land.

Gromov and his two companions had succeeded in landing without attracting immediate attention, but San Jacinto and the nearby hamlet of Hemet would soon buzz with excitement. The first person to reach the plane was Walter Harvey, a 30-year-old rancher from San Jacinto who had been working nearby. Harvey jumped into his car and headed directly to the plane, stopping within a safe distance of the fliers who were standing next to the parked ANT-25. The first thing Mr. Harvey noticed was gasoline leaking from the left wing and onto the fuselage. The fliers greeted the excited rancher enthusiastically but he couldn't understand what they were saying. Gromov pointed to the sky and the ground, apparently trying to explain why they landed at this location. Meanwhile another alert farmer notified county authorities who in turn summoned officers at March Field, about 25 miles northwest of the cow pasture. The Russian flight commander handed Mr. Harvey a slip of paper. Written in English were the words, "Please wire Moscow." Then Major Yumashev produced a map and asked the rancher to point out their location.

The fliers appeared anxious to display what Mr. Harvey thought were passports. In the first "transpolar flight," Chkalov and his two flying comrades did not have any passports when they landed in Vancouver. Gromov and his associates had passports issued July 3, ten days prior to Moscow's announcement of their "flight." If they actually had them on their person when they landed in San Jacinto then they had had about 10 days to get to the archipelago and take the second ANT-25 to America. Gromov may have shown some documents to make a public display of the fact that they carried some official-looking papers. The news media apparently thought the Russians had passports but Mr. Harvey said the documents shown him were unintelligible. Their visas would have been issued by the United States embassy in Moscow, written in English. Did this mean that Gromov and crew also arrived in the U.S. without visas? There is some evidence of this because two more couriers had been dispatched from Moscow within the last week. United States visas identified the couriers as Ian Fridberg-Merkaln and Nikolai Keremetski.

Although the aviators had grown considerable beards, Mr. Harvey later recalled his first impression upon seeing the fliers; they didn't appear exhausted. Ironically, a similar observation was made by George Kozmetsky, the soldier-interpreter in Vancouver, who was the first to meet the fliers Chkalov, Baidukov, and Beliakov. The Soviets threw their arms around Harvey and pounded him enthusiastically on the back, producing cards with the English words, "Bath. Eat. Sleep." Pilot Levanevsky supposedly had helped Gromov with a smattering of handy English words. Curiously enough Gromov said he had been planning a "transpolar trip" to America since 1934, yet he hadn't learned much of the language in advance.

There was a very important reason for sending non-English-speaking aviators to the United States. The Russians wanted to place the bilingual Vartanian inside the U.S. Signal Corps station in Seattle to translate all communications concerning the hoax flights. If the Soviets sent bilingual fliers they wouldn't have any excuse for Vartanian's presence at the central communication hub in Seattle. Sigmund Levanevsky could communicate in English and had traveled extensively in the United States on several occasions. Perhaps this was one of the reasons why Levanevsky was passed by twice in the polar hoaxes despite Soviet announcements he would be the first to utilize the "North Pole Route to America."

Spectators noticed that Yumashev was wearing a heavy leather coat but Gromov and Danilin were lightly dressed, a stark contrast to the polar clothing worn by Chkalov and company on the first "transpolar flight." Henry Sandy, a Hemet city employee and one of the early arrivals, was the first person to communicate with the fliers. Using a common language of German, he was able to speak with Yumashev. The Soviet aviators gave autographs to the welcomers and handed out canned foods and other items as souvenirs. Within 45 minutes of the Russian's landing, American Air Corps Major V.H. Strahm arrived at the cow pasture in a small two-passenger military aircraft from March Field after having dispersed a company of soldiers to guard the Russian plane. The arrival of the first military contingent was none too soon because within 15 minutes thousands of curious spectators began streaming onto the field. The cow pasture was owned by a family named Smith; demonstrating the free enterprise system, a toll charge of 25 cents was collected to enter their property. Not heeding this enterprise, hundreds swarmed over the fences and avoided the toll. In this remote region, one would think it would take longer for crowds to gather, but 4,000 had managed to get there within the first hour. Evidently word traveled fast in these close communities.

Major Strahm assumed control of the situation in the cow pasture and arranged to take the aviators to March Field. The major apparently was in a great hurry to get the Russians to the military complex; instead of waiting for army transportaton he commandeered a civilian's auto. The civilian was B.H. Coy of nearby Hemet, the same man who had alerted the authorities of the unexpected arrival of the Russian plane.

In early questioning, Gromov explained how they had flown the plane beyond March Field, but then continued southward. The Soviet pilot claimed he flew to Los Angeles and circled the city for awhile before running into fog. From there, he said they flew about 130 miles to San Diego, hovering over this area for two or three hours while contemplating a landing. Gromov told March Field officers the visibility over San Diego prevented any possibility of ending the flight at that point; subsequently the fliers chose to cross the border into Mexico and according to their description of the land it was assumed the Russian plane had gone as far as Agua Caliente, meaning "hot water." Hopefully this would not prove to be a bad omen for these displaced fliers. It is curious how the Soviets could claim they went into Mexico when the entire coastal area was fogged in, and since they said they didn't have any maps, how did they know where they had been? Also, going into the Mexican air space for any intention was strange without prior permission. Gromov continued to add mileage onto the flight while the Air Force officials listened intently. The chief pilot tried to explain why they did not want to land in Mexico, saying they preferred to end their air journey on U.S. soil. According to Gromov, the weather over Los Angeles and San Diego was overcast and foggy, forcing them to return to March Field. When Gromov was asked why he had come down in a cow pasture instead of using the concrete landing strip at March, he replied they could not relocate the field on the way back; since the plane was almost out of gas an emergency landing was necessary.

The question is, would the Russian airman have added on those exessive miles, if he had known the ANT was spotted over Roseburg, Oregon at 10:25 the previous night? Gromov had just magnified his flight time by more than five hours and increased the ANT's average speed to 170 mph going to Roseburg, San Jacinto, Los Angeles, San Diego, and on a Mexican "side trip." The sighting at Roseburg by the crew of a commercial airliner was devastating to the mileage claim of the Soviet spokesman. The pilot may not have been aware of the problem because the *New York Times*, the only major newspaper to report the Roseburg sighting, had not hit the streets yet. Perhaps Gromov knew there was a chance they had been seen; but the need to rack up great mileage had greater priority. If challenged on this sighting they would merely have to issue denials. Asked why they had not given their position after the plane reached Canada, Gromov replied, "We did not give our position or report on our trip down the North American coast because it was of no interest to us what people thought. We knew we

were achieving our objective and getting to where we wanted to go."
This pompous answer is an indication the American questions were
beginning to wear on Gromov.

Gromov's manner of speaking must have seemed terribly reckless,
especially after his country had requested the U.S. government to set
up an extensive radio and weather network to assist the fliers. Now here
was their chief pilot and spokesman saying, in effect, that this elaborate
and costly system was not needed. The officials at March Field were not
trying to pry, but only asking reasonable questions expected on such a
"flight." However, Gromov had to come up with an answer to account
for the radio silence they had purposely invoked in order to sneak along
their coastal flight route into California.

Did Gromov think how Tamara, Yumashev's sister, was agonizing
over the radio silence? What if the plane developed problems and was
forced down or crashed, how could emergency agencies locate the
aircraft? The only real gamble for the Soviet fliers, of course, was the
short run from Alaska; and even then they apparently were confident
the flotation equipment on the aircraft would keep them afloat in case
they were forced down at sea.

The United States government followed these "transpolar flights"
with keen interest, yet no high official raised any questions about their
authenticity despite innumerable discrepancies and strange happenings. It was obvious the American government, including the departments of War and State and other key agencies within the Executive
Branch, gave the Russian government total cooperation and assistance
in the "transpolar flights." The U.S. also honored Soviet requests to
keep all information and correspondence confidential. Although the
Soviet requests didn't appear to be warranted, the U.S. stamped all the
file material "Secret." Why were these files made secret? The answers
are buried deep in secret files, some of which have since been purged
clean. One July 7 memorandum sent to Major General Oscar Westover,
deputy chief of the Army Air Corps, arouses curiosity over possible
missing information on the "transpolar flights" and Russian "stations"
in the Franz Josef group. However, a search for the documents enclosed
with the July 7 memo to General Westover was to no avail. It is not
known who wrote the memo to General Westover; all it said was:
"knowing your interest, I enclose bits of fairly precise information
about the Soviet transpolar flight and about their stations in the Franz
Josef group." This "fairly precise information" is missing from the

government's archives; in fact there is no reference to the Russian stations in the Franz Josef group available.

Did the United States government consider the military significance of the alleged Russian polar stations and other northern facilities in the Franz Josef Archipelago? The U.S. was worried about how Russia would align herself in the event of war in Europe and would do almost anything to woo the Russians into the allied camp. The total cooperation by the Executive Branch in helping the Soviets in their transpolar exploits underscored this. Although American aeronautical experts and military intelligence appeared to know the weakness of Russian aviation, they displayed unusual curiosity about the navigational devices they thought were on board the ANT-25s. There were good reasons to believe that top government officials had doubts about the Russian transpolar flights, but publicly the highest authorities praised the Russian achievements as if they were authentic. Strangely enough, the U.S. government never asked the Russians for proof or any documented evidence to verify the "flights" and the so-called polar stations. Russians were never asked to identify the independent observers monitoring the takeoffs. Also, there were no requests for films showing they traversed the pole.

Following the U.S. government's example of accepting claims without verification, the news media and general public also jumped on the band wagon and hailed the Soviet aerial feats and polar explorations without raising questions. Military intelligence directed the Army Air Corps to closely monitor and inspect all navigational equipment on the two ANT-25s. If the Russians were really establishing these northern stations and maintaining them year-round, especially in the "magnetic jungle areas" within the Arctic Circle, they would have needed highly sophisticated and advanced navigational equipment and technology to overcome the severity of the elements and the visibility problems in that part of the world.

The lower echelon (the troops) did ask some fairly penetrating questions but the Russian fliers either brushed them aside with curt answers or gave misleading and outrageous responses – and got away with it. When asked why they didn't have any de-icing equipment on the wings, the fliers said, "in the flight and in making plans for the flight, they did not fly or contemplate flying in any weather which would cause the need for other de-icing equipment on the airplane." Like all other information, the U.S. kept this statement secret.

Gromov's reasons for no de-icers on the fabric-covered wings must have jolted the military inquirer because this equipment was considered an absolute necessity, even on commercial and military aircraft traveling over the much warmer American mainland. Military observers became more interested in how the fliers had negotiated the pole when pilot Gromov said they had no maps on the plane. To be able to make a transpolar flight without maps would certainly require some advanced navigational apparatus not yet developed in the United States and other nations. Walter Harvey reported they had shown him a map and asked their location. Two hours later they told March Field officers they didn't have a map. Maybe the fliers denied having a map to justify not being able to relocate this large military airfield.

Perhaps the next inconsistency can be blamed on the translator because it was so farfetched. The chief pilot said they ran into two cyclones one and a half hours after takeoff (about 150 miles north of Moscow). There was no other confirmation of cyclones in the area on this July 12. A third cyclone was encountered about 300 miles from the North Pole, Gromov said. This is interesting since the fliers' log reported speeds of 200 mph from Rudolph Island to the North Pole. Apparently that cyclone didn't hinder their air speed or force them to bypass the "storm." Cyclones are a rarity if they occur at all in July, and have never been spotted in the polar regions. The previous Soviet fliers reported cyclones in the same area. They had obviously been attempting to identify some unique-type weather or other phenomenon to prove they had flown over the pole.

Gromov continued to baffle American authorities by more outlandish stories concerning the fuel supply, takeoff, landing choice, and leaking gasoline. The Soviet spokesman told high military personnel he had 2,500 gallons of gasoline weighing 15,000 pounds in the wing tanks before leaving Shelkova, but other reports set the gas figure at 2,000 gallons. On takeoff the Russian colonel said he had to use the full 6,237-foot (1,900 meters) runway at Shelkova to get airborne, but Professor Schmidt earlier said the plane lifted off with 600 feet to spare. Little by little the sessions with the U.S. Air Force officers were bringing more things to light. Gromov was asked a second time why he had chosen the pasture over the modern airstrip at March Field. This time he gave an entirely different answer. Instead of staying with his original stories about not being able to relocate the field and a gas shortage, Gromov brazenly told authorities March Field was not long enough because the airplane's brakes had been removed to conserve weight for additional fuel. Air Force inspectors noted the field he did land on was less than half the size of March. Closer examination of the plane showed it never had any provision for brakes.

A formal report went to Air Base headquarters saying there was some reason to doubt these statements. An amazing revelation came to light when it was discovered the engine, after a flight of 62-odd hours, "was absolutely clean of any oil and it gave the general appearance of an engine having just been completely cleaned. The exhaust smudge on the fuselage was exceedingly light." The opinion of all Air Force personnel who inspected the aircraft was the general workmanship "was very poor, welding was poor, riveting unevenly spaced, the heads of rivets generally crushed, inferior painting, apparently brushed on, and the fabric very loose." History shows this information was buried in secret files. It was in the Air Force interest to take a good look at the navigational equipment under the pretext of searching for cameras inside the plane. An in-depth examination of the flight instruments was carried out. This day's ordeal for the fliers was over at last and they could only hope their answers satisfied Air Force officials. Danilin probably would have been concerned if he had known the *New York Times* had used the 1935 photograph identifying him as Nikolai Juroff, the pilot of the ill-fated *Maxim Gorky*.

Later a good breakfast of ham and eggs helped to ease tensions. This was followed by showers. Gregory Gokhman dropped in from San Francisco to serve as the fliers' interpreter. He carried on a lengthy conversation with the aviators while they bathed. Rest was the next thing on the agenda, and then a shopping spree was planned since the trio did not have any dress clothes with them. The inference was that everything had been sacrificed in order to carry more fuel. During the morning's routine both Joseph Stalin and President Roosevelt had wired their congratulations. According to dispatches from Moscow, people were lined up outside the *Izvestia* newspaper offices eager to hear the latest word about the fliers. A "giant" map hanging on the newspaper building plotted the route over which the fliers were said to be flying. News of the successful landing in California was hailed by the press as a "rebuttal of the lies and slander that Russia is a nation of ineffectual people," using this forum to declare the superiority of socialism over capitalism. "Capitalism strangles and wrecks talents. . . . It gives them no freedom for development. Charles Lindbergh opened a new era in aviation by his flight. But he had to escape from his fatherland. . . escape from glory."

Pravda, another arm of Soviet propaganda, warned potential enemies of Russia's capabilities at long-distance bombing. "Our powerful aviation industry can build as many such and even better planes as may be needed...and let our foreign enemies who threaten us with war know that we are much nearer their capitals than we are to Portland and San Jacinto." In a lighter vein Moscow was preparing to welcome back the "heroes" of the first "transpolar" flight. Chkalov, Baidukov, and Beliakov heard the news of Gromov's arrival as they were sailing out of New York Harbor en route home. Each was to receive a brand new Packard as a gift from an unidentified donor.

In keeping with the format of the first flight, the Chamber of Commerce in Los Angeles invited Gromov, Yumashev, and Danilin for lunch. The chief pilot spoke on this occasion, stating: "The Soviet government wanted to demonstrate the practicality of Soviet-engineered aircraft." Gromov should be given some credit, as Chkalov before him, for his great perseverance. Here he was flying a made-over French plane and claiming it as an example of Soviet technology. The chief spokesman told how they were forced to fly high to avoid the ice with only a 24-hour supply of oxygen to make this possible. Newspaper articles had informed the American audience that there was only a ten-hour supply of oxygen on board. Gromov went on to say the motor and navigational system had performed perfectly. The plane was French; the navigation equipment was American-copied or disguised; the motor was probably an Hispano Suiza, a Spanish make converted by the Russians. These facts didn't deter Gromov, judging by a remark aimed at the French: "The French dreamed that they could fly from Paris to San Diego (referring to a second Codos and Rossi attempt). We flew from Moscow to San Diego to show them how to do it." If the Russian pilot had known aviation experts had identified the ANT as a copy of the Dewoitine, would he still have made this comment? Gromov then challenged the Americans to try beating their "record flight" by flying the other way to Moscow via the pole.

The Soviets were given credit for a total nonstop distance of 6,262 miles in 62 hours, about 608 miles farther than Paul Codos and Maurice Rossi. This was announced by the National Aeronautic Association which had formed a committee of officials under the supervision of Edison Mouton. He would be joined by Claude Ryan, builder of Lindbergh's plane; and by two airplane record timers, Ray Booth and Lieutenant Commander L.R. Gray. There was an existing impression that the barograph would be sent to Washington, D.C. for evaluation.

This committee was assigned to remove the sealed, clock-controlled barograph and send it to the nation's capital. However, it appears the committee took it upon itself to recognize the flight and recommend that the FAI accept the feat as a world record, even before any analysis of the barograph reading. Since there had been insufficient time to deliver the barograph instrument to Washington, it was obvious a local decision had been rendered. Ordinarily this procedure might have seemed peculiar, but in the excitement of the moment no one cared.

And since the U.S. government appeared to lend credence to the "historic" happening, why should anyone doubt the authenticity of the flight? Gromov and his two flying comrades must have hoped that the Americans would remain as gracious to them as they had been to the first crew. They were soon to find out as they prepared to travel east to visit President Roosevelt and to tour U.S. factories. Before the end of July the Soviet pilots were scheduled to visit Consolidated, Douglas, Northrup, Boeing, Sikorsky, Glenn Martin, Wright, Pioneer Instrument, Sperry Gyroscope, and NACA Laboratories and Research, a firm associated with Langley Field, a large air force base in Texas. The flying trio were to be accompanied by some heavy names in Russian industry, such as Mikhail Kaganovich, commissar of Heavy Industry; Colonel Vladimir Begunov, military attaché; Stanislav Shumovsky, aeronautical expert; V.M. Petlinev, V.J. Vurgens, and V.K. Bogdon, all said to be knowledgeable in aviation.

CHAPTER 20

Fallen "Falcons"

While Gromov, Yumashev, and Danilin were still touring the U.S. airplane companies and other factories, the Soviets announced preparations for the third flight that was supposed to bring Sigmund Levanevsky and five other airmen to the United States. Levanevsky's attempt with this size of a crew was reported to be a forerunner to regular commercial travel between Russia and the American mainland. A stopover was scheduled at Fairbanks, Alaska, and then his plane, identified merely as a four-motor H-209, would proceed to Edmonton, Alberta in Canada, and finish at Chicago. This announced flight was also veiled in secrecy and recent reports of Levanevsky's arrest further confused the Americans. He was expected to head one or the other of two previous flights and now it was not certain the "Soviet Lindbergh" would come at all; persistent rumors had him falling out of grace with the Stalin regime. It appears Levanevsky was reluctant to play a direct role in piloting one of the hoax flights but he did want to make a legitimate flight to the United States in 1937. Up to this time Levanevsky's function was looking over the latest American planes and recommending aircraft for purchase by the Soviet government. Along with this role the pilot was invaluable in the area of public relations. But if the latest rumors of his arrest were true, the "Soviet Lindbergh" might present some worries to his bosses on whether he would expose the hoaxes. And if the flier was trying to flee the country, he might tell the Americans what was really going on. And since this would be a devastating blow to Russian credibility, the Soviets would not let him leave the country.

It is possible the American government might not give any credence to the idea of hoaxes, but Levanevsky was well acquainted with civilian aviators in the United States. This fact alone increased the chances he would be believed. However, if the flier was a threat to Soviet secrets, why did Stalin and the Kremlin announce he would pilot the next "polar flight" to America? In an interview with the *New York Times* July 10, Levanevsky denied he was under any threat of arrest when asked about his absence from Professor Schmidt's homecoming on June 26. Levanevsky said he had been busy flying, including testing an American plane in the Black Sea port of Sevastopol, near Yalta. The Russians maintained a flight school at Sevastopol. It appears Levanevsky spent considerable time there, a location that offered easy access to many nearby western sanctuaries, particularly by airplane. It was speculated that the flier was attempting to get his family and possibly his close friend General Alksnis out of the country.

At the time when the "polar flights" were scheduled, there may not have been a serious problem concerning Levanevsky and the Kremlin, but a rift with other NSR aviators was possible. Levanevsky, being favored by Stalin, was given a good opportunity to acquire fame from the Mattern and *Cheliuskin* "rescues." Other resources closer to the rescue site near Anadyr were deliberately held back while Levanevsky flew 5,000 miles to "save" the downed American aviator. While Levanevsky was never directly involved in the *Cheliuskin* rescue, he received the "Hero of the Soviet Union" medal. The flier may have acquired a reputation of "I'm too good to lower myself to the level of the hoaxes." Evidently the Soviet pilot went along with these parts of the polar hoaxes because he didn't have to face the Americans. NSR's 1937 polar cruises threw Chkalov and Gromov into the laps of the Americans, something Levanevsky dreaded because of his respected position in the eyes of his American counterparts. Levanevsky must have convinced Stalin that he would be more effective and important to the Kremlin as its aviation representative in the United States.

NSR might have used Levanevsky's close American ties against him by creating doubts of his loyalty, perhaps citing the flier's preference for flying American aircraft. NSR may have convinced Stalin to closely watch the pilot, or at least planted a seed for possible distrust. Stalin had to maintain the loyalty of the NSR staff because he couldn't afford to alienate so many people who knew the inside secrets on the "polar flights." But his personal friendship with Levanevsky, along with the flier's hero status in Russia and the United States, put him in a bind. Levanevsky represented a certain legitimacy as opposed to the fake flights over the pole. Yet if there were any chance of Levanevsky divulging the hoaxes to the Americans and gaining political asylum, Stalin might be brought to his knees, thus discrediting all Russia's newly won fame in "polar explorations and long-distance flying feats." And if it were shown that Russia had stooped to such fraudulent tactics to impress the world, then the real, sad state of its industry and technology would be revealed. Given the ongoing domestic upheavals ravaging the nation, there would be little hope Stalin could survive the consquences. Would Sigmund Levanevsky have to be sacrificed to insure against any public disclosures? Was Levanevsky really a threat at this time? And if so, what could the dictator do about him? The flier was greatly loved by the populace. If anything happened to their hero, especially due to foul play, all hell would break loose.

NSR would continue to use Levanevsky's name in all references to flights to America even though they had no intentions of making him a part of any future transpolar hoaxes and planned to convince the Kremlin chief that it would be dangerous to allow Levanevsky to reach America. This was all going on behind the scenes while Americans were expecting the famous flier to pioneer a publicized commercial airline link between Moscow and America, via the North Pole. Some doubters in America felt Levanevsky would not be making any flights to the United States because of the rumors of his arrest on June 26. This was after the Chkalov "flight" and before Gromov arrived in the United States. But the Soviet government continued to give U.S. officials confidential information of his impending flight.

Regardless of what plane the Soviets said they would use in the third event, they didn't have any aircraft capable of flying nonstop from Moscow to Fairbanks, Alaska, a distance of 3,700 miles. The H-209, or HGI-09, or whatever they called it, couldn't make a nonstop trip to Fairbanks, not even after a refueling stop at Rudolph Island. How was NSR going to get this aircraft to Fairbanks? Surely the Soviets would not crate this 72,000-pound "monster" into the secret camp in the archipelago, fly it "backwards" to Fairbanks, and risk being spotted. The only alternative was to fly the big ship from Anadyr, Siberia, across to Nome, Alaska, a distance of 625 miles; however, Fairbanks was decidedly out of the H-209's range. It was apparent there would not be any four-motor airplane arriving in the United States via Fairbanks or any other route. Levanevsky continued to tell the American press he was flying the third "mission over the pole." He must have known there was not going to be another polar event. The hoaxes, both the flights and the so-called North Pole station, combined to give an impression the Russians would soon establish a commercial airline route between Moscow and America, pioneered by Levanevsky. Pressure to continue this bold venture was now facing a realistic test by using a commercial-type airplane capable of carrying passengers, while reaching altitudes of more than 20,000 feet. The Russians had to "put up or shut up" at this stage of their master plan. Actually on this first test the Soviets said there would only be Levanevsky and a crew of five on board, all aviators.

While Stalin and the NSR organization were trying to figure out how to deal with Levanevsky, Moscow welcomed home the first trio of "transpolar" fliers from the United States. Valery Chkalov, George Baidukov, and Alexander Beliakov had arrived toward the end of July. For some reason Baidukov was chosen to give a major address to the nation, describing the fliers' experiences in America. It appears the confidence in spokesman Chkalov diminished after his poor performance in the United States. For a purpose, undisclosed, the U.S. State Department was interested in knowing the contents of Baidukov's speech to the Soviet people. A man identified as Mr. N. Vishnevsky, of Salt Lake City, Utah, who may have been Russian-born, was enlisted by the State Department to translate Baidukov's speech. (National Archives Files, Sept. 12, 1937). The July 27 speech was more interesting because of what Baidukov didn't say; there was no mention of a "transpolar flight to America." Instead the contents of his talk focused on the physical accomplishments of capitalistic America and the social ills the system produced. Never published in America, the speech is mostly diatribe and politically adjusted by the Kremlin to satisfy Stalin and the Communist line.

The complete translated text of Baidukov's address:

Hello, my country. Hello, fields and rivers, forests and mountains, factories and collective farms. Hello, the united of many nationalities, the families of my people and of our beloved leader, Stalin.

In a short time I have seen half of the world and can assure you, my beloved comrades, that on this earth exists no healthier life, more willing people and prospect than exists here in our country. It is for this reason that regardless of the fabulous luxury of the steamship "Normandy" or the speed and comfort of the bullet fast trains crossing the hot desert of south of America, or the many millions of automobiles and the luxurousness of Paris, we are glad to return to our country.

The capitalistic world is a world of gigantic cities with skyscrapers of marble. Its streets and highways over even the stickiest of swamps sworm with luxurous automobiles. All of this, however, can be tumbled into the swamps by the slightest of disturbance or into the dispair of extremist famine since the people themselves are no part of it. Not only does this grandeur hide the swamps but it hides the poverty of the people of these countries, the oppression of labor without rights and the lowest forms of prostitution.

It is this world of capitalism that writes about our country tales that at best are only lies. We saw many riches and the fat of capitalistic savings. Travel was fast in airplanes with every comfort. These planes and lovely girl stewardesses, who pampered every wish. They were capable of speeds exceeding 300 kilometers per hour. The pullman trains [sic] were fast and comfortable. Their hermetically sealed cars into which no smoke or dust from the hot desert country we crossed could penetrate were air conditioned and one sat in perfect comfort all through the journey.

Twenty million costly automobiles representing an enormous industry sped across these countries constantly and believe me these are beautiful machines. Enormous and beautiful like the dreams of story tellers are the boats that sail their rivers and seas. One of these has a personnel of 1,500 to accommodate 1,400 passengers who of course must carry in their pockets a vast amount of money. This same boat crosses the Atlantic in five days. Yes, I have seen all this and I have bowed my head before the genious of man's mind, but I curse forever those public relations wherein a world of luxury springs out of and creates a world of poverty worse than which our country abolished.

I can not forget the skyscrapers of New York, nor can I forget the great bridges of San Francisco, but I will forever remember the endless strikes with bloodshed, the intolerable treatment of the negroes and lower white elments and the insufferable prostitution of minor, adolescent negro girls which I saw there. Children in want of something better bathed themselves in dirty water running in the paved streets of the big cities.

It was in these countries that I witnessed the greatest of technique with want of justice in its use.

It particularly pleased me to walk in those places in Paris and its outskirts which were the haunts of Vladimir Lenin. Here the proletarian leader began his battle, with the accursed world from which we as a nation severed ourselves in October of 1917.

With loathing I am reminded of the plots of those vile bandits whom the people placed on trial so short a time ago. What did they want? They wanted a world of the calibre of that which exists abroad. They wished to exalt themselves and reduce all others to poverty and to a state without rights.

Those who seek to depart from the way dictated by our leader, Stalin, we must destroy with lightness of heart and without mercy for we are engaged in a war with an alert and watchful enemy. It lies within our power by careful study to create a life on this earth beyond the dreams of man. We now know how to distribute what we have. In time the wealth of this nation and of you the proletariate shall far exceed that abroad.

With the passage of but a little time we will become in many ways the richest people in the world because of the unmeasurable power of our people, because of our leaders and because of our leader and teacher, Comrade Stalin.

Hello, our country! From my heart I embrace you and tightly kiss you.

This must have been the most unpleasant aspect of the entire polar hoax for Baidukov. Facing the Americans was one thing but having to address your own people after a hoax of this magnitude must have been intolerable, particularly when he knew there were civil and military aviators in his country aware of the true nature of the "celebrated flight." It is no wonder Baidukov never mentioned the "transpolar flight" in this first speech. None of these fliers could have forseen the price they would pay for this "glory" but they may have begun to realize there was no way to ever extricate themselves from the polar hoaxes and continue living under the Stalin regime. Could the Soviet fliers have anticipated the demands that would be placed upon them and the tremendous amount of recognition their "flight" would receive in Russia, America, and throughout the world?

Translator Vishnevsky, who said he talked with Baidukov and the other fliers in Ogden, Utah after the so-called transpolar flight, was under the impression the flight ended at Marshall Field, British Columbia. In a cover letter to the U.S. State Department Vishnevsky made reference to the Marshall Field terminus for the flight, never mentioning the Vancouver landing.

While *Pravda* was publishing stories about the first "flight," Levanevsky was supposed to be almost ready to make his "polar attempt." On July 29, Moscow reported that the "Soviet Lindbergh" was standing by waiting for a fair weather signal from NSR's northern radio stations. In addition, the U.S. Signal Corps's giant northland radio network had been sending periodic weather reports for several weeks. Was Levanevsky also going to leave Russia without a passport? Official U.S. documents show Levanevsky did not receive his visa from the American embassy in Moscow until July 31, the same day it was requested by the "People's Commissariat for Foreign Affairs, Moscow." And like the two previous "polar flights," the date of departure and place of entry to the U.S. were "uncertain." The U.S. documents said Levanevsky was directed to fly as an official of the Soviet government in a "special transpolar flight to western United States," with five other men. According to secret exchanges between Russia and the United States, it was first learned on May 29 that Levanevsky was going to make a "transpolar" journey. This bulletin came in conjunction with the proposed Chkalov flight. Shortly after, U.S. weather services began sending data in compliance with a Soviet request. These secret documents gave no indication there was anything amiss with the Levanevsky flight. It was still on.

The only change in the information involving Levanevsky concerned the identification of his airplane. Originally he was to fly a plane marked H-209 but on June 5 the U.S. State Department received word from Moscow that the marking should be changed to HGI-09, which was also a four-motored plane painted red and blue. Levanevsky was keenly aware the HGI-09 or H-209 was developed in 1925. It was called the ANT-4, and it only had a range of approximately 625 miles, about 3,000 miles short of Fairbanks, Alaska, his scheduled refueling stop en route to the mainland. The "Soviet Lindbergh" knew he was not going to leave Russia in this contraption.

The international news media described how Levanevsky was summoned by Stalin to make his request for a "transpolar flight," a scenario with a very familiar ring. The dictator was again placing an NSR pilot in the position of officially requesting to carry out this mission. It is doubtful such a meeting ever occurred because the "Soviet Lindbergh" knew he was not coming to America, at least not in the relic ANT-4 with its limited range. It is more likely Levanevsky had been brought back from Sevastopol at the Black Sea port to Moscow on July 10 and then placed under constant surveillance.

As late as August 1, no technical information concerning the airplane to be used in the proposed third flight was available. Basic data was given such as its gross weight, said to be 72,000 pounds. The engines were described as 34-RNs, probably a spinoff of the M-34s, supposedly able to power the airship to altitudes of almost four miles into the substratosphere. But the most remarkable factor was that the plane, according to the Soviets, could remain in the air for 40 hours. There were no figures offered on fuel load at this time but the Soviets did say six weeks of food rations were to be taken along. The route included a nonstop flight from Moscow to Fairbanks in an estimated time of about 30 hours. A second phase was to take the plane to Edmonton, Canada and then on to Chicago. Additional proof of Russian deception and diversionary tactics are found in Levanevsky's passport application which documented a western United States destination for his flight.

Mikhail V. Beliakov, older brother of Alexander Beliakov who served as Chkalov's navigator, had left Seattle and was ordered to Fairbanks to assist Levanevsky and his crew when they arrived there to refuel. The Russians let it be known the takeoff at Shelkova would be kept secret. The first week in August came and went with no flight. Judging from previous Soviet statements it was getting rather late for a flight over the North Pole because of the greater incidence of storms in the northern arctic. Almost another week passed without word from the NSR administration. Finally, on Friday, August 13, Moscow radio reported Sigmund Levanevsky and a crew of five had left Shelkova 20 hours earlier, the same delayed "takeoff" procedure used in announcing the previous polar hoaxes. Levanevsky's crew consisted of Nikolai Kastanaev, second pilot; Victor Levchenko, navigator; Nikolai Galkovsky, radioman; Gregory Pobegimov and Nikolai Godovikov, both mechanics.

It is extremely suspicious why the Soviet government did not record on film this unprecedented occasion. This was supposedly the first time a commercial airline route was being tested over the North Pole in an effort to link the eastern and western hemispheres; however, the Russians didn't see fit to take motion pictures of the event. Gromov's plane as recorded took off in the dark so there was an excuse in that case, but Levanevsky was supposed to have left Russia about 6:00 p.m., during daylight hours.

Although Professor Schmidt made certain comments on the "transpolar" journey, it did not appear he was supervising the release of information for this event. The news sources reported the four-motored 12-seater craft took off from the airport at 6:13 p.m. Moscow time and arrived over the North Pole at 1:40 the next afternoon. In contrast to the first two hoaxes this latest mythical airship was reported to have left a few hours before nightfall. It is curious the Soviets were not going to take advantage of more daylight. And again a "flight" was launched in the face of very bad weather. Moscow sources said the fliers had to fight 60 mph headwinds. It seems as though those northern stations gathering weather data were not doing very well in assisting any of the flights.

A broadcast, reportedly from the plane at 1:40 p.m. Moscow time on Friday, said, "Flying over the North Pole. Had a very hard time reaching it, beginning at the middle of the Barents Sea. Dense clouds all the time, altitude 6,000 meters (about 20,000 feet), temperature −35 deg., 60 mph winds. Give us weather report on other side of the Pole. Everything in order." The Russian radio reported the H-209 had flown 1,600 miles and reached the pole in 17 hours, later corrected to 19.5 hours. The latter time did correspond with the period between the reported takeoff and arrival at the "pole." One gross error in the Russian bulletin miscalculated the distance to the North Pole. Evidently there was a new operator on duty at NSR because the former radio agents knew the distance was 2,352 miles, not 1,600 miles. This was the first piece of evidence that radio staging was being used. The incorrect distance to the pole was not a result of poor news coverage by American journalists because the Russians verified the 1,600-mile figure in other dispatches. NSR not only started the flight with the wrong distance, but continued to broadcast plane position reports based on this figure, and then their troubles began. Another version of the flight to the pole, a radio message that was supposedly relayed to Seattle, quoted Levanevsky as reporting his time of arrival at the pole to be 5:40 a.m. Saturday PST, (4:40 p.m. Moscow time). This was three hours later than his previous report, reducing his average speed to a more realistic 100 mph. Someone had made some belated calculations on this mythical flight to compensate for the fierce headwinds the "Soviet Lindbergh" had already reported.

Before the fliers reported arriving at the pole, Vartanian in Seattle informed U.S. authorities he had received word from the aviators at 8 a.m. Friday, Moscow time, while the plane was flying over Alexandra Land, 1,750 miles from Shelkova. According to this report the H-209 or HGI-09 had covered this stretch in 13 hours and 47 minutes, averaging 125 mph. The maximum speed of the H-209 is listed in *Jane's Encyclopedia of Aviation* at 128 mph when equipped with four BMW motors. Any Russian engine used on this aircraft would be less efficient. One news report listed the engines as diesel-powered, which would increase efficiency but not speed. Levanevsky had told American news-men he would fly at 20,000 feet, but the maximum ceiling for his plane was 16,400 feet. Levanevsky reported hitting 60 mph headwinds 700 miles before reaching the pole; yet Moscow still claimed the plane flew near its maximum speed. The fierce headwinds would have sharply reduced the average speed; the plane also supposedly took off with 36,000 pounds of fuel (6,000 gallons). To make matters worse, a Moscow radio source said the Russian craft had only averaged 85 mph. Moscow made an obvious error in this average speed because it was computed on the incorrect distance of 1,600 miles to the pole, from the alleged takeoff point at Shelkova Airport.

About one hour after the "North Pole position report," Moscow claimed the H-209 had reported a damaged oil line resulting in the loss of the starboard engine. Perhaps it was a premonition or part of the Moscow script because Levanevsky told a reporter prior to what every-one thought was a transpolar takeoff that the aircraft could fly with one dead engine; it might require dumping some fuel. A second part of this Moscow dispatch indicated a radical loss of altitude from 20,000 to 14,000 feet; but according to the radio dispatch Levanevsky voiced no alarm, noting the plane could proceed safely with the remaining three motors. As in the first two "flights" American and Canadian signal corps stations did not hear any direct messages from the "plane" despite an elaborate communication system, but Moscow and Vartanian, who was temporarily headquartered at the Seattle station, always seemed to receive direct radio coded messages from the "aircraft." On numerous occasions American and Alaskan communication outposts thought they were intercepting plane reports being sent to Moscow. Ironically, there was no evidence supporting this because these stations were not able to establish any radio response from any of the fliers on the three so-called polar crossings, not even acknowledgment of the important weather data being transmitted to them. Things didn't add up in the first two "polar flights" and the latest reports out of Moscow should have raised enough suspicions among U.S. Signal Corps stations to justify a thor-ough investigation.

Anxieties began mounting in the United States and Alaska for the six airmen's safety because no word had come in since the report on the engine failure four hours ago. People had not yet recovered from the apparent loss of Amelia Earhart and now the public believed a terrible fate was looming somewhere in the polar regions for the great "Soviet Lindbergh" and his crew. Could they possibly make it to Fairbanks as announced with only three engines? The loss of one engine was said to have forced the plane down from 20,000 feet to 14,000 feet, lowering the ship into denser clouds where ice would normally form on the wings and the fuselage. It looked bad for the third "transpolar" airplane, at least from the American perspective. Apparently the script writers did not recognize the significance of their own earlier reports or they would have expressed some alarm over a major loss of altitude. Most aviators would describe a 6,000-foot loss in altitude in a polar region as a very serious problem, especially without wing de-icers. Had the fliers identified their position, they would have had a chance of being rescued, assuming they were actually flying in the polar area. The contradictions and discrepancies were nothing new to the U.S. agencies monitoring radio signals from Moscow. Meanwhile, Vartanian, the Russian radio agent, manned the U.S. Signal Corps radio almost around the clock and handled and translated all messages from every station in the communication network.

On the other side of the world the Moscow-Siberian radio connection went on grinding out infrequent reports as to the progress of the mystery ship. Five hours from the pole on the North American side, a "message from the plane" was claimed to have been heard by the Russian station operator at Ft. Schmidt, Siberia, named after Professor Schmidt at NSR. However, there was no mention of its geographic position. Although the U.S. had the best available radio equipment, it seemed odd that only Soviet stations were receiving any information, except Mr. Vartanian in Seattle. At any rate the Anchorage station received what it believed to be a transmission directly from the "polar" plane via the relay outpost in Siberia at 6:44 a.m. PST Saturday, almost 23 hours after the Russians claimed the plane took off from Shelkova. It read, "No bearings!... having trouble with wave bands!!... going down in!!!..." and then silence. There had been no later mention as to whether the plane was aloft or aground. Most of the report was said to be unreadable. Surely these veteran fliers would have had some idea of their location in a real emergency.

While all of this staged drama was going on, unsuspecting well-wishers were gathering at Fairbanks Airport to greet the Russian fliers. But after 30 hours it was obvious the plane was overdue. The Russian authorities did not think the long silence was significant, recalling that an element of silence had also surrounded previous flights. But as the hours ticked by Alaskan bush pilots swung into action. Joe Crosson, a well known "mercy flier" who had brought back the bodies of Wiley

Post and Will Rogers from Point Barrow in 1935, was one of the first to take to the air. He was followed by S.E. Robbins, Murray Stewart, and Roger Williams of trans-Atlantic fame. Other great names in aviation prepared to join the Alaskan air search. Sir Hubert Wilkins from Australia was contacted, and Constantine Oumansky from the Russian embassy personally asked American aviator James Mattern to search for the man who had once come to his rescue in the Siberian wastelands. King Baird offered to bring his pontooned Sikorsky and Vilhjalmur Stefansson announced he too would soon join the arctic search. The consensus of opinion was that the plane was down somewhere south of 83 degrees, north latitude and all the way to the Alaskan mainland, a vast area to search. It seemed the Soviets made sure they kept the search area extremely broad to discourage any meaningful and conclusive search, preempting anyone from claiming the plane had not gone down. And that is the real reason no position reports were given during the final broadcasts and that other earlier position reports were purposely misleading.

After more time had gone by without any word, Soviet sources began saying they were worried; but they expressed an optimistic attitude and confidence in Levanevsky's ability to land the plane on an ice floe. Acknowledging this could mean a "grim finish" for the "Soviet Lindbergh" and his crew of five, NSR notified U.S. agencies assisting in the "flight" that they were taking immediate and extensive measures to save the six men. According to these dispatches two icebreakers and nine airplanes had been ordered into the search. The nine airplanes probably included some being purchased outright or chartered from U.S. factories within the last few hours. All of these were presently or soon to be flown by American pilots to scour the waters north of Point Barrow and some Alaskan mainland areas. The Russians said Mikhail Vodopyanov and two other aviators of North Pole fame had been ordered to Rudolph Island to begin probes over the pole and into the North American arctic. The Soviets said three giant ANT-6s would first have to undergo a three-day servicing before joining the search. It appears the Soviets had not taken any precautions in case there was a need for an aerial search and rescue.

An August 14, *New York Times* article on the missing fliers reported that the "Soviet Government threw all of its enormous Arctic organization into action today in an effort to rescue them." The Russian icebreaker *Krassin* of World War I vintage reported operating somewhere in the Bering Sea was said to be on its way to Point Barrow, carrying three aircraft and a catapult to launch the planes.

One very interesting announcement came from the Soviet government in Moscow. Ivan Papanin and three other men were ordered to prepare a landing field on their drifting station to receive search planes. According to the report, Papanin told Kremlin officials there was plenty of fuel at the station to service planes landing there. This was an astounding revelation since there had been no detailed explanation how they transported huge amounts of fuel to the North Pole. In fact there only had been a total cargo of ten tons of materials unloaded from the four ANT-6s if one were to believe the story of an actual polar landing. Five tons, according to the Russian story, consisted of enough food to supposedly last one year. This left five tons for all the rest of the housing, supplies, radio equipment, etc. There would not be too much cargo space leftover for airplane fuel, not a practical item for a polar camp. Stove oil would be much more useful. Besides, the Soviets didn't have a rescue aircraft ready to fly and even if they did none could have made a round trip to the "search site."

Even if a plane did try to locate the so-called ice floe camp, it would be very difficult to spot it from the air. This fact later drew an interesting comment from aviator-author John Grierson concerning Papanin's alleged North Pole station on an ice floe, in his 1964 *Challenge to the Poles* book. Grierson wrote that it was incredible for this station not to be equipped with a radio beacon to guide rescuers to the floating camp if it became necessary. Grierson noted that he could not believe the Russians with their "extensive knowledge of the arctic" did not know the value of such equipment. He added, "Anyone conversant with polar operations. . . would have known the immense difficulty of picking out an encampment on the ice by visual means." It was also puzzling to the flier why silk tents and hurricane lamps were used by the Papanin party when it was a well known fact these items were not suitable for arctic weather. Grierson did not voice any suspicions about the Soviet claims of a polar camp but he did raise some interesting points others might want to consider in this light. Much of the food taken on the trip was ill-prepared and had caused many episodes of sickness among the four campers, the explorers said later. It appears the so-called scientific planning supposedly going into the polar camp project was actually misrepresented. Even if the Soviets had established some kind of radio station encampment on Rudolph Island, a substitute for a pole station, one would expect food preparation and a radio beacon to be high priorities for human survival. This project, according to NSR and Kremlin spokesmen, had been carefully and scientifically planned for many years. But these deficiencies reflect an absence of sound advance planning and cast doubts on the existence of a polar station. Conventional scientific proof of a Russian polar station was never fully provided.

The maximum duration for Levanevsky's H-209 had been given as 40 hours, carrying 6,000 gallons of diesel. At first American stations believed the fated airship reached Alaska; but after the Alaskan bush pilots logged 100,000 miles this possibility was discounted. Russian estimates of the plane's location was between the latitudes of 83 and 85 degrees. It is apparent this tactic was used to avoid having to send rescue aircraft to the Alaskan area. Even though there was no plane out there to find, the Soviets knew they must go through the motions of an actual search. The greatest aviator in the Soviet Union was supposed to be lost in the most hazardous regions of the world and Stalin must now prove that a supreme effort was going to be executed to save this popular hero. But if the "Soviet Lindbergh" and the other five men were not lost as a result of an airplane incident in the arctic or polar regions, then where were they? Not unlike many other famous Russian citizens they probably were immediately executed shortly after takeoff. What better method than to pretend the country's top flier died in an historic flight.

CHAPTER 21

Search for Levanevsky

In these trying times for the ruling faction it must have been clear to Stalin to either get rid of Levanevsky or take the chance of being ousted himself. If the latter happened he most likely would be imprisoned or even executed by those who succeeded him. Stalin had never let any individual stand in the way of his political ambitions and there was no reason to believe this Soviet flier would be an exception. There was no end to the number of close political associates and friends who fell under the dictator's wrath on his rise to power. If the hoaxes were unmasked, placing Stalin at a disadvantage politically, those seeking revenge would surely find it. Feeling a need to defend this latest of "transpolar flights" in what was described as a brand new airplane, the Russian government moved to defend the choice of aircraft. News articles reported that the plane's designer was Victor Bolkhovitinov and that he, along with some young technicians, spent five months constructing the "H-209" in 1937. A Moscow news article claimed that "Mr. Bolkhovitinoff worked day and night over the plane, going without sleep. He grew thin and did not even take time to shave until his beard became a public scandal. The fliers lured him to their room where the powerful Kastaneyeff (Nikolai Kastanaev) seized and placed him in a chair while Levchenko, Levanevsky's navigator, shaved him forcibly." It is strange the Russians had been planning these flights for years and now must have people working feverishly day and night to prepare the plane for this flight.

The Russians were relying on the Americans and the rest of the world not knowing precisely what kind of plane Levanevsky was supposed to be flying. In truth the model was 12 years old. It was called the

ANT-4 and was designed and completed by August 11, 1925. Actually A.N. Tupolev and not Victor Bolkhovitinov designed the H 209 (ANT-4). Tupolev was greatly influenced by the German Junkers design and fashioned the ANT-4 along the lines of the G-23; however, his was a larger version.

American correspondents talked with Levanevsky and reported witnessing a takeoff during the evening of August 12. The Russian government had relaxed at the last minute its stringent provisions of secrecy and let foreign newsmen observe the final ceremony. It is strange that every time a plane didn't complete a flight neutral observers had been allowed to watch the takeoff, and every time a flight was successfully completed no one witnessed the departure. And for the first time Soviet dignitaries were on hand to send off the fated fliers. By this time General Alksnis knew Levanevsky was never going to come back from the third "polar" adventure. General Alksnis and Levanevsky embraced and held a lengthy kiss on the lips, moments before takeoff. Each sensed the grave danger they faced with Stalin. Was this emotional embrace the final goodbye for both? What were Levanevsky's thoughts at this moment? Did his wife Natalie, at home with their two young children, know her husband's destiny? Did the "Soviet Lindbergh" wonder about his family's fate? The great schemer Stalin had eliminated entire families almost as a matter of routine policy during his rule, and Levanevsky knew this. The Russian people were seeing this third "transpolar" achievement in an entirely different light. If the H-209 were not found with the men safe, the "Soviet Lindbergh" and the crew would have "died in a blaze of glory while trying to connect the old and new world with a new airline route across the top of the world."

The Russians continued to act out a drama of making a third legitimate effort to span the North Pole. The Soviets said that General Alksnis and Stalin had personally inspected the plane before takeoff. Alksnis, as chief of the Air Force, was possibly in a position to make an evaluation of this H-209, but Stalin's appearance is a mystery. He had not bothered to inspect Chkalov and Gromov's ANT-25s prior to the other "flights." Why did he make this unusual appearance on August 12? General Alksnis was already in serious trouble and therefore could have been under heavy pressure to go along with whatever Stalin was plotting. Stalin's presence was to demonstrate his concern for the safety of Levanevsky and his crew. Alksnis was probably forced into making an appearance, apparently in an attempt to disprove rumors of his arrest. Imprisoning the Air Force chief while doing away with his close friend Levanevsky would not have been a good idea. Everything had to appear normal. There was plenty of time to take care of Alksnis later. Stalin had probably convinced the general that nothing would happen to him, but like the thousands of other cases this was not to prove out. First Levanevsky, and then Alksnis was doomed.

There is always a slight possibility Levanevsky was allowed to live among the "walking dead"; however, it is unlikely. As an aviator his ability to flee the country at a moment's notice was too easy. It is of record the plane took off with Levanevsky aboard. The range of the H-209 was about 650 miles at the most, which would enable the "Soviet Lindbergh" to reach Finland. Stalin could not take this chance and likely had placed one or more of Yezhov's secret police on board. The most logical plan would have been for the police to force the plane down in an isolated area and either execute Levanevsky and any other possible witnesses among the crew or imprison them in Siberia. The first option was probably followed since Levanevsky was a very familiar and popular figure throughout Russia. If this execution did take place, Levanevsky was just one more in a long list of Stalin's victims. Following the successful flight hoaxes he moved decisively to stifle other NSR employees or anyone else who might be tempted to expose the truth.

The sophisticated communication system of the American Signal Corps stations and U.S. Weather Services went for naught, but operators continued believing that their services had been valuable. These technicians undoubtedly noticed many peculiar incidents during all the "polar flying" but apparently wrote them off as unexplained happenings. It was one thing to overlook the discrepancies connected to the Chkalov and Gromov flights because the lives of Americans, Canadians, and others were not being endangered in a futile search. But if there had been any hint that Levanevsky was being murdered under the cover of a third "transpolar flight," then the resulting American indignation would have been enormous – enough, perhaps, to reinstate Leon Trotsky's political reputation. High-ranking Soviet officials knew the value of maintaining close relations with the United States. Anyone – including Stalin – who jeopardized this crucial relationship would make a fatal mistake. Russia's salvation depended greatly on importing American technology and other forms of assistance. Stalin was finished if the hoaxes were exposed.

Coincidentally, American tourists were at this time being refused entry into Leningrad – Levanevsky's birthplace. Was Stalin afraid the

Americans might learn something casting doubt on this latest "transpolar" event?

Meanwhile the search for Levanevsky continued without success. On August 16, two days after the scheduled arrival of the H-209, the Soviet embassy reported that a signal "of a weak and irregularly working transmitter," had been heard by its station at Irkutsk, Siberia and relayed to American stations. The Soviets said they were sure the signals were coming from the downed plane. On this day Vartanian had flown to Fairbanks to join Alexander Beliakov's brother in translating messages for the American stations. James Mattern also arrived at about the same time in his new Lockheed Electra to start searching for the Russian airman who had come to his assistance in Siberia. Of course Mattern, like the rest of the volunteer mercy fliers, had no idea Levanevsky's flight was an illusion. All of them were there to risk their lives for a fellow aviator.

Late August storms began clouding the skies north of Barrow, making visibility extremely difficult for the rescue mission. In order to spot a downed plane, searchers must fly very low to scan the waters and islands. There was no sign of Mikhail Vodopyanov's three-plane squadron. Moscow reported that bad weather north of Rudolph Island had prohibited his takeoff while Americans, Canadians, Alaskan bush pilots, and others buzzed the skies over the arctic in a frantic and daring aerial search. The Soviets had just claimed world records for their "polar crossings" to America and boasted their ANT-25s could fly 8,000 miles nonstop through the freezing arctic without wing de-icers. However, no mention was made of using these planes, especially equipped with flotation gear, to join the search for Levanevsky's aircraft. Also, the Russians maintained they had a landing site at their "North Pole Station" where four ANT-6s reportedly made landings on skis, yet there was no mention of this facility during the Levanevsky search.

The Soviets conducted meetings, made plans, and issued numerous public statements about what they intended to do in searching for Levanevsky but no real efforts were forthcoming. Occasionally there would be an announcement of planes on their way across Siberia to Alaska. Soviet fliers, one identified as pilot Vassily Zadkov, flew to Cape Wellen in eastern Siberia; another pilot listed as Alexsei Graziansky was due to fly to Dudinka; and a third pilot, Peter Golovin, flew to Sverdlovsk. All were to wait for further orders. It is doubtful these fliers would be of use in any timely search, judging from their assigned positions. Cape Wellen is across the Bering Strait, in southeastern

Siberia. Dudinka is in north central Russia, about 600 miles inland from the north coast. There are two Sverdlovsks and neither is remotely close to the search area, one being about 1,000 miles northeasterly from Moscow in the Ural Mountains and the other about 400 miles south of Moscow near the Black Sea. Supposedly the fliers were en route toward the search area. Pilot Zadkov arrived at Cape Wellen August 18 and it appears he was the only Soviet-dispatched aviator who would actually engage in the hunt. One other Soviet plane, identified as a BOAR CCC-H 2, flew in from Siberia with four airmen aboard, none of whom could speak English. They arrived at Point Barrow apparently to show the Soviet Union was contributing to the "rescue attempt."

Stalin's next step was added insurance to avoid any personal blame for the death of Levanevsky and the five-member crew consisting of Levchenko, Galkovsky, Kastanaev, Pobegimov, and Godovikov. On August 20, the Soviet government accused "airdrome mechanics of deliberately crippling" the H-209 before takeoff. The mechanics were arrested on sabotage charges and jailed incommunicado. A week later the dictator resurrected the old charge that "wreckers of airplanes" were at it again. Russian authorities declared there had been a plot to interfere with the mass production of aircraft needed to develop a great airline network. Informed people both in Russia and abroad were more convinced that the inferior production system rather than the saboteurs was at fault; however, no one dared challenge the powerful dictator. Stalin wanted to further the belief that Levanevsky was the victim of sabotage by casting suspicion upon the entire industry. If still alive, Levanevsky must have been beside himself with helplessness. If he was already murdered, his spirit might have called out for someone to stop the diabolical Stalin before all of Russia was destroyed.

After the Soviet leader established sabotage as the cause of the H-209's disappearance, the government terminated the search for the missing airmen. The announcement August 30 said, "The Soviet government tonight ordered all search for the missing transpolar plane abandoned." The bulletin added, "it was a virtual certainty that the plane had crashed and that all occupants had been killed." Only 16 days had passed since the disappearance of Levanevsky's plane and now the Russians were giving up efforts to find their much-heralded hero. Two weeks earlier the Russians had been confident the plane and airmen would be found somewhere on an ice floe, reminding everyone six weeks of supplies, tents, warm clothing, and other provisions were on the H-209. After a few days there was a complete reversal and the search was formally reactivated.

What caused the Soviets to change their minds? There were two possible answers; Stalin might have come under criticism by high officials in the Communist Party for ending the search too soon, or an entirely new opportunity opened up to them as a result of this recent hoax flight. The search for Russia's hero provided an excellent excuse for the Soviets to be in the United States studying American methods and technology. The Soviet government had purchased outright or chartered modern American aircraft to use in the "search for Levanevsky." Most of these planes were piloted by Americans; however, sometimes Russian personnel were on board. Weather and communication science were very important to Stalin's regime and both were directly involved in the "Levanevsky search" so why not exploit the situation? The drawback was the necessity of leaving hoax-connected Russians in America. Prolonged exposure to U.S. aviation people might result in a slip of the tongue. Perhaps a few individuals could be trusted. Vartanian had performed well under the circumstances and reportedly had worked for many years in the United States as an employee of Amtorg in New York. Alexander Beliakov's brother Mikhail, presently in Alaska helping Vartanian, might also be trusted. For whatever reason, Stalin decided to appeal to the U.S. government for continued assistance in the "search for Levanevsky" while the Soviets went on pretending to look for the "missing airplane" on their side of the pole.

CHAPTER 22

"Flights of Fancy"

By 1935 it was clear the American government was going to assist the Soviets in strengthening their air transportation systems and A.N. Tupolev, along with many other Russian engineers and technicians, were allowed into American aviation factories to study technological methods and mass production systems. Then along came the hoaxes; did U.S. government officials know beforehand, during, or afterwards what the Soviets were up to? Given all the discrepancies and mistakes related to the three "transpolar flights" (Chkalov's, Gromov's and Levanevsky's), it is difficult to dismiss the American government's cooperation as a naive excercise in diplomatic exchanges. Would the transpolar hoaxes make Hitler hesitate in starting a European war, believing Russia had revolutionary long-range bombing capabilities? Or were the hoaxes a senseless and unproductive scheme serving no purpose except to sustain Stalin in his self-made dictatorship? Only time would tell. It appeared the Kremlin chief was going to weather the storm of protests over the purges, and so far no serious challenge to the "polar flights" had emerged. The dictator had succeeded in moving out the Old Guard and in replacing them with younger people, many of whom were politically naive.

England and France, in particular, followed the "polar" flights with great interest. France's Federation Aeronautique Internationale (FAI) was to determine the authenticity of the polar flights for consideration as world records. The Chkalov venture, according to the FAI, was not long enough to unseat the Codos-Rossi record; however, it was generally conceded that the Gromov crew would soon be recognized as the new world record holders for long-distance nonstop flights. But in

England not everyone was convinced that the two transpolar trips were authentic. After reviewing the alleged Russian transpolar flights the English magazine *The Aeroplane* shocked the world by challenging the Soviet claims in a series of articles beginning September 8, 1937, and continuing into 1938. After the U.S. so diligently tried to avoid trouble with the Soviets, a major aviation magazine was blasting away at the transpolar fraud. In the next few years England expected to benefit from harmonious relations with Russia, but the upstart magazine, *The Aeroplane*, was "throwing the monkey wrench into the machinery." Aeronautical experts associated with the periodical studied the technical data supplied by many sources, including Russian. In their opinion the ANT airplane could not remain airborne for more than 47 hours, given relevant factors including lift-to-drag ratios, horsepower efficiency, gross weight, fuel consumption, headwinds, and other considerations. The English suggested that both ANT-25s had been refueled at some point along the route to America, probably Rudolph Island, where the Russians claimed to have a refueling depot. The British were adamant about the correctness of their figures and finally asked the FAI not to recognize the Gromov flight.

The French organization dismissed *The Aeroplane's* challenge of the Gromov flight and declared the barograph in order, expressing satisfaction with the "Commissaires" who had supervised the flight. *The Aeroplane* fired back saying the barograph readings could be easily faked and suggested the "Commissaires" were all Russians. Although the French did not reply to these charges the editors of the magazine were right on target. All of the barographic devices and readings disappeared from American archives. Originally there were three barographs on Chkalov's plane and one on Gromov's ANT. They were never found. General Marshall was the last person to publicly have in his possession the three instruments from the Vancouver ANT, and Edison Mouton was the last person publicly in charge of the San Jacinto ANT. It is believed all four barographs were sent to authorities in Washington, D.C. and apparently disappeared from their offices. The instruments were probably examined and found to be fraudulent and sent home with the Russian fliers. The results of the evaluations were never divulged to the American public. As it turned out the FAI did acknowledge receiving barographic information direct from a Soviet Aero Club when the application was filed requesting FAI recognition of Gromov's flight as the new world record.

The English were also quick to recognize that the ANT-25 was a "somewhat bastard production," recalling that a French Dewoitine Trait d'Union crashed in Siberia in 1932, and that shortly afterwards the ANT appeared, built along the same lines as the Dewoitine. (The English didn't mention a second Trait d'Union crashing in Siberia.) Despite the technical appraisal offered by *The Aeroplane* London's Aeronautical Society blasted the magazine for suggesting the Russians had cheated, and letters from Europe and elsewhere chastised the English editors for not giving credit where it was due. It is apparent the matter had drawn the ire of high British officials who were more sensitive to the repercussions of a possible hoax than was the independent airplane magazine which called the aerial feats as it saw them, "Flights of Fancy."

The English editors made another interesting presentation concerning the route the Russians claimed to have followed. *The Aeroplane* pointed out the only way the trip could have been accomplished was over a Great Circle Route from Moscow to San Jacinto; the shortest air path between these two points. To do this required passing over Greenland, 700 miles from the North Pole. The Soviet fliers not only claimed they flew directly over the North Pole but insisted that they knew their position at all times. However, Russians and others speaking in defense of the flight's authenticity said the fliers may have been mistaken about this and could have strayed off course. The English answered, "Not 700 miles off course." Apparently the Russian defenders were unaware that Ivan Papanin reported hearing the plane's (Gromov's) motor for four minutes as the aircraft passed over the Pole.

The FAI claimed there was nothing unusual about the barographic information coming directly from Russia. Of course this certainly places into question the organization's ability to determine when a record has been set or broken. This coupled with not demanding proper procedures concerning neutral observers or independent witnesses at takeoff and landings seems to discredit FAI's appraisals of some flights. The Soviets insisted there were foreign observers at the takeoff but did not identify them. Looking back into aviation's past it may be asked how many other so-called records were fraudulent? One might take a closer look at the Codos-Rossi flight which began in New York. Not too many people were aware that the Bleriot passed directly over France, which would have afforded an ideal opportunity to refuel. If the FAI didn't pay much attention to barographs or who was witnessing takeoffs and landings there could have been numerous fraudulent claims.

The searchers in Alaska were aware that the end of September marked six weeks since Levanevsky's H-209 was said to have gone down, meaning food supplies were now exhausted. Stalin had ordered the search terminated even before these so-called supplies would have been exhausted. He was evidently criticized for this order and now went to the other extreme by allowing the search to extend beyond any reasonable period. Many American pilots who had volunteered for the rescue mission began to lose hope of ever finding the six airmen alive. The Russian government continued to allude – without evidence – to the great effort being conducted from the European side. Mikhail Vodopyanov never did arrive in Alaska, nor did any other Soviet airplanes come over the pole to the Alaskan area. Once in a while a Russian plane would seem to stray over from Siberia, stay for a short while and then leave.

The Kremlin could only hope the "transpolar flights" had convinced Hitler that Russia's Air Force was formidable and ready. Actually the opposite was true. The country's military defenses and economic programs were in shambles; the political strife and purges had taken their toll as thousands of technicians and engineers were imprisoned or executed. It is understandable why the Russian government sought a neutrality pact with Germany; the country was simply not ready for war. The Soviets were not able to defend themselves against a Nazi invasion, let alone send forces to help France and England. Japan had already called Stalin's bluff by invading northern China, totally disregarding the Russian retaliatory threat to bomb Tokyo and other major Japanese cities. The chief of staff for the Japanese invasion of northern China was Hideki Tojo, who later assumed dictatorial powers during World War II.

Stalin and his Kremlin staff knew that the moment of truth was at hand; soon Russia's real plight would be obvious unless the country could stay isolated and away from any war entanglements. The only way to accomplish this was for Stalin to come to terms with Hitler, a decision that was bound to alienate the United States government and eliminate Russia's access to American aircraft factories. This would be a terrible price to pay and threatened the future development and security of the nation. But the Soviet dictator was used to making shortsighted decisions; in fact his entire rule was marked by political infighting rather than addressing the basic needs of the country. And now Russia was years away from holding its own in agriculture, industry, and military strength. These deficiencies were forcing the Soviets to make an agreement with Hitler's Germany regardless of its ideologies at the opposite end of the political spectrum. However, this difficult decision must be delayed as long as possible to extract the maximum technology from the Americans. And the bluff of Soviet prowess must continue.

In October Alexander Troyanovsky released a statement from his embassy in Washington, declaring Russia ready for any adversary. However, American newspapers also noted a sudden and unprecedented increase in the purchase of U.S. military hardware and aviation materials. Meanwhile the transpolar scenario continued when A. Vartanian announced from Portland, Oregon that more arctic flights were on the agenda. It appears Mr. Vartanian was reacting to statements made by Admiral Byrd, who had advised the American government two weeks earlier of the impracticality of landing and refueling fields on the polar ice. History has proven him correct because there is no record of any further Soviet activity in this part of the world.

The British periodical *The Aeroplane* continued to lambast the "polar flights," declaring that Russia was systematically doing away with witnesses. A dispatch from Warsaw was cited that announced the execution of A.N. Tupolev, the ANT's "designer," by the Russian secret police on November 19. It was reported the death sentence was imposed on Tupolev at Lubianka prison for his part in overloading the H-209, allegedly causing the death of Levanevsky and five other airmen. *The Aeroplane* cautioned against the validity of the disclosure, pointing out that there appeared to be many "walking dead" in the Soviet Union. This version of the "crash of Levanevsky's plane" is contrary to one of the H-209's "last messages," blaming the malfunction of the airship on a leaky oil line. Curiously the oil line defect was the same problem cited in Levanevsky's 1935 flight. There was no mention of Tupolev having anything to do with the H-209; Victor Bolkhovitinov was said to be in complete charge of this particular airplane. Stalin apparently felt the need to build his case of sabotage in connection to the Levanevsky disappearance. Tupolev's arrest was to remind NSR employees and others of the consequences in store if they divulged any secrets about the hoaxes. People invited death if they spoke up. In blaming Tupolev instead of Bolkhovitinov, it appears Tupolev was chosen as the fall guy despite previous Soviet announcements that Bolkhovitinov was the plane's designer. Everyone connected to the diabolical plot had been carefully woven into the web and were now helpless to divulge the real story.

While the feared dictator had things under control at home, the

NSR organization pretended to search in earnest for the "missing fliers," citing the aerial probes over the North Pole from Rudolph Island. NSR said these search flights would go on indefinitely. Actually none of Vodopyanov's group left Rudolph to search for Levanevsky and his crew until October; bad weather was cited as the problem. And yet those non-Russian aviators were actively looking for the missing plane, particularly Sir Hubert Wilkins, who scoured hundreds of thousands of miles during this stormy season, including four probes 350 miles from the pole. According to Wilkins, he learned of a special frequency by which to contact Levanevsky's plane from Constantine Oumansky, the Russian embassy counselor. This information was apparently offered long after the H-209 was supposed to be down. Why hadn't this data been given to the American stations so they could keep in contact with the plane as it supposedly came over the pole into the North American arctic regions? No U.S. station was ever able to make direct contact with the fated airship. On one occasion a U.S. post believed it was listening to Levanevsky's radio; however, there was no way of knowing for sure this broadcast wasn't being staged from Siberia.

The eventful year of 1937 finally came to an end with the transpolar hoaxes tucked safely away, for the time being at least. The only thing reminiscent of the "transpolar flights" was the four "North Pole campers" who were reported riding an ice floe in the direction of Greenland.

As the year 1938 began, Mikhail Vodopyanov returned again to the public aviation spotlight. He announced on New Year's that there was keen interest by the Russians in establishing a permanent South Pole camp modeled after the one at the North Pole. Here was Vodopyanov talking about flying to the South Pole when he couldn't get his ANT-6 off the ground to help Levanevsky. The versatile Vodopyanov called this new tale "A New Year's Dream" (another "pipe dream") in an interview with *Pravda*. Mikhail Gromov joined in by saying, "We have flown over the North Pole. We will fly over the South Pole. We will fly over both poles, to the stratosphere, wherever our fatherland, party and Stalin send us." Vodopyanov declared, "When the Soviet fliers have established their camp at the South Pole as they did at the North Pole, the world will rotate on a Bolshevist axis." The writer-aviator went on to say, "This year certainly will witness ambitious Soviet aviation exploits. Planes are being developed to fly more than 12,000 miles nonstop." Vartanian had made the same brag; however, he was wise enough not to call the proposed venture a nonstop flight.

Stalin jolted all the actors in the polar scheme as the government suddenly, without publicly identifying anyone by name, made a general charge against NSR personnel having ties to Trotsky, "worming their way into the departments." The government's actions spared the main NSR players, with the exception of Levanevsky and his crew. Even Tupolev, who had been quietly imprisoned, was not branded as a "wrecker" or Trotskyite, and received more humane treatment during his so-called confinement. His wife was permitted to join him in prison, along with a number of airplane designers who assisted Tupolev in designing airplanes during imprisonment in Cell No. 58, at Butyrkyi Prison in Moscow. This was a very unusual and suspicious confinement, ordered by Stalin and his secret police. It is possible the airplane designer actually cooperated in his own arrest to help remove suspicion from Stalin in connection with the disappearance of Sigmund Levanevsky. In addition to the many charges leveled against Tupolev, he was accused of giving the Germans the drawings for the Messerschmitt BF-110. This was also strange since the Germans were the well-recognized designers of this type of aircraft. Tupolev had spent many years copying German, American, and any other foreign aircraft he could get his hands on. Actually Stalin was trying to claim (for Russia) credit for designing the Messerschmitt aircraft. The records show that Tupolev spent a few years in "prison" and when he got out in 1942 Stalin awarded him a high prize for developing the TU-2 bomber.

Nine months had been spent in trying to find the missing Levanevsky and his crew although there was no evidence they ever left Russia in the first place. The Soviets provided the major share of the money for the search project but the United States still came out on the short end of it all in terms of time and resources used in this fruitless endeavor. The U.S. also gave the Soviets a great opportunity to learn more about American planes, communications, and weather forecasting. The American search headquarters in Alaska practically served as a training grounds for Vartanian and Mikhail Beliakov to study the most modern aircraft and support systems used in aerial searches. It also gave Vartanian an excellent opportunity to review aircraft purchased from American companies and later flown by American pilots to Russia. All the search planes used on the American side of the pole were flown by American pilots but Russia had purchased many of them and chartered others. These American pilots and others undoubtedly would have judged the Russian government in harsh terms had they known it was a life-threatening search for six "invisible men" and no missing aircraft.

Fliers from around the world gathered in support of the American and Alaskan bush pilots to save some of their aviator comrades, willingly placing their lives on the line in scouring the dangerous arctic. The idea of the hoaxes may have seemed harmless in the beginning, at least from the Soviet point of view, since the flights from Alaska to the mainland were relatively safe. However, the deception magnified when the Kremlin used a false flight to get rid of Levanevsky, setting off a massive, dangerous search during a stormy season. In the fall of 1937 the U.S. had set a deadline officially terminating American assistance in the search as April 1, 1938, April Fools' Day. One week after the American directive ended U.S. participation in the search, Stalin ordered all Soviet shipping under the control of the Russian secret police. This order included the NSR organization. Nikolai Yezhov whose speciality was doing away with "enemies of the government," was to become the Commissariat of Water Transportation, while retaining his usual position as chief of the NKVD (secret political police). The bulletin from Moscow said Yezhov had been in charge of the Moscow-Volga canal project which was to link the Volga River with the Caspian, White, and Baltic seas. What the news article failed to mention was that the workers in the canal project were 200,000 political and criminal prisoners. Many were slaughtered during the forced labor of digging the canal. Stalin's choice of Yezhov was the beginning of his plan to intimidate the workers of the Northern Sea Route Administration. Evidently Stalin did not feel the elimination of Levanevsky and five others was sufficient insurance. Even the imprisonment of Tupolev did not lessen his dread of the secret being revealed. Now Yezhov, recognized by the citizens themselves as the worst butcher in Russia, had control over all of the NSR employees' lives. If the presence of Yezhov didn't put a damper on things then nothing else would.

Back in the United States, on May 10, General George C. Marshall was ordered to Washington to assume a position with the Army's general staff. It appears his role during the Russian visit in Vancouver had brought him to the attention of the Roosevelt administration. Marshall had regarded his Army career at a standstill upon appointment as commander of the Vancouver Barracks, a conclusion that had been shared by other highly placed sources.

CHAPTER 23

Baidukov Writes
a Book

In the summer of 1938, George Baidukov published his account of the famous "transpolar flight" to Vancouver, Washington. It was entitled *Over The North Pole* and was supposedly based on notes the copilot had compiled during the "flight." It is not known whether the book, released in America and written in the English language, was translated and distributed in Russia. Baidukov obviously disagreed with Chkalov on some very important matters, and these differences should have been noticed by those who supposedly were closely following the "historic" June 20, 1937 event. Chkalov may never have known the contents of the English version, or if he did, no statements were made available to Americans indicating any disagreements. Baidukov claims he did most of the flying, a sharp contrast to what Chkalov said after the ANT arrived in Vancouver. The chief pilot told the world he had not left the controls during the 63-hour journey. Baidukov contends Chkalov was away from the controls for about 47 hours, most of the time sleeping. Baidukov's account was later supported by navigator Beliakov. The copilot seems to rub more sand into his superior's eyes by saying that Chkalov slept as the plane went over the North Pole. Although the flight was only make-believe, it did seem unfair and cruel for Baidukov and Beliakov not to "awaken" Chkalov to share in "this great moment, a once-in-a-lifetime experience." Baidukov defended his decision to let his commander sleep by declaring, "To airmen, the Pole doesn't really mean a damn thing." Even though reality is not being discussed, for argument's sake Chkalov should have been the one to judge whether he wanted to take a peek at the pole or not.

It has been mentioned how Chkalov described in detail the manner in which he brought the ANT-25 in for a landing. *Over The North Pole* contains Baidukov's step-by-step manuevers in bringing the big Russian monoplane down on Pearson Field. Although George Baidukov shows no animosity toward Chkalov, it is obvious he is sending a message to Americans, putting them straight about who really was the most instrumental in the "transpolar flight." Following the Russians' arrival in Vancouver, Chkalov had said more than once how the crew had smoked hundreds of cigarettes in the course of their journey. He was seen lighting up Russian-brand cigarettes; however, Baidukov denies any cigarettes were carried on the plane. On the contrary, the second in command claimed that only pipes were smoked in flight. The first mention came shortly after their "takeoff" from Shelkova Airport when Baidukov wrote, "Valery is sucking on an empty pipe, and both of us want badly to smoke. Too bad there are no cigarettes."

Another interjection on page 31 revealed "Chkalov desperately wants a smoke and has become very irritable. . . . I crawl into the wing and get some pipe tobacco." By saying he crawled into the wing to get tobacco Baidukov is trying to show that a special effort was made to secure tobacco, and thus encourage the reader to believe smoking was not an important nor a frequent thing the fliers did during the trip. On page 69 he says they all shared a single pipe. Baidukov noted this by asking Chkalov for his pipe, "Fill it with 'Capitansky' tobacco," requested Chkalov, as he smoked it with great satisfaction. Another passage from Baidukov's book mentioned looking "down at the Amundsen Straits, completely locked in ice, and the northern shores of Banks Land." The copilot is also mistaking M'Clure Strait for Amundsen Gulf, which is 200 miles farther south. On page 84 Baidukov belabors the cigarette issue, writing, "Smoking his beloved pipe which was given him by Stepanchenko, Valery flies along the coast."

In these passages the author-aviator made a concerted effort to erase the idea that there were cigarettes on the flight, and for a very good reason. The question of possible hidden fuel tanks in the ANT's fuselage was left "up in the air" by Major Burrows; allowing Baidukov to "capitalize" on the situation. The Soviet fliers supposedly loaded enough gasoline at Shelkova to last 100 hours, and after a flight of 63 hours would be expected to have 37 hours, or 740 gallons of fuel remaining – a substantial amount. However, the author could not claim they carried this much fuel in the fuselage and at the same time admit smoking hundreds of cigarettes while almost sitting on top of it. Chkalov was seen smoking Russian cigarettes and told the young soldier-interpreter they had smoked hundreds of them on the trip. Americans noticed Chkalov was a chain-smoker. Possibly some local pilots had expressed amazement when they learned of the excessive smoking in view of the amount of fuel they claimed was aboard. This question might have caused the fliers to attempt to minimize the smoking danger.

After bragging about the extensive arctic weather reporting network, the pilots said they ran into all kinds of bad weather on their "trip." For some reason the Soviets wanted to incorporate the existence of cyclonic storms into their so-called transpolar flight plans. It had been previously believed that such storms only gather after the month of October and occur no farther north than Spitsbergen. NSR may have wanted to come up with some revolutionary discovery about the northern arctic regions to sound more convincing about the flight. To this day science has not recognized this particular phenomenon so far north. The U.S. Weather Bureau, on request, denied the existence of cyclones in the North Pole region, noting the lack of heat energy required to form and sustain cyclones, hurricanes, and other high-wind conditions. There were certain drawbacks in making cyclones a part of the scenario. Why hadn't the North Pole station and other northern outposts reported this problem? And if they did why would anyone take off in the face of such bad weather? Baidukov later attempted to explain away the contradictions. For instance he wrote:

> The three of us bend anxiously over the many charts. There are certain suspicious lines that hint of uncertain weather.... Is it possible that the weather will hold us up? But the meteorologists are as fickle as the weather. First they talk of heavy cyclonic activity over the Arctic and Canadian regions. Then they announce that tomorrow will be unfavorable for the takeoff. But what the hell, will it be any better than it is now? And if it isn't, when is it likely to be? More heated arguments, more differences of opinion. By now it's three o'clock and the decision about the weather must be made soon. We beg them to set down the weather reports in detail, for the 18th, 19th and 20th of June. But the minute we start to examine the details of this sinister business and carefully point by point, attempt to minimize the danger of the severe conditions indicated, the weather, surprisingly enough, rapidly improves. The weathermen laugh at us, but they are willing to agree that even if the

weather is none too good it will be no better in the near future. So the three of us take counsel and then announce to the meteorologists: Tomorrow morning we are off!.... We insist on starting tomorrow, June 18.

This is strange behavior for men about to traverse an area so hazardous and unpredictable climatewise, with no de-icers on the wings, to then complain the flight was being held up.

Obviously the copilot wanted to create a picture of indecision before the "takeoff" at Shelkova. Just prior to the alleged takeoff, Baidukov wrote that "the northern stations did warn of cyclones and storms but the fliers disregarded the reports, it will be no better in the future." This was not a scientific nor sensible observation.

Another claim contrary to science reportedly witnessed by the fliers was the formation of clouds over the polar basin at unheard-of altitudes. Chkalov had told General Marshall they flew over the tops of these formations to avoid icing and in so doing depleted their precious oxygen. The Russian aviator-author did use exceptionally good judgment when he eliminated the Great Slave Lake run. This is where the phantom ANT had to "gallop" about 1,500 miles in 28 minutes to reach the Charlotte Islands. Baidukov was also careful not to touch on some other sensitive situations such as their excessive speed from the North Pole to Prince Patrick Island, and explanations of why the plane was bouncing back and forth over the pole. John Grierson commented on the lack of technical information in *Over The North Pole*, and noted the ever-present small talk; however, closer scrutiny shows Baidukov was feverishly and tirelessly trying to cover up earlier contradictions and discrepancies. Of all the discrepancies he attempted to cover up Baidukov did not tackle one glaring error navigator Beliakov made concerning fuel consumption. Newspaper reporters had noted Beliakov was reporting more fuel was burned during the "flight" to Vancouver Island, Canada, than the total loaded at "takeoff," by about 700 gallons. Radio agent Vartanian, realizing the seriousness of this report, said he didn't know exactly how much gas they started with but suggested an error in transmission was possible.

There is an interesting use of certain photographs in *Over The North Pole*. One photo shows Chkalov enjoying a last cigarette before embarking on this "dangerous" mission. Baidukov used the caption "his last cigarette" in another effort to emphasize the lack of cigarettes during the flight. Chkalov seems to be standing in a light dusting of snow and if so, it is obvious the picture was not taken in the month of June. Another picture in Baidukov's book tempts further analysis. It shows Stalin and Chkalov conversing at an airfield and standing with them the chief of Heavy Industry, Sergei Ordjonikidze. Although the picture is not dated, the reader is led to believe the gathering occurred just prior to the first transpolar hoax in June. Actually Ordjonikidze died February 18, exactly four months prior to the June 18 hoax; his death was listed as suicide from a self-inflicted gunshot wound.

There are some indications that Ordjonikidze enjoyed high credibility and a reputation for truthfulness, but some authorities claimed he was responsible for the brutal and unnecessary executions of many Georgians. In his high position in Heavy Industry and as a member of the Politburo, Ordjonikidze probably was aware that NSR and Stalin were planning a phony long-distance flight to America. He, like others in high office, knew the risk of losing America as a supplier of essential goods and technology if any hoax was exposed. Perhaps he resisted these plans, or at least was uncooperative. Ordjonikidze made numerous appeals to Stalin not to question his loyalty to the Party and thus make him an outcast. The Heavy Industry commissar's older brother had been shot for "wrecking," along with some of his close friends and associates. While under torture some of these victims had signed false accusations against the commissar. When Ordjonikidze appealed to Stalin, the dictator taunted him by presenting these false charges and commented, "Comrade Sergo, look what they are writing about you."

Prior to and after conception of the polar master plan, Stalin's henchman Molotov had persecuted and broken Sergei Ordjonikidze. Stalin was undoubtedly behind the affair because Molotov only acted with the Kremlin chief's blessings, particularly in major decisions.

The apparent suicide set off another Stalin super purge and blood bath, including Ordjonikidze's family members, his close associates, and many leaders in industry and the Politburo. The Kremlin chief apparently staged the photo with himself and Ordjonikidze. Ordjonikidze's bloody body was discovered by his wife, Zinaida Gavrilovna, who heard a gunshot and rushed from a nearby hall into the bedroom where he lay mortally wounded. She telephoned Stalin at his apartment in the same building and he summoned key members of the Politburo, including V.M. Molotov, People's commissar, and Lavrenty Beria, (later to become head of the secret police), before he made his grand entrance. As the Kremlin leaders, family members, and others gathered in the bedroom, Stalin attempted to get the family to say that

Ordjonikidze died of a heart attack, but the victim's wife refused, insisting on the truth in keeping with her late husband's honest character. At one point she cried out, "this must be reported in the press," adding "Sergo loved the truth." Stalin called the bereaved woman an "idiot" and demanded her to "shut up." There were emotional outbursts from Zenaida when she called Beria a "rat," and attempted to slap him before he made a speedy exit. One more person in a position to know what was going on at NSR was now dead.

The photograph showing Stalin with Ordjonikidze was probably taken in March of 1936, at the time Moscow announced a long-distance flight across Siberia. This contrived "flight" was actually to transfer the ANT-25 to Siberia for eventual shipment to Alaska. By posing with Ordjonikidze Stalin could later use the photograph to show the public he was on good terms with the commissar. George Baidukov's book offered the perfect opportunity to use the photograph and pretend it had been taken in 1937 in connection with the "transpolar plans."

The book *Over The North Pole* allowed Stalin to elaborate on the general safety of Levanevsky's airplane in order to remove any doubt concerning his decision to approve the "flight." During the May 25, 1937 meeting with Stalin, Molotov, Voroshilov, Kaganovich, General Alksnis, Levanevsky, and Chkalov, Baidukov was asked his opinion of the plane Levanevsky was scheduled to fly to America. The author-aviator wrote in his 1938 book how he personally tested the Bolkhovitinov-designed plane and noted it had broken "two international records." Pilot Baidukov gave this "mystery" plane high performance marks. Besides not even identifying the plane there was absolutely no documentation on any international records. Now it is known the Bolkhovitinov plane was really an ANT-4 in disguise and was just an average, slow-moving and cumbersome cargo-type aircraft copied by Tupolev from a German model.

This is the very same meeting at which Baidukov commented on the "extraordinary comprehension of technical aeronautical details which both Stalin and Voroshilov showed." The inclusion of this passage is understandable in the light of the Levanevsky tragedy, because Stalin was supposed to have personally inspected the H-209 (ANT-4), and declared it safe for the "transpolar flight." However, it was not in the dictator's interest to show too much expertise in aviation since he wanted to be able to wash his hands of the polar hoaxes if they were exposed. When Baidukov elaborated on Stalin's knowledge of aviation, he wove the dictator, perhaps inadvertently, right into the hoaxes; now it was obvious he knew the capabilities of the ANT-25s, ANT-4s and other aircraft.

Many questions had arisen in America about the poor communications during the two "flights" and it became necessary for the Soviet fliers to offer some explanation. The copilot responded in his book by saying, "Something has happened to Beliakov's radio. All the instruments seem to be in perfect order but there is no reception." This occurs, according to him, a few hundred miles from the North Pole, and he goes on to identify the problem: "It seems that one of us, crawling between the transmitter and the side of the fuselage, had somehow or other torn the antenna loose; that was the reason our reception was so poor. But now, although it has been fixed, no one answers us." Supposedly these "flights" have been in the planning for years, but the antenna wire is laying along the fuselage exposed to anyone crawling about, in spite of the "scores of engineers" inspecting the plane. Baidukov is begging the real question. The problem cited by American signal stations was the almost total lack of transmission from the aircraft, having nothing to do with an antenna. The copilot belatedly claimed Beliakov's sextant broke and they hadn't known where they were heading. Again, this is an obvious ploy to leave open the possibility the fliers flew over Greenland after the English discredited their flight. This contradicts their statements a year earlier when they insisted the plane's position was known at all times.

Some of Baidukov's entries almost suggested there was intrigue taking place. "The newspaper correspondents buttonhole us at every corner. They are excited, but we are still trying to hide from them. Never mind, things will be better for them after we take off.... At the airport gates, all the correspondents are gathered again; a whole battalion of them. And they are terribly put out because we hastily slip right by them to our rooms." All of this is a fabrication because there was no takeoff ceremony and consequently there were no interviews with reporters. In the same vein of secretiveness as the flights were supposedly being planned, the author states, "Late into the winter nights, Valery and I sat up talking, hushing our voices to commonplace shop talk when our wives and children began to be suspicious."

Toward the end of the book and upon nearing Portland the copilot told Chkalov the fuel supply was almost spent. According to Baidukov, Chkalov knew the gas was gone when he told General Marshall there was enough left to reach San Francisco. In later documents the copilot declared, "We have to pump more gas from the main tanks then begin to use the auxiliary tanks in the wings." Instead of the wing tanks containing the main fuel storage, Baidukov is now saying the main tanks are not in the wings; this logically means the main tanks are somewhere in the fuselage. All the evidence, including data from the Soviet Union itself, shows this is not true. However, the author felt it was necessary to account for the missing fuel in this "shell game" maneuver.

A general comparison can be drawn between Baidukov's account of the 1937 "transpolar flight" and the 1936 "in-house flight across Siberia." There were striking similarities in separate books. He describes the 1936 "flight" in a text titled *Chkalov*, circulated in 1977. In the 1936 "transcontinental trip through the Arctic and Siberia," Baidukov told about the fruit freezing, the drinking water turning to ice, an inadequate oxygen supply, encountering cyclones, and low cabin temperatures. The exact same problems were reported in the 1937 "trip." He also talks about propellers and wings icing up and dwells often on outclimbing freezing clouds, which according to weather scientists, were not supposed to occur at such high altitudes. The same pilots made no effort in the 1937 "flight" to adjust to the problems encountered in the earlier "flight." In 1935 Levanevsky reported the heating system in the same ANT-25 made the cabin interior warm enough to allow wearing summer flying gear. And, according to Baidukov the system was improved, yet the water still froze during the 1936 and 1937 "flights." The copilot writes they were still sucking on ice 28 hours after leaving the North Pole. Some of the problems Baidukov said they faced were drawn from previous experiences and from knowledge gained from western arctic explorers, with the exception of the cyclones which no explorer had ever reported witnessing in the arctic during the summer. One could also question why the fliers arrived in Vancouver wearing several layers of regular clothing and arctic gear, when Baidukov said the heating system in the aircraft had been improved for the 1936 "flight."

The question is, did Chkalov ever read the English version of *Over The North Pole* which contradicted many things he had told the Americans? The book was released in the United States during the summer of 1938; however, the Russian translation may not have been available in the Soviet Union until much later, if at all. It is possible the Russian version, if in fact there was such a version, did not contain material offensive to Chkalov. It is apparent to Americans who read the book that Baidukov took over the major role in the 1937 flight ending in Vancouver; but it is not known whether Chkalov was ever aware of this.

In America the chief pilot had Baidukov in a bind of not being able to complain about his insignificant role in the "historic feat." Chkalov, upon arriving, claimed all flying duties for 63 hours and credited Beliakov with manning the radio, leaving Baidukov with no real function. Until he published his book the copilot was not able to take credit for most of the flying and landing.

Once back in Russia the tables turned and Baidukov "sat in the driver's seat," and became the principal spokesman and writer of the "transpolar flight." It is not known why chief pilot Chkalov was relegated to a secondary role, perhaps by choice, or unable to do anything about it. Even though Baidukov takes all the credit, he later writes a book about Chkalov and praises his flight skills and knowledge; but, of course, Chkalov was long dead. The Kremlin probably struck a deal with Baidukov to correct mistakes made under Chkalov's command in return for greater personal credit.

Sir Hubert Wilkins, upon Soviet invitation, traveled to Moscow in June to appear before the Academy of Sciences. The Australian aviator had stayed with the Levanevsky search from beginning to end, showing extraordinary perseverence throughout this dangerous ordeal. Since NSR was never successful in getting Russian planes into the search area, the Kremlin was probably trying to draw out information from Sir Hubert about the American side of the pole, information they didn't possess. Wilkins, of course, had no idea the transpolar flights had been faked and that Levanevsky's so-called flight was a coverup.

About this time Yezhov took over NSR, and only a month later General Alksnis was reported dead at the age of 41, although the cause of death was not announced. Later documents revealed he had been tortured at the "hands" of Yezhov while in confinement for several months, and was subsequently executed July 29. He had been demoted from his Air Force command to a lower civil aeronautical position, which placed him under the control of Yezhov's secret police. His death came almost exactly one year from the date he embraced his friend Levanevsky prior to the flier's "final flight." Perhaps one of the factors keeping him alive this long was the accusation by the British magazine *The Aeroplane* that witnesses to the "polar flights" were rapidly disappearing. The extra few months of life may not have been worth it to the general who was at the mercy of Yezhov and his dreaded secret police.

The following month the Soviet Union invited Charles Lindbergh to view the annual air show and visit aircraft factories throughout the country. Lindbergh and his wife, Ann, accepted the Soviet offer and toured engine factories and certain test laboratories for several days. About the same time a French delegation of experts were also studying the Russian capabilities in aviation. One member was lavish in his praise of the number of planes Russia was producing. He noted that more than 5,000 aircraft were being produced annually, about 20 times more than France was manufacturing. Of course it was in the interest of France to praise Soviet aviation in the hopes of slowing Nazi expansion plans in Europe. Stalin must have been pleased with the French report on his country's aviation strength, but he still had not heard from Lindbergh. When he got his answer, there was no rejoicing among the fliers from NSR. Lindbergh divulged his appraisal of Soviet aircraft during a luncheon in London. In brief, the trans-Atlantic flier told the British attending the luncheon that the German air force was better than the Russian, British, and French combined. The English government was shocked and angered, and blasted the American flier for his defeatist attitude in matters so important to Allied morale and security.

Lindbergh also revealed that the Soviet government had offered him a job as head of the aviation industry, a post he turned down. Lindbergh's public disclosure of this decision enraged many Russian fliers, but curiously the Soviet dictator and the Kremlin staff members did not enter the fray at this time. It was the NSR fliers who took up the battle with the American. On October 10, Valery Chkalov, George Baidukov, Alexander Beliakov, Mikhail Gromov, Sergei Danilin, and other familiar names connected to the "polar" events signed a paper denouncing Lindbergh as a "stupid liar, a lackey, and a flatterer of German fascists." In retrospect it is easy to conclude that the American flier was right on target in evaluating Soviet aviation, but his report came at a time when the Russians were trying to fool the Germans into thinking they were very strong in aerial defense. The Soviet strategy was in the direct interest of England and France, and indirectly the United States, which would be compelled to supply those countries in the event of a war in Europe. Perhaps the U.S. government had not taken Lindbergh into its confidence; however, the aviator usually spoke his mind, and was not known for his diplomacy. Lindbergh's statements about Russian aviation might have wiped out the Soviet propaganda generated by the polar hoaxes. No wonder the NSR people were upset.

Stalin was probably equally disturbed, but it was too early in the prewar game for him to personally attack the prominent American. The Soviet leader still needed the cooperation and support of the American government. Lindbergh never bothered to defend himself against the charges brought forth by Russia, the U.S., and England. Even President Franklin D. Roosevelt publicly criticized him. The day after the NSR's onslaught against the American flier, the Soviet Union announced the replacement of two high officials of the Civilian Air Fleet and 22 pilots, engineers, and technicians were replaced. No specific charges or dispositions were revealed, and since the names of the 22 pilots weren't given, it wasn't known if any were NSR employees. The head of the Civilian Air Fleet, I.F. Tkachev, who had chaired the October 1936 conference setting the stage for the polar hoaxes, apparently retained his position in this latest purge.

December 15, 1938, headline in the *New York Times* "VALERY CHKALOV KILLED IN AIR CRASH!" According to a report from Moscow the star pilot of the previous year's "transpolar flight" was killed while testing a new type of fighter plane near Moscow. The "accident" was attributed to engine failure, causing the plane to strike a telegraph pole. As the ship cartwheeled, the pilot was thrown from the cockpit and died en route to a hospital. While Americans accepted this account of Chkalov's death, another story was unraveling in Moscow, throwing suspicion on the circumstances of the "accident." After Chkalov's death, many high-ranking personnel in the aviation industry were charged with sabotaging the pilot's YAK airplane. The list of those charged included N.M. Kharlamov, chief of TSAGI (the Central Hydro-Aero Dynamics Institute) where Tupolev had worked; a large group of his colleagues headed by V.M. Petliakov, M.M. Miasishchev, and Kovalev, all major airplane designers; and other aviation industry leaders and experimental supervisors. No one has divulged the truth about the death of Chkalov but a pattern of death and imprisonments seems to plague those who were instrumental in the "transpolar flights." One guess is that he probably was telling his close friends about the polar hoaxes and had to be silenced.

Why would the Kremlin want Chkalov dead, this hero of the world, this symbol of the new air-minded Russia? It should be kept in mind that Baidukov's account of the "transpolar flight" differed from that of the chief pilot Chkalov. What was going on in the mind of Chkalov since the Vancouver landing? The death of Gorky may have been the beginning of an obstinate streak in the flier, and the death of Levanevsky and the other five fliers may have weighed heavily on his mind. Was he dissatisfied with his role in the hoaxes and despondent over the deaths and imprisonment of some of his friends? Chkalov liked to socialize and drink. It is possible that he let certain things slip while drinking, thus threatening exposure of the hoaxes. Was this the under-lying factor sealing his doom? It had been good while it lasted, but it took more than being a hero in Russia to be assured of security. To many close observers of the Russian scene, it must have appeared as if Stalin had a "highly contagious disease," because everyone around him "died from it." And now they were saying that Chkalov was a victim of sabotage. He may have been, but who was really the culprit? The most likely suspect was Stalin himself. However, as in other cases where important figures died mysteriously, the dictator moved quickly to demonstrate his support and friendship to the deceased. Chkalov was buried with full honors within the walls of the Kremlin, where only the greatest Soviets found their eternal rest. And although the possibility has to be considered, it is unlikely that Chkalov had the option of joining the "walking dead," because his face was too familiar. And like Levanevsky, he was a pilot who had the means to escape from the country and expose everything. The Soviet government renamed the city of Orenburg, located near the Ural River, 775 miles east of Moscow, in Chkalov's honor.

Apparently Stalin was still not satisfied with how Levanevsky's disappearance might be perceived. Sabotage had already been charged and Tupolev was accused of overloading the plane. Now a new wrinkle was being applied. A radioman identified as M.M. Voznesensky was sentenced to 20 years for failing to give Levanevsky weather data. According to the Moscow dispatch, Voznesensky, operator of a north-ern station 560 miles from the North Pole, purposefully withheld important weather information. It is not hard to imagine how this so-called confession or admission was extracted. Since Levanevsky and the crew were not heard from again who would come forward to testify in the defense of the operator who the Soviets said pleaded guilty to the charge? There may never have been such a person as M.M. Voznesensky; however, if there was, Yezhov must have had him tor-tured until he broke down and told the government what it wanted to hear. It is clear that Stalin wanted to find one more way to absolve himself from complicity in the scheme to get rid of Levanevsky, the people's hero.

Klementy Voroshilov took the opportunity on May Day to tell the world, "We not only know how to fight, we love to fight." History shows that a third necessary ingredient for war was missing, namely, the Soviets didn't have much to fight with, especially bombers and fighter planes. The purpose of Voroshilov's tirade was no doubt to ward off German and Japanese designs on Eurasia.

CHAPTER 24

Revelations of War and Lend-Lease

For the most part the polar hoaxes were now behind Stalin and his staff. The secrets appeared to be safely locked in the Kremlin vault, but would they survive the test of time? The greatest current concern for the Soviets was the continuing build-up of German military power in Europe. Since nothing had really happened to improve Soviet air defenses after the hoaxes, Stalin was forced to seek some type of conciliation with Germany. Russia had to buy enough time to build an aerial umbrella over its western sectors. Germany was beginning to threaten central Europe with its ambitions of reuniting those of Aryan ancestry. Sensing the desperation of the situation, Stalin made his move toward a neutrality pact with the German dictator. This is precisely what Roosevelt and other allied leaders feared. A dreaded ten-year neutrality pact was signed in August of 1939. The truce gave Germany a free hand in Europe, and subsequently placed France and England in a precarious position. Hitler would no longer have to worry about his eastern flank while he moved to consolidate the Aryan population in Europe.

Because of the truce Russia thought she had extra time to bolster her defenses. Stalin figured that whichever side won out in Europe, Germany would be weakened from the conflict. Consequently, Russia could move in and control important buffer territories along her western borders. Almost immediately after the neutrality agreement was in force, Hitler invaded Poland. According to a prearrangement with Hitler, Stalin sent his forces into eastern Poland to "protect" the White Russian and Ukrainian minorities living there. By this time Stalin apparently felt very secure that his regime was well entrenched. With the fear of war drawing the Soviets closer together, Trotsky's influence subsided. It was an opportune time to be rid of him once and for all. Lenin had spoken out against Stalin, feeling that he had usurped too much power, and now his fears were being realized. On August 19, 1940, the assassination of Trotsky, still in exile in Mexico, was ordered by Stalin. This terrorist act was carried out by a member of the household who had gained the displaced leader's trust. The slaying was done with an ice axe inside the Trotsky compound. The outspoken opponent of Stalin suffered until the next day, August 20, before succumbing to injuries.

By June of 1941 the Third Reich controlled the Balkans close to Russia. Soviet intelligence informed Stalin of Hitler's plans to invade their country. Stalin scoffed at the idea and declared that Germany would honor the neutrality pact. But the German armored divisions did come, heavily supported by the powerful Luftwaffe. The Luftwaffe anticipated meeting strong aerial resistance from the Russians because their military had been completely taken in by the propaganda surrounding the polar hoaxes and other reports of the Soviet Union's mass production of hundreds of modern bombers and fighters each month. No one really knows why Hitler broadened the war so early by attacking the Soviet Union. There were even stories circulating that he was following the advice of an astrologer who told him the signs were right.

However, on the first day of the attack the German pilots were surprised to discover the inefficiency of the Russian planes and of the fliers themselves. A count of 1,811 Soviet airplanes were destroyed by the much faster and better armed Messerschmitts. One German officer remarked, "The Red Air Force was nothing but a large cumbersome instrument of small combat value." On some Russian planes the gun sight was merely a hand-painted circle on the wind screen. The situation was so desperate for the Russian fliers that nine pilots rammed their planes into the enemy aircraft in wild fanatic gestures. The Luftwaffe went uncontested while attacking deeper into the Russian interior. Hundreds of Soviet bombers and fighters were destroyed on the ground. (It was later revealed many did not have motors – they were in great shortage.) The clumsy Soviet craft flew in rigid formations only able to fire in frontal attacks, while the Nazi pilots simply picked them off easily. All 21 planes of one fleet were knocked from the skies in a single engagement. The Russian people and particularly all the aviators must have been wondering where all the great Soviet airplanes and technology were hiding while this aerial holocaust was going on.

Most of the "transpolar flight" crews served in the Red Air Force during World War II. Baidukov was in a command position with the Red Air Force; Beliakov directed an aviation school for navigators. The crew of the second "transpolar flight" to America also played military roles during the war with Germany, according to the *Great Soviet Encyclopedia*. Colonel Gromov, who piloted the second "transpolar flight," served as head of the Institute of Flight Research from 1940-1941, then commanded various air force divisions throughout most of the war, holding the rank of colonel general. He ended his wartime service as chief of the Main Directorate for Combat Training of Aviation at the Front. Major Yumashev, Gromov's copilot, was appointed commander of a fighter squadron in July of 1941, rising rapidly to commander of the VI Fighter Air Corps on the Kalinin, Western, and Southwestern fronts. He completed his wartime service as chief of the Main Directorate of Combat Training. Captain Danilin, Gromov's navigator, held the rank of lieutenant general of the Air Force engineers during the early phase of the war and later served as director of the Scientific and Testing Institute of the Air Force Special Services before becoming deputy director of the State Research Institute, where he served from 1944 to 1951.

All of these fliers had acquired extensive knowlege of quality aircraft in America, France, Germany, England, and other technologically advanced nations. They also knew the shortcomings of their own aircraft; so it was no surprise to witness the Luftwaffe's easy destruction of their air force fighters and bombers. They also knew that their pilots and crews were ill trained and no match for the highly skilled Luftwaffe flight crews with superior aircraft. This was graphically underscored every day of aerial combat, particularly during the first few years of the war.

What did the Western nations think when they saw this aerial slaughter taking place? After all, America and other allied nations were led to believe that Soviet aviation technology was very advanced prior to the war; indeed the United States and France helped to publicize Russia's aerial accomplishments, including their aircraft and the skill and daring of their fliers. But, according to Luftwaffe reports, the Soviet aircraft were totally outdated and their pilots seldom demonstrated any semblance of a coordinated plan of execution during combat missions. It was later discovered only the leader of a squadron knew the mission and once his plane was destroyed the rest of the fliers did not know what to do. This was attributed to the practice of secrecy on the part of the military leaders, perhaps because so much distrust was generated by the purges. It took a war to bring out the truth about Soviet aviation capability, but at last it was quite apparent that this industry was extremely antiquated. Since there was no way to protect the ground forces from continued German onslaughts, the Soviets were driven back deep into the interior of the country's western regions.

Because Stalin did not expect Hitler's attack, great numbers were lost due to poor war preparations. On learning of the invasion the dictator declared that all was lost and went into hiding. Depressed, nervous, and off-balanced, Stalin refused to sign any orders from June 23 to July 2, while the German panzer divisions were slaughtering Russian armies on the southwest front. Stalin knew better than anyone the weakened condition of his country. Realizing that his bluffs concerning Soviet aviation had not worked, Stalin gave up prematurely when he saw Hitler's forces spilling unchallenged across his borders. Historians noted that 51 totally unorganized and ill-prepared divisions were annihilated in the first days of the war and 70 additional divisions had losses upwards of 50 percent. While the Germans were advancing, almost at will, Stalin, when he did emerge from isolation (drinking heavily), totally misjudged the enemy's strength and his own defense weaknesses and ordered a full attack on the much stronger and more organized Nazi forces. He gave these desperate orders despite convincing arguments from his own General Staff. Hundreds of thousands of soldiers and civilians were unnecessarily sacrificed by his early indecisions and later bad decisions. Many viewed his actions as cowardly and inept in this hour of emergency.

Molotov and others had to keep the government on an even keel until the distraught Stalin could pull himself together. The Soviet chief had appeared to be a tower of strength, worshipped by the people for his courage and capable leadership, and now he was cringing and afraid to meet the German threat. In time Stalin finally resumed his role as commander-in-chief of the Armed Forces. But just as in the case of Hitler, his obstinacy was the cause of many tactical errors on the various fronts, bringing about untold and needless loss of life. Like his peacetime rule, his efforts in war seemed to constantly waste lives.

The American Lend-Lease Act of 1940 came to the rescue. Congress transferred power to President Roosevelt to provide weapons and other vital war materials to countries opposing Germany and Japan. Russia was included later and thousands and thousands of airplanes and other war equipment were ferried and shipped to the Soviet Union under the lend-lease program. There is no question that without this aid Russia would have fallen under the domination of the Third Reich.

If the United States was not convinced of Russia's deplorable defense capability by the first few months of its war with Germany, it certainly got an eye-opener when the U.S. administration carefully began negotiating with Congress the expansion of the Lend-Lease Act to the USSR. Although public opinion surveys clearly showed that the vast majority of Americans supported the idea of giving Russia arms and munitions to help defeat Hitler armies, many congressmen were very reluctant to support the only Communist country in the world. Caught between helping the Communists and defeating Germany, even the most conservative congressmen finally agreed with Roosevelt to extend lend-lease to the Soviets.

The main question centered on learning exactly the minimum amount of arms and munitions the Russians would need to stave off the advancing German armies in Eastern Europe. The answers startled a reluctant Congress but did not appear to surprise the administration. The Russians needed everything, including food and clothing for the Red Army. Some American observers in Russia tried to sum up the problem by explaining that the Russians "couldn't even perfect a flush toilet."

Technologically, Stalin's forces didn't have any war machinery to combat Germany and what they did have was even outdated by World War I standards, including their aircraft, naval ships, tanks, artillery, small arms, automatic weapons, explosives, communications, anti-aircraft guns, and a wide range of other necessities.

It was interesting that Congress and the administration, at least publicly, didn't ask why the Soviets had such an underdeveloped air force despite widespread claims of superiority in aviation dating back to the mid-1930s. Perhaps this revelation came as no great suprise since the administration had known for years that the Russians wanted to buy American aircraft and obtain patents for many models to copy.

When lend-lease to Russia began in 1941, Stalin repeatedly made requests for aircraft, including bombers, fighters, cargo planes, trainers, and patrol craft. The Americans learned of another deficiency in the Red Air Force upon delivery of aircraft to Fairbanks and Kodiak, Alaska, where Soviet pilots were scheduled to ferry them to Russia. Stalin continued to apply pressure to increase these deliveries, but a logjam quickly developed and many of the aircraft were held up for lengthy periods in Fairbanks and Kodiak due to distribution problems, including a lack of trained Russian pilots. Hundreds of these planes were lost in shipment to Russia, mostly due to pilot errors and unfamiliarity with the aircraft.

Other evidence of the Soviet's backwardness in aviation surfaced when their experts raved over the delivery of outdated P-39, P-40, P-47 and P-63 fighter planes. Although these aircraft were no match for the German Messerschmitts, they were much improved over the Russian Yaks and other outmoded planes being flown by Soviet pilots. The American B-24s and B-25s were similarly praised by the Soviets, but these were class bombers by any standards. However, the Americans did not give Russia any B-17s, the real workhorse of the aerial war against the Axis powers.

The list of materials sent to Russia under the Lend-Lease Act gives a clear picture of the underdeveloped Soviet military defense. Robert Huhn Jones, an author and college professor for many years, does a very credible job of compiling these lend-lease supplies to Russia in his 1969 book *The Roads to Russia*. From early in 1941 and until September 2, 1945, the U.S. sent more than $32 billion in war machinery, food, clothing, and other items to the Soviet Union. This figure does not include transportion costs and heavy losses of cargo due to mishaps, German submarines, or in transit through Iran and other Middle East routes. Nor does it include arms and supplies charged to the Great Britain lend-lease account but sent from England to Russia, an intentional bypass by the administration to calm the critics in Congress.

A general list of materials outlined in *The Roads to Russia* illustrates the magnitude of lend-lease to Russia. The list includes: Railroad transportation equipment (steam and diesel locomotives, flat cars, tank cars, dump cars, rail lines, heavy machinery cars, etc.), metals, chemicals and explosives, petroleum products, sundry machinery, food, clothing and boots, cloth for uniforms, skis, tanks, self-propelled guns, jeeps, land and amphibious trucks, tractors, tank transporters, recovery units, motorcycles, armored scout cars, anti-aircraft guns of all types, a wide range of explosives, and all chemicals to manufacture more explosives, radio stations, receivers, locators, directions finders, altimeters, beacons, compasses, communication wire, barbed wires for combat defense systems, cement mixers, pavers and other construction equipment, generators, metal forming, metal cutting and a myriad of other precision machinery, paper, tires, tubes and other rubber supplies, photographic films, asbestos materials, chemicals of almost every type, and every conceivable food item, measured in thousands of tons to provide a balanced diet to the Russian soliders and citizens. Because of the Soviet's lack of technology and factories, the U.S. simply could not supply it with the raw materials. Almost everything had to be ready for war use. Even the gasoline, lubricating oils, and kerosene had to be refined and delivered in a state of instant readiness for the Red Army, Air Force, and other military units.

Since the underdeveloped Soviet Air Force was annihilated within a few months of the war's opening, the U.S. quickly delivered aircraft to the Russians. The aircraft list included 13,014 fighter craft and more than 4,500 bombers, cargo planes, observation, Navy patrol and trainer-type aircraft, and many extra engines and other spare parts.

While the cost to the United States of this program was extensive, the Russian people were told very little about the American lend-lease program, except when good news was needed to bolster the depressed and war-stricken people. The situation in Russia, particularly during the first two years of the war, was indeed dire. People went hungry and actually froze in their houses and on the streets. Crime was rampant. Gangs of desperate males roamed the streets in search of victims to rob, even stealing food and ration cards from older and other helpless folk. The Russian borders were totally insecure and police were kept busy by the more direct effects of the war. People were not geared to cope with this new criminal element; most of the perpetrators did not have criminal records and many of the police informants would not or could not identify anyone. In addition, the police knew these "robbers" were normally law-abiding and loyal citizens who through desperation had to bring food home to their starving children and family members. German agents infiltrated the open and disorganized cities to stir up rebellion against the government, already in chaos from the invading Nazi air and land forces.

Although the lend-lease program fostered friendly relations between the United States and Russia, ironically in the end the assistance program was a major factor triggering the "Cold War." Stalin and the entire Kremlin became very angry when the United States terminated the Lend-Lease Act with the surrender of Germany in May of 1945. From the Russian perspective, termination of the much-needed assistance to their devastated country was incomprehensible, particularly since their mutual enemies, Germany and Italy, were now enjoying billions of U.S. dollars to rebuild their countries and support their postwar economies and domestic needs. Japan, the other Axis power, was practically rebuilt with American money, technology, and other forms of assistance.

Whereas Stalin and other Russian leaders as late as 1943 acknowledged that their war with Germany would have been lost without the "miracle" of American production, these leaders later discounted the value of the lend-lease program. When the war ended and the "cold war" began, Stalin shifted the credit for their war with Germany to the extreme sacrifices of their soldiers and civilians. The Soviets claimed that their factories produced 35,000 aircraft in 1943, a time when the Russian forces and the country had not recovered from the extreme devastation of the war. In retrospect one might pose an interesting question: If the Russians had produced all those fighters and bombers in just one year, why didn't they use them against Germany? Russia never launched any significant bombing attack on German forces or Germany proper at any time during the war, even when Nazi forces were in full retreat. This belated claim of war production was obviously made to further discount the value of American lend-lease. The United States and England refused to send the B-29 Superfortresses to the Soviet Union, believing from past experiences that these ultra-modern bombers could be put to more effective use under U.S.-Britain control. However, when several Superfortresses were forced down in Soviet territory after bombing runs on Japan in 1944, the Russians confiscated them and interned the crews. A.N. Tupolev, who had been released from prison in 1942, was assigned the task of copying the B-29s for Soviet production as the TU-4. However, the Russian Air Force still could not initiate any significant action in the aerial bombardment of Germany.

The Soviet Union later claimed losses of 20 million people and countless additional millions of wounded in the effort to stem the Nazi invasion. Great numbers might have been spared if Stalin had not severely handicapped the nation by purging many of the best military and technological experts. Some historians maintained that Stalin had purposely eliminated his military officer corps because they challenged his appeasement policies with Hitler, particularly during the period leading to the signing of the 1939 Neutrality Pact. The heavy loss of these key military officers wasn't the only reason the nation was crippled during this period. The USSR simply did not have the war machinery due to the lack of technology. And now it had taken a war to reveal these weaknesses of Soviet aviation and industrial development, further proving the improbability of the so-called aerial feats over the

North Pole. But it is possible the advent of the war saved Stalin's regime because at its conclusion the Russian people hailed him as the great savior of the country. This adulation was to carry over for almost another decade and insure his place as the supreme leader of the largest country in the world.

Joseph Stalin's death on March 5, 1953, gave the Russian people a small light of hope for a more humane leader. He died a jerking and stressful death, typical of heart victims; it might have appeared as if the gods were strangling and punishing him in retribution for his cruel and indiscriminate acts of terror. Although the finest medicine was available to him from abroad, there was a last-ditch crude effort to cure him by the use of leeches placed on his chest. It seemed that his departure might lessen the repressive rule of the Kremlin, but restoration of human rights was to be a slow process. Gradually people caught up in the regime's terror were being repatriated; but the legacy the dictator had left in terms of hate and distrust was bound to prevent any significant breakthroughs toward an enlightened Russia. Even after death Stalin was dangerous; many Russians who came to mourn in Red Square were trampled by the frenzied crowds.

Lavrenty Beria, chief of the secret police since 1938, was quickly charged with numerous crimes against the people, including an allegation that he had been a secret British agent since 1919. There was no public trial, but it is believed Beria was privately executed in the presence of Nikita Khrushchev, Georgii Malenkov, and other high-ranking party officials. Beria was probably killed on orders from Stalin's apparent successor Malenkov who had the support of Molotov, Voroshilov, and Khrushchev. Beria was also hated for his sexual crimes against young girls whom he periodically arranged to have kidnapped from various school grounds. Some victims even committed suicide. Although all the heinous crimes committed under the Stalin regime could not be undone, at least this was a beginning. Perhaps the truth of many matters would now emerge. Maybe someone might bare to the world the story of the polar hoaxes. It wouldn't come from Professor Otto Schmidt because he died in 1956 at the age of 64, apparently from natural causes.

Following World War II the relationship between Russia and the United States deteriorated. Once the war was over their ideological and policy differences emerged once again, further widening the gap despite joint efforts through detente. And the cold war swept in, preventing any meaningful exchanges. The wars in Korea ("United Nations Police Action") and Vietnam and disputes over the nuclear arms race kept the two nations at arm's length, and sometimes at almost sword's length.

CHAPTER 25

Monument to the Soviets

By 1974, 37 years after the "transpolar flights," relations had not improved much between the United States and the Soviet Union, but there was one modest step of reconciliation getting underway in the State of Washington. This effort of improved coexistence was related to the "transpolar flights" of 1937. During Russia's aerial exhibit at the Spokane, Washington World's Fair, Soviet *Sputnik* cosmonauts contacted some Vancouver citizens. The cosmonauts asked why Vancouver had never erected a monument to Chkalov and his crew for the 1937 transpolar flight.

Although there had been an earlier attempt by the city in 1938 to commemorate the event, including official permission by the War Department to erect a stone monument at Pearson Field, this plan did not materialize because of poor relations over ideological differences in the postwar period. But at this later date the meeting during the world's fair was generating new interest in Vancouver. Eventually correspondence between Moscow and Vancouver paved the way for a permanent marker honoring the 1937 flight, to be placed near Pearson Field by June of 1975. The Soviets agreed to design and supply emblems for the monument to be built by the Americans. As a result of the project a group of people organized the Chkalov Committee, selecting the name from the chief Soviet pilot who was killed in 1938. Some of the people who had witnessed the "event" in 1937 became members of the committee. If all went well the commemoration ceremony would take place on June 20, 1975, the day of the flight's anniversary. Various news stories kept the public abreast of the coming program involving numerous

Russian dignitaries, including the two surviving pilots of the "epic achievement."

As the summer of 1975 neared there was considerable interest in Vancouver; the celebration was almost at hand. The print and electronic media coverage of the anticipated meeting with the Russians re-awakened the general population of southwest Washington to the historic moment when Vancouver hosted the famous "transpolar flight" of 1937. Of course many people were either too young or had moved to the city at a later time; however, the flight which had been compared with Lindbergh's ocean crossing to Paris was still of major interest. And the fact that Vancouver, like Paris, was the host city marking the end of such a "famous event" gave the June 20 celebration great prestige. Vancouver had not enjoyed such distinction since the days of the Hudson Bay Company. And what had been achieved often was confused with Canada's much more prominent city of Vancouver, British Columbia. Here was an ideal opportunity to publicize to the world that there was a Vancouver in the United States. Furthermore, the city was forming a unique bond between America and a country heretofore difficult to approach.

One area resident eventually became quite interested in the Russian visit to America. Having heard only bits and pieces about the "famous flight" over the years, Mrs. Alice Hawkins had not paid much attention to Vancouver's involvement in the now famous event. At this time the papers were full of news about the "famous" Russian landing in Vancouver as it was being relived during these few days left before the Russians arrived. One evening Mrs. Hawkins was watching television and learning of the final preparations for hosting the Russians when a peculiar feeling came over her. The announcer was telling how the Soviet pilots had crossed over the North Pole and arrived in Vancouver in June of 1937. As he spoke about airplanes and Russians Mrs. Hawkins' attention became more focused on the broadcast. There was something she was trying to recall. It had to do with airplanes and Russians. It seemed someone had told her a story relating to this – perhaps a conversation had taken place a long time ago, she mused. What was it? The question kept nagging at her, refusing to be swept aside.

Then there was a sudden flashback, a conversation with an Indian man many years ago! Yes, that was it. An Indian friend had told her a story about Russians and airplane parts. It was in Alaska. When was that? she asked herself while probing her memory for the year when the Indian told her this story. She had not seen her Indian friends, the Eyles, for ten years; but one day in 1946 as she was passing their home some of the family members were in the yard. Upon seeing her they had come to the gate to talk. A nice-looking man, about 28 years old, joined the group shortly, and after a moment's recall she recognized him as Frank Eyle. Now, 29 years later, Mrs. Hawkins remembered what Frank had told her. Her mind jumped back and forth between this long-ago conversation and the television broadcast. Could it be? Was there a connection between what Frank had told me and this Vancouver thing? Her thoughts were almost too scary to say aloud. What could all this mean? The possibilities disturbed her and she became instantly apprehensive and concerned. It was crazy to entertain such thoughts. There was probably nothing to it. But she knew in a few minutes the subject couldn't be discarded just like that. The housewife began to analyze the situation, hoping to think it through logically, and perhaps hoping it would all go away. She might be the only person in the world who was considering that the Russian polar flight to Vancouver could be a hoax. Mrs. Hawkins knew she could not chance telling anyone about this because they surely would think her to be a lunatic. There was no proof that her 1946 conversation and the 1937 flight had any connection. She believed the year mentioned by her Indian friend was 1937, when he had helped the Russians. Could it all be a coincidence? she asked herself.

In the final analysis, there was really nothing much to be gained by telling the public this story, Mrs. Hawkins was convinced. Vancouver was preparing for perhaps its finest hour. There was no reason to spoil this treasured event and enrage the citizens by telling her story. After confiding in her husband it was decided the story should be dropped. She went about her chores and pushed the episode from her mind, or tried to.

A year-long effort had gone into the plans to bring the Russian delegation to Vancouver. The Soviet Communist Party leader, Leonid Brezhnev, had been invited but there was no official word of acceptance. The Vancouver citizens had done their part by having the monument in place to honor the fliers when they arrived. Right at this very moment a four-motor Russian jet was en route to America. Its route over the North Pole was supposed to be in recognition of the first "transpolar flight" of 1937. About 25 Soviet dignitaries and news people were accompanying copilot George Baidukov, navigator Alexander

Beliakov, and the 52-year-old son of the late Valery Chkalov who had served as chief pilot for the first "transpolar flight." As the Soviet passenger jet was in flight Baidukov referred frequently to his book, *Over The North Pole*, while "reliving the experiences of the first flight." Navigator Beliakov had brought along a flight log to use as a reference, probably not wanting to trust his memory in the presence of so many reporters. The same stories about the radiator freezing up, the lack of oxygen, and how their radio quit functioning were retold.

As the 500-mile-an-hour plane crossed the pole the delegation rose from their seats and toasted the fliers. The medium-sized jet followed the very same route claimed in 1937, passing over Banks Land and the Mackenzie district in the Northwest Territories of Canada. From there the jet turned west toward the Pacific coast from the same point where Chkalov and Baidukov said they had decided to fly over the rugged Mackenzie mountains. The newsmen and camera personnel hung on every word as microphones were held close to the old fliers. Great Slave Lake and northern Alberta were hundreds of miles away to the southeast, but these embarrassing landmarks had long been forgotten. With repeated gestures the old copilot told the delegation how they flew down the coast in darkness and overcast, requiring Baidukov to negotiate this stretch by "blind flying." Motion pictures were taken inside the jetliner to record the "retracing" of the "polar route."

And then this 1975 real transpolar flight was over when the big jet came down at Everett, Washington. The trip had taken 11 hours. This was a unique experience for Baidukov and Beliakov, marking their first crossing over the pole. Everett Field is owned by the Boeing Company, which had prepared a ceremony on the eve of June 18, two days before the Vancouver commemoration. On June 19, the fliers and the rest of the delegation boarded private airplanes for a trip to Vancouver, the now-famous terminus of the first "transpolar flight." At 1:30 p.m. PST airplanes began landing at Pearson Field. In a few minutes an Aero Commander carrying the celebrated pilots arrived. Out stepped George Baidukov, now 69 years old, and Alexander Beliakov, 78, looking considerably different to the old-timers who had witnessed their visit in 1937. Baidukov had done especially well in his career since then. He presently held the rank of colonel general in the Soviet Air Force, and had been for many years the chief of Aeroflot, the government's civilian airline carrier. Beliakov had retired from a professorship in aviation navigation many years earlier. Both appeared to be in fairly good health, but the older celebrity needed to lie down on occasion to gain back some strength.

On the next day, June 20, the anniversary of the 1937 landing was at hand. Soviet Ambassador to the United States Anatoly Dobrynin had brought two Russian officials from Washington, D.C. Ambassador Dobrynin was appearing in the same capacity as his 1937 predecessor, Ambassador Alexander Troyanovsky. The Russian delegation included Counsel General Alexander Zinchuk and his wife from the Russian consulate in San Francisco. Eighteen news people and camera crews from the Soviet Union had been recording the entire proceedings. They would continue to cover the commemoration of the monument and other events as they took place. One thing on the agenda was to rename a city street after Chkalov, in the presence of his son Igor. More than 1,000 people gathered at the site where the monument had been erected. This particular place had been donated by Washington State and was located not far from where the flight had ended – off a main highway along the Columbia River. There to represent the State of Washington was Governor Daniel Evans and Secretary of State Bruce Chapman. Representing the City of Vancouver was Mayor James Gallagher.

The year 1975 also marked the 150th anniversary of Vancouver's existence as a city; however, it was known as Fort Vancouver for many years. Ten members of the Chkalov Committee were on hand, proudly promoting the historic event. They had been the driving force behind the movement to build a monument to the Russian achievement. The usual speeches were given, expressing hope for a better relationship and peaceful objectives between the two countries. Gifts were exchanged between the officials from both countries, mostly in the form of souvenirs of the "historic" flight. Finally the strings were pulled and the monument was unveiled. It stood about 20 feet high and had the Soviet-designed plaque imbedded in the stone work. The bronze emblem contained a picture model of the "famous" ANT-25, the plane used in the "polar" trip. There was also a description denoting the date of the flight and the destination. Oddly enough, one of the plaques, inscribed with Russian lettering, listed Portland, Oregon, as the official terminus of the flight instead of Vancouver. It appears the Soviets chose the larger city as more prestigious.

Still following in the footsteps of the 1937 itinerary, the delegation attended a luncheon hosted by the Portland Chamber of Commerce. Then, just as in 1937, the Soviets boarded a commercial airliner to San

Francisco for still another fete. On June 22 the party was scheduled to be in Washington, D.C. for a special meeting with President Gerald Ford. A large gathering stood outside while the President addressed the audience from the White House steps, speaking in recognition of the bonds established by the fliers in their 1937 "achievement." Moscow was the next stop and the great anniversary program would come to a close.

Two years later in 1977, exchanges between the Chkalov Committee and the Russian fliers were kept alive with a dual ceremony performed at Vancouver and a small Russian town designated as Chkalovskaya, located about 20 miles from Moscow. This site is not to be confused with Chkalovsk, located near the Volga River and 300 miles from the capital city. Chkalovskaya was expressly established for the 1977 exchange. It is interesting the Soviets did not invite the visiting members of the Vancouver Chkalov Committee into the birthplace of Valery Chkalov where the museum is located and the ANT-25 is on "display." However, only one member of the Chkalov Committee has ever been allowed in the city of Chkalovsk. There are only poor roads into the city so this visitor was transported there by helicopter. Judging by Chkalovsk's inaccessibility, the Russian government apparently does not want to make the museum public. So the Soviets set up a substitute city outside of Moscow for its part of the dual ceremony. According to reports, 8,000 Russian citizens and a five-member delegation from the Chkalov Committee attended the occasion, while in Vancouver there was a more modest program to celebrate the June 20 event, witnessed by a small number of city officials who welcomed a former Soviet Air Force general.

In the interim between 1977 and 1983 no significant exchanges took place while the cold war got a little colder. Although there was nothing so grandiose as the 1975 event, some personal contacts were maintained by members of the Chkalov Committee and the Soviet fliers and their families. The Russians had been invited many times to return to Vancouver but for various reasons the invitations were declined. Some members of the Chkalov Committee were interested in keeping the contacts going in the hopes some trade agreements could be initiated. Whatever was to follow, it would have to proceed without the presence of Alexander Beliakov, who died December 2, 1982. Now only one of the flier-witnesses was still alive – George Baidukov; however, the "transpolar affair" was not over yet.

CHAPTER 26

"The Best Job
I Ever Had"

By 1983 the "peace movement" was gaining momentum throughout the world. The people of many nations had finally begun to speak up and march against the buildup of nuclear arms. Thousands of cities in America began developing their peace advocate programs; and more and more of these groups were exhibiting strong opposition to the arms race. In Vancouver, a cross section of people such as lawyers, ministers, businessmen, and other community leaders, joined with the rank and file to protest continued growth of the atomic arsenal in America. People were also looking for ways to develop better relations with the Soviet Union. One program in particular that gained interest was the Ground Zero Pairing Project designed to establish sister cities in Russia and the United States, with the intentions of building cultural, social, and educational bonds. Vancouver had an advantage in considering Sister City status because of the "transpolar" event. Thanks to the Chkalov Committee a solid foundation was already in place. All they needed to do was build on this base.

The author, although not a member of any specific arms-control organization, was very much interested in the objectives of the universal peace movement. The merits of the sister city concept began to be discussed in Vancouver as an ideal way to lessen tensions between the two most powerfully armed nations in the world. Yes, Vancouver should have a sister city was the conclusion, and one choice was Chkalovsk, the birthplace of Valery Chkalov who had been credited with the "transpolar flight" ending in Vancouver. The issue of a sister city was under study by a small Ground Zero Paring Project Committee in Vancouver early in 1983, and many families, including the author's, discussed the merits of this program during this time.

One day a visitor dropped by the author's home when the sister city proposal was being discussed, with the probability that Chkalovsk would be named as Vancouver's selection. When the visitor heard the "transpolar" event being reviewed, he was compelled to relate an unusual story told to him by his grandmother, Alice Hawkins. According to the young visitor, the children and grandchildren of Mrs. Hawkins had been sworn to silence about this story for the past eight years. But this young man couldn't seem to hold back any longer. His account was startling because it cast serious doubts on whether there had actually been a bona fide flight over the North Pole to Vancouver in 1937.

If the story had any truth it could have serious impact on the sister city project and might prove embarrassing to the city and the officials making the selection of Chkalovsk. The young man telling the story was known to the author as a sensible and stable individual with high credibility. His revelation didn't cause immediate alarm but it was felt there was enough to the story to quietly raise the issue at the next meeting of the sister city committee. As a precaution the proper people were notified of the situation by a member of this committee, my sister Mary Ellen. After studying the new information provided, the special committee didn't feel any changes in their sister city plan were warranted. Tentatively, the Russian city of Chkalovsk was still being eyed as Vancouver's choice.

In July 1983 the young man happened to visit again and was asked to retell his grandmother's extraordinary tale about the Russians. His second account of the story was consistent with what he told earlier. He earnestly believed that his grandmother secretly felt the Russian flight had been a hoax. The question emerged, What if grandmother Hawkins was right? Wouldn't it be better to play it safe than be sorry in the selection of Chkalovsk as Vancouver's sister city? Again, the committee didn't take the rumor seriously and the author, at the request of his family, decided to personally take a look at the "historic event" by examining newspapers, books, and other articles about the 1937 "transpolar flight." This seemed appropriate.

The author had not been present when the "transpolar flight" occurred, and really knew nothing about Vancouver's role in the famous flight 46 years earlier, except what was recalled from the 1975 anniversary ceremony. The need to satisfy curiosity and gain a better perspec-

tive in this "historic event," demanded that some hours be spent studying microfilms at the local library, gathering various materials and
talking informally with people who had been present during the landing
of the Russian plane at Vancouver. The first discrepancy in the "polar
flight" to catch the eye was the small amount of gasoline left in the
ANT-25 aircraft after the so-called harrowing trip across the North
Pole. Less than 11 gallons were drained from the Russian plane when
2,000 gallons were said to have been loaded at the Shelkova airfield near
Moscow. In addition, the Soviet officials in charge of the flight claimed
that the ANT-25 could remain aloft for 100 hours with this amount of
fuel. Since the fliers were eventually credited for 63 hours and 17
minutes of air time, it is rather academic for anyone to ask, "Where was
the remaining fuel?" – approximately 37 flying hours were missing.

In addition to the fuel situation there were also some disturbing
discrepancies and contradictions concerning the plane's reported positions while en route, and its speed. Moreover, it was impossible to
blame the discrepancies on the American news media since a Russian
translator was supervising all press releases. There were many other
puzzling factors seemingly suggesting that some basic irregularities and
inconsistencies were running throughout the entire affair.

On the strength of what was learned a greater interest in Mrs.
Hawkins' story evolved, creating additional curiosity. The coincidence
of her account and the discrepancies uncovered increased the chance
that a great hoax had been pulled on the American people. At any rate it
would not do any harm to confront the lady, who was now crowding her
70th year. What was she like? Would she be rational or someone with an
overactive imagination? It would be interesting to meet Mrs. Hawkins
face to face. Motivated by this increased interest, wheels were put in
motion to arrange a meeting. Her grandson was approached and asked
about the possibility of speaking with her. He had already told his
grandmother that he had let her story out. She was not exactly pleased;
however, the lady was moderate in her reprimand of him. It was agreed
the grandson would carry our request to talk with Mrs. Hawkins at her
convenience.

In a few days, contact with the grandson was made, at which time
he let it be known that his grandmother was willing to see us. Her phone
number was provided and subsequently the call took place. The request
to discuss the story directly with Mrs. Hawkins was met with a warm
welcome and my sister and I were invited to come. Mrs. Hawkins' home
was located on the outskirts of Vancouver and well off the beaten path of

the more traveled roads. As our car approached her home she came out on the porch and gave a friendly wave and pleasant greeting. On drawing nearer it was obvious this woman was an alert and kindly sort of person. She graciously welcomed us into her home and introduced her husband. At first Mrs. Hawkins appeared a little reserved, perhaps because of the nature of our visit. No one rushed into the story about the Russians; the time was spent getting acquainted and exchanging family stories. Finally the discussion strayed into the history of her family. This opened the door to the period when the Russians had supposedly flown to Vancouver in 1937.

It was learned that Mrs. Hawkins was getting reacquainted with neighbors she had not seen for the past ten years. On one occasion while revisting in her old neighborhood she passed by the old Eyle home. The year was 1946. Some members of this Native American family were in the yard when she approached, and they came to the gate to greet her. A nice-looking man approached and asked if she remembered him. After a moment or two she did remember his first name – it was Frank, now age 28.

"How have you been?" she inquired.

"Fine," he replied.

"What have you been doing over these past years – since I've been away?"

"Well, I've had a number of jobs, mostly saw mills and construction type things, you know, nothing really steady." And then his face noticeably brightened as he said, "The best job I ever had was working for some Russians up near Sitka, Alaska in 1937."

Mrs. Hawkins found this interesting and she waited for him to explain further.

"Some other guys [Indians] and I got hired to carry crated airplane parts from a boat onto land. We helped them assemble an airplane. The Russians paid us very well and gave us all the vodka that we could drink."

Mrs. Hawkins got the impression from Frank that they had been asked not to say anything about the work they did. Why had he told Mrs. Hawkins? Perhaps the ten years since it happened made the difference. Possibly he had wanted to say something of particular interest to the visitor – something more impressive than the ordinary jobs. She thought Frank was about 18 years old when he went to Alaska. Mrs. Hawkins, on being asked, did not believe Frank Eyle had ever made any connection between what had happened in Alaska and the

Russian "transpolar flight." She said nothing had registered with her either until 1975 when the "transpolar" commemoration was being planned in Vancouver. That was all there was to the story, which had already been heard from her grandson; but it was important to hear it firsthand for a better evaluation. She was genuine; that was for sure. The fact that she never told the episode outside her own family is proof there was no ulterior motive behind the story. If the grandson had not revealed what young Eyle had said, it is doubtful Mrs. Hawkins would ever have told this unusual tale outside of her family, mainly because she felt no one would believe it anyway. Mrs. Hawkins knew what had been told her wasn't proof the Russian polar flight was a hoax and there was no way to question Frank Eyle since he had died 11 years ago.

The U.S. government had recognized the flight as authentic in 1937 and nothing ever surfaced to cast any doubt on the historic achievement. With government sanction and military approval of the "transpolar flight" there was every reason for the citizens of Vancouver to continue honoring the historic event. It was a credit to the Chkalov Committee to demonstrate American appreciation for the accomplishments of another country. It seemed the U.S. was always in the spotlight in these affairs. Lindbergh had received a tumultuous welcome abroad, and now Americans had risen to the occasion for the Russian fliers. If the English magazine *The Aeroplane* had been quoted in U.S. publications, would it have made a difference in the way Americans accepted the "transpolar flight?" Probably not, unless there was some official criticism from the American government or aviation experts.

The public sector was simply not aware there was anything wrong with the 1937 Russian flight story. But now 46 years later there was a question about its legitimacy. It was recognized that Mrs. Hawkins was sincere and that she had related the story in a believable manner. Now it was time to check on Frank Eyle's background and credibility. It was quickly confirmed he had died in 1972 at the age of 53 or 54 from alcohol abuse. The last years of his life were spent with Rosemary Kalama, his niece, who looked after him. Through personal communications with her it was learned that Frank had several brothers still residing in the Pacific Northwest.

Inquiries were sent to them asking whether Frank had ever been in Alaska, and if so did he ever mention working for any Russians. At the same time about 100 other relatives, friends, and acquaintances were contacted, many of whom still resided near the old Eyle homestead. The Eyles were one of the few Indian families in the area who chose to live away from the reservation located in eastern Washington. Their home and acreage was in Charter Oaks, a small rural sector north of Vancouver. All of these people, including the county sheriff who was in office in 1937, were asked to describe the Eyle boy when he was in his late teens. Everyone without exception said that Frank was truthful and reliable. It was also the consensus of those interviewed that he was a private person who did not volunteer much about himself. Bill Koitzsch's property borders on the old Eyle homestead. Frank and Bill attended the same school and were at the Hemlock CCC camp in Washington state at the same time. Bill claims that young Frank was honest. Confirmation that Frank Eyle had been in Alaska during the period in question eventually came from his brother John, who lived in central Washington. This information was provided by Ed Hill, publicity director for the National Association of Civilian Conservation Corps (CCC) Alumni in Yakima, Washington. One possible explanation why no one else knew Frank's whereabouts was he had quit high school before graduation to enlist in the CCC. President Roosevelt had allocated new monies for work projects in Alaska and utilized the CCC for manpower. Indian recruits were sometimes used in special projects to preserve Indian culture and heritage in Alaska, including construction and preservation of ancestral gravesites, totem poles, sweathouses, artifacts, and other cultural facilities.

Frank Eyle had told Mrs. Hawkins he had been employed by a group of Russians to assist them in unloading crated airplane parts and carrying them to a site south of Sitka. This raised a question of whether there was suitable terrain to allow a large, wide-winged airplane to take off. The search for a possible takeoff site near the city of Sitka on Baranof Island had to be expanded when it was learned that Indians commonly refer to the entire island of Baranof as Sitka. This meant one of many islands in the archipelago might have been the location where crated airplane parts could have been assembled. The "transpolar route" declared by the Soviets passed over Chichagof and south to Baranof, Prince of Wales and Charlotte Island [sic] in the archipelago en route to the United States and Vancouver, Washington. It is logical to consider that somewhere along this line of flight was a 1937 campsite where two airplanes possibly were assembled. Having the route run directly over the camp would have allowed the ANT-25s the convenience of lifting off and being right on target to America. Did Frank Eyle, a citizen from Vancouver, Washington, end up unknowingly helping the Russians to complete what became recognized as the first "transpolar flight" to span two continents? Did the Russians in southeast Alaska believe all of their workers were native Alaskans, and consequently overlook the possibility one was an American mainlander? Moreover, the chance that one of the workers would be from Vancouver, the terminus of the Russian flight, defied all reasonable odds. And as it turned out Frank Eyle's casual remark to Mrs. Hawkins led the way to uncovering the true story about the 1937 polar adventures. Ironically it wasn't a Russian who exposed the transpolar hoaxes but someone who unknowingly gave it away.

Frank Eyle had no idea his "off-the-cuff" remark to Mrs. Hawkins would someday lead to a massive investigation of the 1937 Russian polar claims. He went to his grave oblivious of his participation in an extraordinary event. And now this unassuming and private person unknowingly had etched his name in the history books. Young Eyle grew up in Charter Oaks, just north of Battle Ground, in Clark County where Vancouver is the county seat. Eyle's parents homesteaded a large flattened knoll overlooking a fork of the Lewis River. This is where he spent his early years, attending a country school, fishing the nearby waters, and exploring the beautiful, rolling and forested hills of Charter Oaks. The Eyle family, like other Indian families, decided to settle in the Battle Ground area rather than on government reservations.

Satisfied that Frank Eyle had told the truth, a more extensive investigation was conducted on all of the 1937 Russian polar claims. Newspaper articles, books, and other materials were photocopied and gathered together to get a clearer picture of the Russian flights to America. Two flights, not one, had come to America in that "historic year." A second Russian flight had ended in San Jacinto, California.

After studying the materials carefully it became more and more evident that things were not adding up. Something was wrong. What to do? The primary motive for investigating the flights in the first place was to make sure that Chkalovsk was an appropriate sister city, but more time was needed to determine this. The committee was still going ahead with their original choice of Chkalovsk. A decision was made to present some of the preliminary findings about the Russian "transpolar flights" to the news media.

Realizing local newspapers would not be very receptive to a suggestion that the Russian flights they helped publicize might be hoaxes, it was decided to approach a less provincial newspaper outside of the area. By previous contacts we knew of an experienced journalist and former staff writer for the local Vancouver daily newspaper who was now writing for the *Seattle Times*. We thought this might be the right person to approach about this controversial new twist to the 1937 Russian "transpolar flight" ending in Vancouver. The reporter's name is Bill Dietrich. Judging from his stint with the *The Columbian* in Vancouver, he was not afraid to tackle an explosive issue. Reporter Dietrich showed an interest in the story and agreed to meet with us in Vancouver. Mr. Dietrich arrived in the late morning and stayed most of the afternoon, examining various documents and other circumstantial evidence presented in support of our belief that the 1937 flights could have been faked. He was interested in our story and suggested any additional documents or information concerning the subject be sent to the *Seattle Times* office. The reporter was also asked if he would like to talk by telephone to the lady without knowing her name. He accepted this offer and spent some time asking her questions before departing.

Once it appeared a news story was forthcoming, an effort was made to secure all of the materials printed on the "polar flights." It was imperative to obtain everything possible about the aircraft used in this period to acquaint ourselves with capabilities, limitations, and aeronautical specifications. After considerable footwork it was discovered that most of the U.S. government's records about the "transpolar" events were in government archives in Washington, D.C. A request was sent out under the Freedom of Information Act to obtain all relevant information filed by the various governmental branches involved in the "flights." It was learned that the records were held under the auspices of the General Services Administration (GSA), so inquiries were directed there.

While awaiting the GSA's response, numerous local and statewide pilots, engineers, and others connected with aviation were interviewed in the hopes of learning more about long-distance flying and airplanes. It seemed most of the local aviators shied away from the idea of the flights being faked, probably due to the controversial and potentially explosive subject. Apparently, there also is a loyalty and respect among fliers regardless of their nationalities, at least this was a feeling coming across during interviews. It was explained that at this time in the research, only technical information was being sought concerning the capabilities of contemporary airplanes of the 1930s – that no names were going to be used in connection with information obtained. Still many aviation personnel declined to offer anything substantive. Questions about barographs, fuel capacity, horsepower, high-altitude flying, oxygen consumption, gas mileage, de-icers, compasses, magnetic deviations, headwinds, polar cyclones, drag-lift ratios etc, were posed to aviation people. Not getting much technical assistance from these sources, it was necessary to consult books and periodicals for specific data on the subjects.

Research was to be interrupted on October 23, 1983. On this particular Sunday, the *Seattle Times* broke the story about the possible transpolar hoax. Almost one full page was devoted to a general review of the historic event and the recent "cloud" casting doubts on the flight's authenticity. A reprint of the wide-wing ANT-25 and the three Soviet airmen dominated the page. The impact of the news article and the famous photographs of the Russian airplane and fliers were now being viewed in a questionable light. The article included (anonymously) Mrs. Hawkins' story about her Indian friend helping the Russians haul airplane parts into the Sitka area. Generally, the *Seattle Times* concluded that most of the official sources connected directly with the flight agreed it was authentic but the article raised a number of unanswered questions and noted some discrepancies, leaving the truth still in doubt. It was hoped that this article being carried by international news services would help slow down the movement to choose Chkalovsk as Vancouver's sister city. However, the local newspapers did not choose to pick up the *Times*' story from the wire services. This was understandable since these were the same newspapers that originally reported the success of the "transpolar flight" and its historical landing in Vancouver, undoubtedly the most significant event for this city in the twentieth century.

Area newspapers did, however, print brief accounts of the Indian story. The Portland *Oregonian*'s coverage was designed to discredit the hoax theory and take a defensive position in the controversy. The reaction of some of the Chkalov Committee members indicated they were quite disturbed by the suggestion that the flight was not authentic. A few of the more verbal ones expressed their displeasure in the local media; however, generally, in view of the circumstances, most people seemed to take a wait and see posture. Many of the people whose lives had been directly affected by the 1937 landing had since died and other newcomers joined in the effort to keep the issue alive. From this endeavor sprang the Chkalov Flight Committee. One of the main objectives today revolves around the development of trade relations with Russia, at least this is what some observers believe. Despite efforts on the part of the Vancouver committee, no trade agreements have directly resulted from this relationship; but renewed social contacts have been established through the committee's actions since 1975.

After the *Seattle Times* news article broke on October 23, several members of the Chkalov Committee invited any doubters of the "flight" to a viewing of a motion picture film, purporting to be actual footage of the transpolar flight takeoff from Shelkova Airport in Russia, on June 18, 1937. The "film" was definitely an important document since there were no neutral observers present; neither was the American ambassador to Russia, who under the circumstances would be expected to attend such historically important events. The Soviets claimed foreign newspapers were represented at the takeoff ceremony but didn't identify any newspaper or reporter specifically. There were several parts to the film; one segment showed the Vancouver landing, another a scene near the takeoff area, while a third depicted the 1975 flight retracing the alleged 1937 flight route over the North Pole to America. Finally, there was a segment showing the dedication of the monument in Vancouver and the fliers' reception by President Gerald Ford at the White House.

Three Russians had no doubt landed a plane on American soil; however, the "takeoff" from Shelkova was rather puzzling, to say the least. This segment of the film only took a few minutes. The three fliers, dressed similarly to the way they appeared when arriving in Vancouver, were shown in the film to be quickly exiting an auto, supposedly at the Shelkova Airport; then posing very briefly in front of an ANT-25; followed by a film clip of them embracing A.N. Tupolev, the aircraft designer. The film does not catch the fliers actually boarding an ANT-25, but leaves the impression they boarded it and flew off in "predawn hours toward the North Pole." No government officials or other dignitaries from either Russia or America were identified in the film. Instead, about 25 to 30 folk who looked like peasants could be seen milling around a takeoff area. The "Shelkova takeoff" film clip was brief, difficult to follow, and therefore no significant discrepancies were identified. However, the film presentation didn't portray a scene one would expect in depicting an unprecedented and historic attempt to circumvent half the globe via the North Pole. At this particular time it was not realized this document held the key to determining once and for all whether the "transpolar flight" to Vancouver was a hoax or not.

CHAPTER 27

Vancouver Revisited

In 1983, one month after the *Seattle Times* published the transpolar flight hoax theory, the national Ground Zero Pairing Project Committee announced that 800 cities and towns across the United States would mail out their city portraits to communities in the Soviet Union for possible sister city relationships, but U.S. government red tape delayed the mailings of these portfolios and some cities never did cut through the "tape." The American cities tried to match their geography, populations, and economic characteristics with Russian townships. Vancouver has mailed its portrait to Chkalovsk with the prospects of cementing a sister city relationship with that Russian city but no formal answer has been received from the Soviets. The "Sister City" program began when leaders of nuclear arms reduction committees and other peace advocates decided that government efforts to defuse tensions between the two superpowers had failed and they hoped their people-to-people approach would be more effective in promoting peace and in stopping the nuclear arms race.

On the same day this program was publicly aired, the United States government moved to rule Clark County, where Vancouver is located, out of bounds to the Soviets. According to the U.S. State Department, the U.S. began closing certain regions of the nation to the Soviets in response to Russian closure of many areas of the USSR to foreign visitors, a practice beginning 30 years ago. Although there is no proof, it is possible Vancouver and Clark County were deemed closed to the Russians because the city of Chkalovsk had never been opened to American visitors. During the 1975 commemoration a large Soviet delegation had been allowed in Vancouver and the Portland area, while on the other hand, only one person from the United States has ever been permitted into the city of Chkalovsk; Alan L. Cole, of Portland, a member of the Chkalov committtee, who has made frequent trips to Russia, said he visited Chkalovsk in February of 1984, and saw the ANT-25, stored in a "quonset hut" structure along with other memorabilia from the "transpolar flight," including a 1937 American automobile given to Chkalov by an anonymous American donor.

Most countries would do everything possible to develop and promote their achievements, but the Russians have not even seen fit to build an accessible road into this area with a population of more than 50,000.

On several occasions the Russians have circulated reports that Chkalov's ANT-25 would be displayed publicly, including at the 1986 Exposition in Vancouver, British Columbia, but this failed to materialize. Another report indicated that the aircraft will be brought to Vancouver, Washington for the 50th anniversary of the "transpolar flight" that ended in that city June 20, 1937. But this was cancelled. The latest report claims the Russians were seriously considering displaying a scaled-down model of the plane at Vancouver's celebration of the "flight." This too was cancelled. Aviation experts and others investigating the questionable transpolar flights would welcome an opportunity to closely inspect the ANT-25 to determine if the aircraft was even capable of making such a long-distance flight.

Vancouver citizens have been involved in extensive planning to observe what they believe was an historic aviation achievement that placed the city on the map 50 years ago. The city is sponsoring many activities to commemorate this event and plans to host a Russian delegation. The local Chkalov committee is expecting George Baidukov, co-pilot on the "flight" to make an appearance, along with others connected with the various cultural, social, and economic exchange programs between Vancouver and Russia. An American delegation is preparing to honor the Soviet pilots June 8-19 in Russia and visiting three major cities – Leningrad, Kiev and Moscow. But again, the Americans will not be allowed into Chkalovsk. Vancouver has even invited President Ronald Reagan and Soviet Premier Mikhail Gorbachev to its anniversary.

The State of Alaska will observe the 50th anniversary of another "transpolar" flight in which Levanevsky's plane was supposedly lost over the North Pole in August of 1937, setting off a massive aerial and ground search lasting eight months. The Arctic Institute of North

America, along with the University of Alaska, aviation organizations, and other associations are jointly sponsoring this anniversary by staging many historic, and media events, and other activities in August of 1987. There is serious interest among some aviation enthusiasts to conduct new searches for the "missing" aircraft, a risky enterprise since research has shown there is no plane to be found.

The "transpolar flight" observances, particularly exchange programs, will be impacted by the fact that Chkalovsk is a closed USSR area to outsiders, and there was previous controversy about the United States government closure of Vancouver and the rest of Clark County. However, the first announcement by the U.S. State Department banning Soviets from Clark County, Washington area had been misinterpreted by the local media and officials. When the U.S. policy was clarified it did allow Soviet tourists to visit the closed area but Russian nationals temporarily living or stationed in the United States would be barred. The clarified policy allowed Vancouver to host a Russian delegation and plans were being formulated to ask the Soviet government to allow an American delegation to visit Chkalovsk. Early in December of 1983, 19 citizens of the USSR arrived in Portland as representatives of the Friendship Society, an organization active in developing harmonious relations between the countries. It was fitting for the group to pay a visit to the Chkalov Monument in Vancouver. However, when the delegation arrived with their American hosts they found the 20-foot stone tribute had been defaced with swastikas, anti-communist profanity and human excrement. Red-faced and surprised local citizens reacted sharply, calling the vandalism "sick." The embarrassment didn't stop the ceremony and later in the day the speeches by local committee members and Soviet delegates stressed the need for improved relations between the superpowers. This was not the first time something like this had happened. A similar act of vandalism had occurred at the monument when martial law was invoked in Poland in 1981.

But now it was understood that a Soviet delegation could visit Vancouver in June of 1984, an event apparently prompted by the recent news articles questioning the authenticity of the "transpolar flight." The date of this event didn't correspond to any anniversary time frame but committee members were obviously trying to keep the questioned flight alive in Vancouver and San Jacinto, California by promoting various activities. The rededication of the "Chkalov Monument" was the official reason given for the June celebration, nine years after it was erected and dedicated in a 1975 ceremony near Pearson Field, and 47 years following the "transpolar flight" to Vancouver. At the time of these December announcements, four members of the Chkalov Transpolar Flight Committee were in the Soviet Union to celebrate the tenth anniversary of the formation of the Chkalov committee and to attend the 80th birthday in memory of Valery Chkalov, according to press reports. The American delegation arrived in Moscow at the time the Soviet President, Yuri Andropov, lay dying. The news reports said the Vancouver delegation was not given permission to enter Chkalovsk.

As a prelude to the anticipated Soviet visit in June the local newspapers carried an historical review of General George C. Marshall's career. David Morrissey capsulized the noted soldier-statesman's public life with a special emphasis on Marshall's short stint as commander of Vancouver Barracks at the time of the "transpolar flight." The journalist wrote, "Marshall realized the pilots, exhausted after 63 hours of flying, might accidentally say something in a press conference they later regretted. . . rather than risk a slip of the tongue that might trigger an international incident, Marshall told the hundreds of reporters a press conference would wait until the fliers were rested. . .with the aviators' arrival, Marshall was unexpectedly thrust into a delicate international situation, which he handled skillfully." As Marshall's biographer, Forrest C. Pogue wrote how the incident "may have aided his career more than anything else. It put him in the news from coast-to-coast. He handled a difficult job exceedingly well." There is little argument Marshall was one of the most outstanding men of his time, not only from a leadership point of view, but also on the basis of human kindness and an unflawed character. The fact that he as a soldier was awarded the Nobel Peace Prize, primarily because of his Marshall Plan (an international relief program for war-torn countries), is testimony of his great depth.

Marshall's wife Katherine was also held in high esteem, particularly by the citizens of Vancouver. In June, a local writer recalled some of Mrs. Marshall's experiences on that eventful Sunday morning, "In 1937 there was a knock at my door and the orderly said, 'Mrs. Marshall, the Russian plane is circling the Vancouver airfield. It is landing here. General Marshall has gone to meet it and says to have breakfast for the fliers." According to the general's wife, "Three men walked, or more exactly, staggered into the house. They wore huge parkas of fur, only their faces showing and these were so streaked with oil and dirt, so haggard and covered with beards, that the men hardly looked human."

Baidukov must have realized that people would find it hard to believe the three fliers had bathed and put on clean clothes just 63 hours ago and in his book *Over The North Pole* he attempted to account for this discrepancy. The author told about pumping too much oil at one particular time during the flight and how the liquid had overflowed onto the floor of the plane, requiring the airmen to clean up the mess. But there was one thing Baidukov failed to address; this was the peculiar smell emitting from their clothing. This offensive odor was described by General Marshall's maid who likened it to chicken manure and skunk smell. Although there is no reason to think Mrs. Marshall was aware anything was wrong, it is interesting to note her description of the men as they "staggered into the house." With the help of a translator Mrs. Marshall learned what the fliers were requesting. They were "calling for cognac," she said.

Of all the Americans involved in the Russian story General Marshall had been placed in the most difficult position. Other high officials were far enough removed from the scene at Pearson and the barracks not to worry; however, the general was forced to deal both personally and officially with his numerous Russian vistors. Marshall's superiors, no doubt, were watching his every move as he struggled to keep a handle on this explosive situation. For two hectic days when the fliers stayed at the Marshall residence they were fair game for the American radio and news people but the general rose to the occasion and avoided any problems. It took well into July to get the Russian plane on its way back to the USSR. Each commander of a military installation keeps a daily report, so it is interesting to speculate on what General Marshall wrote after each day's experiences with the Russians. We probably will never know because these reports have been reported missing from the military archives. If this proves to be the case, perhaps Marshall entered information and observations which might have proven to be embarrassing to the higher-ups. Were these records purposely destroyed? If the general had noticed and recorded things he believed to be wrong with the Russian claims, he would have been exercising his routine duty and responsibility. If others destroyed these records it does not reflect negatively on General Marshall. The missing daily reports might indicate that the commander at Vancouver had entered an honest assessment of the situation. If anyone can be blamed for covering up the probability of a hoax it would be those officials who were in charge of the major departments of the government.

No matter who is to blame and what national security or foreign interests were served by a cover-up, the people of Vancouver have been hurt the most. After the U.S. government recognized the polar flights as official, the citizens of this small community displayed unselfish appreciation for what they believed was one of the greatest aviation feats ever accomplished by man. Americans were used to such laurels as illustrated by Lindbergh's mastery over the Atlantic in 1927. The French showed their international character when thousands greeted the young aviator in Paris. Ten years later the American reception in Vancouver was equally genuine and sincere. Vancouver had been caught in a helpless situation, the victim of international political circumstances as Russia targeted the small city.

Now 47 years later the Vancouver committee would host only one surviving flier from the original trio to commemorate the "transpolar flight." As the Russians promised, a delegation arrived in Vancouver in time for the June 20 ceremony. Ironically this anniversary was also beset by rain and clouds, the same climatic conditions copilot Baidukov claimed forced them to land in Vancouver rather than their intended destination of San Francisco. The remaining flier had not come alone to the commemoration. Igor Chkalov once again represented his deceased father at the ceremonies, along with the wife and daughter of the late Alexander Beliakov. It is interesting to contemplate whether Igor, Ina, Beliakov's wife, and Irina, his daughter, knew about the hoaxes. Perhaps they did not and were truly enjoying their visit to America. If they did know, the ordeal of coming to honor the event must have weighed heavily upon them. Baidukov showed greater weariness than he did in 1975, dragging himself through the ceremonies. Chkalov, due to his early death, was spared all of this, and at least Beliakov didn't have to make another trip to celebrate this phony rededication. But once again the famous copilot was asked to recall the most dangerous journey of the times. He made some errors in his statements to the press, which could be attributed to a failing memory as he was now 75 years old. Baidukov said this time that they had turned their ANT-25 airplane back toward Vancouver at Medford, Oregon, instead of at Eugene as previously claimed. He also related how the frozen engine had been thawed by hot water from the thermos, yet on another occasion he identified the contents as lemonade. Still another version described how Chkalov broke into rubber sacks and salvaged some water inside a layer of ice. The aging copilot said the brakes had been removed to save weight but Army investigators had long ago determined that the aircraft never had provisions for brakes. Perhaps this would be the last time he would be expected to make this difficult trip to Vancouver, where he had to relive this illusionary flight.

The Soviets had brought along many gifts to be donated to Vancouver's museums. Among these items was an hour-long videotape including segments from the 1975 flight when Baidukov and Beliakov retraced their "polar flight of 1937" in a modern jet aircraft. Several reels of this tape were provided for showing on American television. It would have been better for the preservation of the Soviets' secrets if they had never brought this film to America. It would soon prove to be their downfall in keeping their long-held hoax secret. Perhaps time had made the Russians a little careless.

While Vancouver was hosting the Soviets on this 1984 occasion, little Hemet, California was carrying on a similar celebration in honor of Gromov's landing in nearby San Jacinto Valley. Both events were occurring on the 47th anniversary. It was obvious some coordinated effort had been made between citizens of Vancouver and Hemet to celebrate at the same time. Had the Indian story prompted the two cities to revive these "historical occasions?" The Hemet celebration was nothing in comparison to Vancouver's events, being limited to a few people and news articles. However, there were plans to send a delegation to Moscow to meet with Mikhail Gromov, now 85, and with Andrew Yumashev and Sergei Danilin (Nikolai Juroff), both 82.

At any rate the 1984 celebrations were finally over. Would this be the end of it all? San Jacinto and Hemet had never made too much of the flight after Gromov landed his ANT-25 in a cow pasture there in 1937, but Vancouver showed signs they would not let go so easily. Baidukov had to be very tired of carrying on this charade, considering his advanced age and failing health. On a governmental level perhaps the only man still living who is knowledgeable of the hoaxes is V.M. Molotov, the once famous premier of the Soviet Union. At this writing there is an attempt to reinstate this long deposed political figure, who was such a close henchman of Stalin. This man was at least indirectly responsible for the deaths of Levanevsky and his companions, and many more people who were associated with the hoaxes. There were some other key and trusted government officials who knew about the hoaxes but evidently took their secrets to the grave. Of the six aviators involved in the two "transpolar flights" only one, Chkalov, met an early death. In the course of their lives, in view of the splendid manner in which the Americans honored them, they must have felt some shame in being a part of the fraud. However, it cannot be forgotten the dire circumstances of those times. "Russia must be saved from her enemies." On this basis the fliers might have excused themselves, believing they were true heroes of the Soviet Union. This philosophy might have been the only way the fliers could justify their actions and personal involvement while remaining silent.

CHAPTER 28

Hoaxes Exposed

There had always been an interest in making a detailed examination of the so-called historic films of the Shelkova takeoff. An ongoing effort had been made to obtain a copy of the one shown in 1983. The 35-millimeter film had been used to produce video tapes with the assistance of a local cable company. The cable version became available and it was examined for possible clues to determine whether it was an authentic documentary. Up to this time much information had been gathered indicating deception had been used in the "transpolar flight."

As mentioned, the film and now the tapes, were composed of various segments, one of which was supposed to document the 1937 departure from Shelkova Airport. Other proof the flight was actually achieved was never offered by the Soviet government. The American ambassador to Russia, Joseph Davies, was admittedly absent, and no other specific names were listed as neutral observers at the June 18 takeoff ceremony. To make matters worse, the three barographs carried on the plane to Vancouver disappeared. These instruments are not tamper-proof, but it appeared strange the proper authorities did not make an offering of the barographs as proof of the flights or retain them as evidence. It is surmised the barographs were indeed passed on to the proper authorities in Washington, D.C. but now they are nowhere to be found. Not wanting to risk an international incident American officials probably returned the instruments to Russian officials for return to their country.

Despite extensive media and governmental acceptance of the polar flights to America there never was any concrete evidence or even circumstantial proof of any takeoffs, the first reported as being 4:05

a.m., June 18, and the second at 3:22 a.m., July 12, 1937, both from Shelkova Airport near Moscow. The film now circulating in the United States was the only "proof" offered to corroborate the Russian claims of the first flight. Attention at this point was directed at the film, mainly to determine its authenticity. The particular segment showing the pre-takeoff preparations and the lift off was of primary interest. The scene opened with a full view of the ANT-25, and it was presumed the locality being depicted was the Shelkova Airport, with a concrete runway. Beyond the plane in the far background could be seen a black sedan with people in the act of leaving the vehicle. The cameras quickly zoomed in on the automobile and Baidukov with coat in hand made his exit. He appeared dressed as he was after landing an ANT-25, June 20, 1937 at the Pearson airfield in Vancouver. The other two aviators, Chkalov and Beliakov, were not readily distinguishable in this scene. The camera followed the three pilots making their way toward the airplane with a small group of people gathered behind them. One other person in the small crowd was carrying a camera but the film didn't record the presence of battalions of newsmen and reporters Baidukov described in his book.

It was noted that the cameras always stayed focused on the fliers' upper torsos, but then there was an apparent splice in the brief and disjointed film. Three "sets of legs" in motion appeared in composite form on the film, and the "legs" were wearing mukluks. It is obvious the film had been spliced and the mukluk portion imposed upon the primary film. There was no question this was the case because the people who had been standing behind the fliers suddenly disappeared when the mukluks came into view. The camera refocused on the upper torsos of the fliers with another film splice. It was not clear whether the "legs wearing the mukluks" correctly matched the fliers' torsos. Another obvious clue that the film had been "doctored up" emerged when it was discovered the ANT-25 engine was running but the propeller wasn't moving. Why the film splicing? Was this a clue the takeoff was staged and the film was only a composite of at least two separate takeoff scenes? This departure from good film making might have been excused; however, there were more serious transgressions.

Below the monstrous wings of the ANT, shadows were easily recognizable. Here was something inexcusable that couldn't be overlooked in this film. The time of "takeoff" was almost an hour before sunrise and the presence of sun shadows under the big airplane couldn't be possible this early in the morning. The only way shadows could form directly below the wings is to have flood lights positioned well above the plane but they would have had to move with the aircraft taking off, an absurb situation. There was another big problem with the shadows; the sky was clearly blue and illuminated by the highly positioned sun, indicating the film was shot about noon, not 4:05 a.m. There were a number of noticeable direct sunspots and their reflections on the aircraft fuselage and wings, further proving this was not a predawn scene. The so-called document of authenticity was "coming apart at the seams," or the splices.

The motion picture continues showing the fliers preparing to board the plane. A.N. Tupolev is apparently the only person of renown at the ceremony. No one from the Soviet hierarchy is identified in the film, moreover the 25 to 30 people in attendance seem to be from the "lower class." Baidukov in his writings said hundreds of well-wishers were on hand to bid them farewell. As the aviators filed by to receive Tupolev's embrace and kiss on the cheek, something about the fuselage didn't appear right, something was missing. When the camera focused on the right tail section to record Tupolev's farewell to Chkalov, the first flier to be embraced, the distinguishable Russian lettering translating as "Route of Stalin" was not there. Both sides of the ANT brought to Vancouver had "Route of Stalin" painted in large letters on the fuselage. There was no mistake about the missing lettering when Tupolev moved to embrace Baidukov and then Beliakov, both scenes exposing more of the right side of the fuselage. Still no lettering appeared. It was absolutely conclusive: The right side of the plane's fuselage was devoid of any lettering. This was critical to the film's credibility. The Russian transpolar claims were false! The Vancouver transpolar flight claims were tumbling down!

It was unbelievable that the Soviets would offer this film as a true portrayal of the 1937 takeoff. The film or tapes given to the Vancouver museums and certain indiviudals were coverage of another event, probably the 1936 Siberian run. As the film progressed, the fliers prepare to board the craft, and within seconds the viewers see the wide-winged monoplane lumbering forward along the concrete runway. Scenes change so rapidly they gave the appearance of more disjointed segments and splicing, undoubtedly due to editing designed to deceive. As the ANT proceeded down the runway slowly gathering speed it was clearly not moving down an elevated runway as stated by other Russian reports concerning Shelkova Airport. The big monoplane gathered speed and rushed away from the camera taking its shadows along with it. Slowly into the air it climbed supposedly on its way to the United States via the North Pole. But we will leave all these film discrepancies to the experts for scientific examination. The experts did just this and submitted their findings and analyses, based on the film supplied by the Russian government to the Americans.

Capitol City Video of Salem, Oregon, was asked to examine the film and give its conclusions and conjectures. This firm, held in high standing with the American courts and possessing an aviation background, submitted the following report:

The video tape you supplied is most interesting indeed. It raises many questions, some we can answer and some we cannot. From all the transcripts we read and through conversations with you [author and investigators], we have reached the following opinions:

1. It is of record that the transpolar flight took off at 4:05 a.m. Moscow time, which brings serious cloud to mind, said Richard L. Bias, a forensic video specialist. "The plane shown in the video tape casts a long shadow, meaning from wingtip to wingtip. This means the sun, or a light as bright as the sun, was directly overhead of the moving airplane. It is our opinion that artificial lighting technology was not available to anyone in 1937. All the film is adequately lit, the sky is bright, it is a clear day, no clouds, no snow, no rain, and the sun is approximately at the 11 or 12 o'clock position in the sky.

2. The plane shown on the ground and in the takeoff in this video tape had no writing on the fuselage on the starboard side. It is of record that the plane that landed in Vancouver had writing on both sides, starboard and port. (The Russian lettering was black in color and about one foot in height and was translated from the words *Stalinskiy marshrut* [Route of Stalin], inscribed on both sides of the fuselage.)

3. It is of record that the Russians claim the transpolar flight took off on a very steep decline, meaning they took off downhill, because the plane was so heavily laden with fuel they needed that extra boost. The plane that took off in the film supplied by the Russian government took off on a flat plain.

4. For what it is worth the Russian pilot logged in his flight ledger that he raised his landing gear as soon as the plane lifted off. In the film supplied us the landing gear stayed down until the plane was out of sight.

5. According to the Russian pilot's book, he took off directly from the airport heading north. But a question comes to mind in the film supplied to us, because it shows the Russian airplane flying

by a group of bystanders about 50 feet to 75 feet off the ground and the people do not show in the original takeoff footage. So it is our contention the pilot had to have circled the field and flew over the peoples' heads or other footage was spliced in.

6. Although this film supplied to us was edited in 1975, and a lot of the original footage was shot, we presume, in 1937, there are too many errors in the edit, meaning if all film was shot at the same time within a matter of minutes that it took the plane to take off, there should not be as many discrepancies in the lighting and camera angles. By that we mean in order for them to have this many edits of the takeoff, they would have had to had as many as nine camera shootings from nine different angles and nine different lighting effects. This means the time of day, time of year, and weather conditions will determine whether you have a high density film or low density film. Through our years of experience we have gathered enough knowledge and expertise to know when errors have been made in lighting. There are several edits in this tape that were taken at different times of the year. Some of the footage has high resolution, high density, meaning it was taken in bright sunlight, and other footage was taken in low light which could mean it was cloudy, a different time of day, etc. As we said, there are a lot of errors. So in our opinion all the footage on this film was not taken on the same day, or under the same lighting conditions. It had to be taken at different times of the day and more than likely different times of the year and under different weather conditions.

7. The plane that took off in 1937 did not have a wire loop antenna affixed to the fuselage directly in back of the cockpit and the plane that landed in Vancouver had a two-foot circumference wire loop antenna affixed to the fuselage directly in back of the cockpit. Although you will have to research this fact it may have been detectable but we doubt that very seriously.

8. From the pictures we have observed that were taken immediately after the plane landed in Vancouver, it seems that the plane itself is very clean. No exhaust trail on the underside of the plane is visible and it is shiny. This brings serious questions in our minds that they must have stopped and washed the airplane and had it painted because there was writing on both sides of the airplane and it was whistle clean. Also, the question about the antenna.

Forensic expert Bias concluded that his firm could "go on and on about other errors in the tape but it would be conjecture on our part. Going by the facts above, it is our opinion that there were several different pieces of footage [reference to the takeoff] used, meaning they were taken at different times and under different lighting, and all spliced together to make this film. More than likely two different airplanes and several different time frames."

Efforts to obtain the original film were not successful. It was once reported that copies of the original film had been given to certain museums, but upon checking these sources none acknowledged this.

When the fliers had boarded the ANT, as depicted in the film, they had done so from the left side of the plane, the side with the Russian inscription translated as "Route of Stalin." There were no such markings on the right side. The right side of the fuselage was clearly visible when the airplane was still on the ground and after takeoff. Then how did the plane arriving in Vancouver clearly bear the markings of "Route of Stalin" on both sides of the aircraft? Obviously, it was either a different plane or the film was taken when the plane carried markings only on the left side. If one assumed the Russian film creators were attempting to match the so-called takeoff ceremony from Russia to America with the "transpolar crossing" and landing in Vancouver, they did a terrible job. The planes did not match. But something could have happened to change the choice of the aircraft they were assembling in Alaska, throwing the film creators in a hopeless bind. What could have gone wrong?

Some students of aviation, in studying photographs of the Chkalov plane after it landed in Vancouver, questioned whether the aircraft had matching wings, giving some validity to the damaged wing theory. The Russians said one ANT-25 wing had been damaged one month prior to the alleged takeoff but had undergone repairs in time for the June flight. Baidukov claimed this ANT-25 was parked on the runway and was struck on the wing by another airplane during landing. But this belated revelation came in 1977 from copilot Baidukov, 40 years later, possibly prompted by questions posed during his 1975 visit to Vancouver on why there was a slight difference in the wing ribbing and contour. (The first plane, flown by Chkalov, arrived with the wing identification number N 025, changed from its original number of 025. Was there an exchange of wings between the Chkalov and Gromov planes? We will leave all of this for speculation.)

At last the long ordeal was over for George Baidukov, the only surviving flier of the Vancouver transpolar hoax. His failing health may exclude him from having to face the Americans again. It must have been difficult to accept the wonderful and caring treatment bestowed upon him when he knew the honors were undeserved. Just how the old copilot perceived himself among family and friends is hard to ascertain. The hoaxes could always be rationalized as a patriotic act to help save Russia from the German war menace. Even American citizens ought to be able to understand this. It also should be obvious the Soviet Union for decades has misrepresented her military and industrial strength in order to ward off those elements, real or imaginary, threatening their country from within and from the outside.

In spite of all the years gone by since the 1937 hoaxes, not much has really changed in the Soviet Union. The country still has problems feeding its people, evidenced by the huge grain shipments from the United States. Russia's railroad system is still in disrepair and there are plans now to purchase many locomotives from foreign companies.

In 1984 the Soviets announced a second trans-Siberian railroad had been completed; this one constructed to the north of the original line finished in 1904. However, further study of the recently completed project revealed much of the work is still unfinished. Miles of tunnels have not yet been built and there are many problems with the roadbeds supporting the rail ties, probably due to the freezing and thawing of the terrain. At this time the electrification of the line had not been started. Also, most of the distance covered by the railroad line allows only one-way traffic because there is but one track. To complicate construction of the project, many workers are unhappy with management and are eager to return to their homes in the warmer southwestern regions of the country. The workers' complaints center on poor food and housing.

The country's water transportation systems have not been greatly improved in the Siberian region. The same problems with the ice packs in the north channel exist in these times as well. And shipping by air has always been a very expensive mode of transporting cargo. It is apparent the USSR has not solved its dilemma by constructing efficient communication and transportation networks. Although the nation is well endowed with natural resources such as oil, coal, timber, and gold, it has not been easy to extract these valuable raw materials from their arctic sources. Rivers also remain frozen for much of the year, further inhibiting the movement of manufactured goods and supplies. Although the USSR does not have a large population for the size of its country, there is sufficient manpower to get the work done, indicating that the government is to blame for the stagnant development of the country's resources. Repressive government policies have discouraged people from free and creative participation in the nation's industries.

This problem plagues the Soviet Union today just as it did during the time of Stalin, minus the harsh cruelty of his regime.

In his own way the Soviet dictator set about to do something to improve Russia's image in the eyes of his people and the more developed countries, regardless of how many people were hurt. Ever since Levanevsky's aborted flight Stalin had seriously begun to use the NSR organization to conduct hoax flights in an attempt to impress the rest of the world. He also knew such activity would serve to distract the Russian people from his own political conduct. The dictator as early as 1935 was committed to an accelerated reign of terror against many political factions and individuals. There was also the realization that the Soviet Union was not keeping pace industrially nor militarily with her neighboring enemies – Germany and Japan. Because of the size and population diversity of his country Stalin was frightened into making certain moves to bring the citizens of Russia under tighter control.

Motivated by fear, "the great schemer" unleashed the purges through his butcher Yezhof. All the intellectuals and professionals Stalin feared were subsequently brought down. These were the people that nations normally depend on to chart future direction and progress necessary for survival of any government. Now a good share of that needed expertise was lost forever. Only a few people close to Stalin, such as Molotov and Voroshilov, escaped his petty wrath. Molotov is still a survivor, for at this writing he, at the age of 94, is being reinstated in the Communist Party.

Stalin's close affiliation with the Northern Sea Route Administration was a key factor leading to the hoaxes. Professor Schmidt's work in the arctic and the use of airplanes in this project set the stage for the transpolar deceptions. The international military situation and the domestic picture, as the Soviet leaders perceived them, provided the motivation and rationalization for Stalin to act. It was imperative for the decrepit aviation industry to be upgraded either by hook or by crook. Perhaps no other major leader in history would have risked his entire political career on one decision to deceive the world. Stalin's everyday tactics were an exercise in deceit and a study of his earlier life reveals he tended toward criminality; maybe this helps explain his decision to go ahead with the hoaxes. But for the various reasons mentioned and others not known the Soviet dictator decided to take his country on a "shortcut to fame."

Hitler was not fooled for long by Russia's claims in aviation because the German Luftwaffe quickly slaughtered Soviet vintage aerial squadrons. Realistically there was not much gained by over advertising Soviet prowess in aviation because it did not deter the German armies and air force, in spite of the neutrality pact between the two countries. The ravages of the Third Reich claimed millions of Russian lives; however, many of these could be charged off to Stalin for his near-destruction of the country in the prewar years. The "transpolar flights" were the only bright light of the period.

If there had been any regrets it would have to be the untimely death of Chkalov and the missing Levanevsky and crew. Did any of the survivors ever feel partially responsible for what happened to these fliers? Valery Chkalov and George Baidukov were young men who happened to be in the wrong place at the wrong time, particularly since they were pilots. Forces beyond their control or ability to understand were factors helping to fashion their roles in the hoaxes. Baidukov enjoyed many materialistic advantages because of his cooperation, but usually there is a price to pay.

Look in the eyes of Baidukov. One can almost detect the anquish, even the fear, of a man who got too close to absolute power, not strong enough to overcome this evil dictator's clutches: Too naive and un-sophisticated to guard against his treachery and scheming tactics. Too inexperienced to understand the magnitude of the situation and the eternal web he wove around his life. Was it all worth it?

Did the fliers feel any remorse or sense of guilt for their roles? Did they live in constant fear and wonder what punishments might befall them if exposed? Were their lives better or worse for having deceived the world, their families, and fellow countrymen? Did they believe that their lives and aviation had been compromised? It is interesting to speculate on just who knew of these polar secrets, particularly among family members. One of the amazing aspects of this entire polar affair was the number of people who had to be involved, yet nothing was ever leaked to the outside world, an indication of the repressive environment existing throughout Russian history. They are masters at hiding their skeletons.

It would be easy to condemn and moralize about these greatest of aviation and polar exploration hoaxes. It is much more difficult to make an objective assessment of the U.S. government and media roles in this unbelievable distortion of world history. The U.S. government un-doubtedly had a "hidden agenda" in helping the Russian propaganda machine. But there is no excuse for the apparent blindness of the

American media in not exercising standard journalistic caution and not making routine inquiries when the "transpolar flights" disclosed so many flagrant discrepancies, contradictions, omissions of fact, gross errors, and literally hundreds of other "warning flags" that trained reporters and editors should have immediately recognized, particularly the large metropolitan newspapers, international wire services, radio networks, news magazines, and others in the communication field.

How would this revelation change history and more specifically, what would be its effect, if any, on Soviet-American relations? Nothing was gained by the Russian polar hoaxes in terms of forestalling and altering the course of the war. In fact this false propaganda may well have lengthened and strengthened the repressive regime of Joseph Stalin. It probably would have been better to have exposed the hoaxes in 1937 in the hope that new leadership would emerge that was perhaps more realistic, humane, and dedicated to less antagonistic relationships with the rest of the world. By the United States government's failure to uncover and expose the hoaxes, Stalin was able to insure his political future and continue eliminating anyone who challenged his policies. In this sense the United States government actually contributed to Stalin's power to the detriment of millions of people who lost their lives needlessly.

If there is any lesson to be learned from the 1937 hoaxes, it is that much of the secrecy imposed by governments is pointless and often very harmful to a free society. When the Soviet government asked the United States War Department to keep all the "transpolar flight" correspondence confidential, someone should have discouraged this arrangement and proposed that all flights be carried out in full public review and inspections, including accessing all information to the worldwide news media and aeronautical aviation agencies. Since the United States was the scheduled terminus for the "transpolar flights," this government had a clear-cut responsibility to insure the authenticity of the record-seeking and historical events.

There could have and should have been follow-up investigations by the U.S. Army Air Corps to verify the Russian flight claims, especially with reference to the barographs, plane position reports, performance of the aircraft used, and numerous other questions, including many raised by *The Aeroplane*, the English aviation magazine. Instead, the U.S. merely filed all reports under its Secret Classification and discarded its own air force technicians' questions about these flights. Certainly the U.S. Army Air Corps, all the intelligence agencies, and those from other Western nations knew that the Russians did not have aircraft capable of flying nonstop for distances required in the transpolar crossings. If the United States government and the military/ commercial aircraft builders believed the M-34 engine powering the ANT-25s could fly these outlandish distances, every effort would have been made immediately to acquire these engines. There is no evidence of any Western government trying to acquire these motors or the patents to build them. In fact, it was public knowledge during this period that the Russians wanted U.S. and other Western nations' aircraft, and purchased many planes from these countries.

Too often governments do or don't do various things in the so-called interest of national security and diplomatic causes. Perhaps, a new approach based on truthfulness would lead people on a more productive path and therefore produce honest and meaningful sister city relationships between peoples throughout the world. Since war is no longer recognized as a solution to the world's problems, particularly in this dangerous nuclear age, governments must find ways to cooperate and live peacefully together, and this most certainly will require honest exchanges between nations regardless of ideologies. It will also require a renewed dedication to human rights. People must be allowed to move about freely, both in their own country and the world. We should be struggling to build nations where people want to get in rather than to get out. First Secretary Mikhail Gorbachev seems to be offering an alternative to the Stalinist and post-Stalinist repression. Hopefully, the new Soviet leader will relax the constraint of free travel in the years ahead.

Unfortunately history has demonstrated how war and the fear of war have led to the practice of international spying and an obsession with secrecy. If war isn't an answer then secrecy as practiced by nations today is outmoded and serves no purpose, leaving no logical reason to withhold advanced technology from anyone. Indeed it would be in the interest of the world at large to join in solving major problems concerning food, health, the environment, and other social concerns lessening the quality of life on earth and in space. These are not idealistic proposals but absolutely necessary goals to preserve the earth and ensure the survival of the human race.

REFERENCE NOTES

Books

Baidukov, George, *Over the Pole* (New York: Harcourt & Brace, 1938), pp. 1-200.

Bonney, Walter T., *The Heritage of Kitty Hawk* (New York: W.W. Norton & Co. Inc., 1962), pp. 188-89.

Calvert, Commander James, USN, *Surface at the Pole* (New York: McGraw-Hill Book Co., 1960), pp. 166-209.

Cavendish, Marshall, *The Illustrated Encyclopedia of Aviation* (New York & London: 1979), pp. 2,221-32.

Cooke, David C., *The Story of Aviation* (New York: Archer House, 1958), pp. 64-5 and pp. 86-112.

DeLear, Frank J., *Famous First Flights Across the Atlantic* (New York: Dowd Mead & Co., 1979), pp. 121-41.

DeLeeuw, Hendrix, *Flying Horse to Man in the Moon* (New York: St.Martin's Press, 1963), pp. 73-97 and pp. 104-11.

Donovan, Frank, *The Early Eagles* (New York: Dowd Mead & Co., 1962), pp. 278-91.

Dwiggins, Don, *The Air Devils* (New York: J.B. Lippincott Co., 1966), pp. 176-86.

Faber, Harold, *Soldier & Statesman* (New York: Ariel Books, 1984), pp. 70-79.

Fairhall, David, *Russian Sea Power* (Boston: Gambit Incorporated, 1971), pp. 28-53.

Garber, Paul E., *National Aeronautical Collections* (Washington, D.C.: Smithsonian Institution's National Art Museum, 1965), pp. 48-51.

Gilbert, James, *World's Worst Aircraft* (New York: St. Martin's Press, 1973), pp. 8-12.

Great Soviet Encyclopedia (New York: Macmillan & Co.), Vols. 5, 7, 8, 10, 13, 14, 15, 16, 19, 20, 22, 23, 26, 29.

Green, Fitzhugh, *Peary, The Man Who Refused to Fail* (New York: G.P. Putnam's Sons, 1926), pp. 286-309.

Grierson, John, *Challenge to the Poles* (Hamden, Conn., Archon Books, 1964), pp. 456-84.

Grolier Educational Corporation, *Jane's Encyclopedia of Aviation* (Danbury, Conn., 1980), Vol. 4, pp. 690-700.

Higham, Robert, *Air Power: A Concise History* (New York: St. Martin's Press, 1972), pp. 210-13.

Hooftman, Hugo, *Russia's Aircraft* (Fallbrook, California: Aero Publishers Inc., 1965), pp. 142-44.

Hunt, William R., *To Stand at the Pole* (New York: Stein & Day Publishing, 1981), pp. 246-51.

Jablonski, Edward, *Atlantic Fever* (New York: Macmillan & Co., 1972), pp. 249-53.

Jane's All the World's Aircraft (New York: The Macmillan Co., 1932-1942), USSR aircraft sections.

Jane's All the World's Aircraft (London: Sampson, Low, Marston, 1939), p. 214.

Jones, Robert Huhn, *Road to Russia* (Norman, Oklahoma: University of Oklahoma Press, 1969), pp. 275-95.

Kilmarx, Robert, *A History of Soviet Air Power* (New York: Frederick A. Praeger Publishing, 1962), pp. 118-71.

Link, Arthur S. and William B. Catton, *American Epoch History of the U.S. Since 1900* (New York: Alfred Knopf Publishing, 1973), Vol. 2, pp. 232-34.

Littlepage, John D. and DeMaree Bess, *In Search of Soviet Gold* (New York: Harcourt, Brace & Co., 1937), pp. 3-12 and pp. 116-32.

Lydolph, Paul, *Geography of the U.S.S.R.* (New York: John Wiley & Sons, 1964), pp. 350-52.

Mason, H.M. Jr., *Bold Men, Far Horizons* (Philadelphia/New York: J.B. Lippincott & Co., 1966), pp. 124-25 and pp. 179-85.

Marshall, Katherine Tupper, *Together* (New York: Tupper & Love Inc., 1946), pp. 24-29.

McCauley, Martin, *The Soviet Union Since 1917* (London/New York: Longman Publishing, 1964), pp. 350-52 and pp. 387-89.

Medvedev, Roy A., *Let History Judge* (New York: Vintage Books, 1973), pp. 193-239.

Millar, R.E., *Geography of the U.S.S.R.* (New York: Macmillan & Co., Ltd./St. Martin's Press, 1964), pp. 42-7, pp. 108-13, pp. 308-09, and pp. 356-61.

Mitchell, Mairin, *The Maritime History of Russia* (London: Sidgwick & Jackson Ltd., 1949), pp. 218-81.

Mosely, Leonard, *Marshall* (New York: Hearst Books, 1982), pp. 114-15.

Nobile, Umberto, *My Polar Flights* (New York: G.P. Putnam's Sons, 1961), pp. 142-51.

Ovseyenko, Antonov, *Time of Stalin* (New York: Harper Colophon Books, 1980), pp. 130-134, pp. 205-09, and pp. 210-13.

Pogue, Forrest T., *George C. Marshall, 1880-1939* (New York: Viking Press, 1963), pp. 300-16.

Potter, Jean, *The Flying North* (New York: Macmillan & Co., 1947), pp. 66-67.

Rae, John B., *Climb to Greatness* (Cambridge: MIT Press, 1968), pp. 72-81.

Salnikov, Yu. P., *A Life Given to the Arctic: Sigizmund Levanevsky* (Moscow: Political Literature, 1984), pp. 131-46.

Simmons, George, *Target Arctic* (New York: Chilton Books, 1965), pp. 248-308.

Solzhenitsyn, Aleksander I., *The Gulag Archipelago* (New York: Harper & Row, Publishers, 1975), Vol. 2, p. 333 and p. 687.

Stefansson, Vilhjalmur, *Unsolved Mysteries of the Arctic* (New York: Macmillan & Co., 1939), pp. 322-27.

Stefansson, Vilhjalmur, *The Friendly Arctic* (New York: Macmillan & Co., 1943), p. 688 and p. 713.

Sunderman, James, *Early Air Pioneers* (New York: Franklin Watts Inc., 1961), pp. 253-63.

Taylor, John W.R., *The Lore of Flight* (New York: Cresent Books, 1976), pp. 408-17.

Time/Life's Epic of Flight (New York: Time/Life Inc., 1980).

Periodicals

The Aeroplane, London, England, September 8, 1937.

Columbian, Vancouver, Washington, June, July, August, 1937.

Columbian, Sunday Magazine, Vancouver, Washington, David Morrissey, May 27, 1975.

Hemet News, San Jacinto, California, July, 1937.

New York Times, New York, N.Y., July, August, 1935.

New York Times, New York, N.Y., May, June, July, August,
    September, 1937.
Oregon Journal, Portland, Oregon, June, July, 1937.
Oregonian, Portland, Oregon, June, July, August, September, 1937.
Oregonian, Northwest Magazine, Portland, Oregon, Leveritt Richards,
    June 1975.
Polar Times, Cambridge, England, October, 1937.
San Francisco Chronicle, San Francisco, California, June, July, 1937.
Washington Post, Washington, D.C., June, July, 1937.
Clark County History, Fort Vancouver Historical Society, (Vancouver,
    Washington: Pioneer Printing), 1968, pp. 299-323; 1976,
    pp. 21-42 and pp. 53-87; 1978, pp. 33-37; 1980, pp. 73-74.

Official Flight Log

Navigator's Flight Log Book, Alexander Beliakov, June 17-19, 1937.

U.S. Government Documents

U.S. State Department Central Decimal File, Record Group 165,
1930-39, 811.79661, 250 pages; 861.248/109, one page; 811.111,
eight pages, compiled by the Military Intelligence Division, War
Department, relating to Soviet overflight of U.S. territory in 1937.

U.S. Weather Bureau, Departments of Agriculture/Commerce, files
040.4, 410.3 and 030.6, about 180 pages of documents relating to
weather and communications specially implemented for the
"transpolar flights."

Canadian Government Documents

Canadian National Defense, Record Group (RG) 24, Volume 3569,
File H.Q.C. 6933, 1044-55-4, 65 pages; and RG 24, Volume 5206,
File H.Q.C. 15-27-4, 200 pages, all relating to the "transpolar
flights" and Levanevsky rescue attempts of 1937.

Forensic Report

A 1987 study of film supplied by the Russian government purporting
to depict departure of the "transpolar flight" that flew from Russia to
Vancouver, Washington via the North Pole June 18-20, 1937, by
Richard L. Bias, forensic video specialist, Salem, Oregon.

GLOSSARY

The Aeroplane. Periodical published in England that reviewed the 1937 Russian transpolar flights and judged them to be hoaxes.

Alaskan Plan. A plan devised by the Northern Sea Route Administration (NSRA) and Stalin to secretly fly airplanes from the Alexander Archipelago in order to fake nonstop flights from Russia to the United States.

Alcock, John. Pilot who flew across the North Atlantic in 1919 with Arthur Brown.

Alexander Archipelago. A chain of hundreds of islands in southeastern Alaska.

Alksnis, Iakov (Jacob). A general who commanded the Soviet air force during the "transpolar flights" to America.

Amtorg Trading Company. A New York-based Russian-American import/export firm.

Amundsen, Roald (1872-1928). Norwegian explorer credited with first reaching the South Pole in 1911 and with supposedly crossing over the North Pole in a dirigible.

Amur River. Waterway separating Manchuria and other parts of China from the USSR.

ANT-4. Russian airplane copied from the German Junkers G-23.

ANT-6. Russian airplane copied from various Junkers models.

ANT-25. Russian airplane converted from the French Dewoitine's Trait d'Union D 33.

Arnold, Henry (Hap). American general who commanded the U.S. Army Air Corps during the "transpolar flights."

Baidukov, George. Copilot who accompanied Valery Chkalov and Alexander Beliakov on first "transpolar flight" ending in Vancouver, Washington June 20, 1937.

Barograph. An instrument attached to aircraft to measure barometric pressures at various altitudes.

Balbo, Italo. Italian general who commanded 25 clipper-type airplanes on a 1933 flight from Italy to the United States.

Baranof, Alexander. First Russian governor of Alaska.

Baranof Island. One of the larger islands in the northern region of the Alexander Archipelago.

Beliakov, Alexander. Navigator who accompanied Valery Chkalov and George Baidukov on first "transpolar flight" from Moscow to Vancouver, Washington.

Berdnik, Vassily. An airplane engineer who claimed to have assembled the ANT-25 (Chkalov's plane) in Moscow.

Bleriot. French long-distance airplane used by Paul Codos and Maurice Rossi in a flight from New York City to Syria in 1933.

Bolkhovitinov, Victor. Russian engineer who claimed to have designed Levanevsky's H-209.

Bond, Carlton. An Army Air Corps lieutenant present at the FBI meeting that told of a forthcoming Russian airplane landing at Vancouver, Washington.

Brown, Arthur. Pilot who accompanied John Alcock in crossing the North Atlantic in 1919.

Bullitt, William C. American ambassador to Russia in 1935 when Levanevsky made his alleged attempt to fly from Moscow to the United States via the North Pole.

Burrows, Paul. Air Corps major who commanded Pearson Field in Vancouver when a "transpolar flight" landed there June 20, 1937.

Byrd, Richard Evelyn. American Navy admiral who claimed to have flown over the North Pole from Greenland May 8-9, 1926.

Civilian Conservation Corps (CCC). A U.S. government program designed to employ young men in public works projects during the economic depression of the 1930s.

Cheliuskin (Chelyuskin). A Danish reinforced freighter named after an eighteenth century Russian explorer, Semen Ivanovich Cheliuskin, and used in arctic waters by the Northern Sea Route Administration.

Chkalov, Valery. Chief pilot on the first "transpolar flight" ending in Vancouver, Washington June 20, 1937.

Chkalovsk. Russian city about 75 miles east of Gorki near the Volga River, a city named after Pilot Chkalov who was credited with flying the first nonstop flight from Russia to the United States, via the North Pole, ending in Vancouver, Washington, June 20, 1937.

Chkalovskaya. A small temporary suburb developed specifically to host American delegations from Vancouver, Washington in observance of the 1937 "transpolar flight."

Chkalov, Igor. Son of Chief Pilot Valery Chkalov.

Codos, Paul. French pilot who flew with Maurice Rossi in establishing a new long-distance world record in 1933, flying in a Bleriot from New York to Syria via France.

Coffey, Harry. Represented the National Aeronautical Association during the "transpolar flight" that ended in Vancouver, Washington June 20, 1937.

Cook, Dr. Frederick Albert. Claimed to have reached the North Pole just prior to Navy Commander Robert Edwin Peary's expedition to the pole April 6, 1909.

Crosson, Joe. Alaskan bush pilot who made several aerial missions in the search for Levanevsky in the polar region in 1937.

Danilin, Sergei. Russian navigator who flew on the "transpolar flight" that ended in San Jacinto, California, July 14, 1937.

Davies, Joseph E. American ambassador to Russia during the 1937 "transpolar" events.

Denny, Harold. *New York Times* correspondent who was on assignment in Moscow during the "transpolar" events.

Dewoitine Company. French aircraft firm that designed and built the Trait d'Union D 33s, two of which were salvaged and converted by the Russians to ANT-25s.

Dietrich, Bill. *Seattle Times* reporter who first wrote a story about the possibility of the transpolar flights being hoaxes, based on information supplied by the author of *Russia's Shortcut to Fame.*

Doret, Marcel. French pilot who crashed two Dewoitine Trait d'Union D 33 aircraft in Russia in the early 1930s.

Duranty, Walter. *New York Times* correspondent in Moscow who was on assignment during the years of the infamous Russian purges under Dictator Stalin.

Earhart, Amelia (Putnam). Noted American aviatrix who established a number of flight records before disappearing in the South Pacific in 1937.

Eyle, Frank. Native American from Charter Oaks near Vancouver, Washington who reportedly assisted Russians in unloading airplane parts in Alaska.

Federation Aeronautique Internationale (FAI). French organization that officially sanctioned airplane records.

Faymonville, Philip. Military attaché assigned to the American embassy in Moscow during the "polar flights" of 1937.

Fedorov, Eugene. Magnetologist and one of four Soviet explorers who supposedly was flown to a Russian North Pole camp in May of 1937.

Fitzmaurice, James. Irish pilot, who, along with the Germans Gunther von Heunefeld and Herman Koehle, commanded an Irish Free State Air Force plane (Junkers Bremen) in the first successful west to east flight across the Atlantic in 1928.

Franz Josef Land. Island group that includes Hooker and Rudolph islands, 600 miles from the Soviet side of the North Pole.

General Services Administration (GSA). The U.S. agency in charge of the National Archives and Records Service.

Gokhman, Gregory. Acting counsul for the Soviet embassy in Washington, D.C. during the 1937 "transpolar" events.

Goose Island. Island above Queen Charlotte Island where Levanevsky said he landed to wait out adverse weather during a 1936 flight from Alameda, California to Moscow, via the Alexander Archipelago.

Gorky, Maxim. Known as the "Poor People's Poet," who became disillusioned with Stalin, and was the namesake of the *Maxim Gorky*, the largest aircraft ever built by 1934.

Greenwich Time. The official time used in precise navigation by ships and airplanes as determined by the most important observatory located at Greenwich, England, on the prime meridian in latitude +51 degrees 28' 38.4" N.

Gregg, Willis. Chief of the U.S. Weather Service during the "transpolar flights" of 1937.

Gromov, Mikhail. Chief pilot of the "transpolar flight" from Russia to San Jacinto, California via the North Pole, July 12-14, 1937.

Ground Zero Pairing Project. A national organization established to match cities in Russia and United States for sister city relationships as part of an overall peace initiative program.

Hitler, Adolph. Führer of the Third Reich who attempted to rebuild the German empire by military means from 1934 to 1945.

Hooker Island. One of the first arctic bases established by Russians within the Franz Josef group.

Izvestia. Official Soviet news agency.

Juroff, Nicolai. Last-minute substitute pilot of the *Maxim Gorky* who supposedly died when the mammoth craft crashed near Moscow in 1935. (There was a question about his death because a photograph published by the *New York Times* in 1937 identified him as Sergei Danilin, navigator on the "transpolar flight" that landed in San Jacinto, California in July of 1937.)

K-37 Junkers. A German aircraft model that may have been converted to the *Land of the Soviets*, a Russian aircraft that flew to Vancouver, Washington in 1929.

Kaganovich, Lazar. Russian Commissar of Transportation.

Kaganovich, Mikhail. Russian Chairman of Heavy Industry.

Kalama, Rosemary. Niece of Frank Eyle who cared for him during the last 14 years of his life.

Kelly, Oakley D. A U.S. Army Air Corps lieutenant who commanded Pearson Field, Vancouver, Washington, when the Russian *Land of the Soviets* arrived there in 1929; he also was credited with breaking an endurance record in a flight from New York to San Diego in May of 1923.

Khrushchev, Nikita. Russian official present during "transpolar" events of 1937, becoming the first secretary of the Communist Party and Soviet premier after Stalin's death in 1953.

Koehle, Herman. A German airman who accompanied James Fitzmaurice during the first successful east to west crossing of the Atlantic in 1928.

Kozmetsky, George. ROTC student fluent in the Russian language who happened to be at Pearson Field when a Russian airplane supposedly flew from Russia to Vancouver, Washington, June 18-20, 1937.

Krenkel, Ernest. A radio operator said to have been one of four Russian explorers who was left at the North Pole May 22, 1937.

Kviring, E.J. Director of Soviet state planning commission who predicted in 1929 that Russia would take the industrial and technical lead from the United States within a few years.

Land of the Soviets. A Soviet-owned aircraft believed to have been a converted German Junkers K-37.

Lenin, V.I. Communist leader following the Russian Revolution.

Levanevsky, Sigmund. A pilot who became known as the "Soviet Lindbergh," and gained hero status after participating in the rescue of survivors of the *Cheliuskin* in 1934.

Levchenko, Victor. A navigator who accompanied Sigmund Levanevsky on a 1936 flight from Alameda, California to Russia.

Lindbergh, Charles A. An American colonel in the U.S. Army Air Corps who gained international fame when he became the first to fly a single engine aircraft solo across the Atlantic from New York to France in 1927.

Littlepage, John D. An American mining engineer hired by the Soviet government to supervise Russia's gold mining operations from 1928 to 1937.

Mamay, Tamara Yumashev. American immigrant and sister of Andrew Yumashev, who lived in the San Francisco Bay area.

Markham, Beryl. An English aviatrix who flew solo across the North Atlantic from east to west in 1936.

Marshall, George C. A general and commander of Vancouver's Army Barracks during the Russian "transpolar flight" that landed there June 20, 1937; eventually Army chief of staff, secretary of state, secretary of defense, special ambassador to China, architect of the Marshall Plan in Europe and winner of the Nobel Peace Prize.

Marshall, Katherine Tupper. Wife of General Marshall who hosted the Russian fliers after they landed at Pearson Field in Vancouver, June 20, 1937.

Mattern, James. American test pilot and record seeker who was rescued by Russian pilot Sigmund Levanevsky in 1933 and who later participated in the search for Levanevsky who supposedly disappeared on a flight over the North Pole in August of 1937.

Medvedev, Roy A. A Russian dissident and author of *Let History Judge*, whose writings in 1971 disclosed the true personality of Stalin and the horrors of his reign.

Mitsubishi K 1/2. Japanese modification of the Junkers K-37 aircraft.

Molotov, V.M. Premier of the People's Commissars who served during the 1937 "transpolar flights" and during Stalin's purges.

Mouton, Edison. Representative of National Aeronautical Association and one of the last persons to have possession of barograph recordings from Gromov's ANT-25, which landed at San Jacinto, California, supposedly after flying nonstop from Russia in July of 1937.

Nansen, Fridtjof. Norwegian arctic explorer, naturalist, and statesman, 1861-1930.

Northeast Passage. Russia believed for a number of years that there was a warm water route through the arctic but it was never discovered.

Northern Sea Route Administration (NSRA). Russian organization established to develop a shipping lane along the northern coast from Murmansk to the Bering Strait and later promoted hoax transpolar flights from Russia to the United States via the North Pole.

Ordjonikidze, Gregory. Soviet Heavy Industry commissar who died under mysterious circumstances.

Orenburg & Oblast. The name of a region near the Ural Mountains in western Siberia that was changed to "Chkalov" in 1938 after Chkalov was credited for the "transpolar flight" from Russia to Vancouver, Washington in 1937. The region was renamed Orenburg & Oblast in 1957.

Oumansky, Constantine. Counselor in the Soviet embassy in Washington, D.C. who was in charge of coordinating Russian fliers' presence in the United States during the 1937 "transpolar flights."

Papanin, Ivan. Supervised three Russian explorers who supposedly were left at the North Pole in 1937.

Pearson Field. A U.S. Army Air Corps airport at Vancouver, Washington, where a "transpolar flight" ended June 20, 1937.

Peary, Robert E. Navy Commander who led an expedition to the North Pole, April 6, 1909, later promoted to admiral.

Post, Wiley. American aviator who broke many world flight records, spending considerable time flying in the arctic. He died in a plane crash with actor/humorist Will Rogers August 15, 1935, at Point Barrow, Alaska.

Pravda. Soviet news agency.

Roosevelt, Franklin Delano. President of the United States from 1933 to 1945, serving during the "transpolar flights" of 1937.

Rossi, Maurice. French pilot who accompanied Paul Codos on nonstop flight from New York to Syria via France in 1933.

Route of Stalin. A name given to a Russian ANT-25 aircraft that the Soviets claimed flew nonstop from Russia over the North Pole to Vancouver, Washington, June 18-20, 1937.

Rudolph Island. One of the islands in the Franz Josef group that is situated about 550 miles from the North Pole, the nearest land mass to that pole.

Ryan, Claude. Leading American aircraft manufacturer, and builder of the plane flown by Charles A. Lindbergh in his historic Atlantic crossing in 1927.

San Jacinto. A California city east of Los Angeles that was the terminus of a Russian "transpolar flight" in July of 1937.

Schmidt, Dr. Otto J. Professor and later director of the Northern Sea Route Administration, which tried in vain to open a year-round sea lane from Russia's northern coast to the Bering Strait, and promoted the "transpolar flights" in the 1930s.

Serebrovsky, Alexander. Russian commissar of oil and gold mining, and a leading industrialist who hired John D. Littlepage, an American, to supervise gold mining operations from 1928 to 1937.

Shelkova Airport. A Russian military field, 25 miles northeast of Moscow, where the NSRA planned its "transpolar" events.

Shestakov, Semion. Russian pilot of the *Land of the Soviets*, a large aircraft that flew from Moscow to New York after making numerous refueling and maintenance stops, including one landing at Vancouver, Washington October 16, 1929.

Shirshov, Peter. A hydrologist and one of four explorers said to have been left at the North Pole in 1937, also performed services as a medical doctor without formal training, including amputations and other surgical procedures.

Sikorsky, Igor. Russian immigrant who became a leader in American aircraft design and development with a speciality in helicopters.

Sitka, Alaska. Capital of Baranof Island and mentioned in Frank Eyle's story about helping Russians unload airplane parts in that area in 1937.

Slepnev, M.T. Accompanied Levanevsky during the *Cheliuskin* rescue from a base near Nome, Alaska in 1934.

Spirit of St. Louis. Name given to Charles A. Lindbergh's plane used to fly from New York to France in 1927.

Spitzbergen. Island 600 miles from the North Pole on the Russian side.

Stefansson, Vilhjalmur. U.S. arctic explorer (born in Canada) who became president of the New York Explorer's Club.

Stalin, Joseph. General secretary of the USSR Communist Party from 1922 and Soviet premier from 1941 to his death in 1953, later condemned by modern rulers for purges and other human rights violations.

Strahm, Victor. U.S. Army Air Corps major stationed at March Field, who greeted the "transpolar flight" crew when their plane landed at nearby San Jacinto, California, July 14, 1937.

Swan Island. Portland, Oregon municipal airport across the Columbia River from Vancouver's Pearson Field, an airport used by Charles A. Lindbergh while on tour following his historic 1927 flight in the *Spirit of St. Louis.*

TSAGI. Translated from Russian to Central Hydro-Aero Dynamics Institute, an "industrial complex" near Moscow.

Trotsky, Leon. Exiled Russian political leader who opposed Stalin's rule for many years.

Troyanovsky, Alexander. Russian ambassador to the United States during "transpolar" events.

Troyanovsky, Mark. Son of Ambassador Troyanovsky who photographed and wrote articles about the alleged Soviet camp at the North Pole.

Udd Island. An island in the Amur River that the Soviets claimed was the terminus to an alleged Russian flight from Shelkova, near Moscow, in July 1936. The plane was reportedly piloted by Valery Chkalov, the same pilot who was credited with flying a nonstop flight from Russia to the United States in 1937.

Vancouver, Washington. A southwest Washington city that served as a terminus for a Soviet aircraft that was credited with flying nonstop from Russia to Pearson Field at Vancouver via the North Pole, June 18-20, 1937, and also served as the terminus of a 1929 flight by Semion Shestakov.

Vartanian, A.A. A Russian identified by the media as a trading representative with Amtorg Company, a New York-based export/import firm, and assigned as a radio agent by the Soviets to direct communications with the ANT-25s that supposedly flew the "transpolar flights" in 1937. (However, recent queries to Amtorg Company officials failed to confirm that Vartanian was ever affiliated or conducted any business with that firm.)

Vodopyanov, Mikhail. Pilot/author who supposedly landed the first Russian plane at the North Pole in 1937.

Voroshilov, Klementy. Commissar of defense and close friend of Stalin, who acted as a go-between for NSRA and the Kremlin concerning the hoax flights.

Waterfall, Alaska. Coastal city on southwestern section of Prince of Wales Island, the city where Shestakov changed an engine on his *Land of the Soviets* plane that eventually landed at Vancouver's Pearson Field October 16, 1929.

Wilkins, Sir Hubert. Australian aviator, famous for numerous world-record flights and a leader in conducting aerial searches for Sigmund Levanevsky's aircraft that the Soviets claimed disappeared over the North Pole in a flight from Russia to the United States in August of 1937. No trace of the aircraft or its six-member crew was ever found.

Yagoda, Henry. Chief of Soviet secret police during the planning stages of the "transpolar flights."

Yeshov, Nicolai. Succeeded Yagoda as chief of the secret police and served during the "transpolar" events.

Yumashev, Andrew. A pilot who accompanied Gromov during a "transpolar flight" that terminated at San Jacinto, California July 14, 1937.